Cruising America Online® 2.5

Other Prima Visual Learning Guides

Internet for Windows: America Online 2.5 Edition
PowerPoint for Windows 95: The Visual Learning Guide
Windows 95: The Visual Learning Guide
Word for Windows 95: The Visual Learning Guide
Excel for Windows 95: The Visual Learning Guide
WinComm PRO: The Visual Learning Guide
PROCOMM PLUS for Windows: The Visual Learning Guide
WordPerfect 6.1 for Windows: The Visual Learning Guide
Word 6 for the Mac: The Visual Learning Guide
Cruising America Online
Quicken for Windows: The Visual Learning Guide
1-2-3 for Windows: The Visual Learning Guide
ACT! 2.0 for Windows: The Visual Learning Guide
Excel for the Mac: The Visual Learning Guide
Windows 3.1: The Visual Learning Guide
Excel 5 for Windows: The Visual Learning Guide
PowerPoint: The Visual Learning Guide
Word for Windows 6: The Visual Learning Guide
WordPerfect 6 for Windows: The Visual Learning Guide
WinFax PRO: The Visual Learning Guide

Upcoming Books!

Access for Windows 95: The Visual Learning Guide
Internet for Windows, The Microsoft Network Edition
Quicken 5 for Windows: The Visual Learning Guide

How to Order:

Individual orders and quantity discounts are available from the publisher, Prima Publishing, P.O. Box 1260BK, Rocklin, CA 95677-1260; (916) 632-4400. For quantity orders, include information on your letterhead concerning the intended use of the books and the number of books you wish to purchase.

Cruising America Online® 2.5

Grace Joely Beatty, Ph.D.
David C. Gardner, Ph.D.
David A. Sauer, M.S.

PRIMA PUBLISHING

P™, Visual Learning Guides™, and "The Fastest, Easiest Way to Learn"™ are trademarks of Prima Publishing, a division of Prima Communications, Inc. Prima Publishing™ is a trademark of Prima Communications.

© 1995 by The Gardner Beatty Group. All rights reserved. No part of this book may be reproduced or transmitted in any form or by any means, electronic or mechanical, including photocopying, recording, or by any information storage or retrieval system without written permission from Prima Publishing, except for the inclusion of quotations in a review.

Project Editor: Jeff Ennis

If you have problems installing or running America Online® (version 2.5) contact America Online, Inc. at (800) 827-3338. Prima Publishing cannot provide software support.

Prima Publishing and the authors have attempted throughout this book to distinguish proprietary trademarks from descriptive terms by following the capitalization style used by the manufacturer.

Information contained in this book has been obtained by Prima Publishing from sources believed to be reliable. However, because of the possibility of human or mechanical error by our sources, Prima Publishing, or others, the Publisher does not guarantee the accuracy, adequacy, or completeness of any information and is not responsible for any errors or omissions or the results obtained from use of such information.

ISBN: 7615-0302-1
Library of Congress Catalog Card Number: 95-70669
Printed in the United States of America
95 96 97 98 BB 10 9 8 7 6 5 4 3 2 1

Acknowledgments

We are deeply indebted to reviewers around the country who gave generously of their time to test every step in the manuscript. Linda Beatty, Carolyn Holder, and J.D. Maple cannot be thanked enough! In addition to manuscript testing, Linda and Carolyn added significantly to many chapters. Linda Beatty created the original artwork.

We are personally and professionally delighted to work with everyone at Prima Publishing.

Cal Callahan and David Coburn, technical editors; Carol Venolia, copy editor; Prima Creative Services, interior layout; and Paul Page, cover design, contributed to the final product. George Thomson helped us through the tricky technical stuff.

Bill Gladstone and Matt Wagner of Waterside Productions created the idea for this series. Their faith in us has never wavered.

Joseph and Shirley Beatty made this series possible. We can never repay them.

Asher Schapiro has always been there when we needed him.

Paula Gardner Capaldo and David Capaldo have been terrific. Thanks, Joshua and Jessica, for being such wonderful kids!

Thanks to Cyrus and Jemmie for their invaluable moral support.

We could not have met the deadlines without the technical support of Ray Holder, our electrical genius, Diana M. Balelo, Frank E. Straw, Daniel W. Terhark and Martin J. O'Keefe of Computer Service & Maintenance, our computer wizards.

Contents

Customize Your Learning

Prima Visual Learning Guides are not like any other computer books you have ever seen. They are based on our years in the classroom, our corporate consulting, and our research at Boston University on the best ways to teach technical information to non-technical learners. Most important, this series is based on the feedback of a panel of reviewers from across the country who range in computer knowledge from "panicked at the thought" to sophisticated.

Each chapter is illustrated with color screens to guide you through every task. The combination of screens, step-by-step instructions, and pointers makes it impossible for you to get lost or confused as you follow along on your own computer.

LET US KNOW...

We truly hope you'll enjoy using the book and America Online® 2.5. Let us know how you feel about our book and whether there are any changes or improvements we can make. You can contact us through Prima Publishing, 3875 Atherton Road, Rocklin, CA, 95765, or send us an e-mail letter. Our Internet address is write.bks@aol.com. Thanks for buying the book. Have fun!

Joely Beatty, David Gardner, and David Sauer

PART I: USING E-MAIL

CHAPTER

CHAPTER 1

Sending E-Mail

You can use America Online's (AOL) mail service to send electronic mail to anyone in the world who has an AOL account. Because charges can add up quickly, we recommend that you compose your mail messages offline before you actually sign on to America Online. Mail cannot be typed with fancy formatting, so if you want to send a word-processed document or a graphics file, see Chapter 8, "Sending and Receiving Files." In this chapter, you will do the following:

✔ Save money by composing mail offline
✔ Send e-mail to one or more people
✔ Send carbon copies
✔ Read mail sent
✔ Print a copy of mail sent
✔ Automatically save mail to your Personal Filing Cabinet

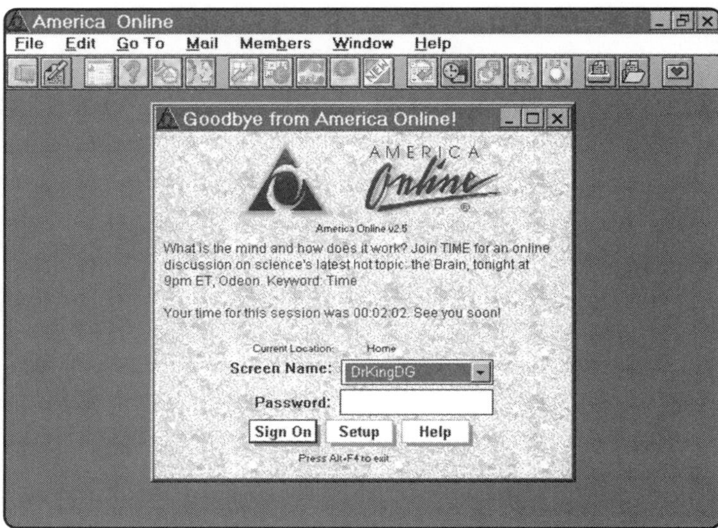

OPENING AMERICA ONLINE

1. **Open** the **America Online** program if you have not already done so, but do not connect to the service.

COMPOSING MAIL OFFLINE

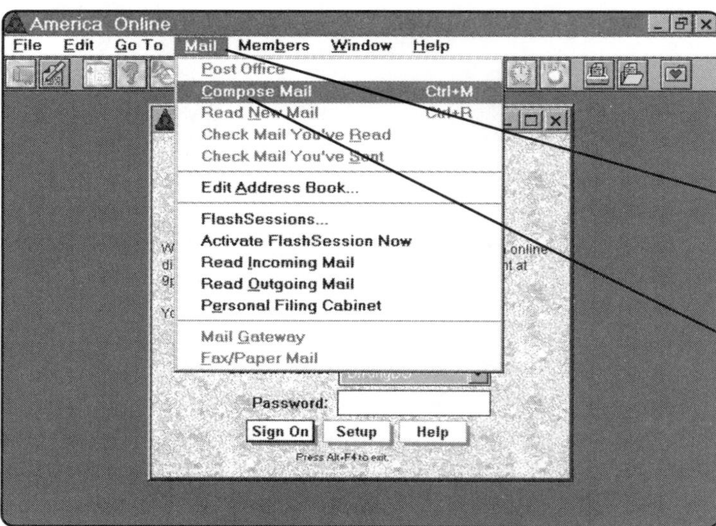

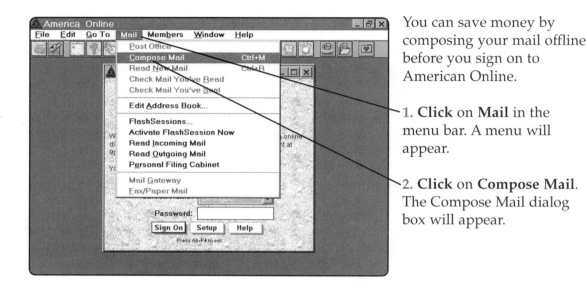

You can save money by composing your mail offline before you sign on to American Online.

1. **Click** on **Mail** in the menu bar. A menu will appear.

2. **Click** on **Compose Mail**. The Compose Mail dialog box will appear.

ADDRESSING MAIL

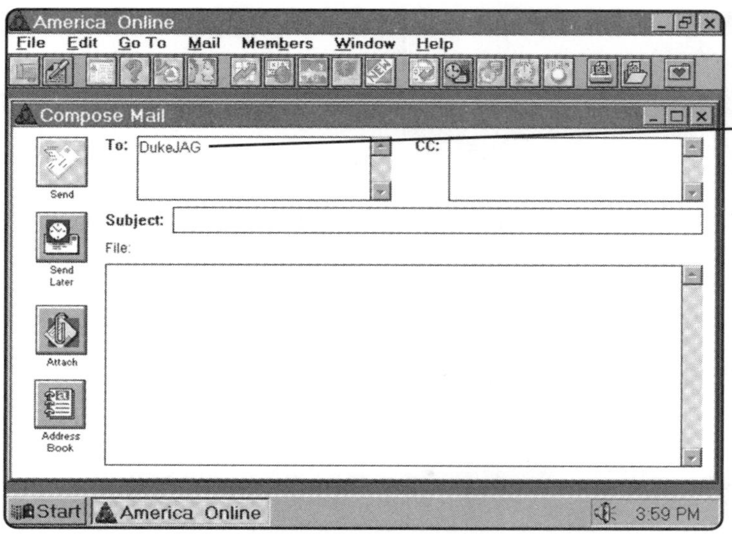

You can send the same letter to more than one person.

1. **Type** the **screen name** of the **first person** who will get the mail message. In this example, it is DukeJAG.

2. **Type** a **comma** to seperate this address from the next. *Don't put a space between the comma and the second address.*

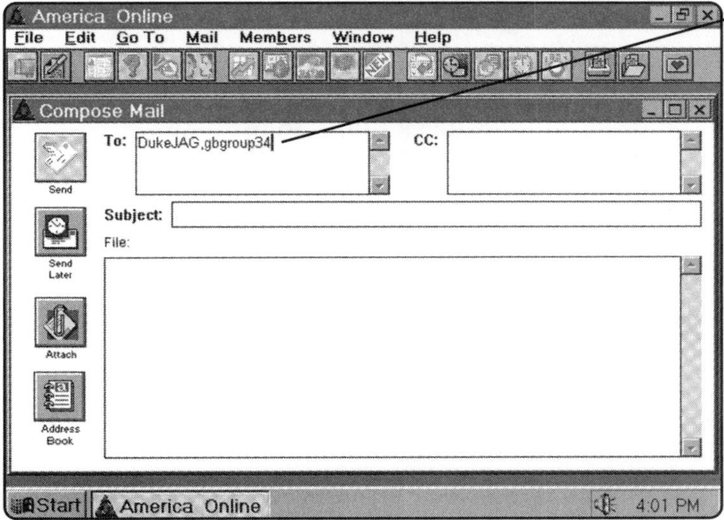

3. **Type** the **screen name** of the **second person** who will get this letter. In this example, it is gbgroup34.

4. **Repeat steps 2 and 3** for each name you want to add to the To list. If you regularly send mail to the same group of people, you can create a group name and include all appropriate people in the group. See the section entitled "Adding a Group Address" in Chapter 3.

Note: When you send AOL mail to multiple AOL recipients, AOL will list the names of all recipients on every person's copy of the letter so that everyone knows who got copies of the letter.

Sending a Carbon Copy

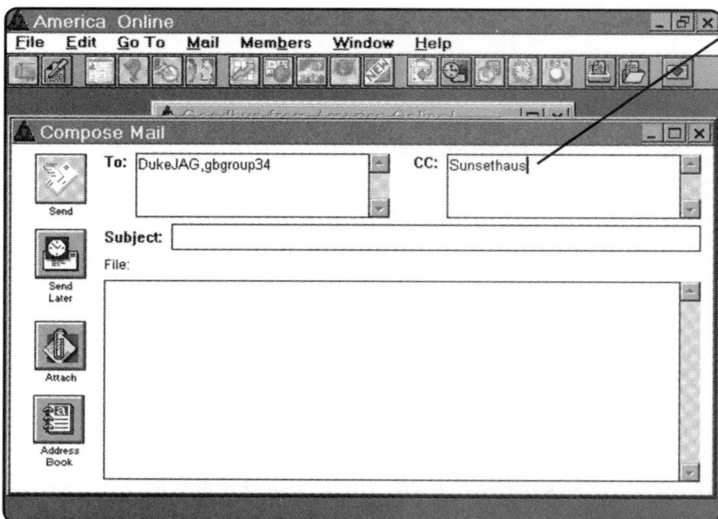

1. **Press** the **Tab key** to move the cursor to the CC field.

2. If you want to send a copy of this letter to someone, **type** that person's **screen name** in the CC box.

Depending on your age, you may be asking, "What the heck is a carbon copy? If you want the person to get a copy, why not put the name in the To list?"

The term "carbon copy" comes from the time when letters were typed on a typewriter and copies were made using a piece of carbon paper. Hence, a *carbon copy*.

In terms of business etiquette, there is a difference between listing someone's name as a carbon copy recipient and putting multiple names in the To line. Let's say that you are heading an interdepartmental project team and you want to send the final report to all involved department heads as well as a department head who is not directly involved in the project. The names of involved department heads should be in the To line (perhaps in alphabetical order if they are all equal in rank), and the name of the other department head should be in the CC line.

Typing a Subject and Message

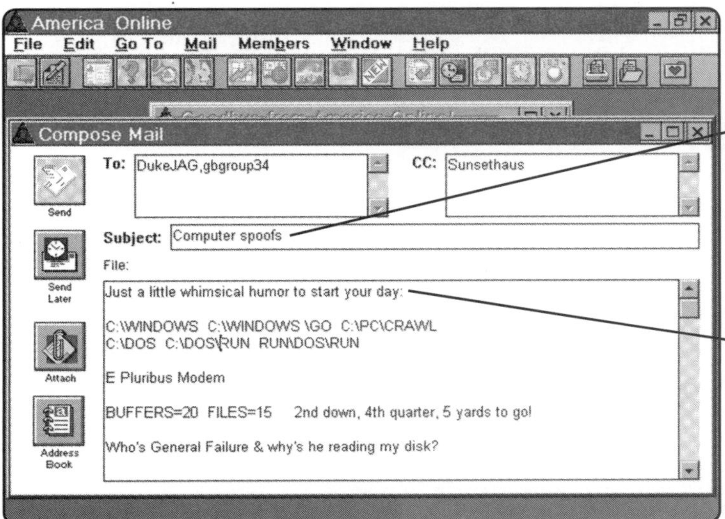

The Subject is required for AOL mail.

1. **Press** the **Tab key** to move to the **Subject** field. Type the **subject** of your message. It should have no more than 32 characters.

2. **Press** the **Tab** key to move to the **File** field. **Type** your **message**. The message cannot be more than 32K, (about eight pages). If your message is longer, you'll have to divide it and use several e-mails.

Minimizing Your Message

You have to sign on to AOL to send mail.

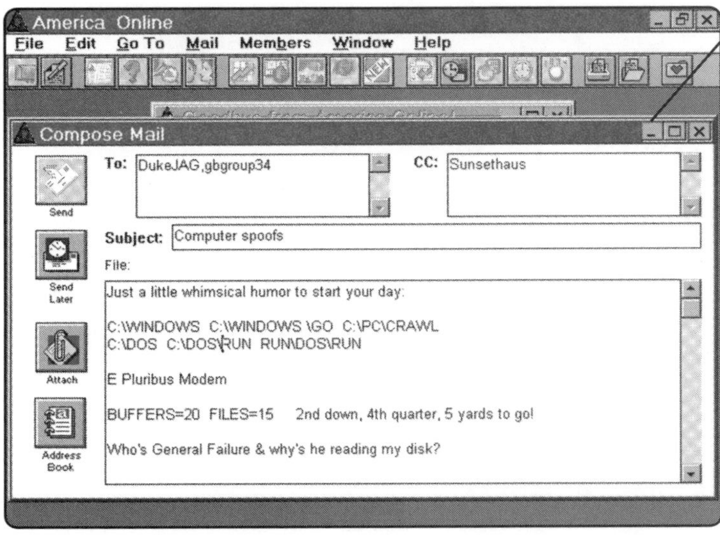

1. **Click** on the **Minimize button** (▁, or ▼ if you're using Windows 3.1) to minimize the dialog box at the bottom of your screen. The Welcome dialog box will reappear. You can write and minimize as many messages as you want before you sign on to AOL.

Note: You can also click on Send Later and schedule a FlashSession. See Chapter 7 for information on using FlashSessions.

SIGNING ON TO AMERICA ONLINE

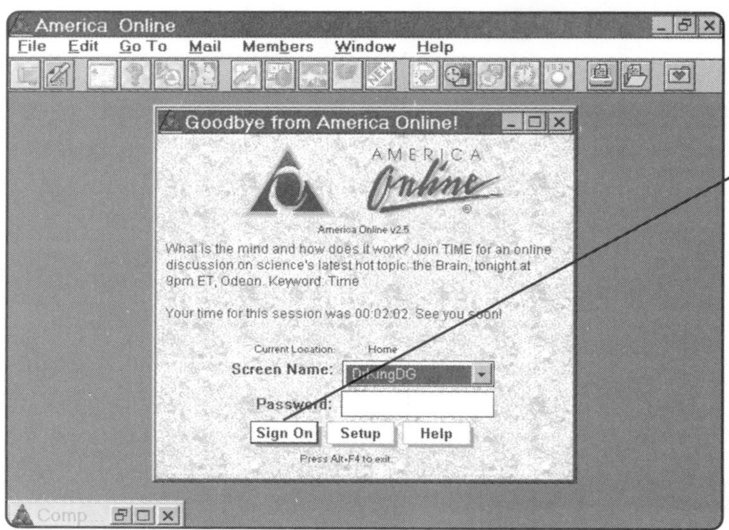

Now that you've finished composing mail, you're ready to sign on.

1. **Click** on **Sign On**. The America Online logo will appear as you hear the usual connecting noises.

SENDING MAIL

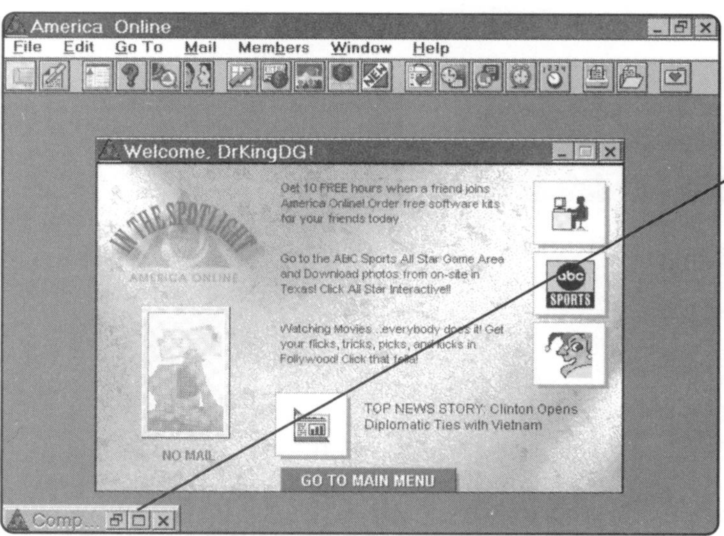

You must first maximize the Compose Mail icon so you can send the mail.

1. **Click** on the **Restore button**, or, if you're using Windows 3.1, **click twice** on the **Compose Mail icon** at the bottom of your screen. The Compose Mail dialog box will appear on your screen with your mail message.

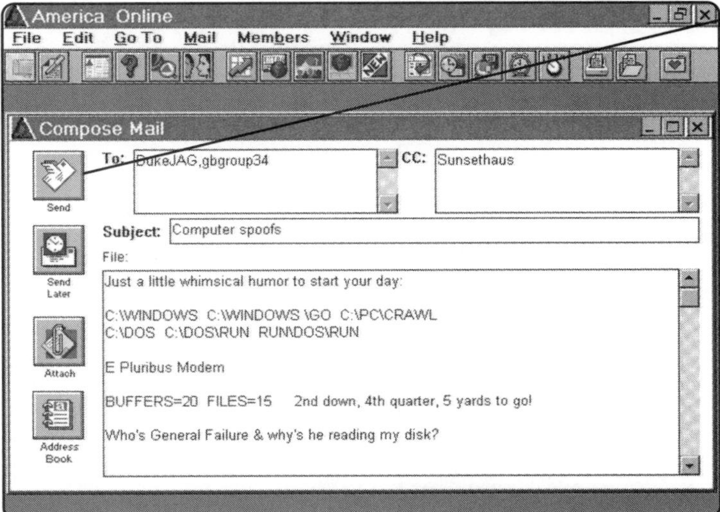

2. **Click** on **Send**. When your mail has been sent, you will see the message below.

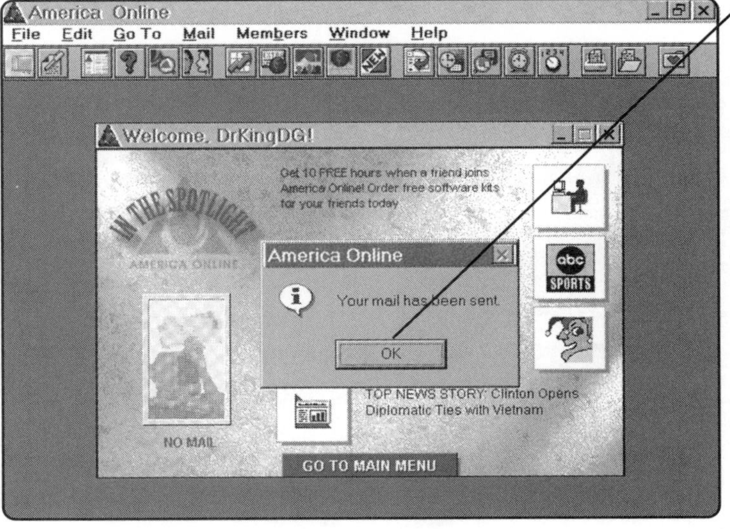

3. **Click** on **OK** to close this message box.

CHECKING OUTGOING MAIL

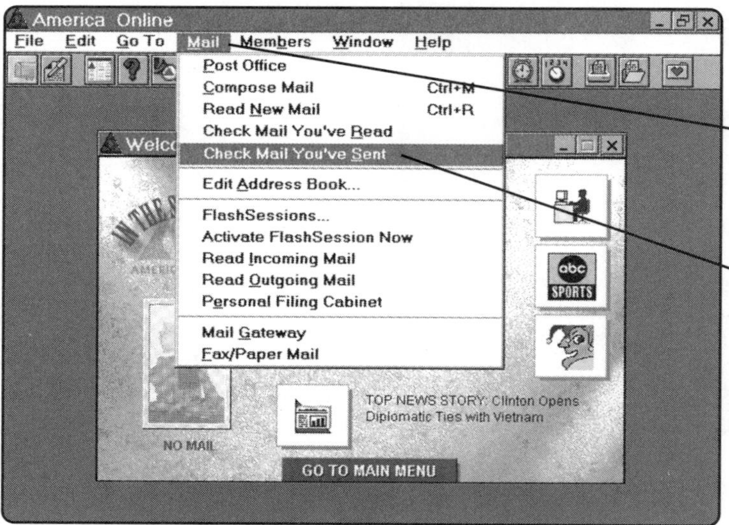

You can read mail you've sent.

1. **Click** on **Mail** in the menu bar. A menu will appear.

2. **Click** on **Check Mail You've Sent**. The Outgoing Mail dialog box will appear with a listing of mail you've sent.

Showing Status

You can check to see whether someone has read his or her mail. (This feature does not apply to Internet Mail).

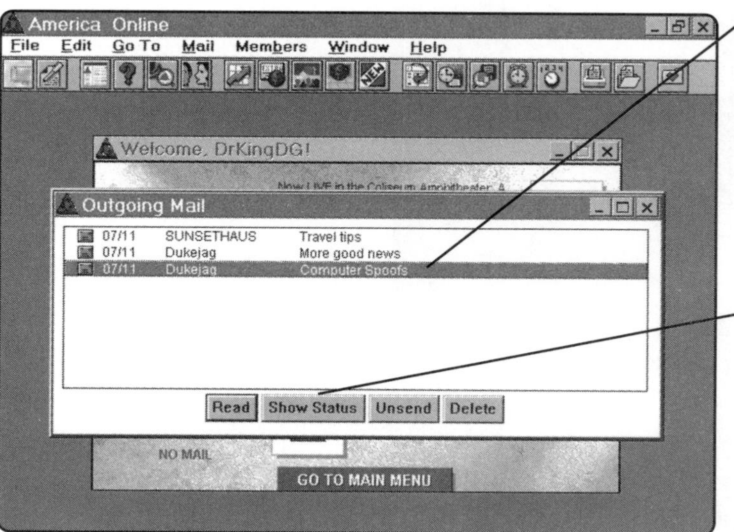

1. **Click** on the **letter** you want to check on to highlight it. Notice that only the first recipient is listed in the Outgoing Mail dialog box even though you sent the letter to several people.

2. **Click** on **Show Status.** The Show Status dialog box will appear.

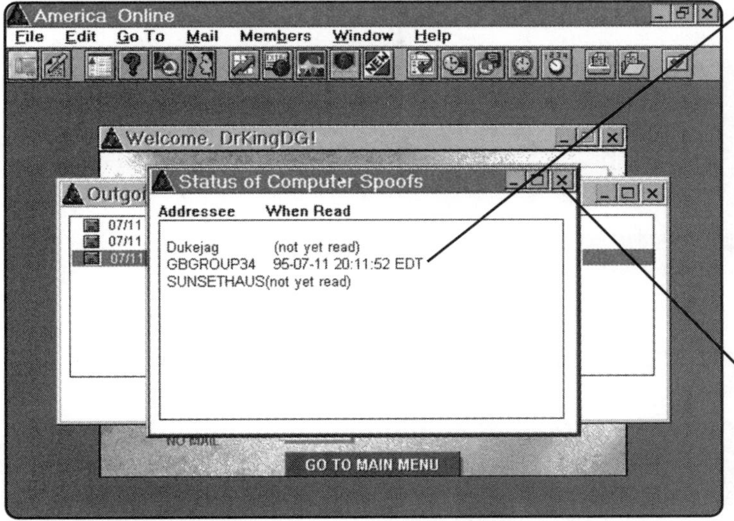

Notice that this window shows the names of the three people we sent the letter to earlier in this chapter. The letter has been read by only one of its recipients. The list shows the date and time it was read by GBGROUP34.

3. **Click** on the **Close box** ([X]) in the right corner of the title bar, or, if you're using WIndows 3.1, **click twice** on the **Control menu box** ([X]) in the left corner of the title bar. The dialog box will close. We will only give the Windows 95 step for closing dialog boxes in the rest of the chapter.

Unsending Mail

If the mail has not been read, you can "unsend" it. Once it has been read (by any one of the people to whom it was addressed), you cannot unsend it. The Unsend feature applies only to mail sent to other AOL members. It doesn't apply to Internet mail, which will be discussed in Chapter 2.

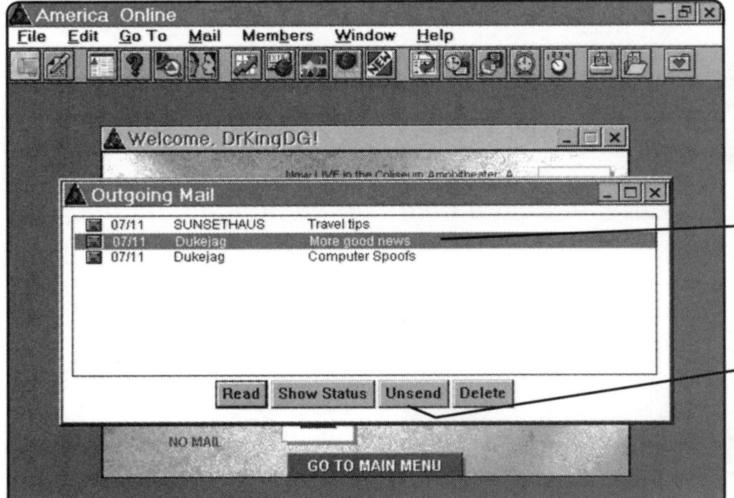

1. **Click** on the **letter** you want to unsend to highlight it.

2. **Click** on **Unsend.** A message box will appear.

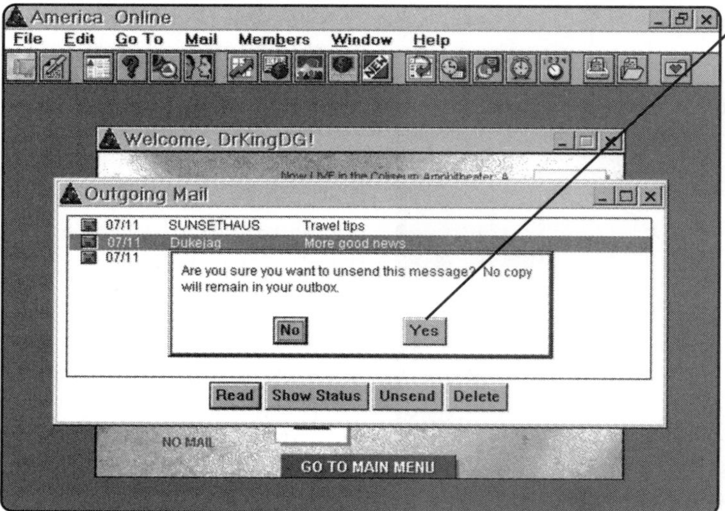

3. **Click** on **Yes**.

4. Another message box will appear. **Click** on **OK**. The message box will disappear.

READING A LETTER YOU'VE SENT

If you send a letter to a group of people, only the first person in the To box will show in the Outgoing Mail dialog box.

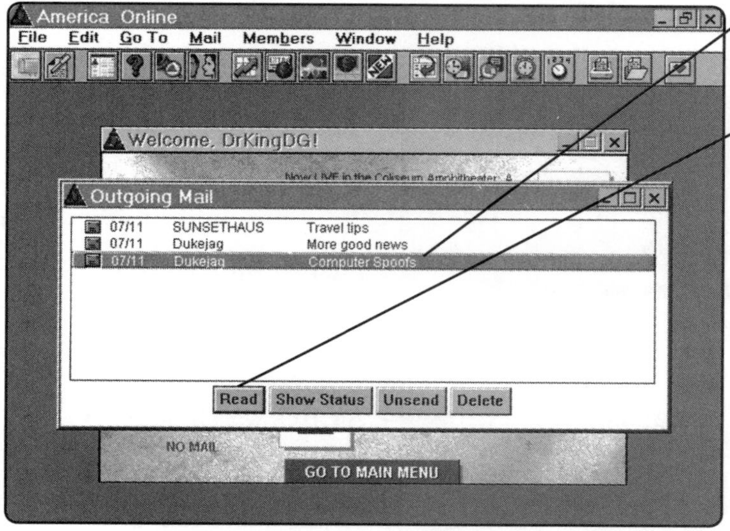

1. **Click** on the **letter** you want to read.

2. **Click** on the **Read button**. The letter will appear on your screen.

Mail will stay on this list for seven days. If you send lots of mail, you may want to use the Delete button to delete it sooner. The Delete button only deletes highlighted items from this list. It has no effect on the status of mail that has been sent.

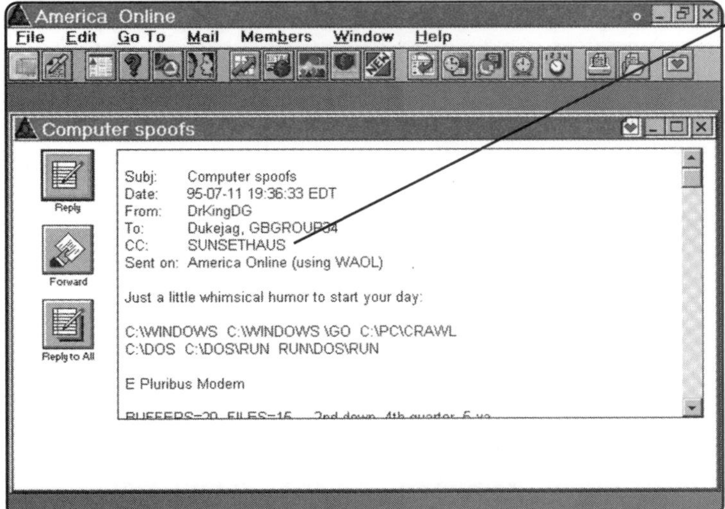

Notice that the two original recipients and the carbon-copy recipient are shown in your e-mail letter.

Note: This view is the only view that gives you this header information.

PRINTING A LETTER

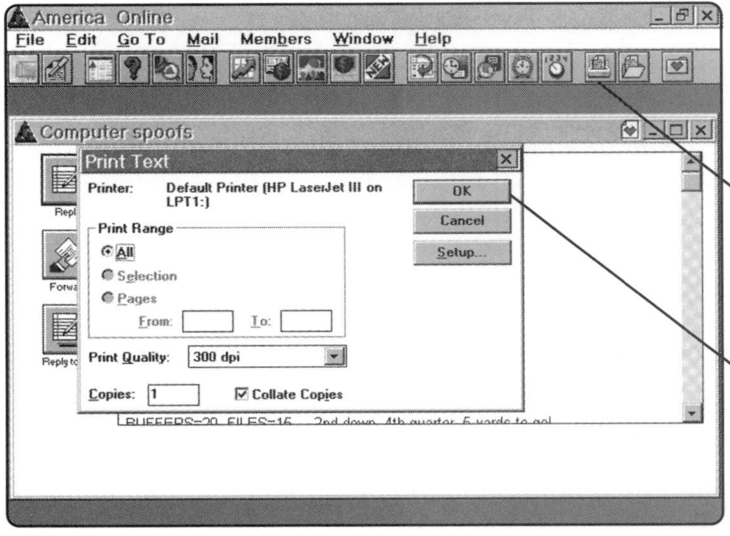

You can print a copy of outgoing mail after you have opened it in the Read view, as you did above.

1. **Click** on the **Print** icon. It's the third from the right. The print dialog box will appear.

2. **Click** on **OK**. The letter will print.

3. **Click** on the **Close box** (**X**) in the right corners of the title bars to close the letter and Outgoing Mail dialog boxes.

SAVING COPIES OF YOUR E-MAIL

Copies of mail you send and receive can be saved automatically in your Personal Filing Cabinet.

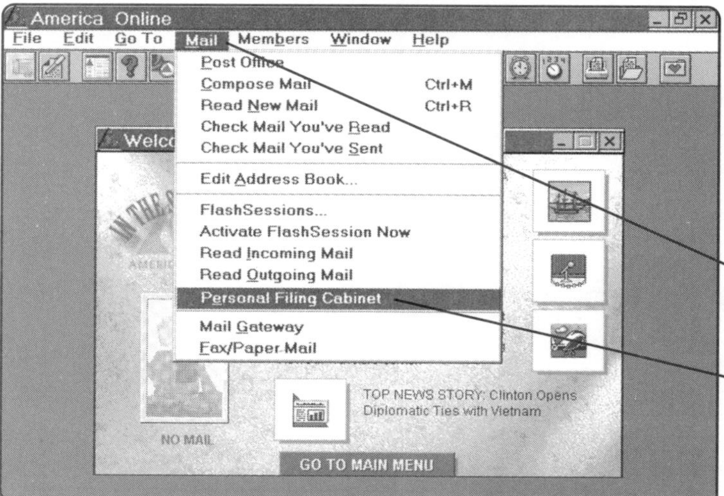

Opening the Personal Filing Cabinet

1. **Click** on **Mail** in the menu bar. A menu will appear.

2. **Click** on **Personal Filing Cabinet**. The Personal Filing Cabinet dialog box will appear.

Setting Personal Filing Cabinet Preferences

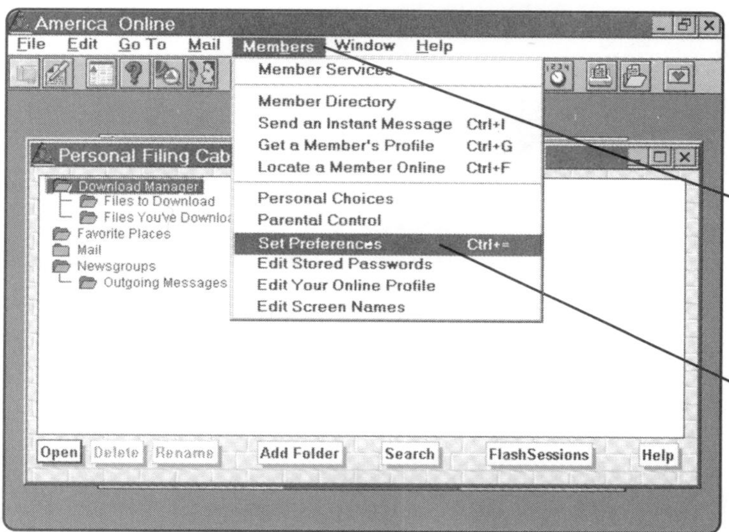

AOL allows you to set your File Cabinet preference and use the Filing Cabinet both on or offline.

1. **Click** on **Members** in the menu bar. A menu will appear.

2. **Click** on **Set Preferences.** The Preferences dialog box will appear.

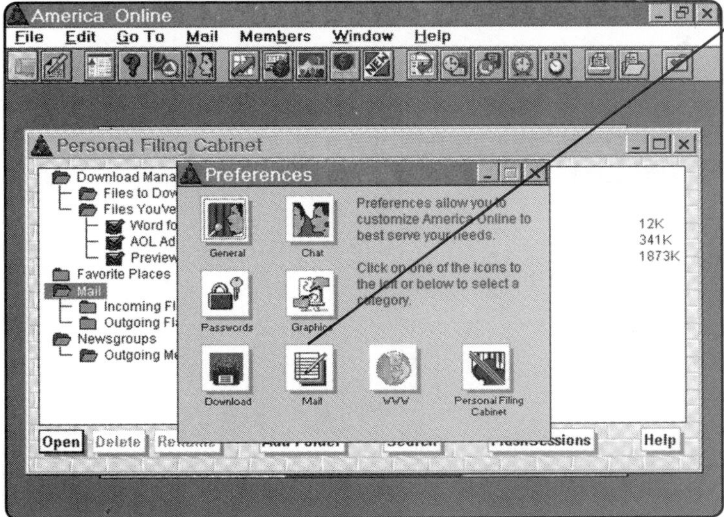

3. **Click** on **Mail**. The Mail Preferences dialog box will appear.

These settings allow you to automatically store copies of e-mail you send and receive in your Personal File Cabinet. You can sort or delete these saved messages offline to save on connection charges.

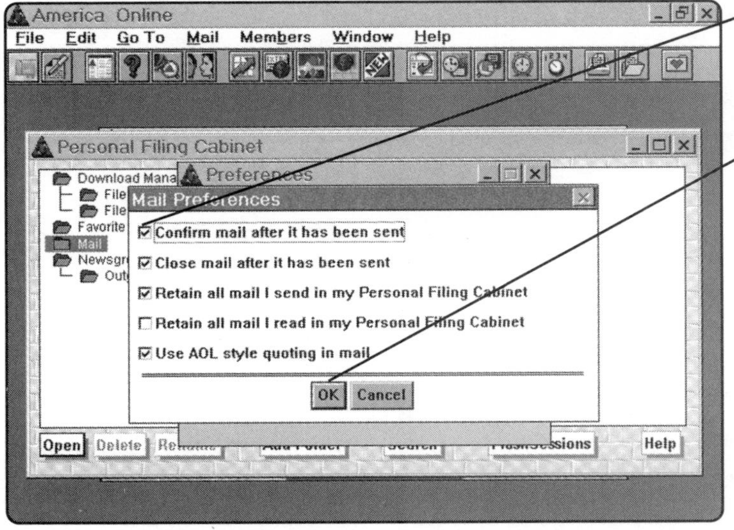

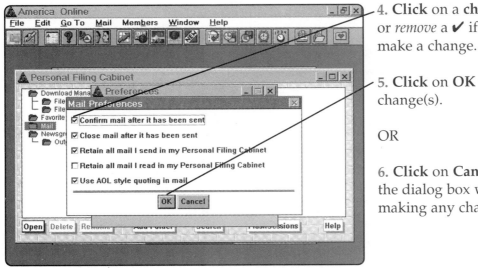

4. **Click** on a **choice** to *place* or *remove* a ✔ if you want to make a change.

5. **Click** on **OK** to save your change(s).

OR

6. **Click** on **Cancel** to close the dialog box without making any changes.

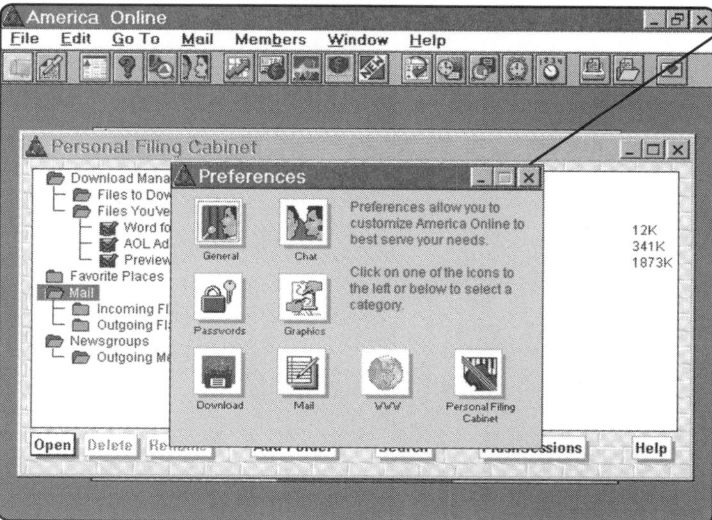

7. **Click** on the ☒ in the right corner of the title bar. The Preferences dialog box will close.

Viewing Your Mail

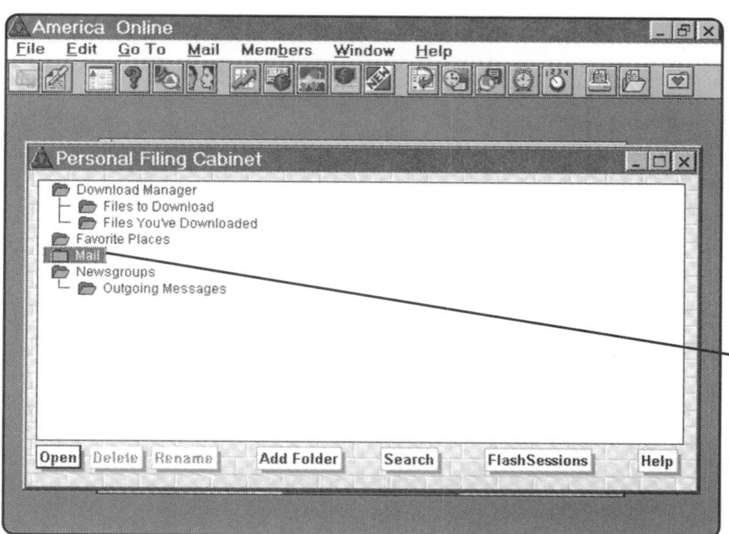

If you choose to have copies of your e-mail automatically saved, a folder named *Archives* will be created for you the first time you subsequently send or receive e-mail. Your copies will be stored in it.

1. **Click twice** on **Mail**. The Mail folders will appear.

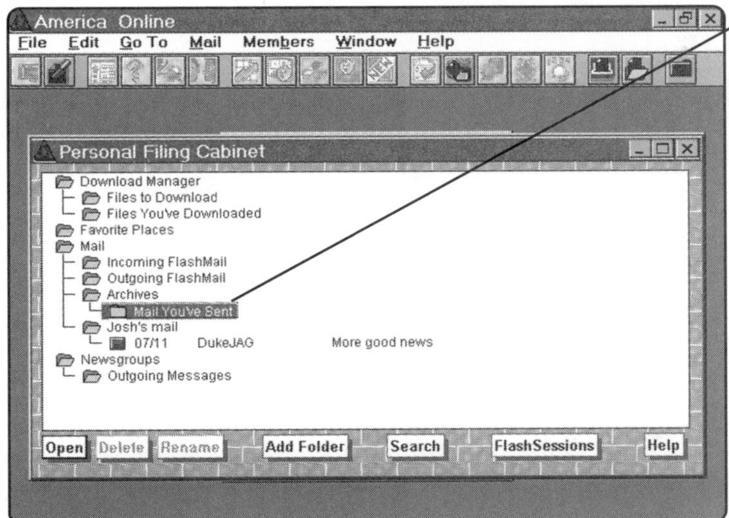

2. **Click twice** on **Mail You've Sent**. A list of the mail you have sent will appear.

Adding Folders

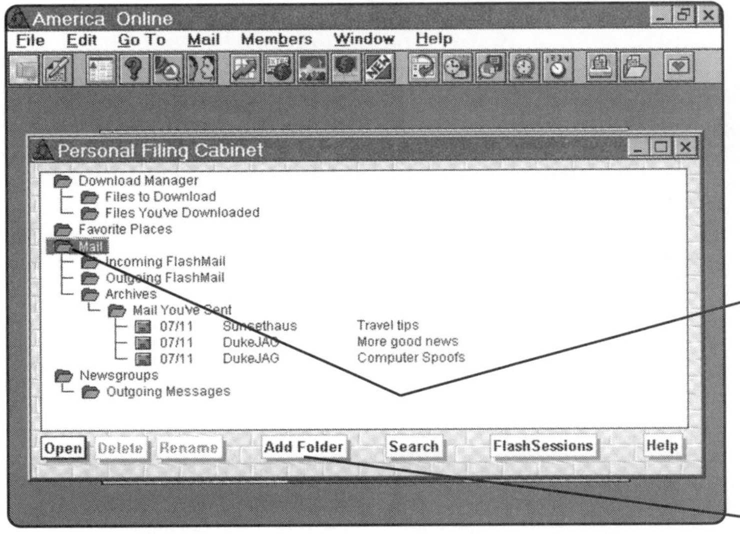

You may want to create separate folders for each person you correspond with, or make folders to organize other items in your Personal File Cabinet. It couldn't be easier.

1. **Click** on the **heading** to which you want to add a folder. In this example, we've selected Mail.

2. **Click** on **Add Folder**. The New Folder dialog box will appear.

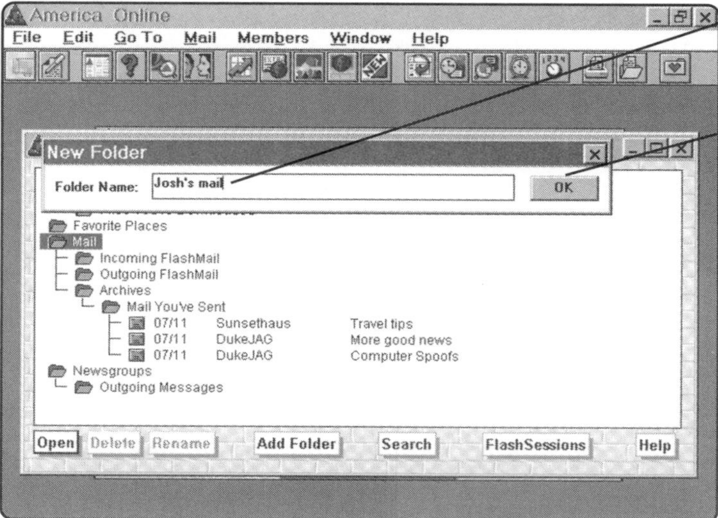

3. **Type** a **name** for the folder.
4. **Click** on **OK**. The dialog box will close and a new folder with the name you typed will appear under the heading you selected.

Moving Files Using Drag-and-Drop

E-mail can easily be moved between folders using standard drag-and-drop techniques.

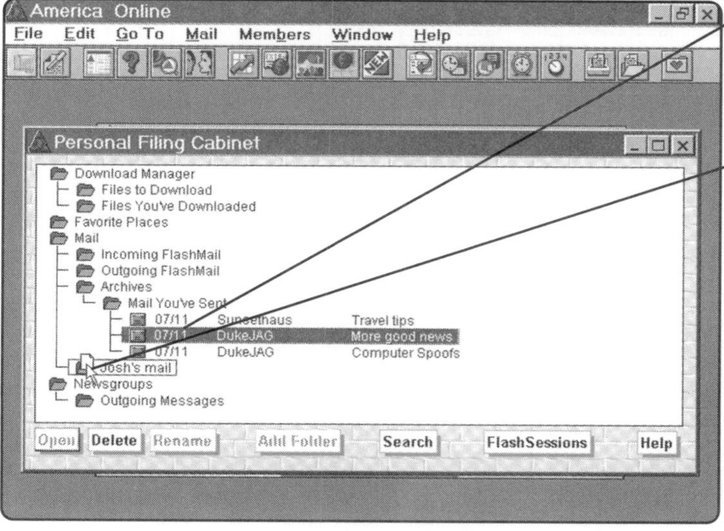

1. **Click** on the **letter** that you want to move. The selection will become highlighted.
2. **Press and hold** the mouse button as you drag the icon to the new folder.
3. When the icon is over the new folder and a box appears around the new folder, **release** the **mouse button**. Your file will move to the new folder.

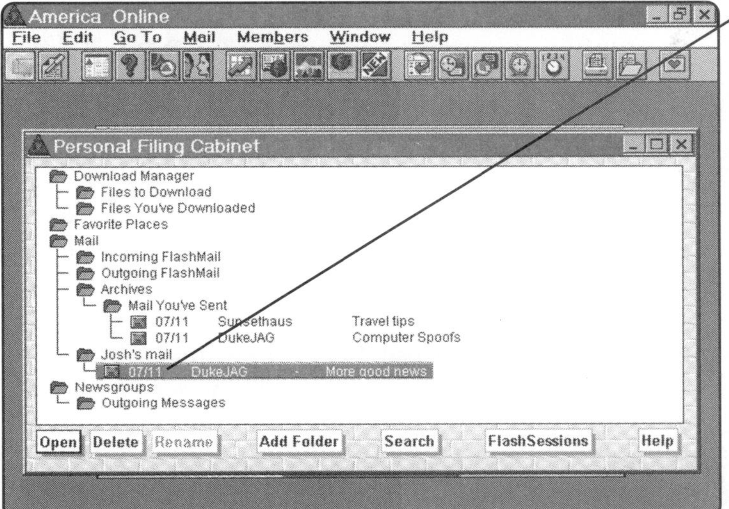

Notice that the file is now in the new folder.

Have fun making additional folders to keep all of your letters sorted.

CLOSING AMERICA ONLINE

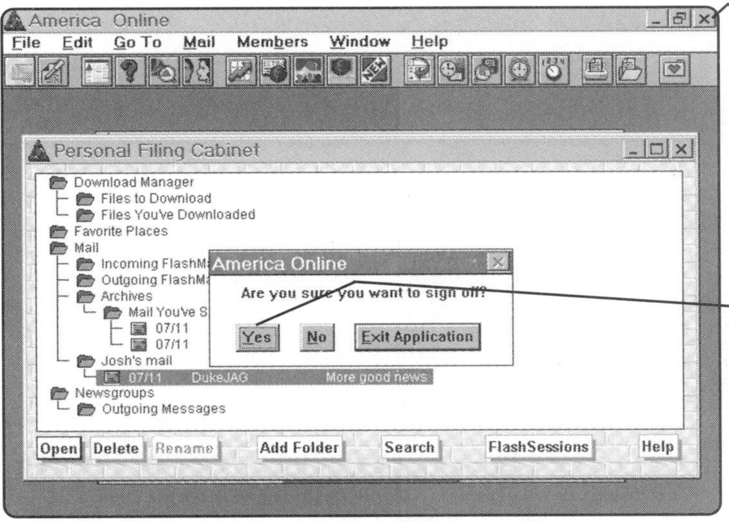

1. **Click** on the **Close button** in the right corner of the America Online title bar. A dialog box will appear.

2. **Click** on **Yes**. You will be disconnected from the online service, but the AOL program will still be running.

RECAPPING

- ✔ Use fast, efficient e-mail to send letters to one or more people simultaneously.
- ✔ Use the Personal Filing Cabinet to organize your e-mail.

Sending Internet Mail

If you want to correspond with someone who is on another online service, such as CompuServe, Applelink, or Prodigy, you can use AOL's connection to the Internet to send the mail. You don't have to do anything special to send Internet mail. The process is the same as sending mail to other AOL members. The determining factor in whether mail is AOL mail or Internet mail is the address. Internet addresses (or screen names) have a specific format. In this chapter, you will do the following:

✔ Learn how Internet addresses work
✔ Make an online address into an Internet address
✔ Address and send an Internet letter
✔ Automatically save mail to your Personal Filing Cabinet

UNDERSTANDING INTERNET ADDRESSES

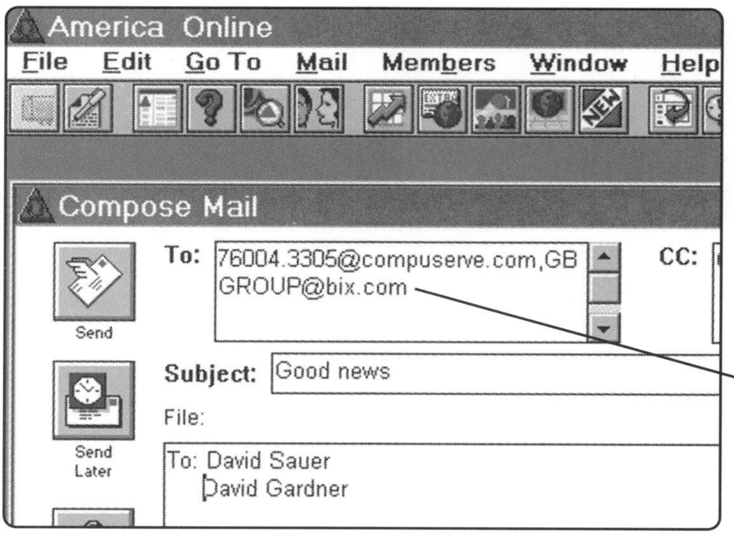

The first rule of sending Internet e-mail is to have the person give you his or her address. There is no easy way to look up someone's Internet address because there is no comprehensive directory of Internet names and addresses.

Internet addresses can be confusing at first glance, but they do have a logical format. Let's take a closer look at the parts of the Internet address.

❶ The first part of the address is the person's name, e.g. bbunny or efudd.

❷ The person's name is always followed by @, for "at."

Examples of Internet Addresses

❶ ❷ ❸
bbunny@acs.bu.edu
efudd@crsa.bu.edu
❺ ❹

The part of the address after the @ depends on how complicated the address is. For example, if you live in an apartment building, your address has more parts to it than if you live in a single house, because you have to give your apartment number as well as your street address. The same is true of an Internet address. It actually helps to look at the last element in the address first.

❸ The last element in these addresses is "edu." This is one of six major categories that describe the types of Internet accounts. The six categories, or *domains*, are listed to the left. The EDU domain name tells you that these are educational accounts.

Internet Categories

COM = Commercial
EDU = Educational
GOV = Government
MIL = Military
NET = Networks
ORG = Organizations

You may also see 2-letter country codes, such as US for the United States, CN for Canada, JP for Japan

❹ The next-to-last part of the address (bu) tells you that this is a Boston University account.

❺ The two Boston University addresses have different letters after @ because Boston University has many different computers connected to the Internet.

Each of these parts of the address is followed by a period (.), called a "dot" in online talk, or *dotspeak*. The dot separates the parts of the address. If you want to sound like one of the "in" crowd, read the first name above as "bbunny at acs dot bu dot edu."

Making an Online Address Into an Internet Address

As a member of AOL, you have to add elements to your AOL address to make it an Internet address. This is true of the addresses in all online services. For most online services, there is one simple formula:

Making an Online Service Address Into an Internet Address

1234567@mcimail.com (an MCI Mail address)

WRITEBKS@AOL.COM (an AOL address)

Jeannie2@genie.com (a GEnie address)

21147.123@compuserve.com (a CompuServe address)

❶ Type the person's screen name or identification number (also called a "userid");

❷ Type @ after the individual's name;

❸ Type the name of the online service;

❹ Type a dot;

❺ Type "com" to identify it as a commercial service.

There are some things you should notice about these Internet addresses:

✔ It doesn't matter whether you type the name in all upper-case letters, all lower-case letters, or a combination. Addresses are not case-sensitive. WRITEBKS is the same as WriteBks and writebks.

✔ A CompuServe userid has a comma (21147,123). The Internet doesn't recognize commas so the comma must be changed to a dot (21147.123).

Addressing and Sending an Internet Letter

Composing Internet mail through America Online involves the same process as composing mail to AOL members. In this example, we will show you the format of an Internet letter. If you want to send the letter now, you'll have to sign on to AOL.

1. **Click** on the **Compose Mail icon** in the Flash Bar. It's the second one from the left. A Compose Mail dialog box will appear.

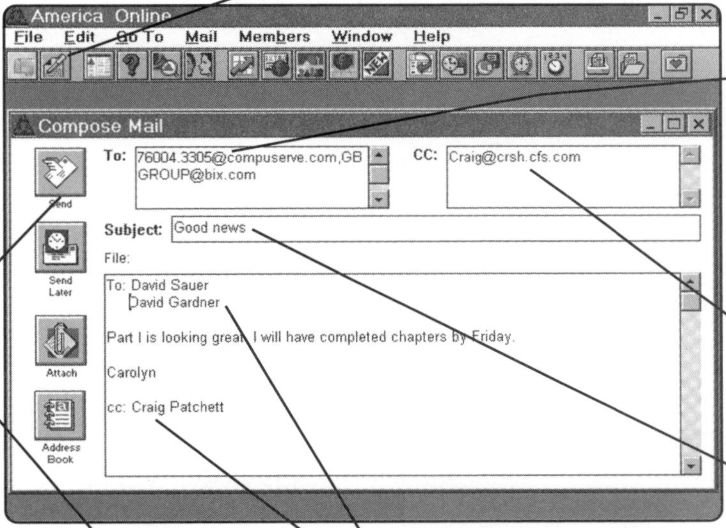

2. **Type** the **Internet address** of the **recipient(s)** in the To line at the top of the letter. Remember, for multiple recipients you do not put a space after the comma.

3. **Type** the **Internet address** of any one to whom you want to send a carbon copy.

4. **Type** a **subject.**

5. **Type** the **message.**

Notice that we have listed all recipients at the top of the letter, and the carbon-copy recipient at the bottom so that everyone will know who got copies. This is because Internet mail sent through AOL doesn't show multiple or carbon-copy recipients. Internet mail will send a letter to each person, but will put his or her name as the only name in the To line of the letter.

6. **Click** on **Send**. A message box will appear saying that your mail has been sent. **Click** on **OK**.

SAVING COPIES OF YOUR E-MAIL

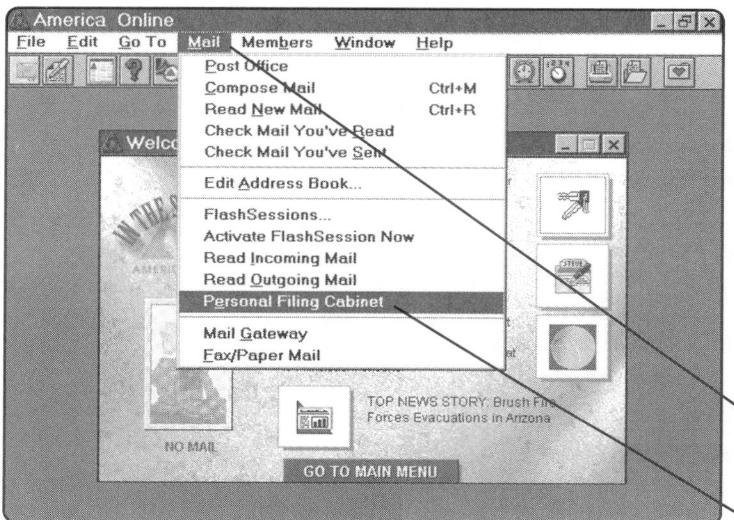

Copies of mail you send and receive can be saved automatically in your Personal Filing Cabinet. See Chapter 1 for details on setting your Mail preferences to do this. Saved copies can be viewed by opening the Personal Filing Cabinet.

1. **Click** on **Mail** in the menu bar. A menu will appear.

2. **Click** on **Personal Filing Cabinet**. The Personal Filing Cabinet dialog box will appear.

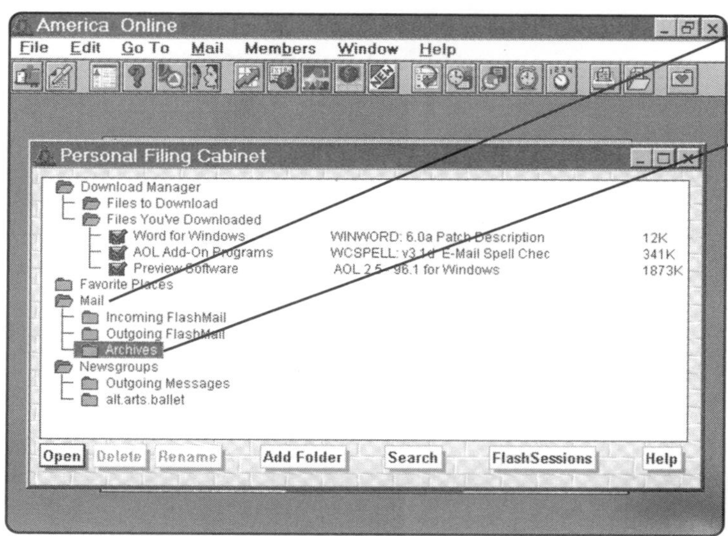

3. **Click twice** on **Mail.** The Archives folder will appear.

4. **Click twice** on **Archives**. The Archives folder will open.

5. **Click twice** on **Mail You've Sent**. A list of the mail you've sent will appear.

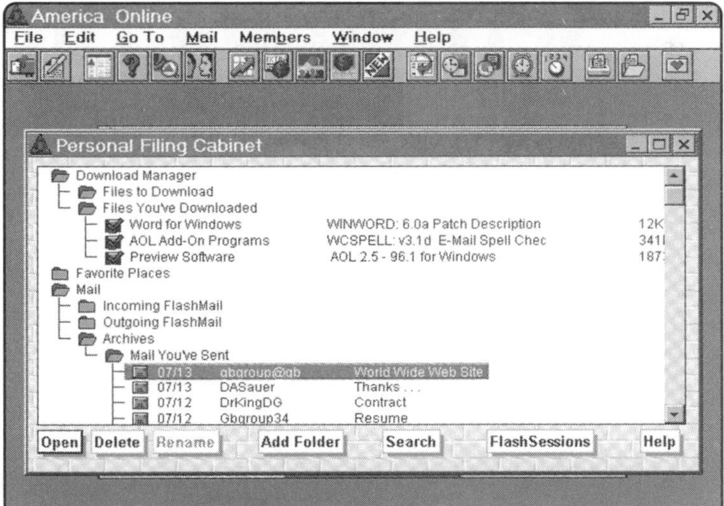

We've set our Mail preferences to save only copies of sent mail, so there's no folder for mail that we've read. To view the mail, just click twice on it.

Closing the Cabinet

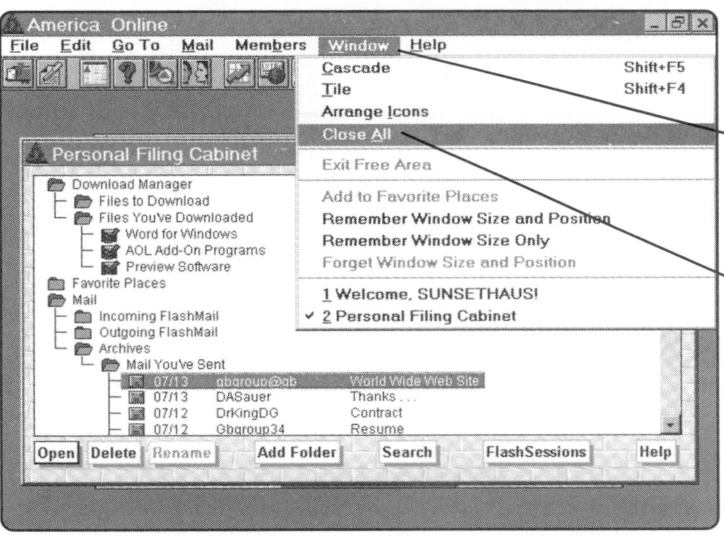

1. **Click** on **Window** in the menu bar. A menu will appear.

2. **Click** on **Close All**. All of the open dialog boxes will close.

RECAPPING

✔ Use Internet e-mail to keep in touch with friends and colleagues throughout the world.

✔ Use the Personal Filing Cabinet to keep track of your e-mail.

Setting Up the Address Book

America Online's Address Book makes it easy to send e-mail by keeping your addresses handy. In this chapter, you will do the following:

- ✔ Add names and addresses to your AOL Address Book
- ✔ Modify an address
- ✔ Delete an address
- ✔ Add a Group address
- ✔ Use the Address Book to address an e-mail letter
- ✔ Search for a member online
- ✔ Create your own member profile

ADDING NAMES AND ADDRESSES

You can open and edit the Address Book without being connected to America Online's computer. This means you can do all of your address book maintenance off-line at no charge!

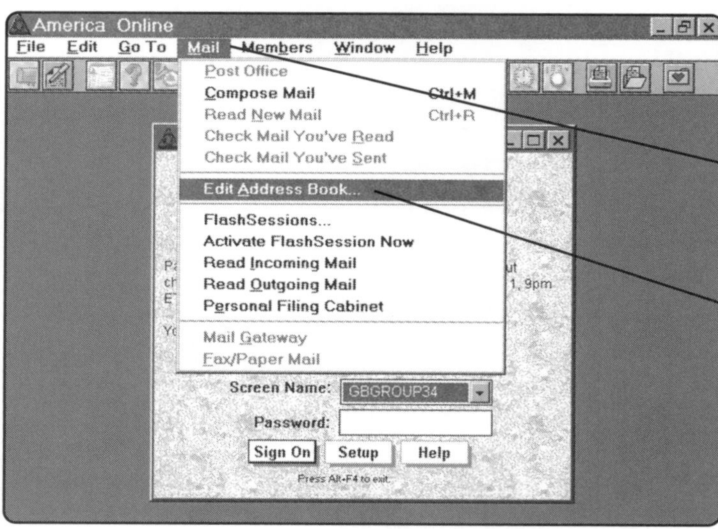

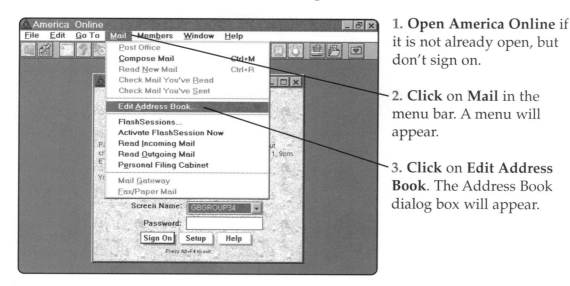

1. **Open America Online** if it is not already open, but don't sign on.

2. **Click** on **Mail** in the menu bar. A menu will appear.

3. **Click** on **Edit Address Book**. The Address Book dialog box will appear.

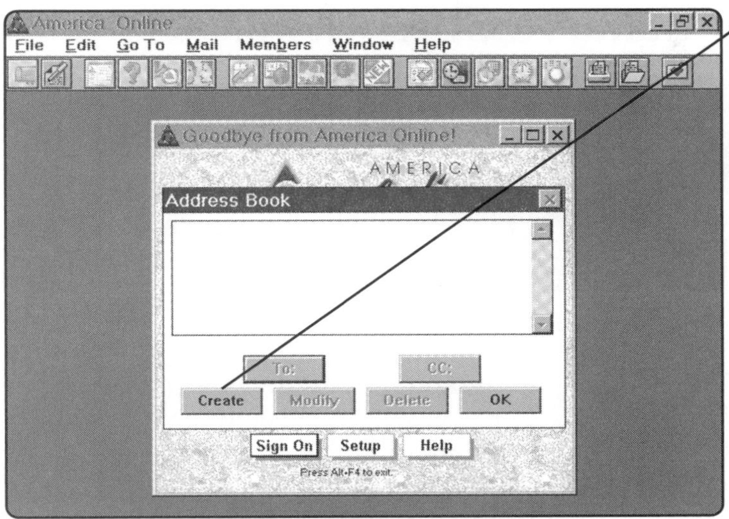

4. **Click** on **Create**. The Address Group dialog box will appear. The cursor will be flashing in the Group Name box.

5. **Type** the person's **name** and **press** the **Tab key** on your keyboard. The cursor will move to the Screen Names box.

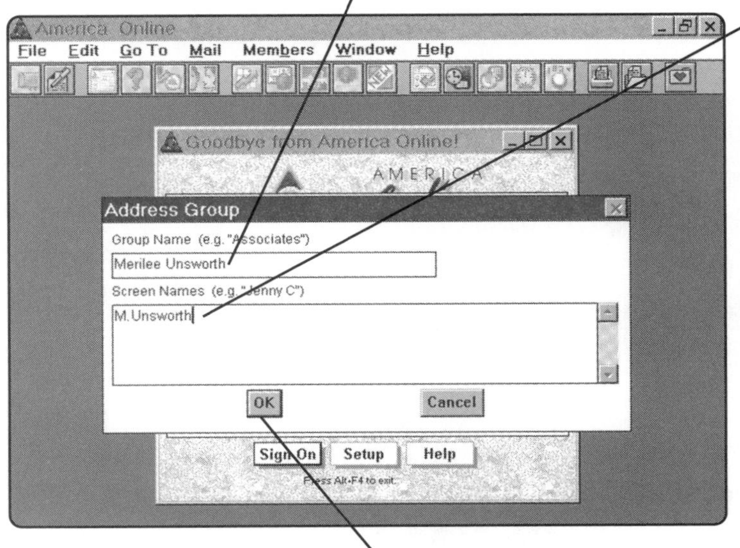

6. **Type** the person's **screen name** here. (Merilee Unsworth's screen name should not have a period between M and Unsworth. Type it incorrectly here, though, so that you can learn how to correct a name later in this chapter.) AOL names are not case sensitive, so it doesn't matter whether you type in all upper-case or lower-case letters, or a combination of upper- and lower-case.

7. **Click** on **OK**. The Address Book dialog box will appear.

Adding Another Name

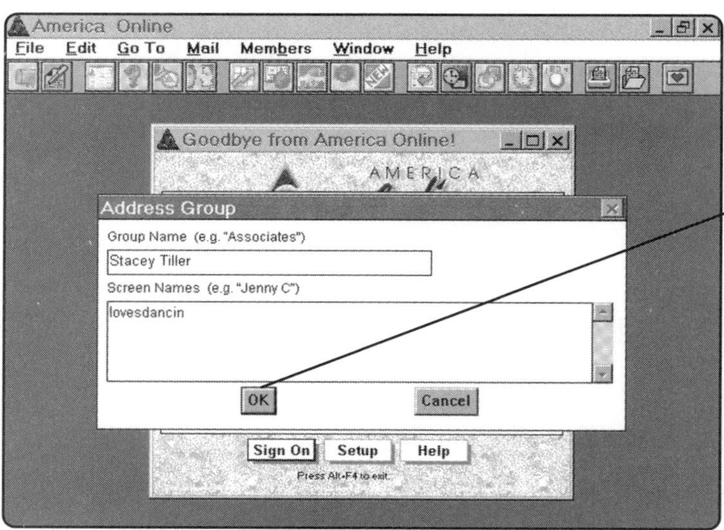

1. **Repeat steps 4–6** in the previous section to add a second group and screen name.

2. **Click** on **OK**. The Address Book dialog box will appear.

Notice that the names in the screen below are not in alphabetical order. *The AOL Address Book adds names only in order of entry*. The last name entered goes to the bottom of the list. For this reason we keep our e-mail address list up to date in a Word table so that we can alphabetize the names automatically. Then, periodically, we delete most of the names from the AOL Address Book and re-enter them in alphabetical order. We hope AOL will improve the software so that you can sort the names in the address book!

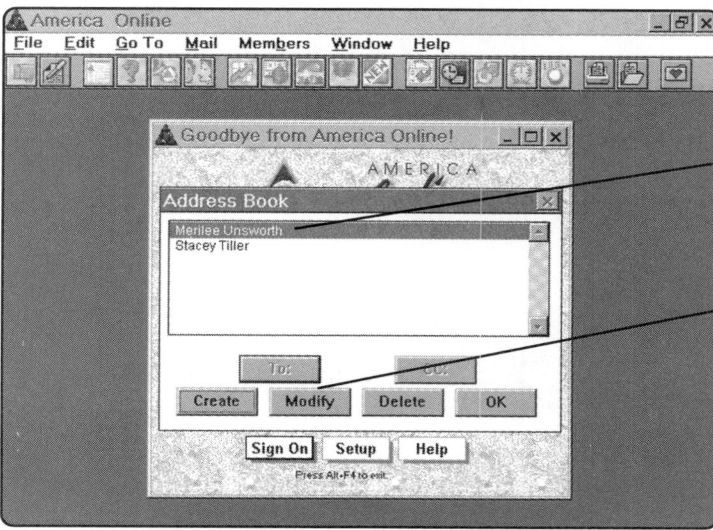

EDITING AN ADDRESS

1. **Click** on the **name** of the person whose address you want to **edit.**

2. **Click** on **Modify**. The Address Group dialog box will appear. The cursor will be flashing in the Screen Name box.

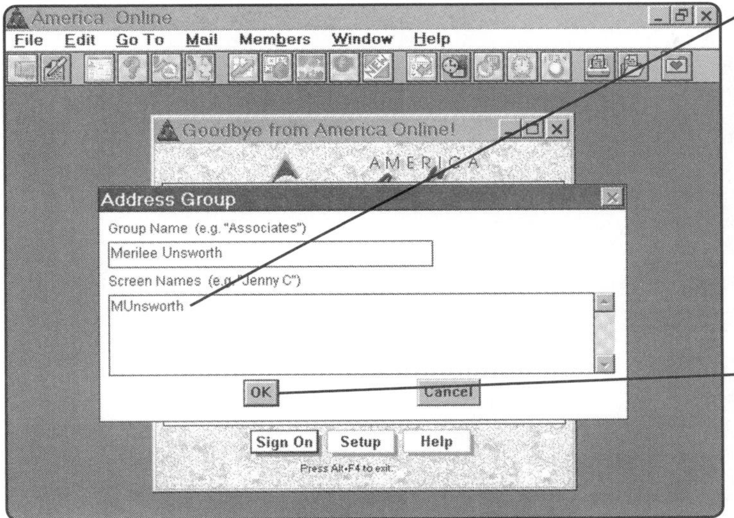

3. **Press and hold** the mouse button and **drag** it to the **left** to **highlight** the **screen name**.

4. **Type** the **correct name.** In this example, there should not be a period after the letter C.

5. **Click** on **OK**. The Address Book dialog box will appear.

DELETING AN ADDRESS

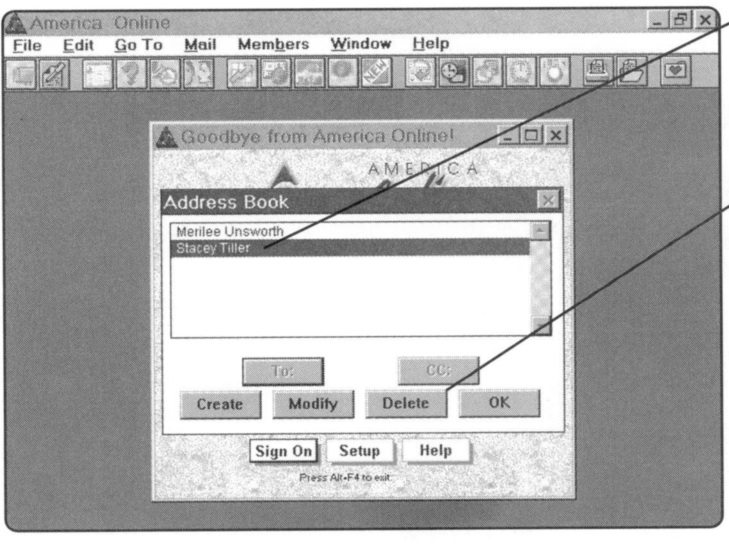

1. **Click** on the **name** of the person whose address you want to **delete** from your address book.

2. **Click** on **Delete**. The Delete dialog box will appear.

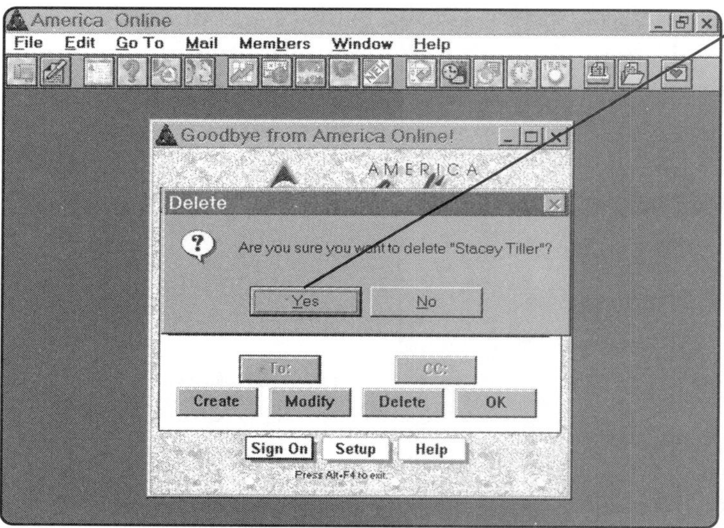

3. Click on **Yes**. The dialog box will disappear.

ADDING A GROUP ADDRESS

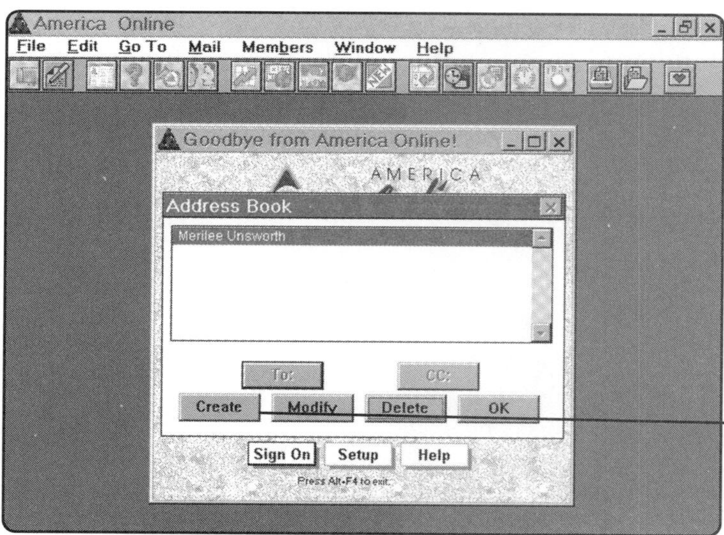

If you regularly send mail to the same group of people, you can create a group address and add the names of all appropriate people to the group. Thereafter, when you send mail to the group, a copy of the letter will automatically be sent to everyone in the group.

1. Click on **Create**. The Address Group dialog box will appear. The cursor will be flashing in the Group Name box.

2. **Type** the **group name** (your choice) and **press** the **Tab key** on your keyboard. The cursor will move to the Screen Names box.

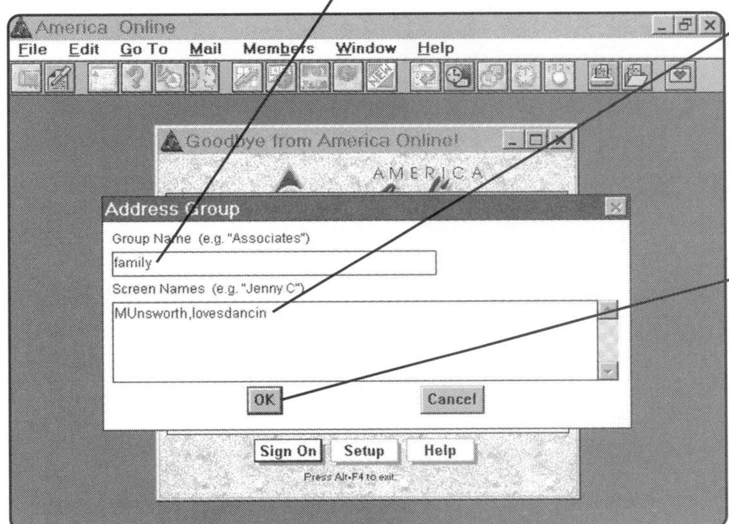

3. **Type** the **screen name** of each person you want in the group. *Separate each address with a comma. Don't put a space before or after the comma.*

4. **Click** on **OK**. The Address Book dialog box will appear. You now have a group address. You use it just like a single address but it addresses your letter to each member listed in the group.

CLOSING THE ADDRESS BOOK

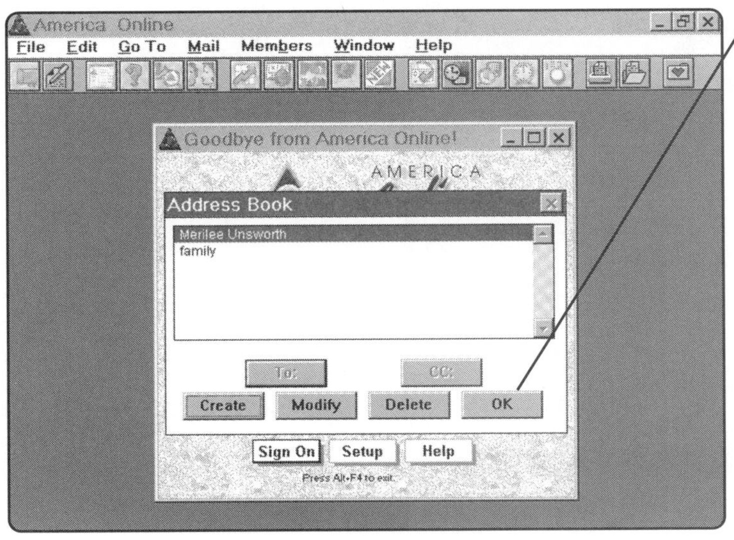

1. **Click** on **OK**. The Address Book dialog box will disappear.

USING THE ADDRESS BOOK

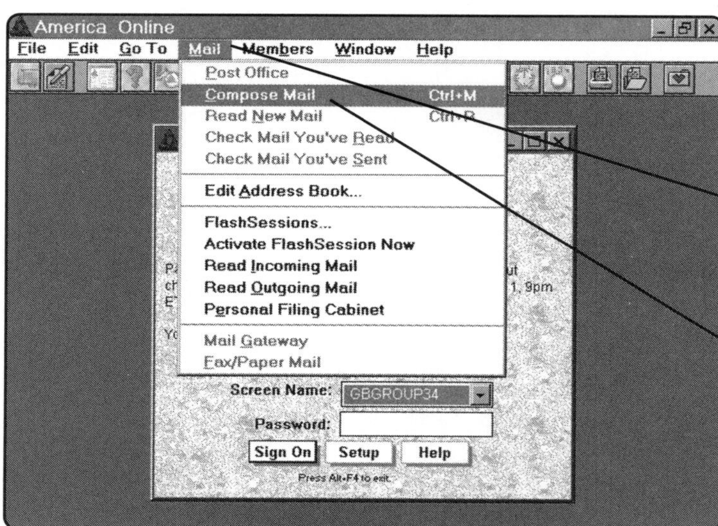

You can use the Address Book to send an original letter or a carbon copy of the letter.

1. **Click** on **Mail** in the menu bar. A menu will appear.

2. **Click** on **Compose Mail**. The Compose Mail dialog box will appear.

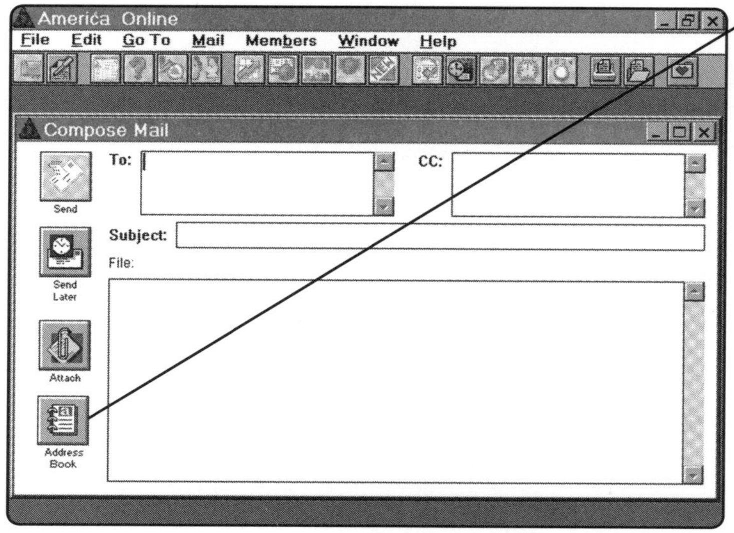

3. **Click** on the **Address Book icon**. The Address Book dialog box will appear.

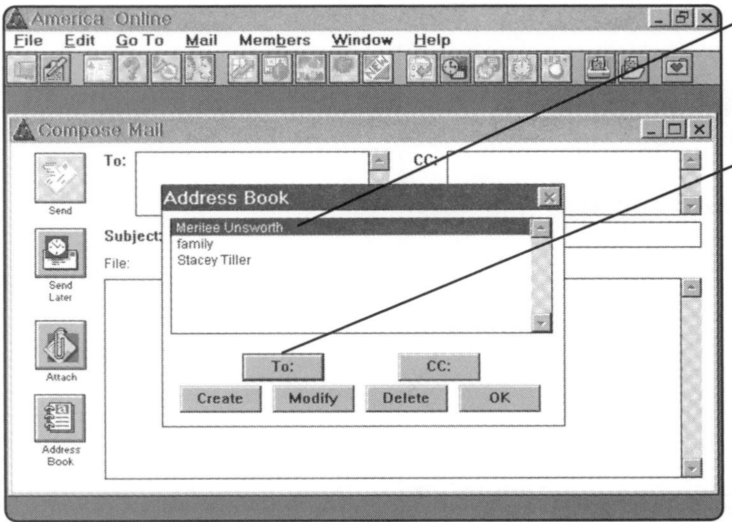

4. **Click** on the **name** of the person to whom you want to **send** a letter.

5. **Click** on the **To button**. The person's screen name that you chose will appear in the To box of the Compose Mail dialog box.

Note: If you click on the group address, the result will be the same except that more than one address will appear in the To box.

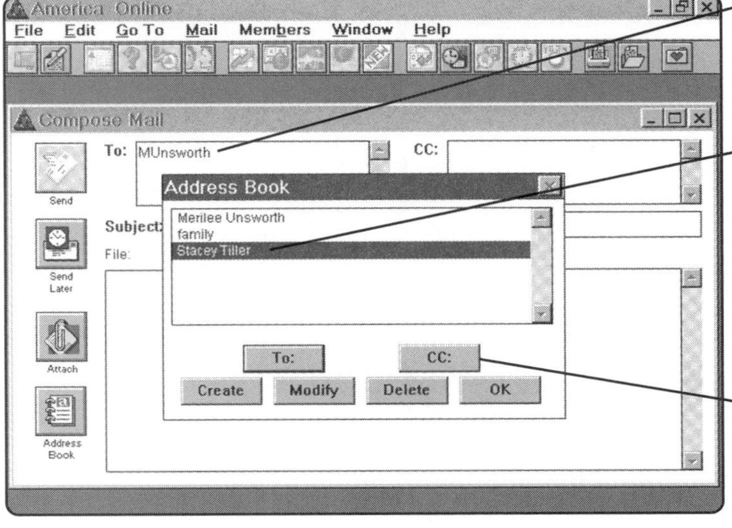

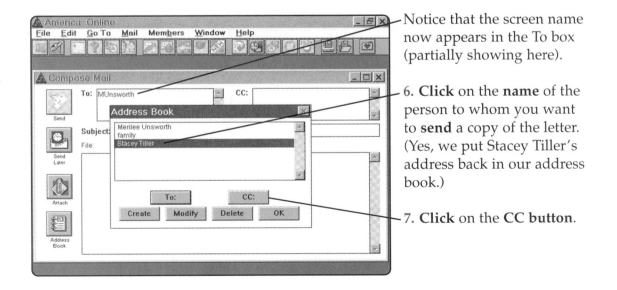

Notice that the screen name now appears in the To box (partially showing here).

6. **Click** on the **name** of the person to whom you want to **send** a copy of the letter. (Yes, we put Stacey Tiller's address back in our address book.)

7. **Click** on the **CC button**.

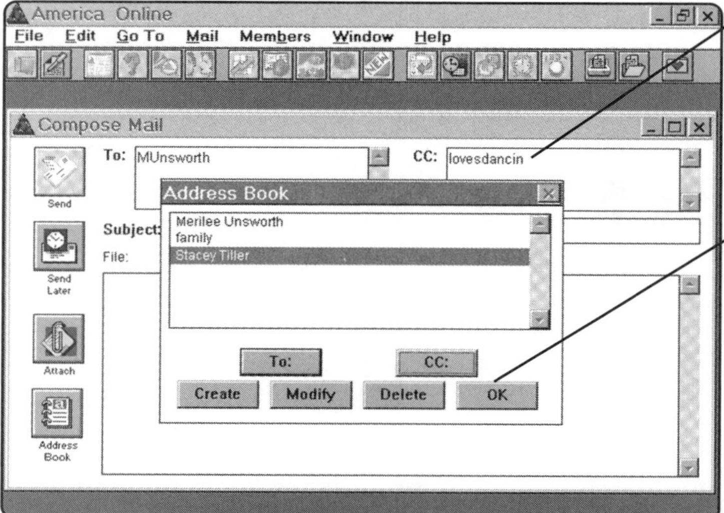

Notice that a screen name now appears in the CC box (partially showing here) of the Compose Mail dialog box.

8. **Click** on **OK**. The Address Book dialog box will close and the Compose Mail dialog box will appear.

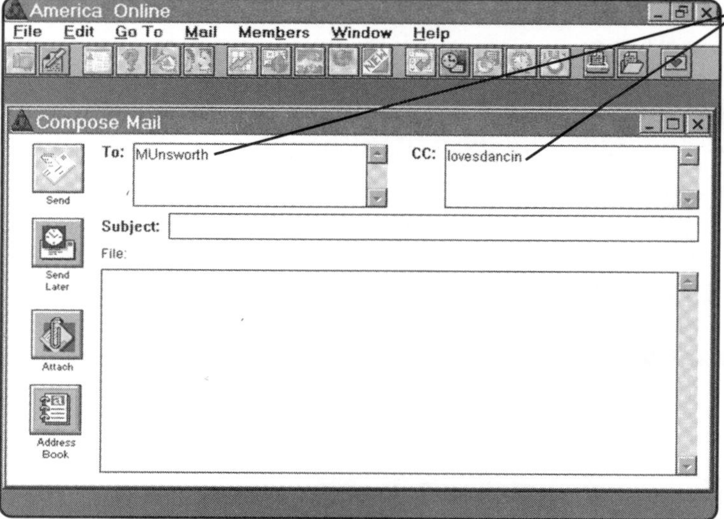

Notice that the Address Book has done its job!

9. **Repeat steps** on pages 7 thru 9 in Chapter 1 to finish composing and sending the e-mail letter.

Note: You can add, modify or delete names from the Address Book at any time, online or not, even when you are composing a letter.

SEARCHING FOR A MEMBER'S E-MAIL ADDRESS

Before you can search for a member's address, you must be signed on to America Online. Once online, you can search for a member by first or last name. You can also search by using descriptive words. For example, when we searched for "author," we got a list of people who had the word *author* in their profiles. The list also included those who had the word *authority* in their profile and who were not authors. In this section, you will search for a member whose name is "Al Gore."

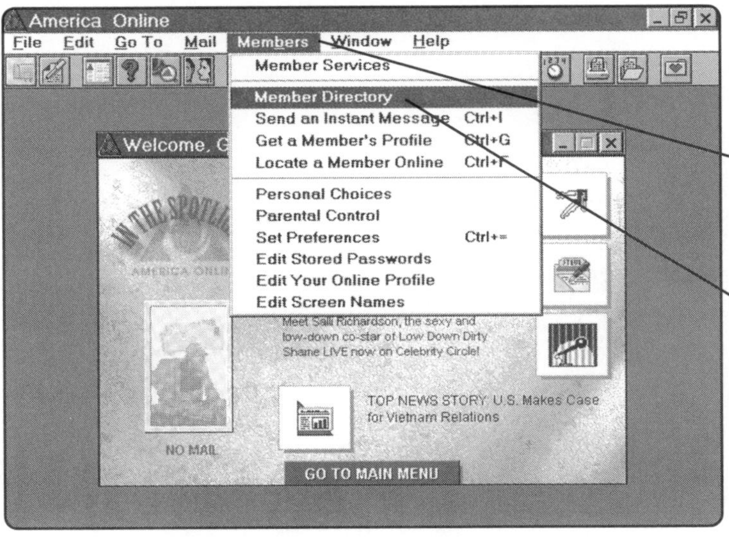

1. **Sign on** to **America Online** if you have not already done so.
2. **Click** on **Members** in the menu bar. A menu will appear.
3. **Click** on **Member Directory.** A Member Directory dialog box will appear.

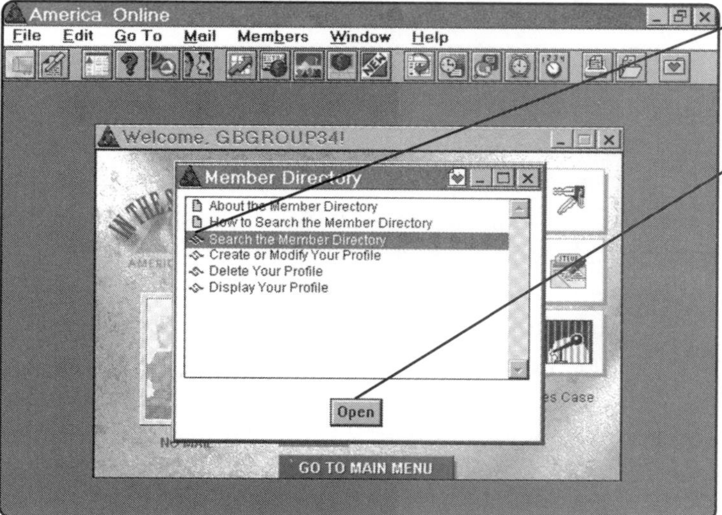

4. **Click** on **Search the Member Directory** to highlight it.

5. **Click** on **Open**. Another Search Member Directory dialog box will appear.

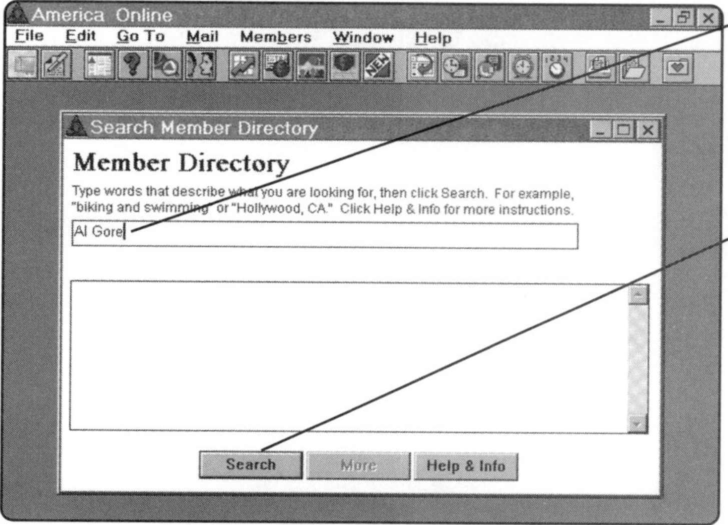

6. **Type** the **name** of the member you are looking for in the text box. In this example, we used the name "Al Gore."

7. **Click** on **Search.** A list of names that have "Al Gore" somewhere in their profiles will appear. The list is not in alphabetical order.

Checking the Profile

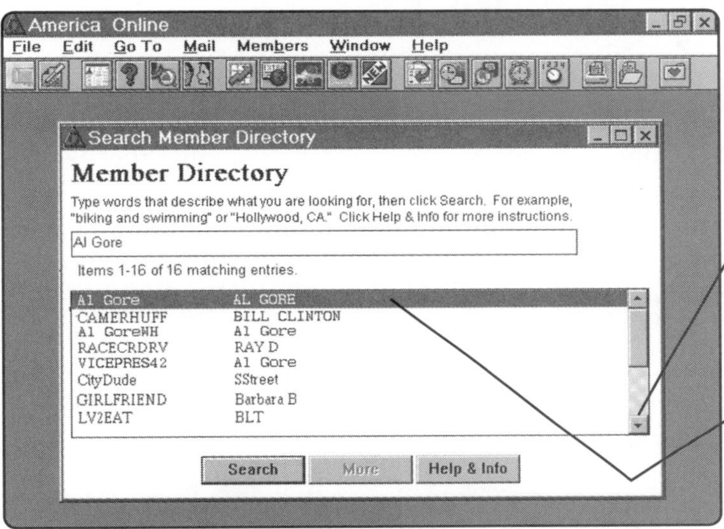

Isn't it amazing that all these people have "Al Gore" in their profiles. (We changed the names you see in this example.)

1. **Click** on the ▼ to scroll down the list until you find the name of the person for whom you are searching.

2. **Click twice** on the **name**. The Member Profile dialog box will appear.

3. **Read** the **profile** to see if it describes the person you want to find. If so, move on to the next step.

4. **Repeat Steps 2-7** on pages 26 and 27 to add the name to your Address Book.

5. **Click** on the **Close buttons** (☒) in the right corners of the title bars, or, if you're using Windows 3.1, **click twice** on the **Control menu boxes** in the left corners of the title bars to close the windows and return to the main menu.

Note: You have to fill out a personal profile to be in the member directory. If you cannot find a particular member, that person has not filled out a profile.

FILLING OUT A PERSONAL PROFILE

As a member of America Online, you have the option of filling out a personal profile that will be placed in the online member directory. The personal profile operates like a telephone book. A telephone book is divided into white and yellow pages (the white pages are an alphabetic list of names and addresses, and the yellow pages contain subject categories). The AOL "book" lists members by name as well as by each of the categories in the member profile, such as occupation or hobbies. In this section, you will learn how to fill out a member profile.

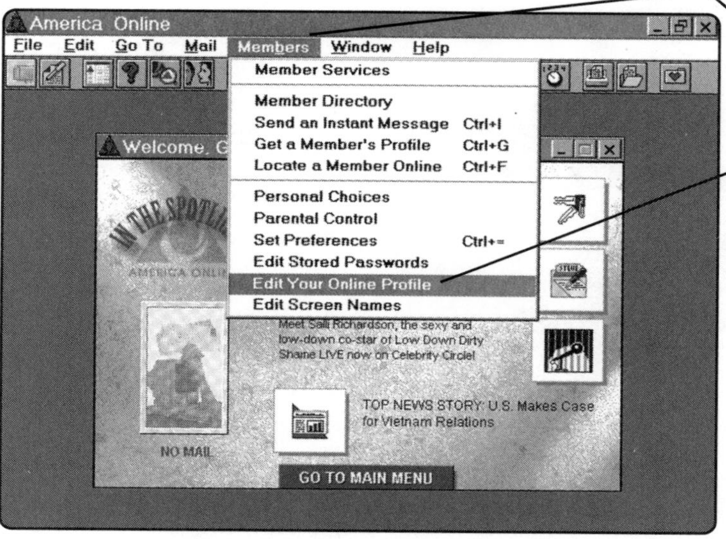

1. **Click** on **Members** in the menu bar. A menu will appear.

2. **Click** on **Edit Your Online Profile.** An Edit Your Online Profile dialog box will appear.

Notice that the electronic directory has already placed into the first two lines of your member profile the information previously available to the computer network when you registered with AOL.

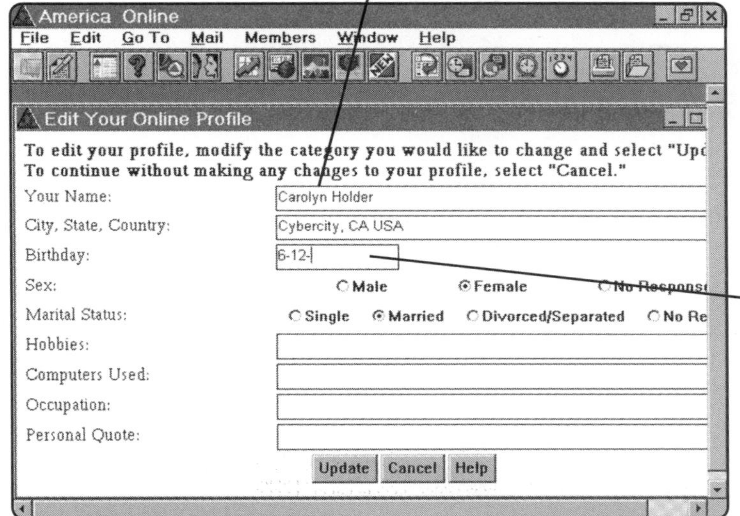

Note: if you are concerned about having your name and the specific city where you live available online, you can make the address more general, e.g. Ohio, or not fill it in at all.

3. **Type** in the **information** you want to make available to AOL members. Press the Tab key to move the cursor down the page. You can also use your mouse to click in the text boxes individually.

4. **Click** on **Update.** An AOL dialog box will appear.

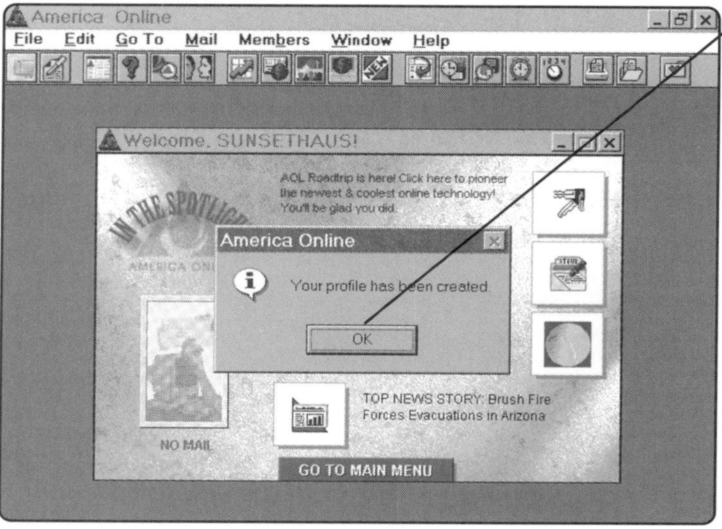

5. **Click** on **OK.** Your profile will be added to the member directory.

CLOSING AMERICA ONLINE

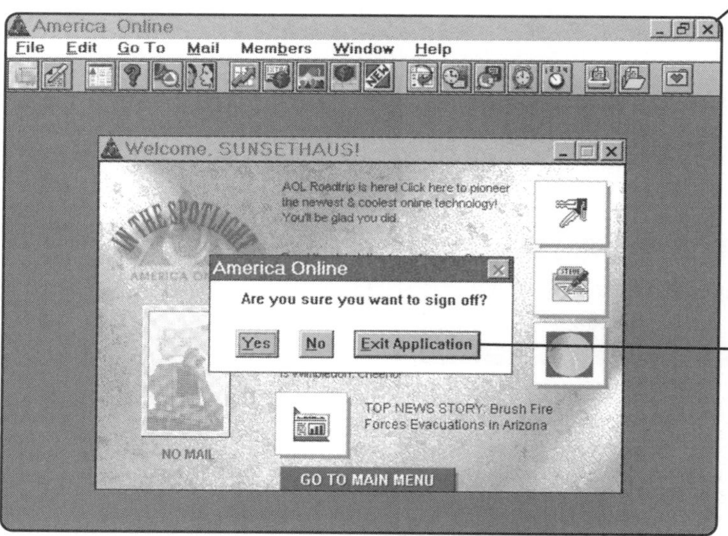

1. **Click** on the **Close button** (X) in the right corner of the America Online title bar, or (Windows 3.1), **click twice** on the **Control menu box** in the left corner of the title bar. A dialog box will appear.

2. **Click** on **Exit Application** to disconnect and close AOL. If you click on Yes, you'll be disconnected from AOL, but the program will remain open.

RECAPPING

✔ Create an Address Book with e-mail addresses.

✔ Complete your AOL member profile.

CHAPTER

4

Replying to and Forwarding Mail

No more peeking in the mailbox to see if the mail has arrived! America Online automatically notifies you when you have mail. Once you are notified, reading, replying to, and forwarding e-mail is quick and easy! In this chapter, you will do the following:

✔ Read mail
✔ Reply to a letter
✔ Use a quote from mail you've received in your reply
✔ Forward a letter
✔ Re-read old mail
✔ Delete old mail
✔ Keep old mail as new

READING YOUR MAIL

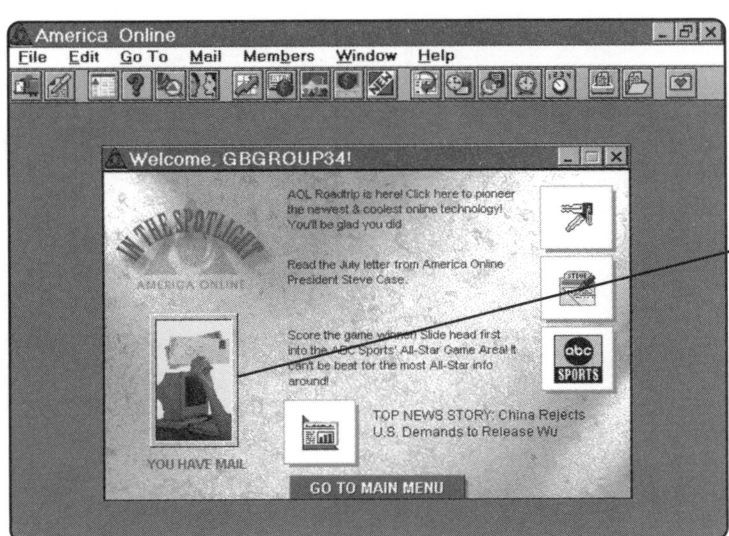

1. **Open** and **sign on** to **America Online** if you have not already done so. If you have mail, the Mail icon will let you know.

2. **Click** on the **You Have Mail icon.** The New Mail dialog box will appear.

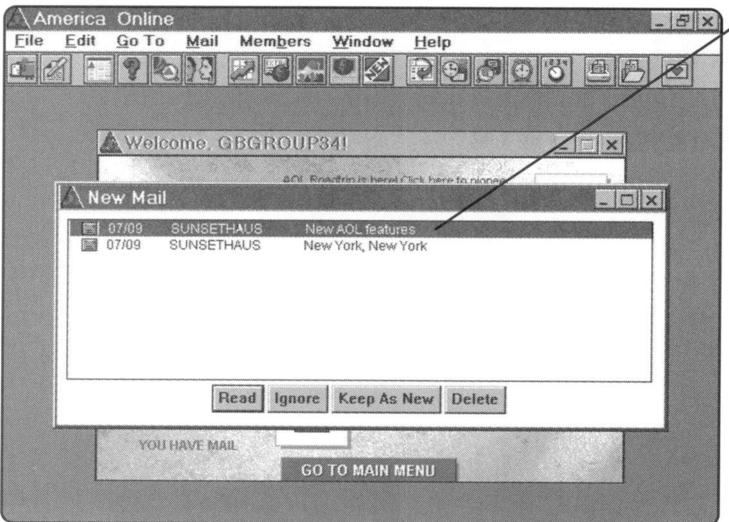

3. **Click twice** on the **letter** you want to read. The letter will appear on the screen.

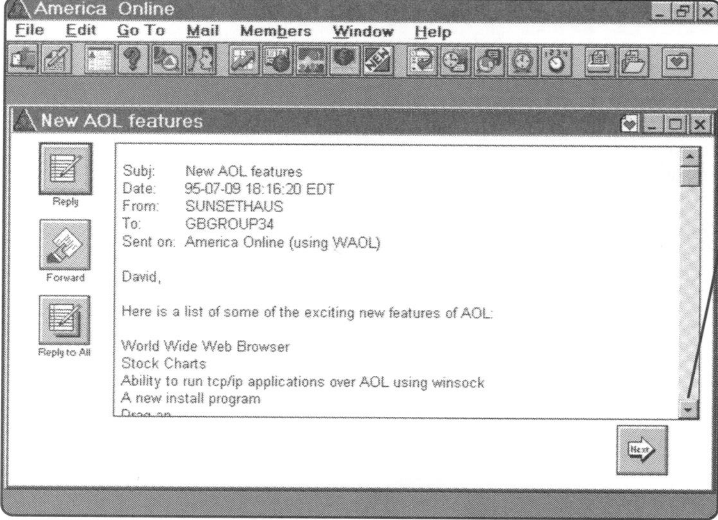

Reading the Letter

1. **Click repeatedly** on the ▼ to scroll through the letter to read it all online.

See Chapter 1 for the steps required to print a letter or to set up your Personal Filing Cabinet to save copies of e-mail that you receive.

REPLYING TO A LETTER

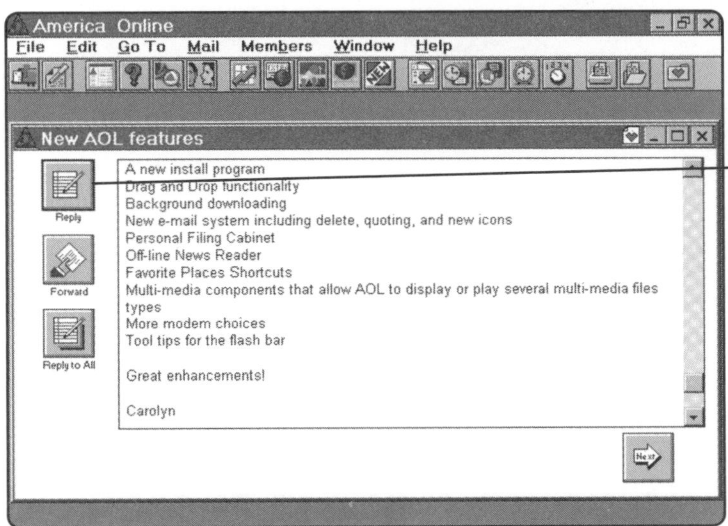

While a letter is open on your screen, you can reply very easily.

1. **Click** on **Reply.** A Compose Mail dialog box will appear.

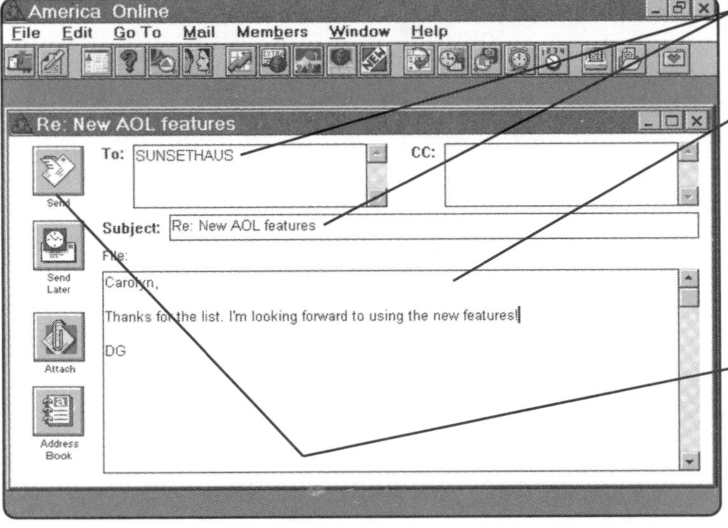

Notice that the address and subject are already filled in.

2. **Type** your **reply**. This is no different than sending a letter from scratch except that the address and subject are already filled in for you.
3. **Click** on **Send**. A message box will appear, saying that your mail has been sent.

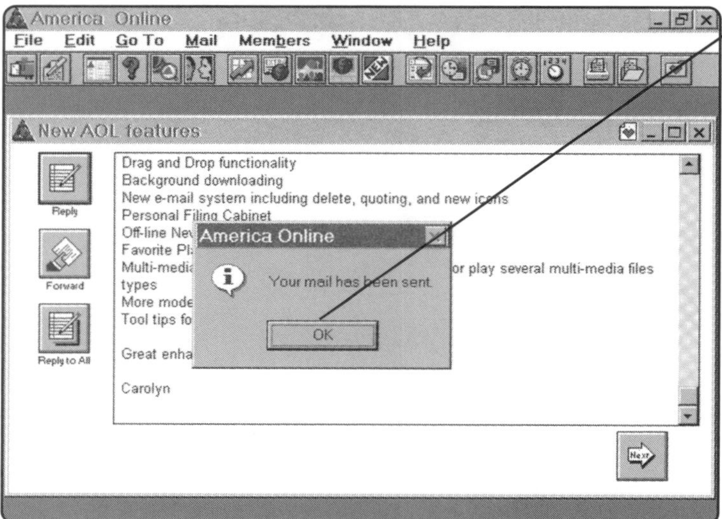

4. **Click** on **OK**. The dialog box will close.

INCLUDING A QUOTE FROM ANOTHER LETTER IN A REPLY

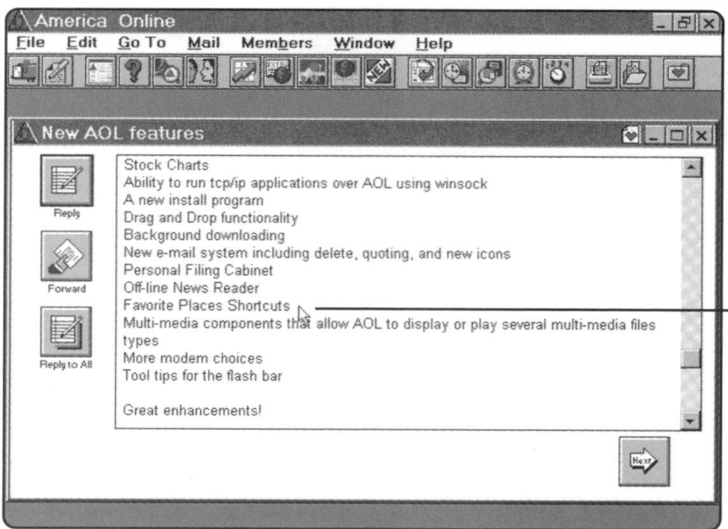

If you decide that you want to include a quote from the letter you're replying to, you can use AOL's "AutoQuote" feature. The letter you want to quote from must be open.

1. **Place** the **mouse arrow** at the end of the text you want to quote.

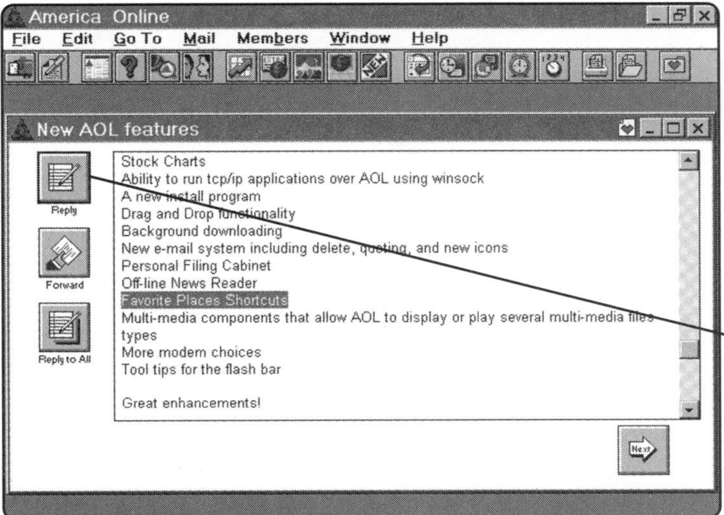

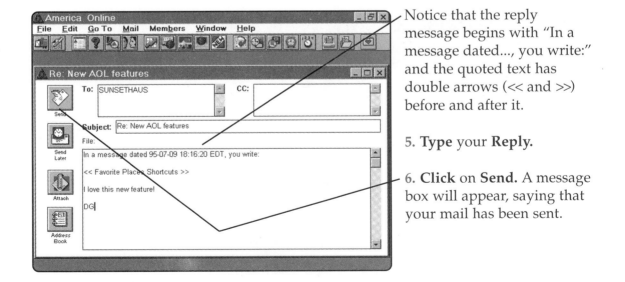

2. **Press and hold** the mouse button and **drag** the cursor back and up over the text. The text will become highlighted as you do this.

3. **Release** the **mouse button.**

4. **Click** on **Reply.** A reply dialog box will appear with the address, subject, and the text you want to quote filled in.

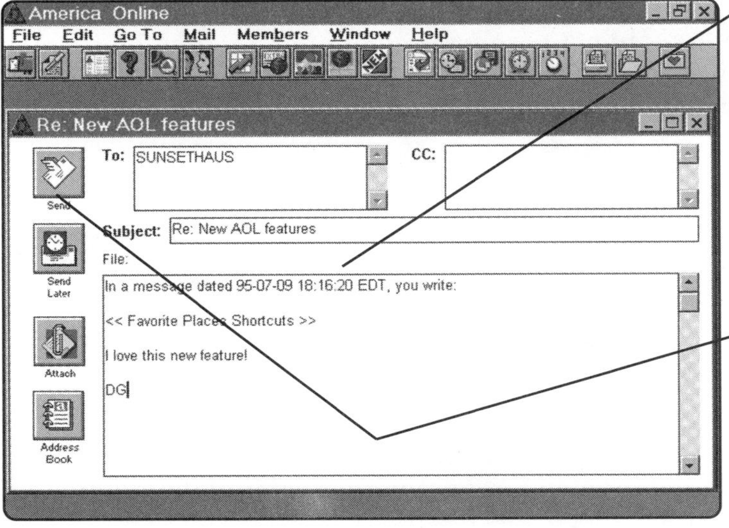

Notice that the reply message begins with "In a message dated..., you write:" and the quoted text has double arrows (<< and >>) before and after it.

5. **Type** your **Reply.**

6. **Click** on **Send.** A message box will appear, saying that your mail has been sent.

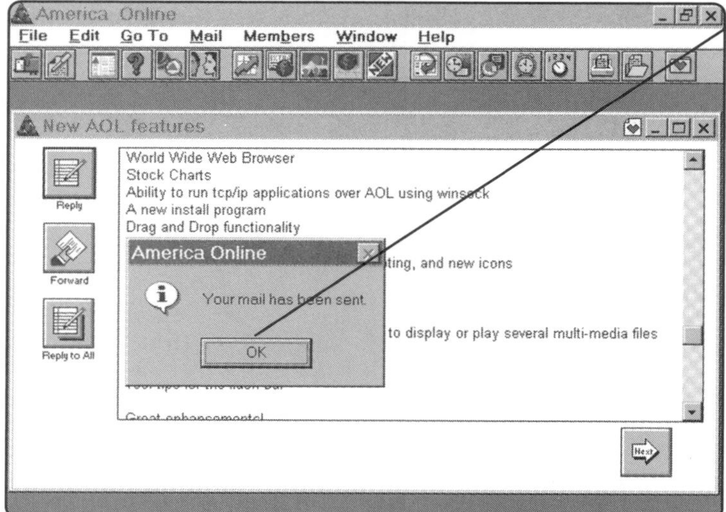

7. **Click** on **OK**. The dialog box will close.

FORWARDING E-MAIL

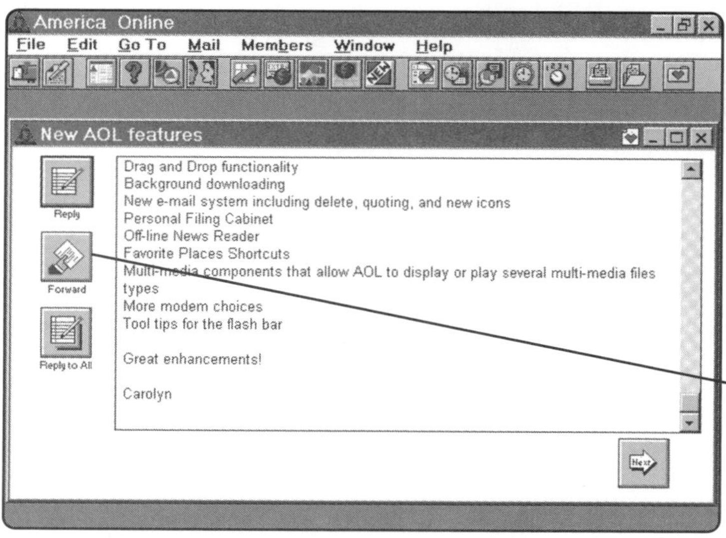

You can send a copy of any letter you receive to a third person. This is called *forwarding* mail. When you forward mail, you have to type a message to go with it. The letter you want to forward must be open on your screen.

1. While the letter is open on your screen, **click** on the **Forward icon.** A mail dialog box will appear.

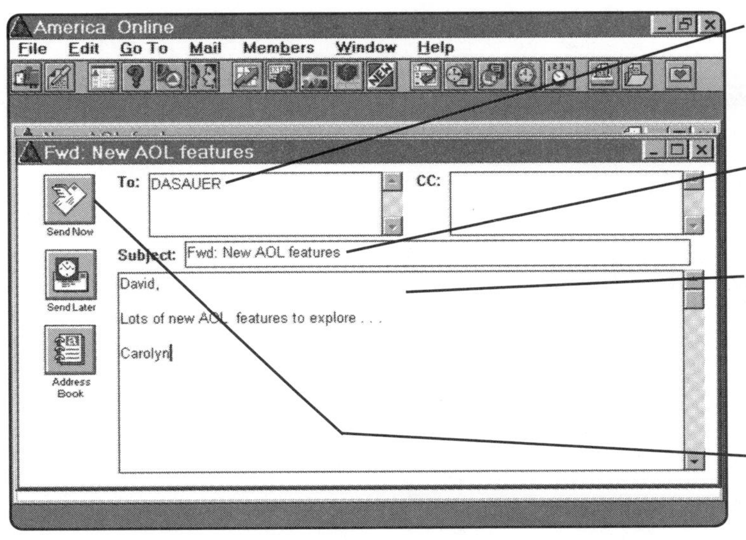

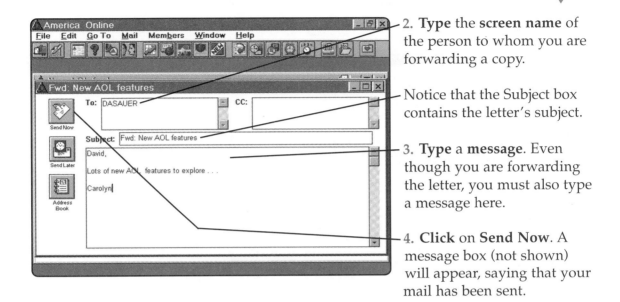

2. **Type** the **screen name** of the person to whom you are forwarding a copy.

Notice that the Subject box contains the letter's subject.

3. **Type** a **message**. Even though you are forwarding the letter, you must also type a message here.

4. **Click** on **Send Now**. A message box (not shown) will appear, saying that your mail has been sent.

5. **Click** on **OK**. The message box will disappear.

The forwarded letter will be identified as "Fwd: (subject)" in the recipient's mailbox. The letter will have your message at the top of the page and the forwarded message at the bottom.

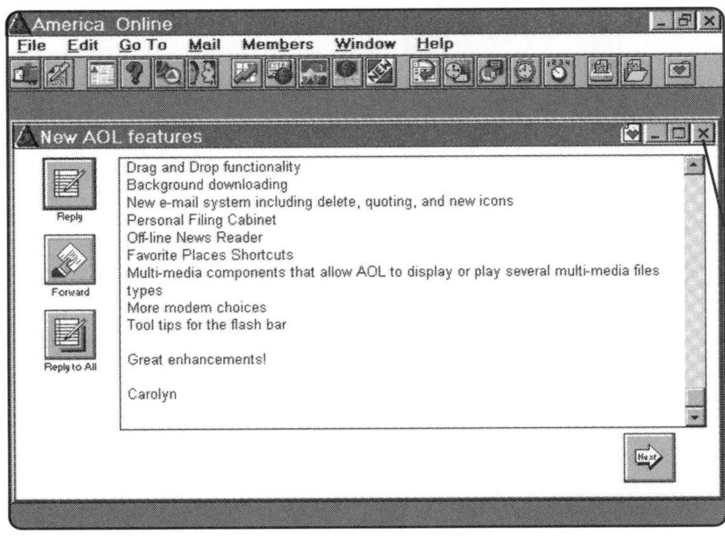

FINISHING READING YOUR MAIL

1. **Click** on the **Next button**. The next unread letter will appear.

2. When you've finished, **click** on the **Close button** (X) in the right corner, or (Windows 3.1), **click twice** on the **Control menu box** in the left corner of the letter on your screen. It will close.

Closing the New Mail Box

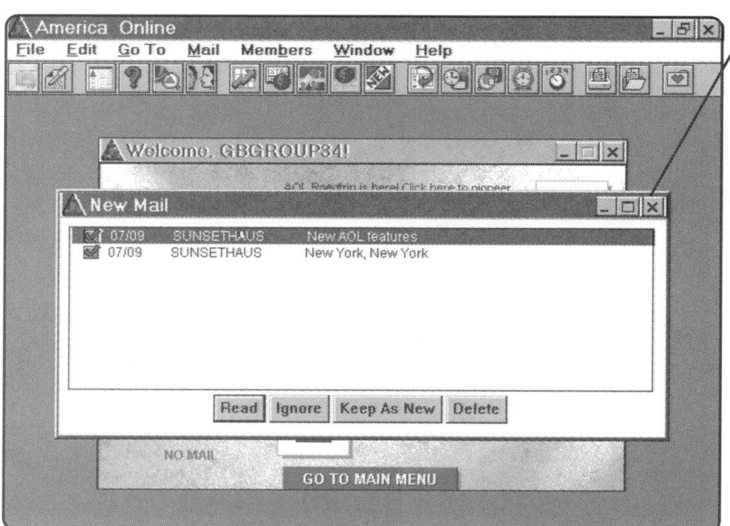

1. **Click** on the **Close Button** ([X]) in the right corner of the New Mail title bar, or, if you're using Windows 3.1, **click twice** on the **Control menu box** in the left corner of the title bar to close the dialog box. We will only give the Windows 95 step for closing dialog boxes in the rest of this chapter.

READING OLD MAIL

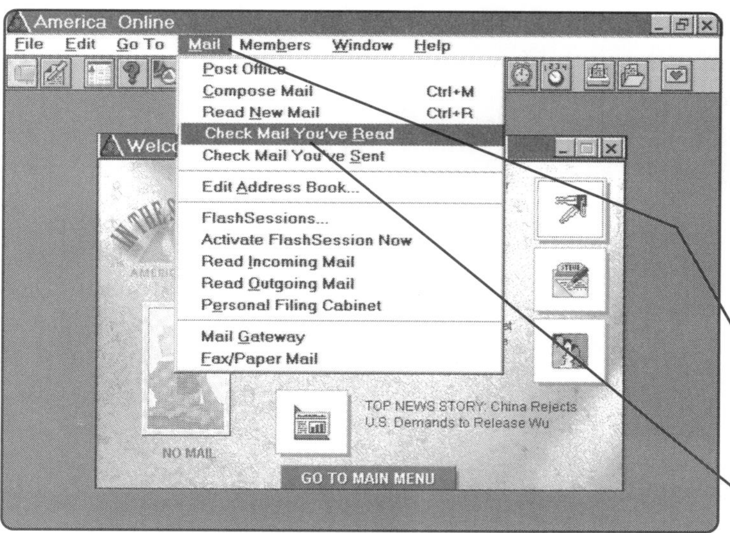

America Online will automatically delete each letter seven days after you have read it. Until it is deleted you can re-read it, delete it yourself, or recode it to appear to AOL as unread (new) mail.

1. **Click** on **Mail** in the menu bar. A menu will appear.
2. **Click** on the **Check Mail You've Read**. The Old Mail dialog box will appear.

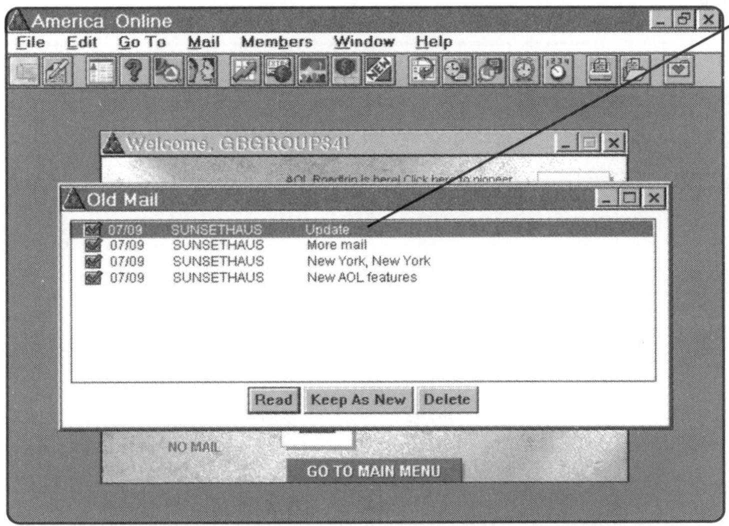

3. **Click twice** on the **letter** you want **to re-read**. It will open like the letter in the "Reading the Letter" section, earlier in this chapter.

Once the letter is open, you can read it, print it, reply to it, or forward it just as if it were "new mail."

DELETING MAIL YOU'VE READ

If you want to beat AOL to the punch, you can delete letters before they are seven days old. It takes only a couple of clicks of the mouse.

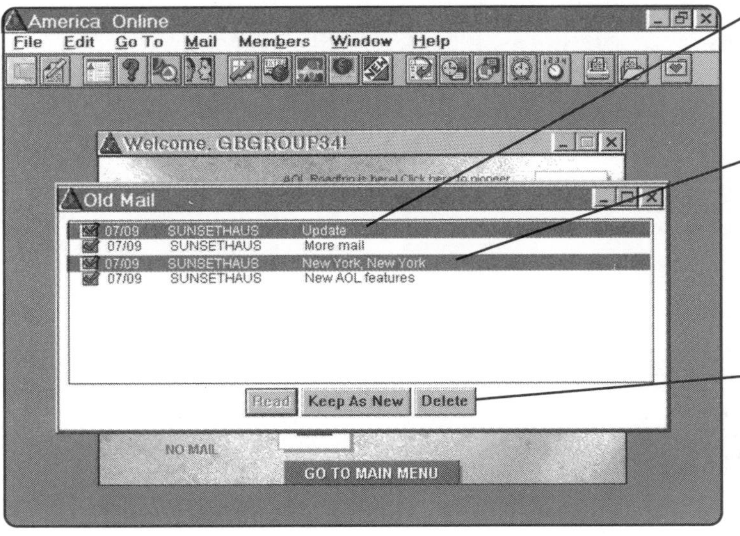

1. **Click** on the **first letter** you want to **delete** to highlight it.
2. If you want to **delete another** piece of mail, **click** on the **letter** to highlight it while holding down the **Ctrl key**.
3. **Click** on the **Delete button**. The letters will be deleted from your list.

MAKING THE OLD "NEW"

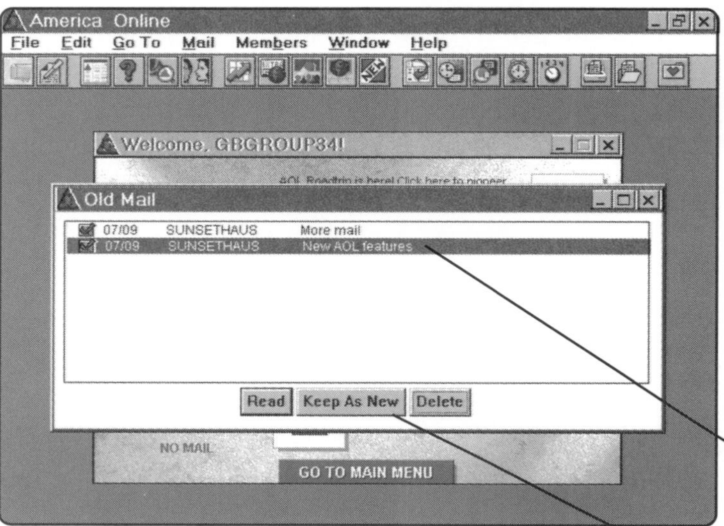

You can make a letter you have read appear as unread to the AOL computer. AOL will not delete *unread* mail for five weeks, so you can use this option to hold a letter. For example, if you are out of town, your secretary can screen your mail and mark specific letters "Keep As New."

1. **Click** on the **letter** you want to keep as new to highlight it.

2. **Click** on the **Keep As New button**. The mail will remain in your mailbox.

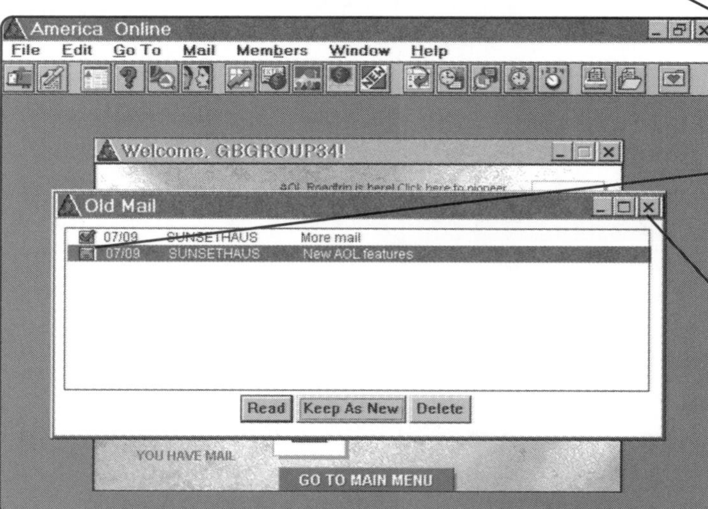

Notice that the ✔ has been removed indicating that the letter is new mail.

3. **Click** on the **Close button** (☒) on the Old Mail title bar to close the dialog box.

RECAPPING

✔ Check your mailbox and respond to your mail.

✔ Use the direct quote feature when replying.

Sending and Receiving Instant Messages

If you and another AOL member are online at the same time, you can send private messages back and forth to each other instantly. In this chapter, you will do the following:

✔ Check to see if an AOL member is online
✔ Chat with another AOL member using Instant Messages

CHECKING WHO'S ONLINE

You can't send an instant message to a member unless he or she is online. In this section you will check to see who is online.

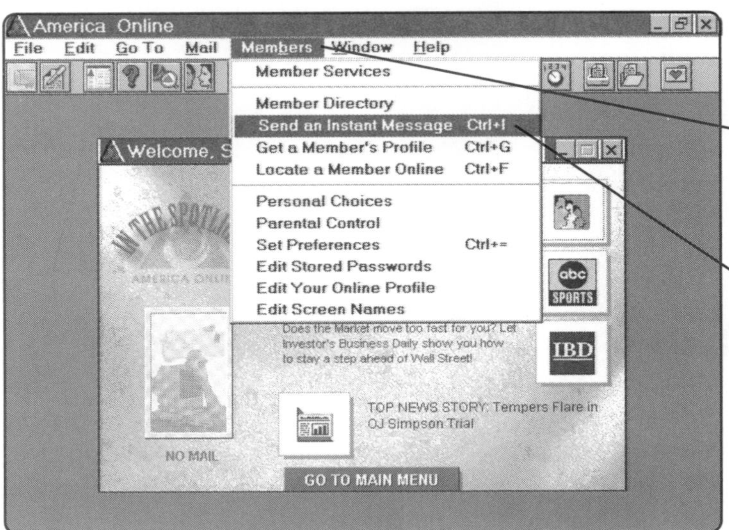

1. **Open AOL** if you have not already done this.
2. **Click** on **Members** in the menu bar. A pull-down menu will appear.
3. **Click** on **Send an Instant Message**. The Send Instant Message dialog box will appear.

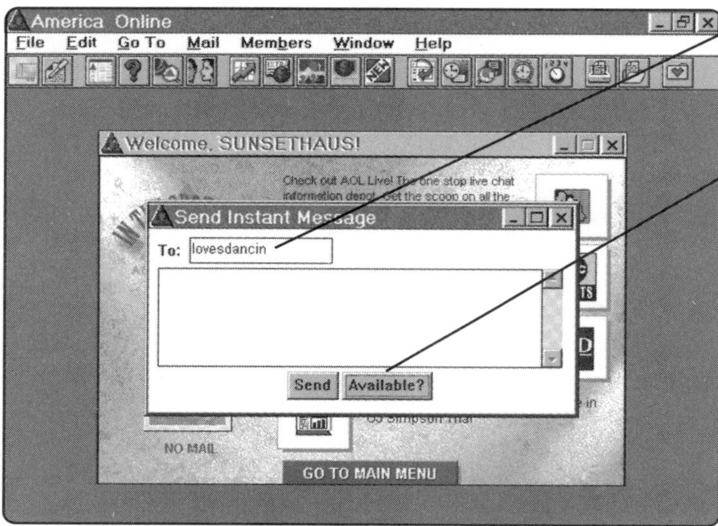

4. **Type** the **screen name** of the person on whom you want to check.

5. **Click** on **Available?** An America Online dialog box will appear.

In this case, "lovesdancin" is not online.

6. **Click** on **OK**. The dialog box will close and the Send Instant Message dialog box will reappear.

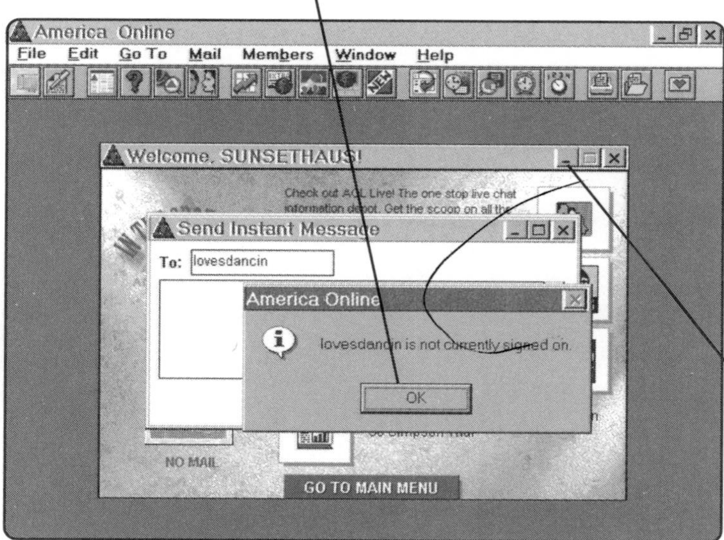

Reducing Clutter on Your Screen

If you find the multiple layers of dialog boxes confusing, you can "clean up" your screen.

1. **Click** on the **Minimize buttons** (▁, or ▼ in Windows 3.1) of the Welcome window and the Main Menu. They will be reduced to icons at the bottom of your screen, as you will see for the person receiving the message in the next section. This will give you an uncluttered screen. You can get them back by clicking on the maximize button, or (Windows 3.1) by clicking twice on each icon.

SENDING AN INSTANT MESSAGE

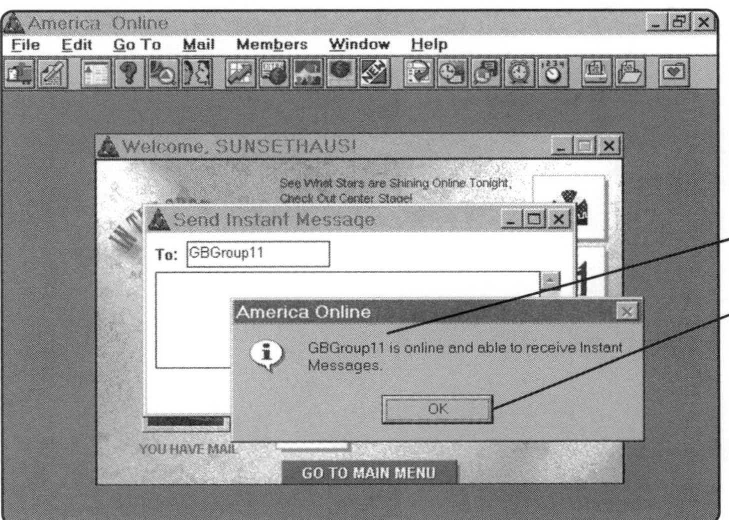

1. **Repeat steps 4 and 5** in the previous section to check to see if someone else is online. In this example, we checked on GBGroup11.

He's online!

2. **Click** on **OK**. The America Online dialog box will close. The Send Instant Message dialog box will reappear.

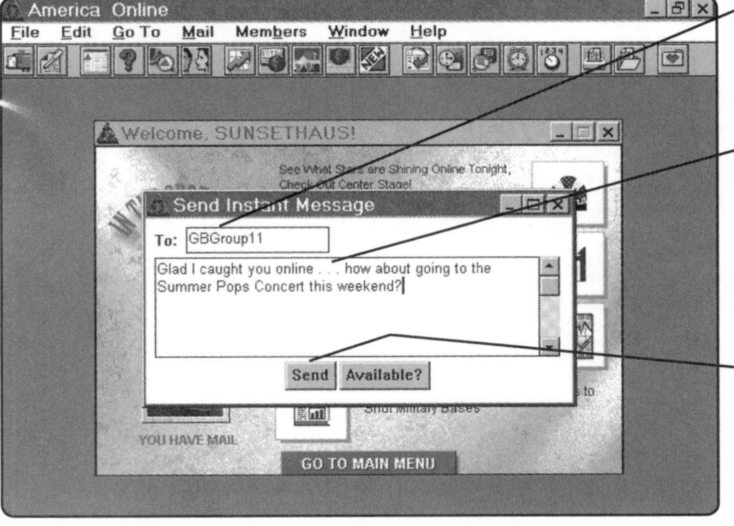

You typed the screen name in step 1 above so you don't have to retype it.

3. **Click** inside the **message box** to set the cursor if it is not already there.

4. **Type** a **message**.

5. **Click** on **Send**. The dialog box will disappear.

RESPONDING TO AN INSTANT MESSAGE

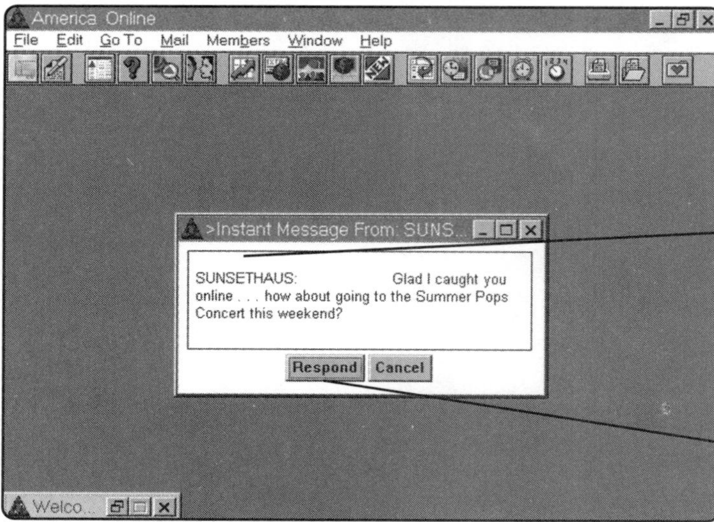

This screen is what the recipient sees. A dialog box like this one will pop up no matter what the person is doing on AOL.

Notice that the message shows the sender's name.

The recipient will do the following:

1. **Click** on **Respond**. A drop-down box will appear.

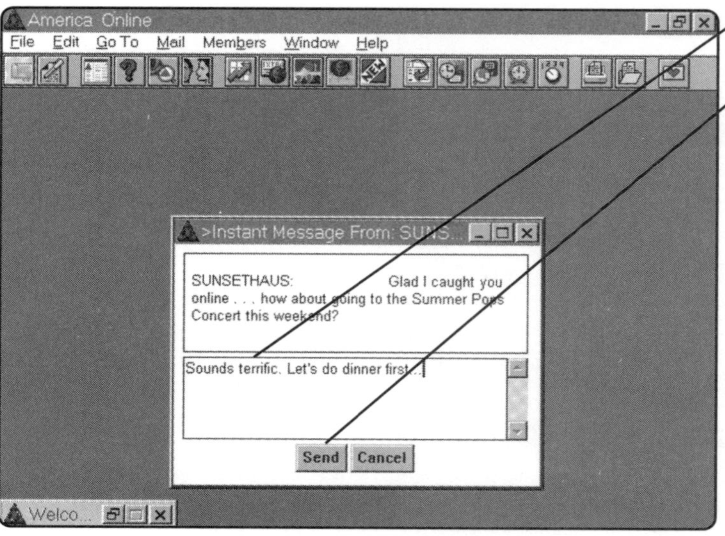

2. **Type** the **response**.

3. **Click** on **Send**.

A record of the conversation appears in the upper part of the Instant Message box. You can print the conversation in an Instant Message box by clicking on the Print button while the Instant Message box is open. You will get a printed copy of both sides of the conversation.

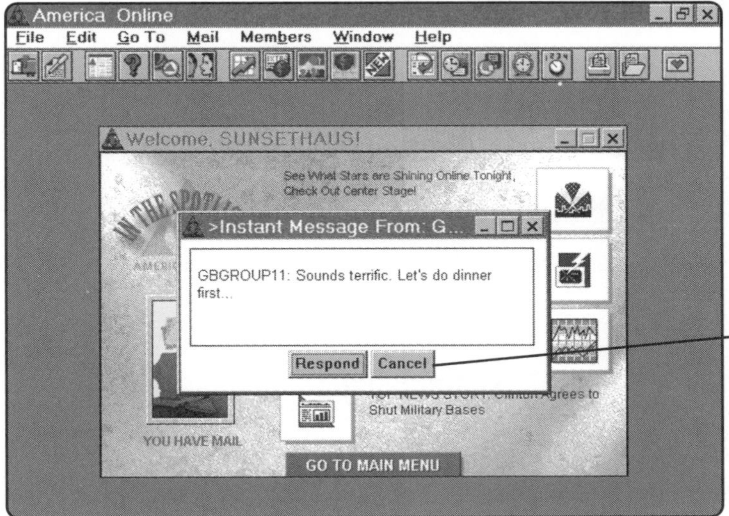

Meanwhile...

You, as the originator of this session, receive an answer.

1. **Repeat steps 1-3** in the previous section, to continue chatting.

2. When you've finished the session, **click** on **Cancel** to close the Instant Message dialog box and end the session.

CONTROLLING MESSAGES

You can turn Instant Messages (IM's) off and on.

1. **Repeat steps 2 and 3** at the beginning of this chapter to bring up the Send Instant Message dialog box.

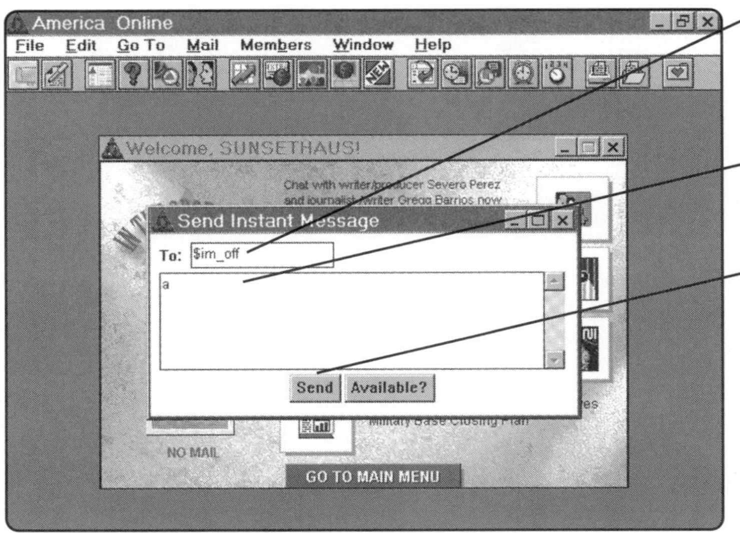

2. **Type $im_off** (lower case, with an underline between the words) in the **To box**.

3. **Type any character** in the **message box**.

4. **Click** on **Send**. You will see a message box (not shown here) saying, "You are now ignoring Instant Messages."

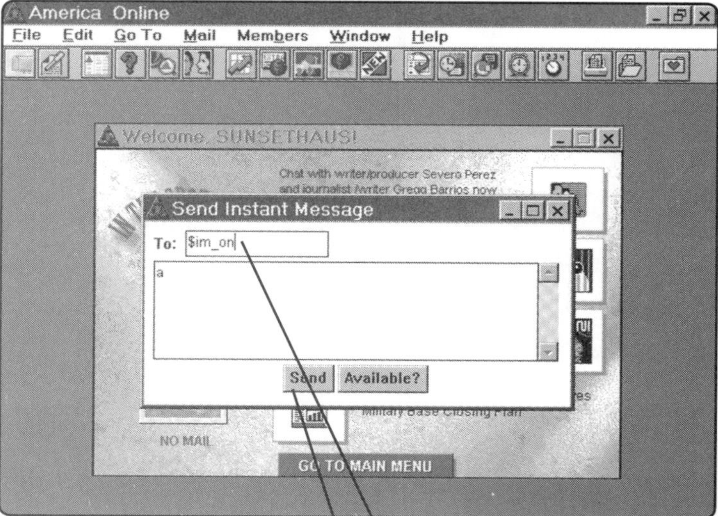

5. **Click** on **OK**. The message box will close. A member sending you an Instant Message will be informed that you cannot receive it.

Instant Messages are blocked only until the end of *this session* or until you turn them back on with the following steps.

6. **Open** the **Send Instant Message box**.

7. **Type $im_on** in the **To box**.

8. **Type any character** in the **message box**.

9. **Click** on **Send**. You'll get a message box (not shown here) saying, "You are no longer ignoring Instant Messages."

10. **Click** on **OK**, then close the Instant Message box.

RECAPPING

✔ Use Instant Messages to chat with friends online.

CHAPTER

6

Checking Spelling

When we first started using e-mail, we found that America Online did not offer a spell-check option. At first we used our word processing program to compose e-mail and then used the Windows Clipboard to copy and paste the text into America Online's Compose Mail window. This method turned out to be such a colossal pain in the neck that we skipped spell-checking all together. Then one day we found Next Generation Software's spell-check program. It's yours for the asking on AOL! In this chapter, you will do the following:

✔ Get a copy of (download) Spell Check to your computer from AOL
✔ Set up Spell Check
✔ Check the spelling in an e-mail letter

GETTING SPELL CHECK

Spell Check is a shareware program. This means you can get a review copy through America Online and try it. If you like ie and continue to use it, send a modest fee to the developer for a registered copy. In this section, you will download Spell Check.

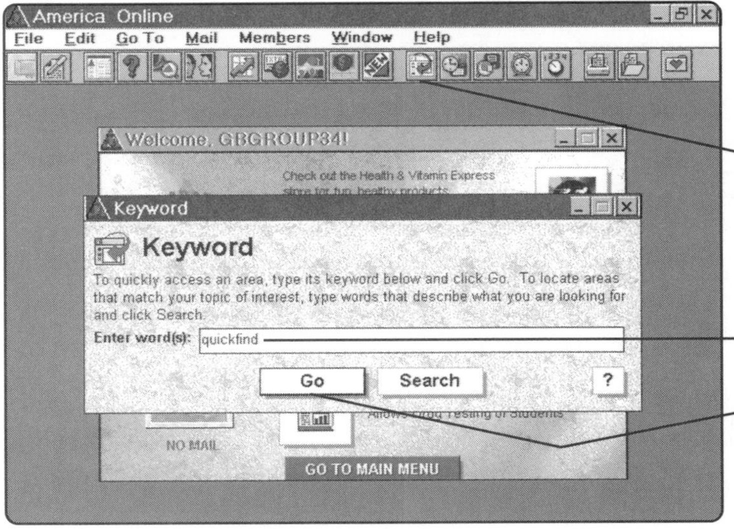

America Online
File Edit Go To Mail Members Window Help
Welcome, GBGROUP34!
Keyword
Keyword
To quickly access an area, type its keyword below and click Go. To locate areas that match your topic of interest, type words that describe what you are looking for and click Search.
Enter word(s): quickfind
Go
Search
?
NO MAIL
GO TO MAIN MENU

1. **Open** and **sign on** to **America Online** if you have not already done this.

2. **Click** on the **Keyboard button** on the toolbar. The Go To Keyboard dialog bx will appear.

3. **Type quickfind.**

4. **Click** on **Go.** The File Search dialog box will appear.

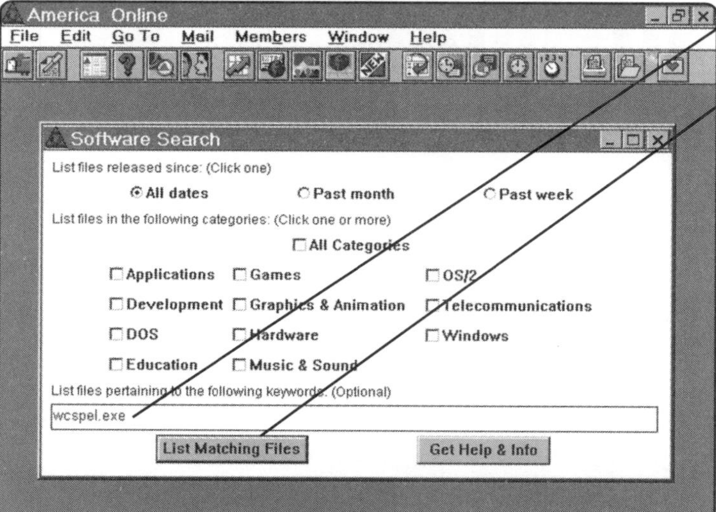

5. **Type wcspel.exe.**

6. **Click** on **List Matching Files**. After a few moments, the File Search Results dialog box will appear with the file highlighted.

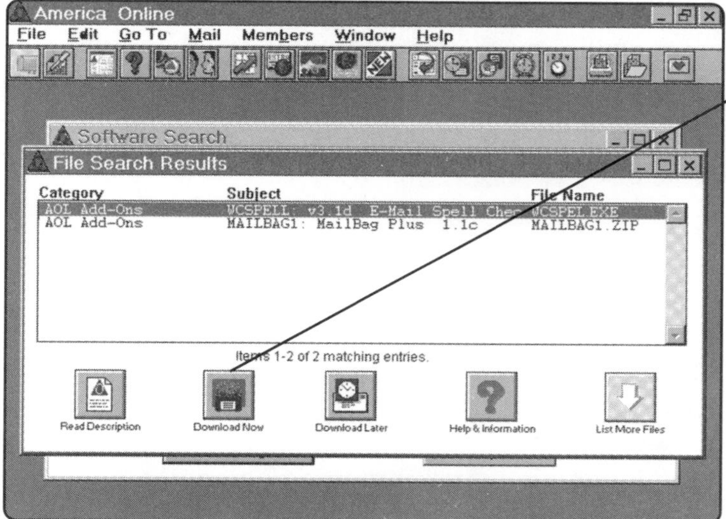

Downloading

1. **Click** on **Download Now.** The Download Manager dialog box will appear.

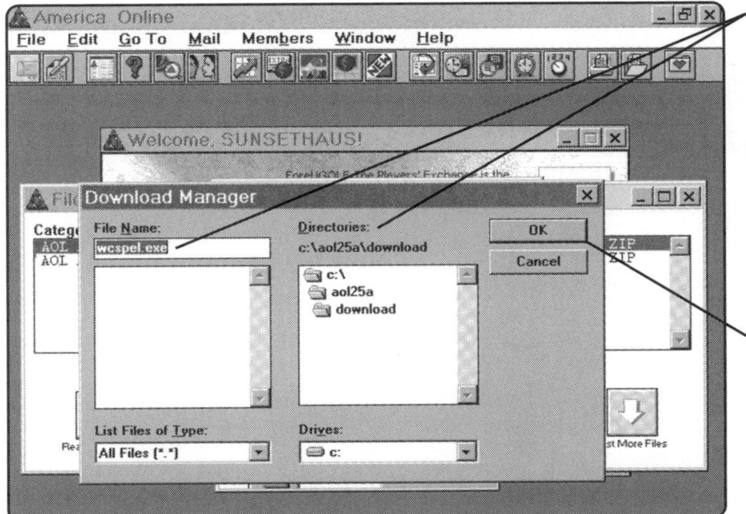

The dialog box tells you that the wcspel.exe file will be downloaded automatically to AOL's download subdirectory on the C drive. (Your drive letter may be different if you installed AOL on another drive.)

2. **Click** on **OK**. The File Transfer dialog box will appear.

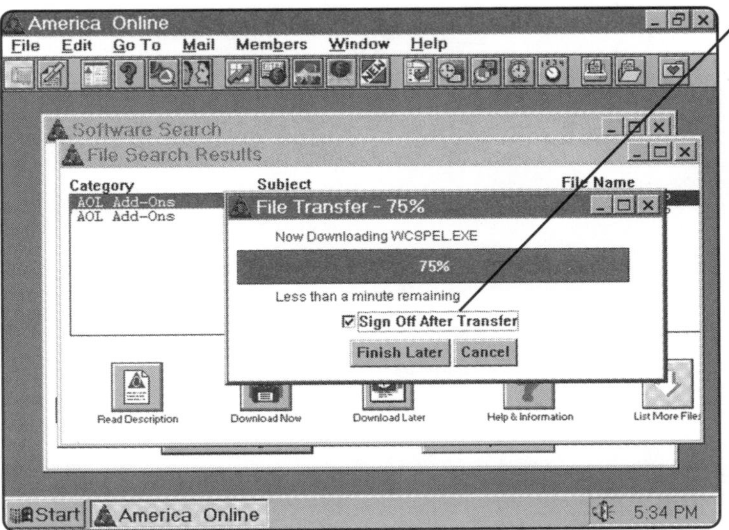

3. **Click** on **Sign Off After Transfer** to put a ✔ in the box. It will take about five minutes to complete the download. Then, after the file is transferred, the Goodbye America Online dialog box will appear. A message box about extracting files may flash by so fast you can hardly read it, and you will be disconnected from AOL.

Note: "Sign Off After Transfer" when downloading a file is optional and lets you leave your computer unattended without fear of running up connection charges. If you are going to follow along in this chapter, please use this option.

CLOSING AMERICA ONLINE

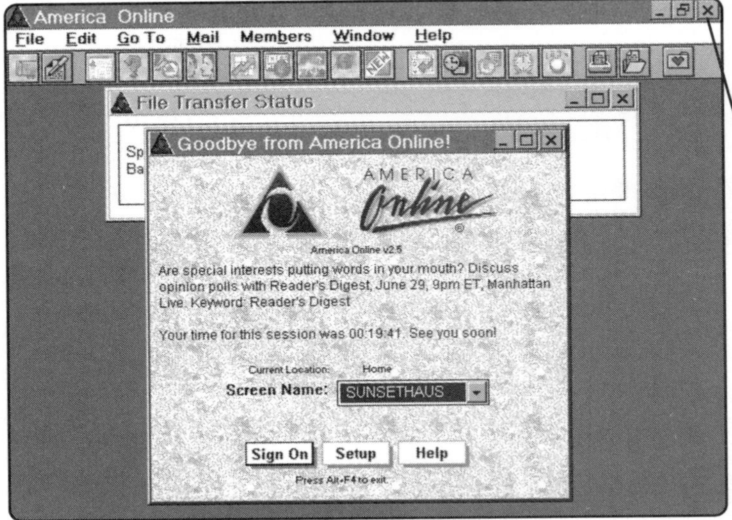

1. **Click** on the **Close button** (☒) in the right corner of the title bar, or, if you're using Windows 3.1, **click twice** on the **Control menu box** in the left corner of the title bar to close AOL. We will only give the Windows 95 step for closing open dialog boxes and windows in the rest of this chapter.

SEARCHING FOR THE WCSPEL.EXE FILE

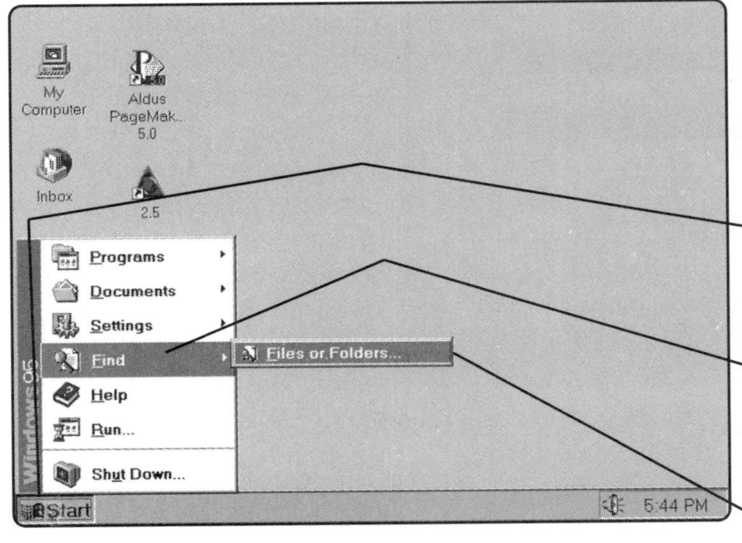

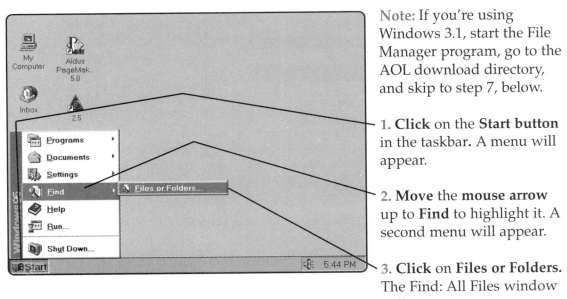

Note: If you're using Windows 3.1, start the File Manager program, go to the AOL download directory, and skip to step 7, below.

1. **Click** on the **Start button** in the taskbar**.** A menu will appear.
2. **Move** the **mouse arrow** up to **Find** to highlight it. A second menu will appear.
3. **Click** on **Files or Folders.** The Find: All Files window will appear.

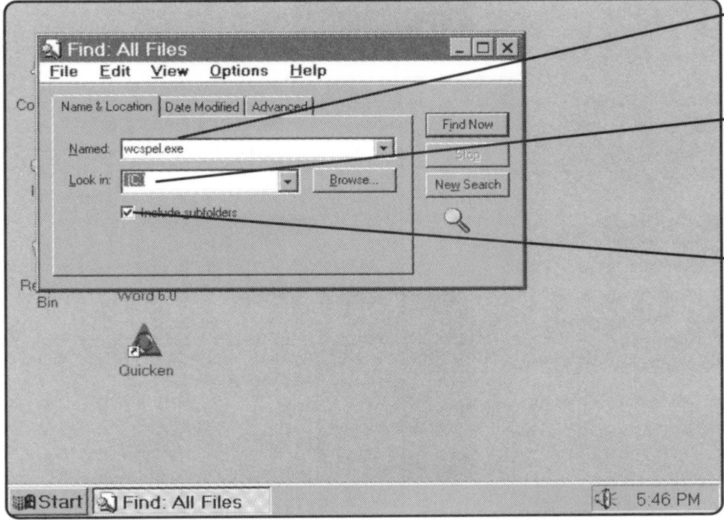

4. **Type wcspel.exe** in the **Named text box**.

Make sure the correct drive is selected in the Look in text box.

5. **Click** on the **Include subfolders box** to put a ✔ in it, if there isn't one there already.

6. **Click** on the **Find Now button.**

Your computer will begin searching for your file.

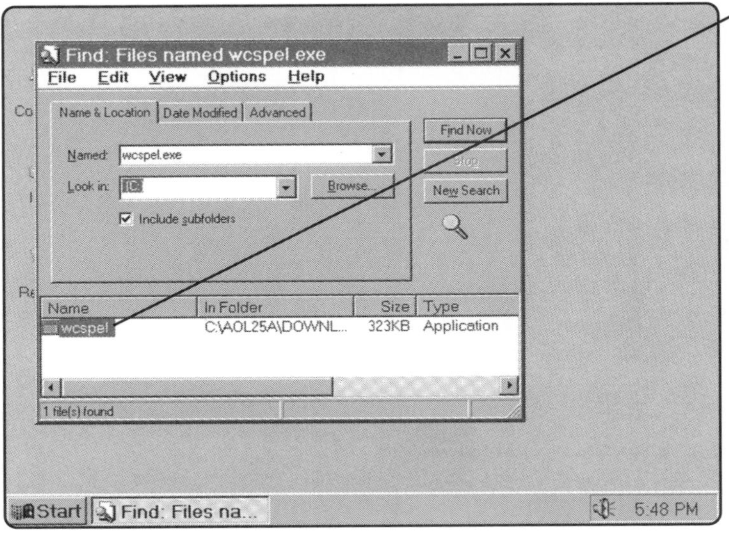

7. Once the search is complete and your file has been located, **click twice** on **wcspel**. If you're using Windows 3.1 and File Manager, the file will be listed as "wcspel.exe." The WinZip Self-Extractor dialog box will appear.

Unzipping the Setup file

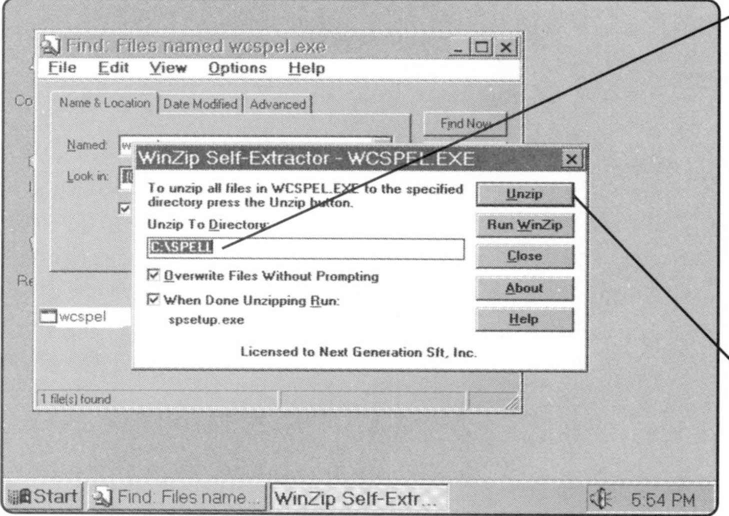

The self-extractor program will automatically create a new Spell directory for you. If you have a previous version of Spell Check on your computer, type in the name of the directory that the previous version is in to extract the file there.

1. **Click** on **Unzip.** It will just take a few seconds to unzip the file.

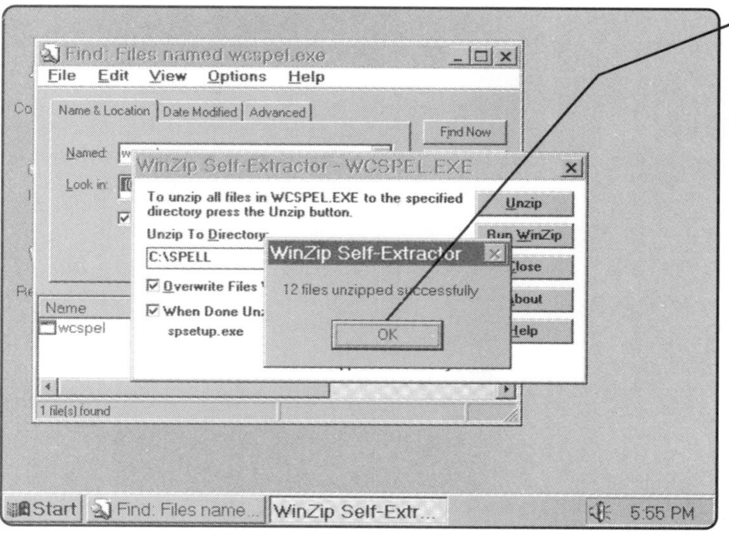

2. **Click** on **OK** to close the message box and the WinZip Self-Extractor dialog box. Leave the Setup Utility dialog box open.

CREATING THE SPELL CHECK ICON

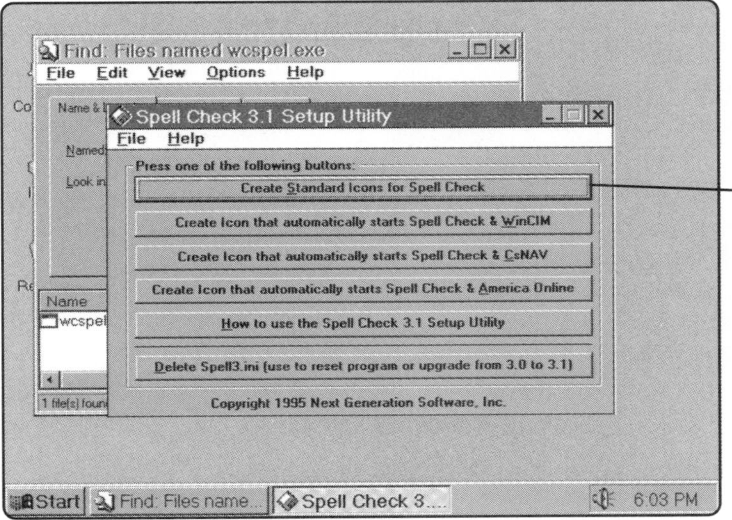

In this section, you will create an icon for Spell Check and place it on your desktop.

1. **Click** on the **Create Standard Icons for Spell Check button.** A Spell Check icon group window will appear.

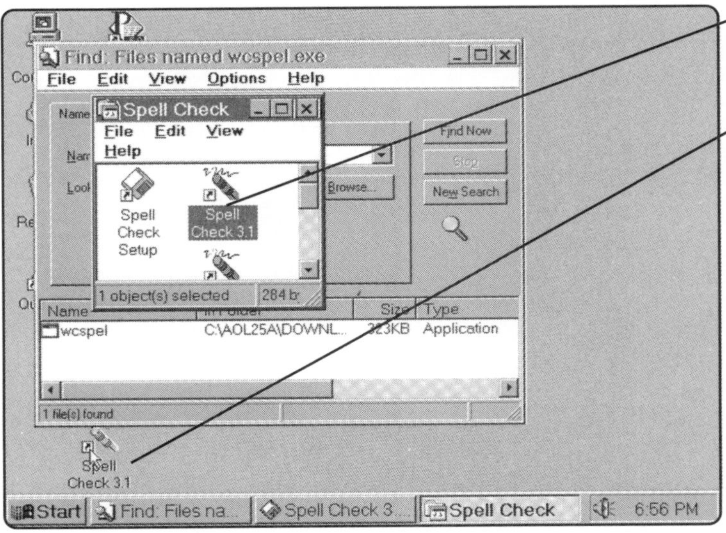

2. **Click** on the **Spell Check 3.1 icon** to highlight it.

3. **Press and hold** the mouse button as you **drag** the **icon** to your desktop.

Note: If you're using Windows 3.1, you may wish to leave the icon where it is or drag it to the group folder where your AOL icon is located.

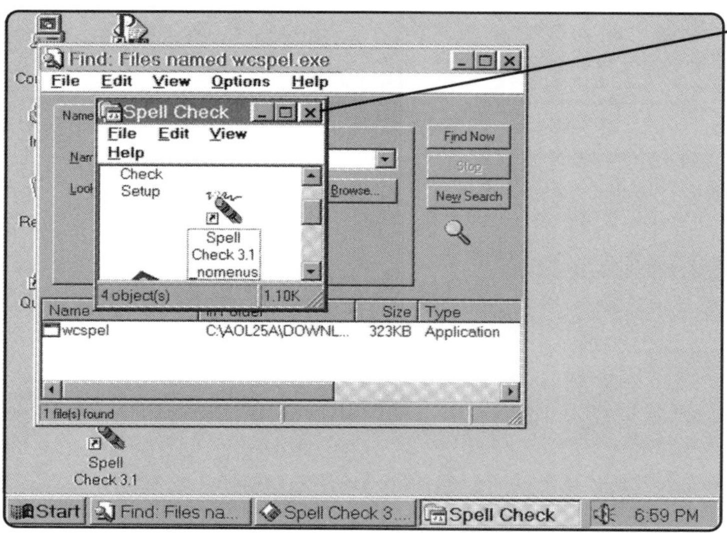

4. **Click** on the **Close buttons** (☒) in the right corners of the title bars, or, if you're using Windows 3.1, **click twice** on the **Control menu boxes** in the left corners of the title bars to close the open dialog boxes. We will only give the Windows 95 step for closing open dialog boxes and windows in the rest of this chapter.

DELETING THE SPELL3.INI FILE — FOR UPGRADE USERS ONLY

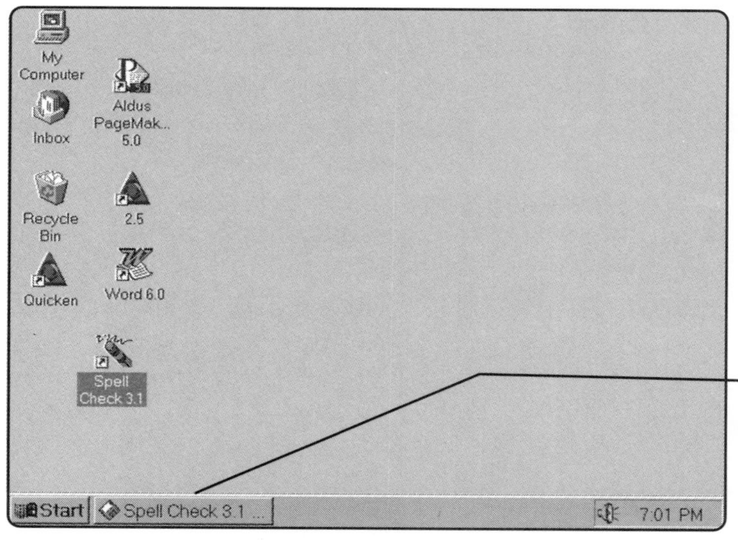

If this is your first installation of Spell Check, take a break and then go on to the next section. However, if you are upgrading from a previous version of Spell Check, you will need to do a little "housekeeping" first.

1. **Click** on the **Spell Check 3.1 button** on the taskbar. The Setup Utility window will appear. If you are using Windows 3.1, click twice on the Spell Check icon.

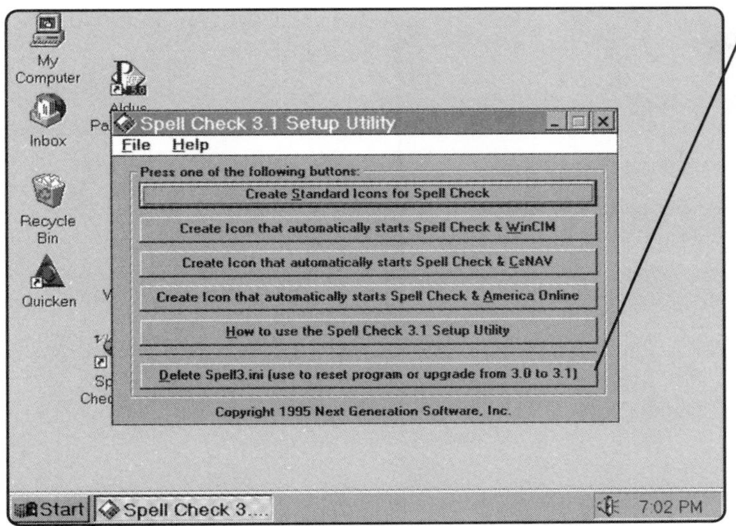

2. **Click** on the **Delete Spell3.ini button.** Another Setup Utility window will appear.

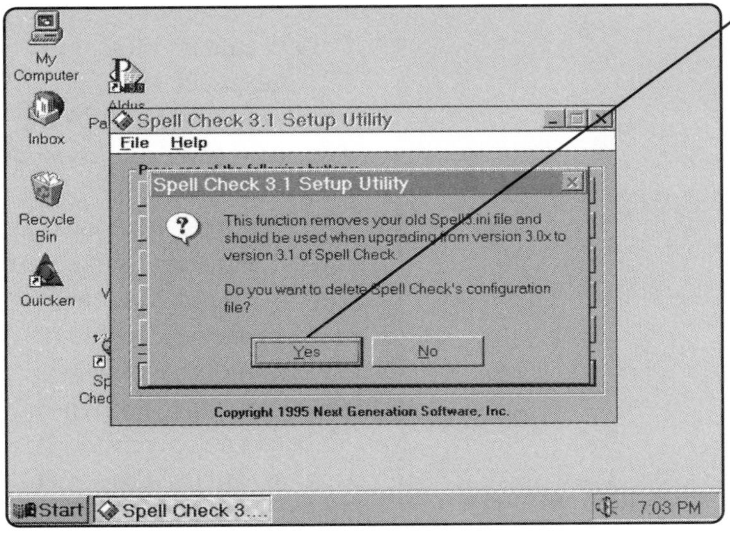

3. **Click** on **Yes**. Another Setup Utility dialog box will appear.

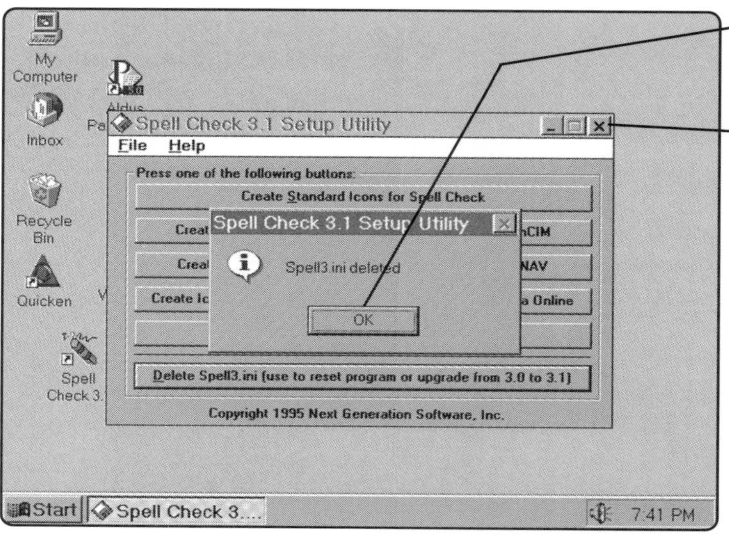

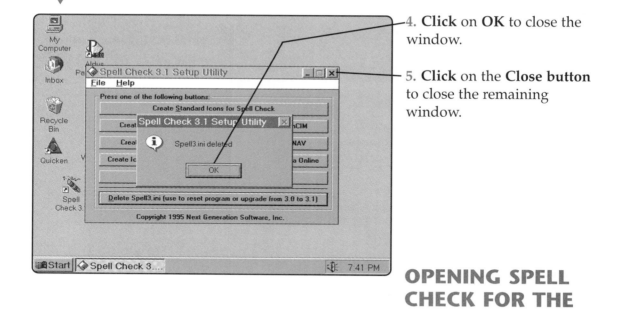

4. **Click** on **OK** to close the window.

5. **Click** on the **Close button** to close the remaining window.

OPENING SPELL CHECK FOR THE FIRST TIME

1. **Click twice** on the **Spell Check icon**. A Spell Check 3.1 Setup dialog box will appear.

Note: You may get an error message saying "Cannot find VBRUN300.DLL." If this happens, click on Close in the message box. Another "Cannot find..." message box will appear. Click on OK. Next, repeat steps 1-8 in the previous section to download vbrun300.dll from AOL and use File Manager to put it in your c:\windows\system directory. If you need help with this process, send an e-mail message to Next Generation Software. They will help you solve the problem. Their AOL screen name is NEXTGENSFT.

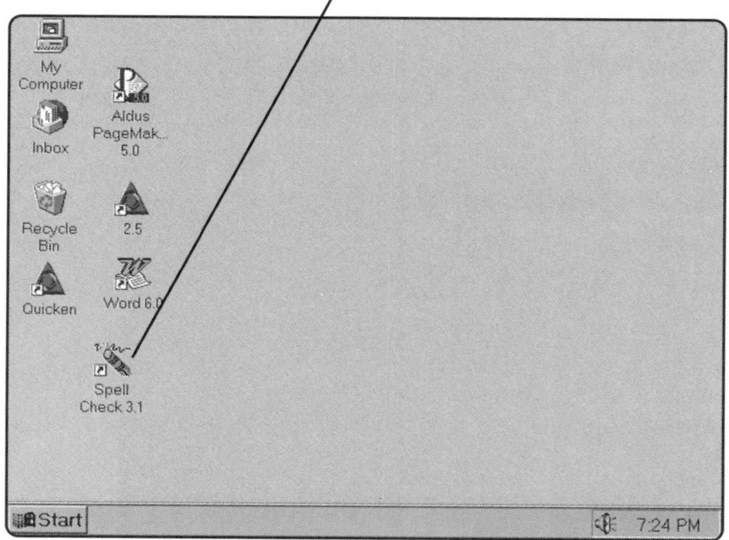

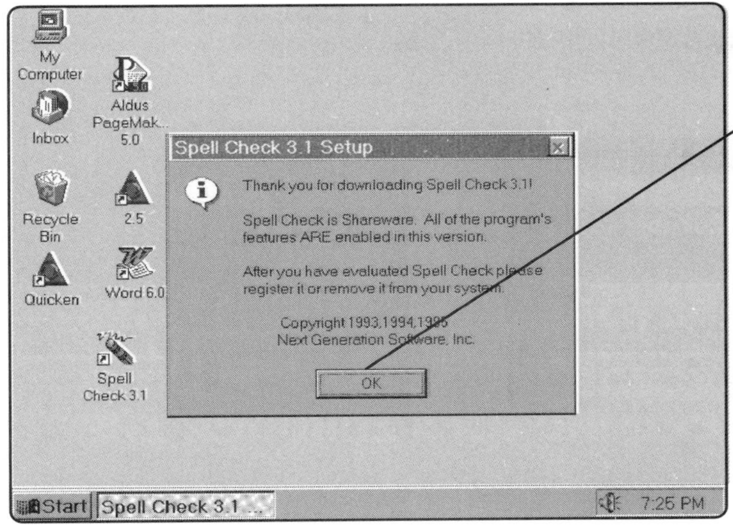

You will now get a series of introductory messages.

2. **Click** on **OK**. Another Setup message will appear.

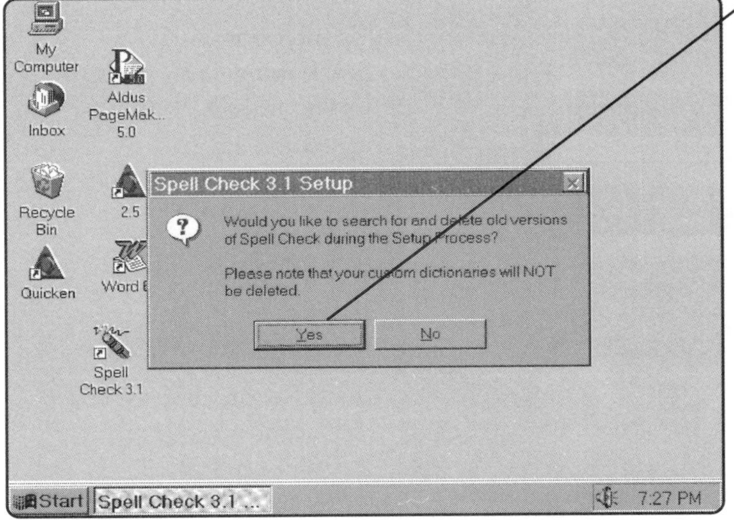

3. **Click** on **Yes.** Another message box will appear.

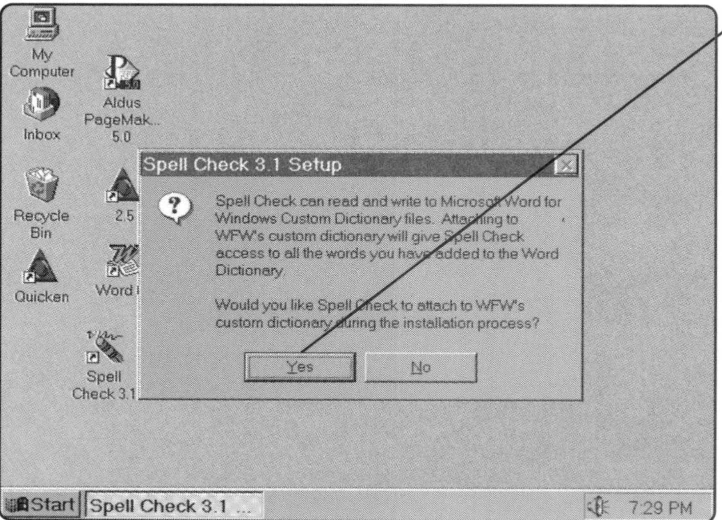

4. Click on **Yes**. The last Setup message box will appear.

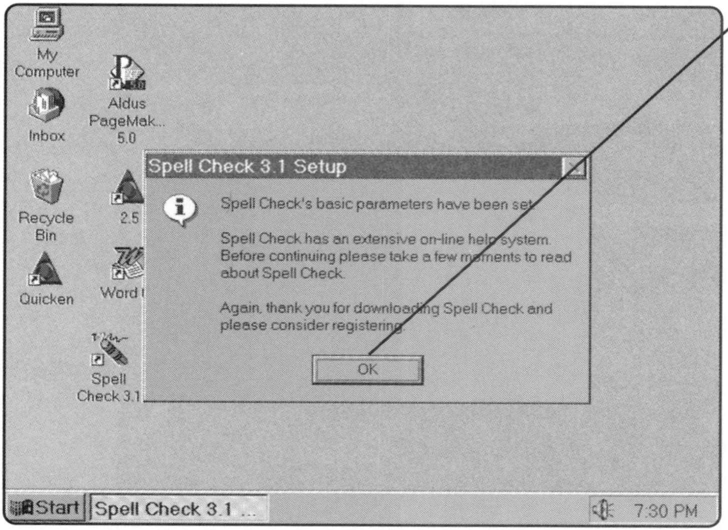

5. Click on **OK**. A Help System dialog box will appear.

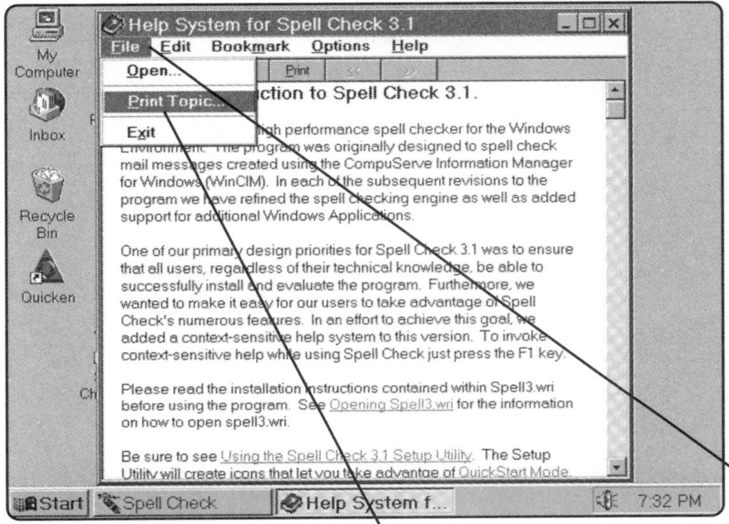

Printing Help Topics

Your window may be a different size than the one you see in this example.

You can learn the names of the programs for which Spell Check provides spell checking by printing the current topic screen.

1. **Click** on **File** in the menu bar. A menu will appear.

2. **Click** on **Print Topic**. When the Print Menu dialog box appears, click on OK. You'll see a Print message box, then the "Quick Introduction" page will print.

Closing the Help Window

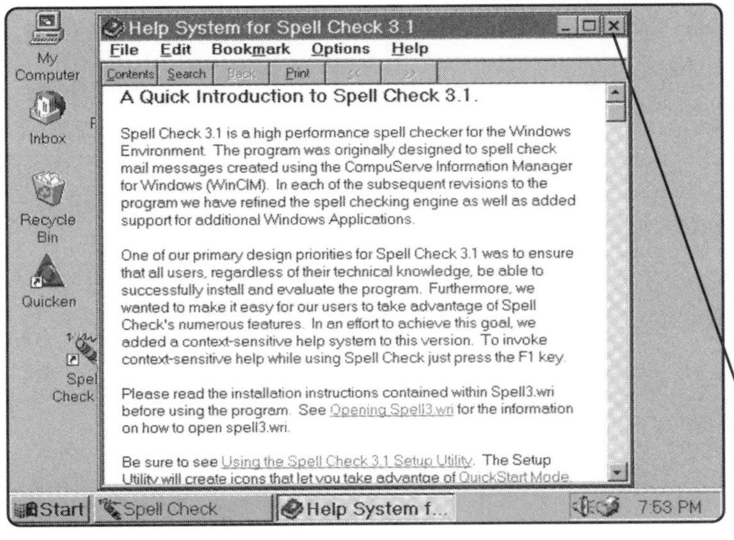

You should return to Spell Check's online help later for information on how to customize the program for your personal use. You can, for instance, set it up to include a custom closing, such as your name and address, for your e-mail each time it checks your spelling.

1. **Click** on the **Close Button** (x) in the right corner of the title bar to close the Help window.

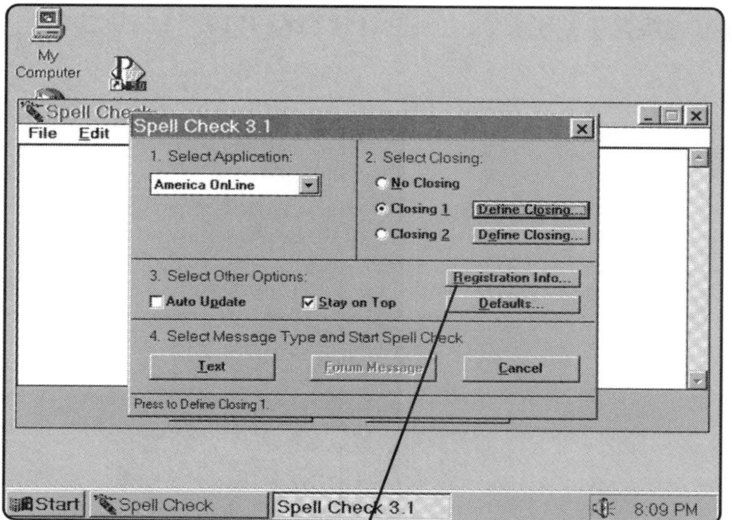

Registering Spell Check

You can register now or you can skip this section for the moment, work with the program, and register later if you like it. If you decide to use Spell Check, make certain that you pay for a registered copy. It's only fair.

1. **Click** on the **Spell Check icon** on the taskbar. If you're using Windows 3.1, click twice on the Spell Check icon. The Spell Check dialog box will open.

2. **Click** on the **Registration Info button**. The Registration Information dialog box will appear.

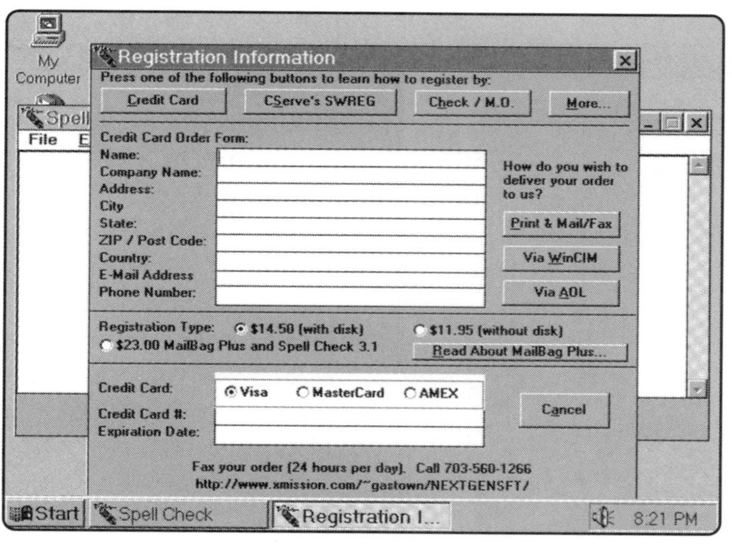

Complete the Registration Information now, choosing to pay by check or credit card. If you do not wish to complete the registration at this time, click on the Cancel button. You can always return to the Registration Information dialog box in the future.

CLOSING SPELL CHECK

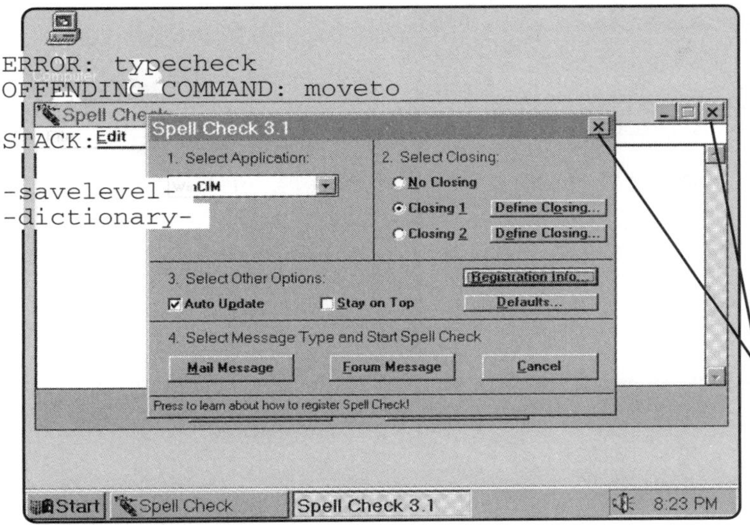

You will close Spell Check now so that in the next section you can see what the process of opening Spell Check and AOL will be like. In the section that follows, you will learn to use Spell Check to check the spelling in your AOL e-mail.

1. **Click** on the **Close buttons** (☒) in the right corners of the title bars to close both dialog boxes.

USING SPELL CHECK

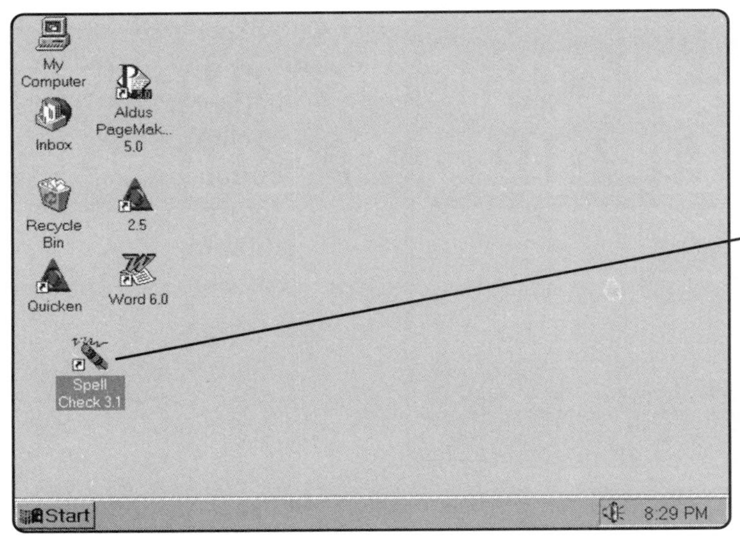

It is a good idea to open Spell Check first so that you don't forget to have it running when you are ready to use it.

1. **Click twice** on the **Spell Check program icon**. It will appear on your taskbar, or, if you're using Windows 3.1, it will appear as a minimized icon.

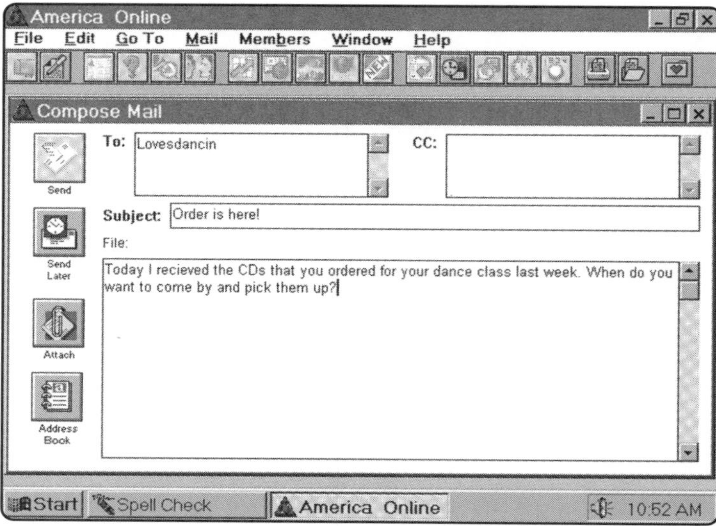

2. **Follow** the **steps** in the **beginning of Chapter 1** to open AOL offline and compose a letter. Misspell some words on purpose so you can try out Spell Check. This screen shows our example of a letter with a misspelled word in it.

Starting Spell Check

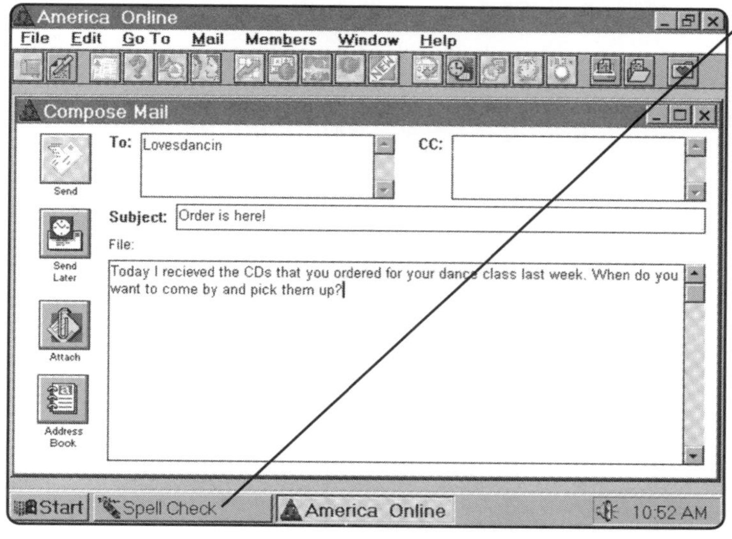

1. **Click** on the **Spell Check button** on the taskbar. If you are using Windows 3.1, click twice on the minimized Spell Check icon. The Spell Check window will appear.

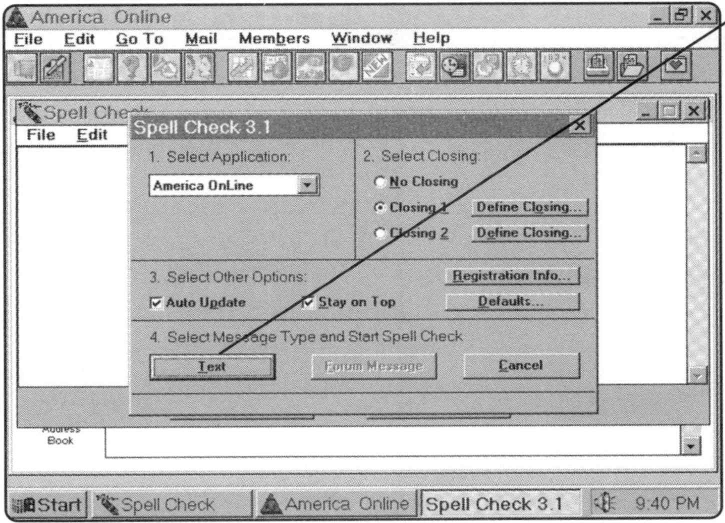

2. **Click** on the **Text button**. Another Spell Check dialog box will appear showing the first misspelled or unrecognized word in your letter.

Correcting Misspelled Words

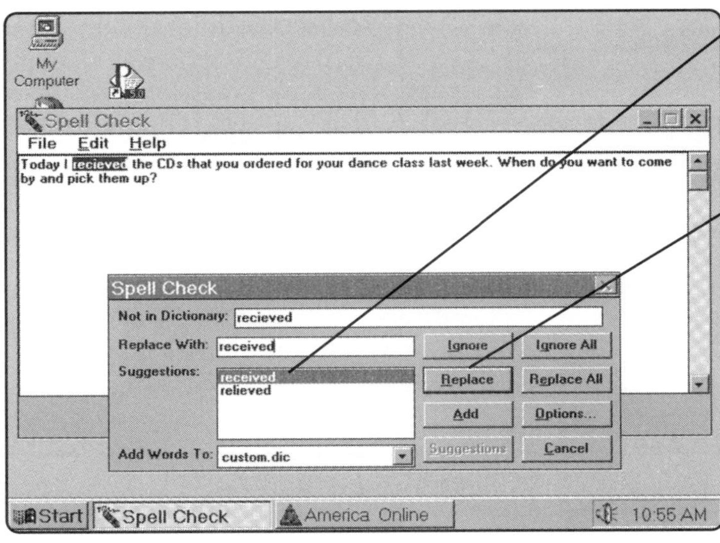

1. **Click** on the **correctly spelled word**. In this example, the correct word is "received."

2. **Click** on **Replace**. Spell Check will highlight the next word that is misspelled or that it does not recognize.

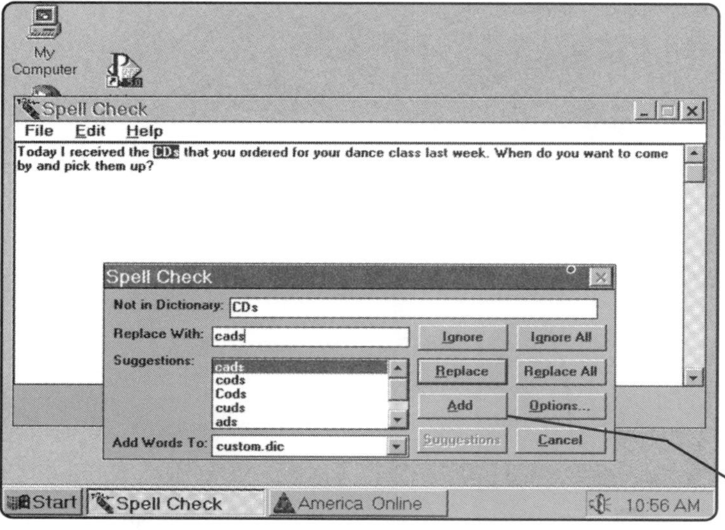

Adding a Word to the Dictionary

A spell-checker can't spell. No kidding. It can only check to see if a word is one that it recognizes (i.e., if it matches a word in its dictionary). Because it doesn't recognize the word "CDs" we'll add it to our dictionary in this example.

1. **Click** on **Add**. "CDs" will be added to your Spell Check dictionary. If you set up a closing, it will be added to the bottom of your letter.

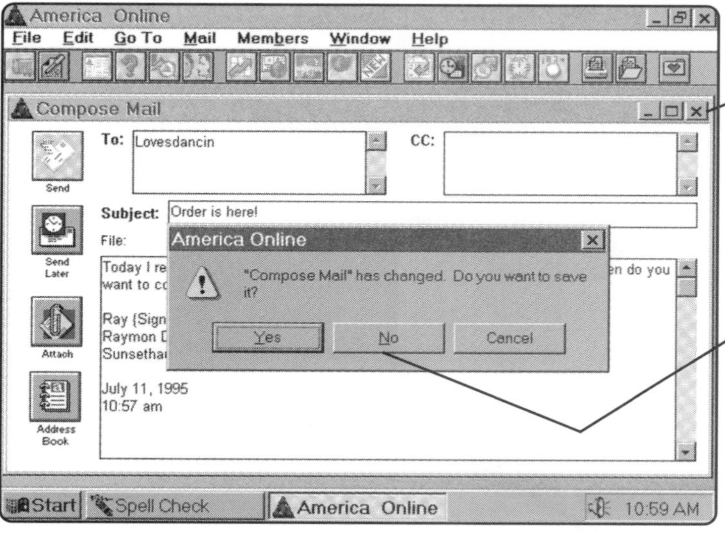

2. **Click** on the **Close box** (☒) in the right corner of the Compose Mail title bar to close the dialog box. An AOL dialog box will appear.

3. **Click** on **No**. The Compose Mail window will close.

RECAPPING

✔ Use Spell Check to keep your letters A+!

CHAPTER 7

Using FlashSessions

If you send and receive a lot of mail, using America Online's FlashSession feature will save you much online time and money! You can schedule FlashSessions to turn on automatically, sign on to AOL, get and send mail, and then turn itself off — all while you're doing other things. You can then read your new mail offline. In this chapter, you will do the following:

- ✔ Set up your FlashSession preferences
- ✔ Send mail, receive mail, and download files automatically
- ✔ Read your mail offline
- ✔ Schedule a FlashSession

OPENING FLASHSESSIONS FOR THE FIRST TIME

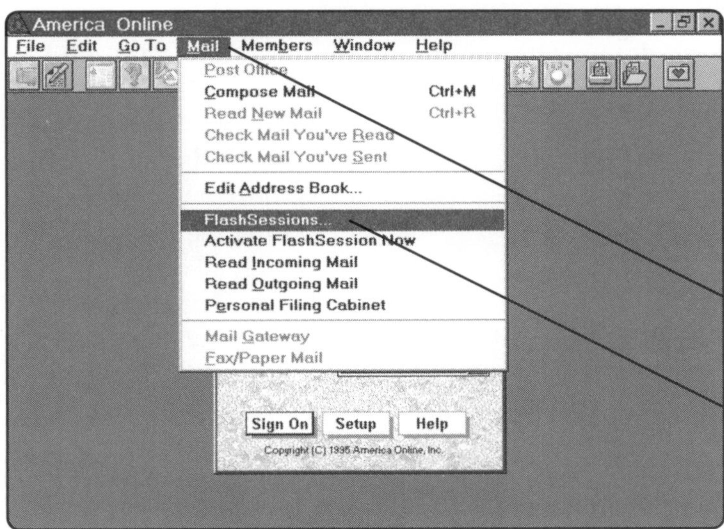

The first time you open FlashSessions, AOL walks you through a series of basic setup dialog boxes.

1. **Open America Online** but don't sign on.
2. **Click** on **Mail**. A Mail menu will appear.
3. **Click** on **FlashSessions**. A FlashSessions Walk-Through dialog box will appear.

Note: If you have opened FlashSessions before, you will get the regular FlashSessions dialog box. At that dialog box, you can click on the "Walk Me Through" icon to duplicate the following steps.

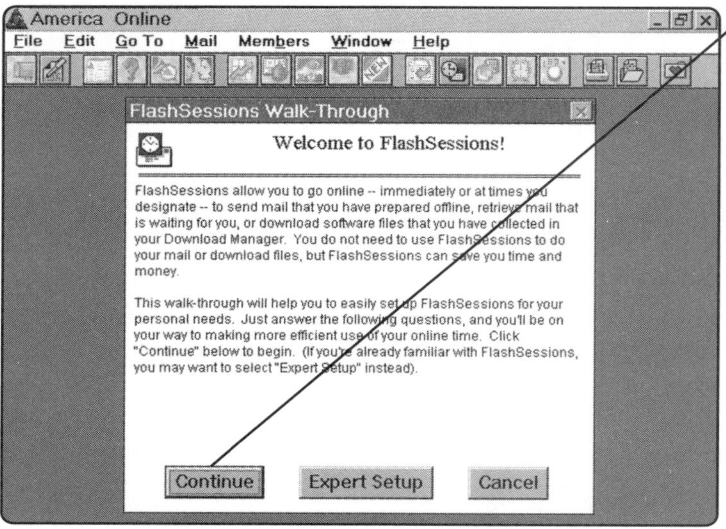

4. **Click** on **Continue** after you read the Welcome message. Another FlashSessions Walk-Through dialog box will appear.

Setting Initial FlashSession Options

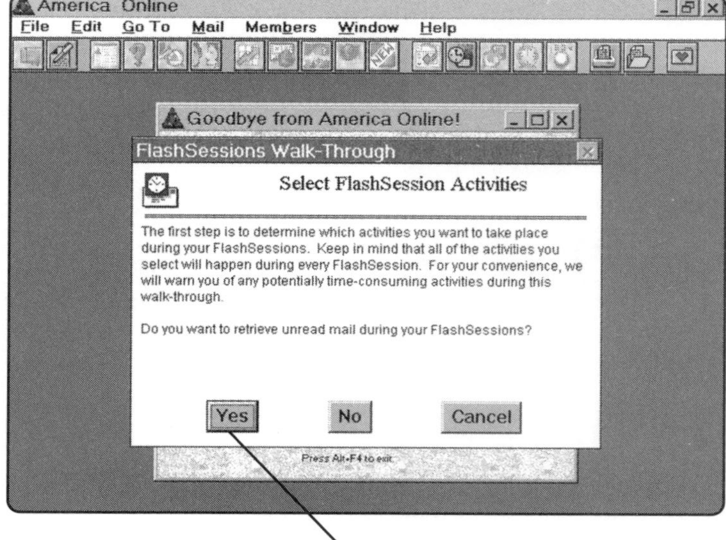

In this example, you will select the basic options for a FlashSession that sends and receives mail, downloads files, and sends and receives newsgroup messages. It doesn't matter if you don't have any mail or files to send or receive. This is just to show you how FlashSession setup is done. You will be able to change the options later to suit your needs. This dialog box asks if you want to use FlashSessions to get your mail.

1. **Click** on **Yes**. Another FlashSessions Walk-Through dialog box will appear.

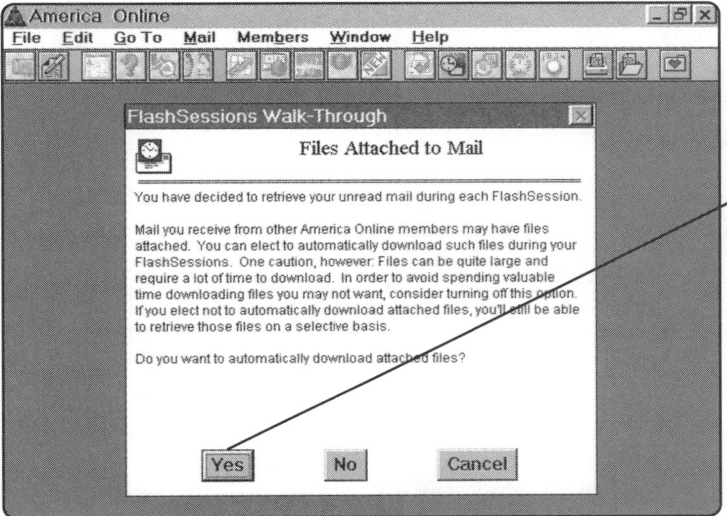

America Online
File Edit Go To Mail Members Window Help
FlashSessions Walk-Through
Files Attached to Mail
You have decided to retrieve your unread mail during each FlashSession.
Mail you receive from other America Online members may have files attached. You can elect to automatically download such files during your FlashSessions. One caution, however: Files can be quite large and require a lot of time to download. In order to avoid spending valuable time downloading files you may not want, consider turning off this option. If you elect not to automatically download attached files, you'll still be able to retrieve those files on a selective basis.
Do you want to automatically download attached files?
Yes
No
Cancel

This dialog box asks if you want FlashSessions to download any files that may be attached to your mail.

2. **Click** on **Yes**. Another FlashSessions Walk-Through dialog box will appear.

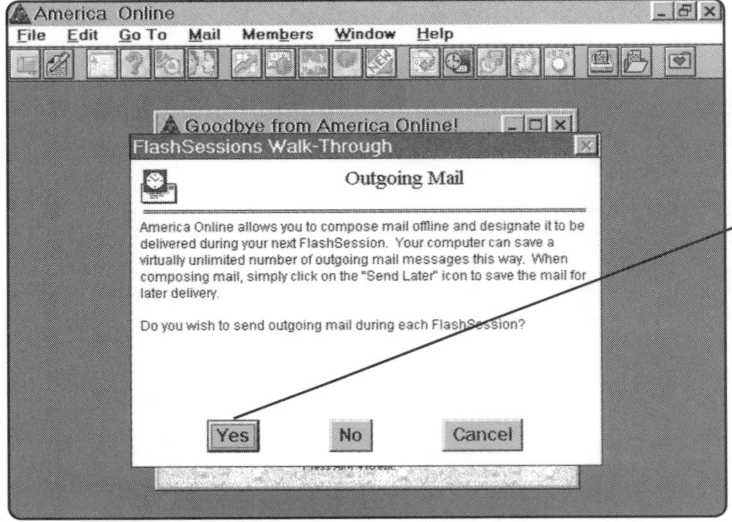

America Online
File Edit Go To Mail Members Window Help
Goodbye from America Online!
FlashSessions Walk-Through
Outgoing Mail
America Online allows you to compose mail offline and designate it to be delivered during your next FlashSession. Your computer can save a virtually unlimited number of outgoing mail messages this way. When composing mail, simply click on the "Send Later" icon to save the mail for later delivery.
Do you wish to send outgoing mail during each FlashSession?
Yes
No
Cancel

This dialog box asks if you want FlashSessions to automatically send mail that you have composed offline. (See Chapter 1.)

3. **Click** on **Yes**. Another FlashSessions Walk-Through dialog box will appear.

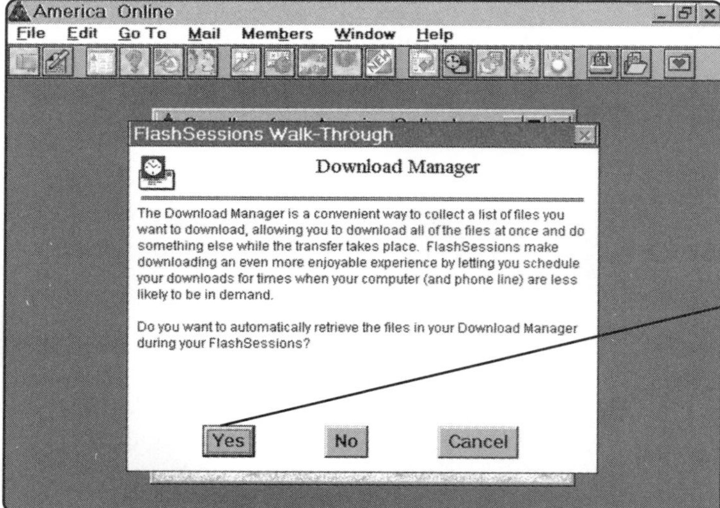

This dialog box asks if you want FlashSessions to automatically download any files that you may have selected to download later while you were previously connected to AOL.

4. **Click** on **Yes**. Another FlashSessions Walk-Through dialog box will appear.

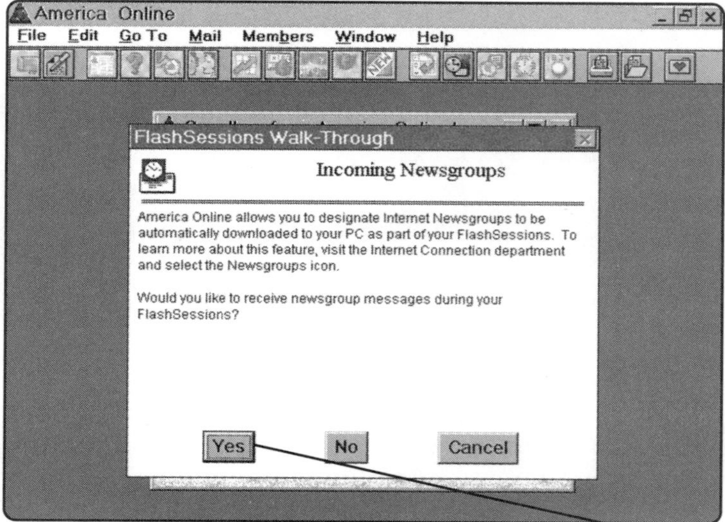

This dialog box asks if you want FlashSessions to automatically retrieve your unread Internet newsgroup messages.

Note: This is not the only step involved for retrieving newsgroup messages. You also have to go to the Internet newsgroups area and designate which newsgroups you want to read offline.

5. **Click** on **Yes**. Another FlashSessions Walk-Through dialog box will appear.

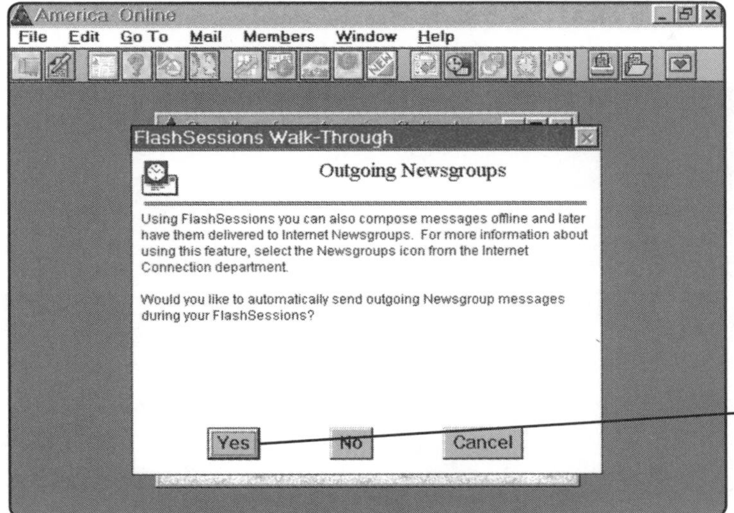

This dialog box asks if you want FlashSessions to automatically send any replies that you have made offline to newsgroup messages. To learn more about newsgroups, refer to the *Visual Learning Guide, Internet for Windows: The America Online Edition*.

6. **Click** on **Yes**. Another FlashSessions Walk-Through dialog box will appear.

Setting Up FlashSessions for Different Screen Names

If you have more than one AOL screen name, you can set FlashSessions to run for each screen name. AOL will connect and disconnect for each screen name's session in turn. However, in this section, you will set up FlashSessions to run with only one screen name.

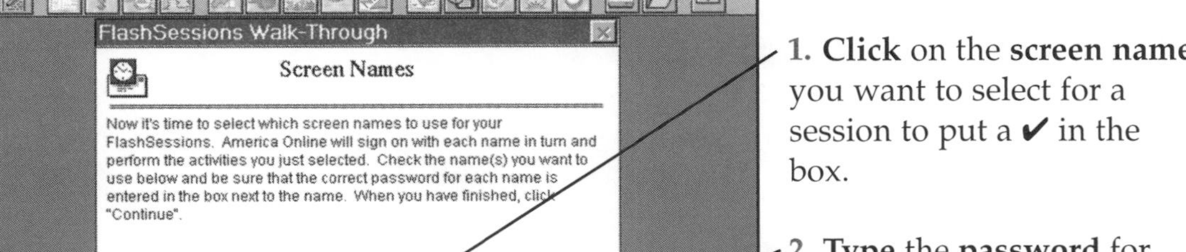

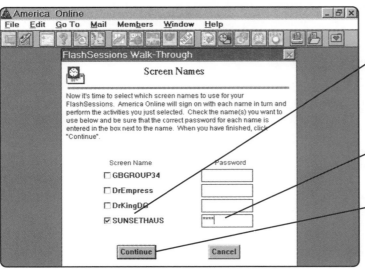

1. **Click** on the **screen name** you want to select for a session to put a ✔ in the box.
2. **Type** the **password** for the selected screen name.
3. **Click** on **Continue**. Another FlashSessions Walk-Through dialog box will appear.

Finishing the Walk-Through

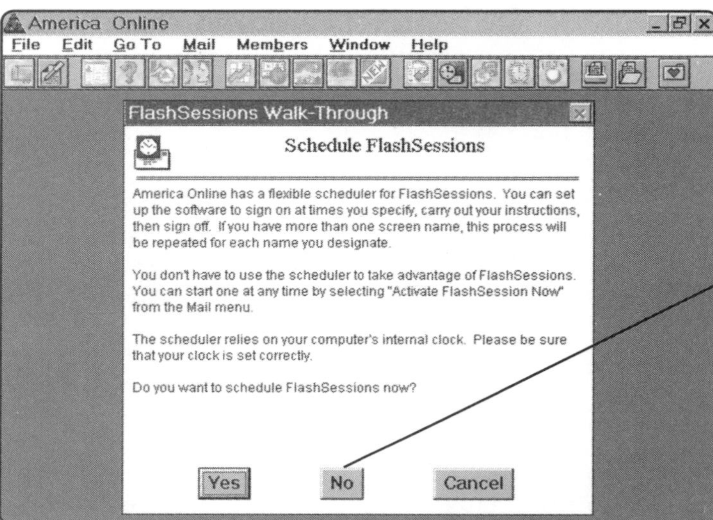

Now it's time to complete your first FlashSessions Walk-Through. This dialog box asks if you want to schedule a FlashSession now. We'll do this later.

1. **Click** on **No**. Another FlashSessions Walk-Through dialog box will appear.

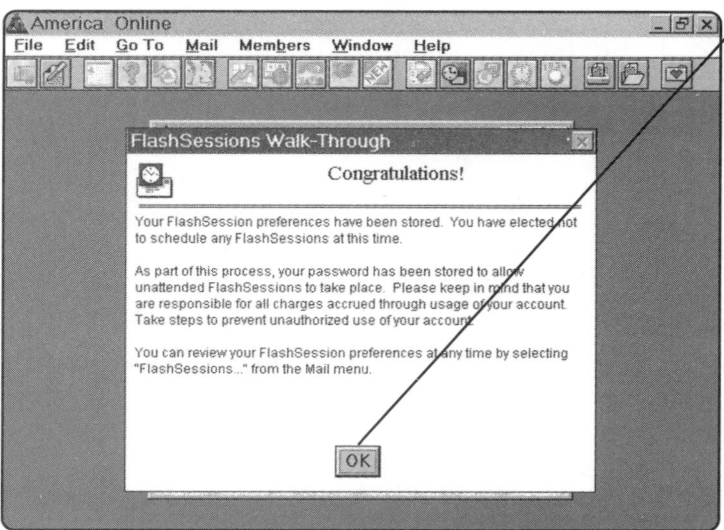

2. **Click** on **OK**. The Welcome dialog box will reappear.

SETTING UP A FLASHSESSION

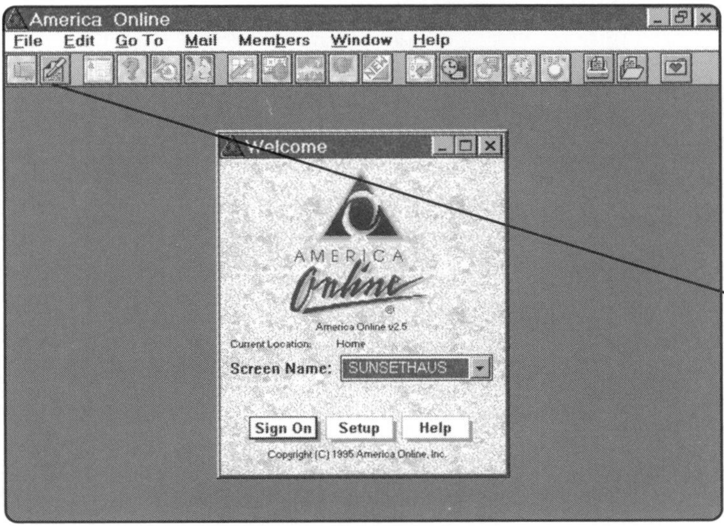

In the example in this section, you will send mail and receive mail automatically. In addition, in this example, you will download a file attached to an e-mail letter.

1. **Click** on the **Compose Mail icon** in the Flash Bar. The Compose Mail dialog box will appear.

Composing Mail for a FlashSession

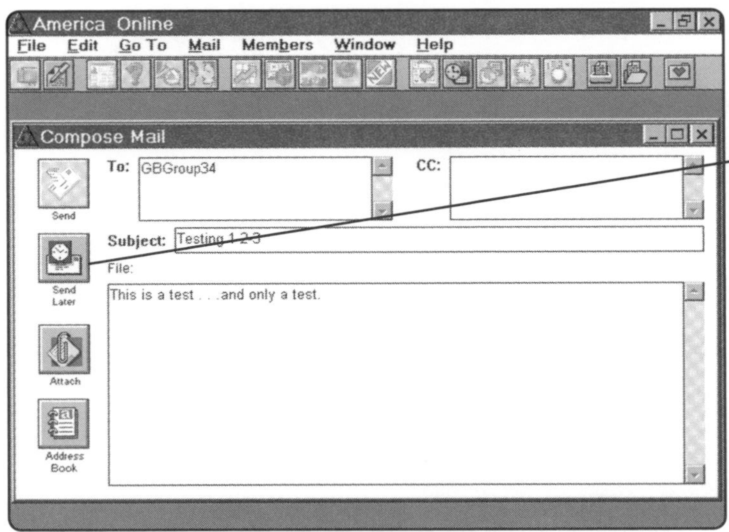

1. **Compose** the **letter.** See Chapter 1 if you need help composing a letter.
2. **Click** on **Send Later**. An America Online dialog box will appear.

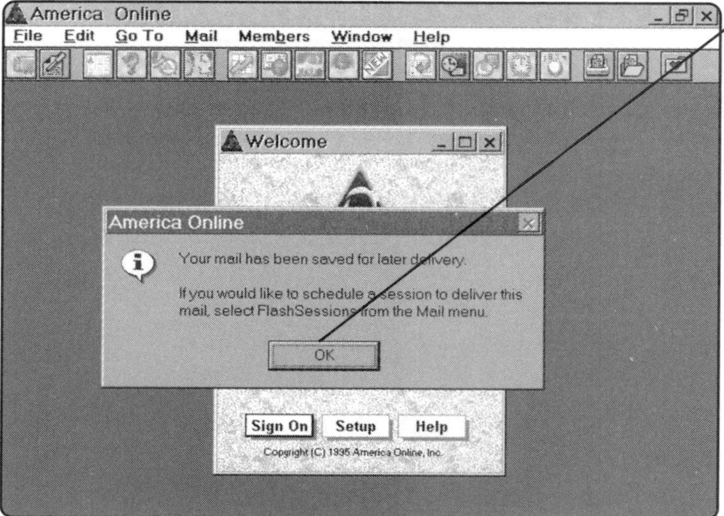

3. **Click** on **OK.** The dialog box will close.

Changing Session Options

Earlier, in the Walk-Through, you set up FlashSessions to perform all of the basic options. It's very easy to change these options before beginning a FlashSession.

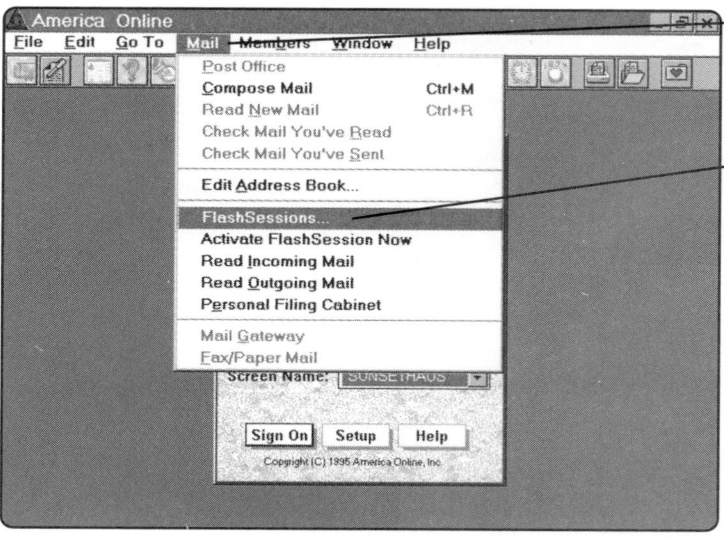

1. **Click** on **Mail** in the menu bar. A Mail menu will appear.

2. **Click** on **FlashSessions**. The FlashSessions dialog box will appear.

Note: If you wanted to start a FlashSession without making any changes to your setup, you would click instead on Activate FlashSession Now.

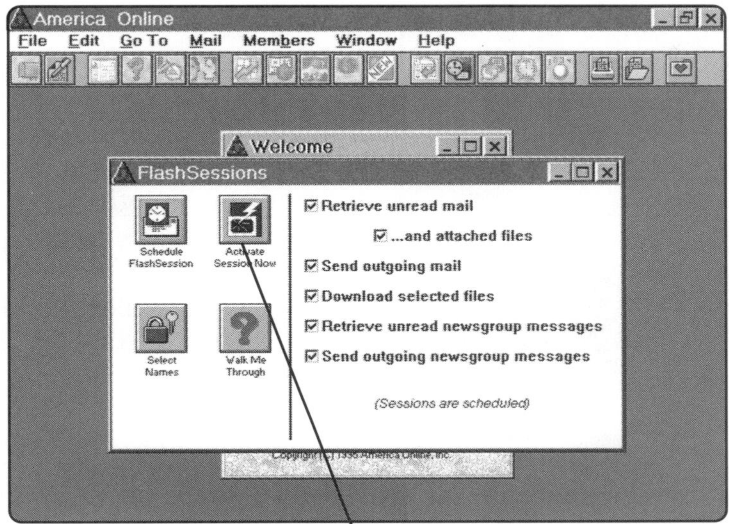

3. Click on any **options** to *add or remove* the ✔ from the box.

Note: If you want to use AOL's "Walk Through" again, click on Walk Me Through in this dialog box.

RUNNING A FLASHSESSION

1. Click on the **Activate Session Now** icon in the FlashSessions dialog box. The Activate FlashSession Now dialog box will appear.

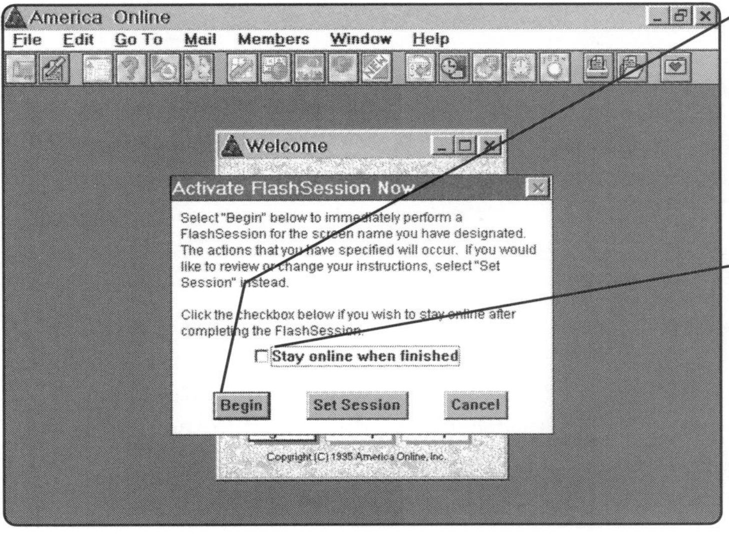

2. Click on **Begin**. The sign-on process will begin and an America Online Flash-Session Status dialog box will appear in the background.

Note: If you want to stay online after the FlashSession is finished, click on Stay online to put a ✔ in the box. In this example, we did not choose to stay online.

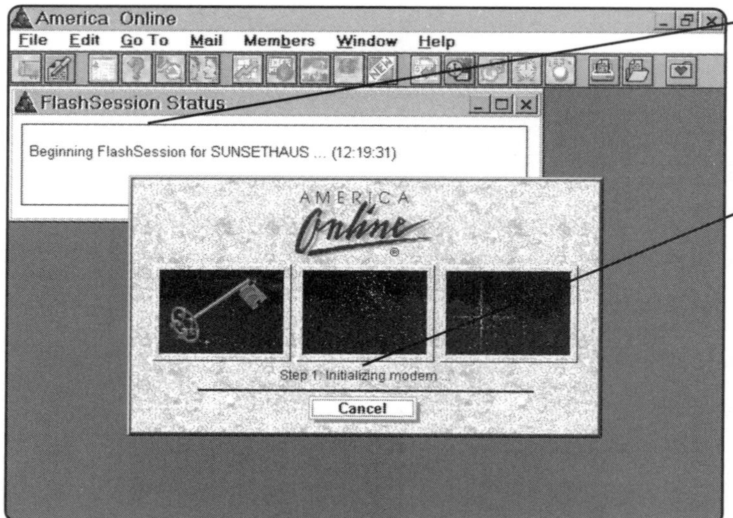

Notice the dialog box. It will record every action taken in the FlashSession as each action occurs.

AOL will go through the normal steps in the connecting process as it starts the FlashSession.

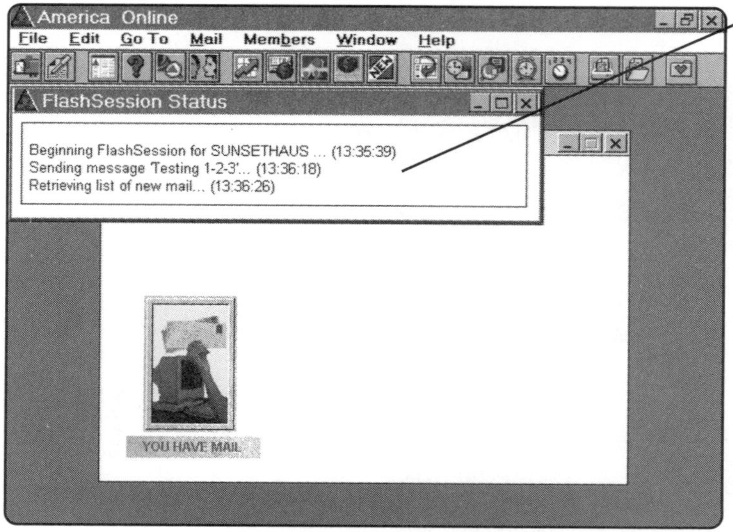

While you are online, the status of the FlashSession is continually updated as AOL performs the tasks you have assigned to this session. In this example, it starts by sending the message we composed a few pages back. Once the session is complete, AOL will disconnect automatically and the Goodbye From America Online dialog box will appear.

Reading the FlashSession Log

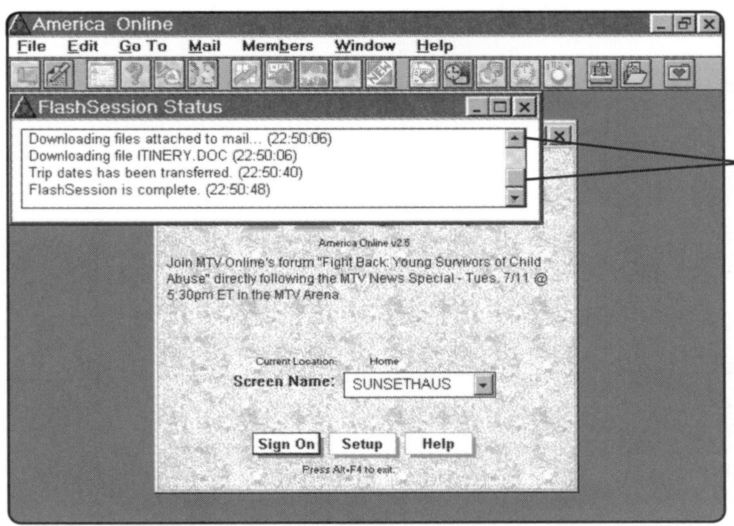

You can review the FlashSession to see if all the tasks were completed.

1. **Click** on the ▲ or ▼ to scroll up or down to review the FlashSession results.

2. **Click** on the ☒ in the right corner of the title bar, or, if you're using Windows 3.1, **click twice** on the Control menu box (⊟) in the left corner of the title bar to close the FlashSession Status dialog box. We will only give the Windows 95 step for closing dialog boxes in the rest of the chapter.

READING INCOMING MAIL AND MESSAGES OFFLINE

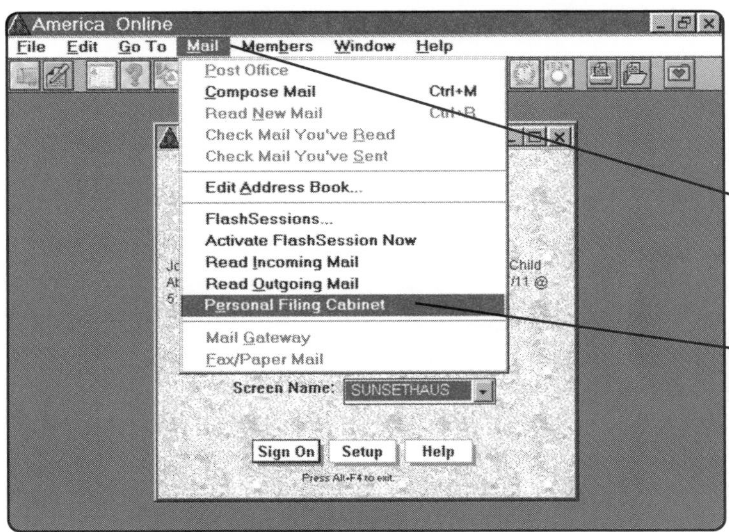

In this section, you will read, print, save, and delete the mail you just retrieved in your first FlashSession.

1. **Click** on **Mail** in the menu bar. The Mail menu will appear.

2. **Click** on **Personal Filing Cabinet**. The Personal Filing Cabinet dialog box will appear.

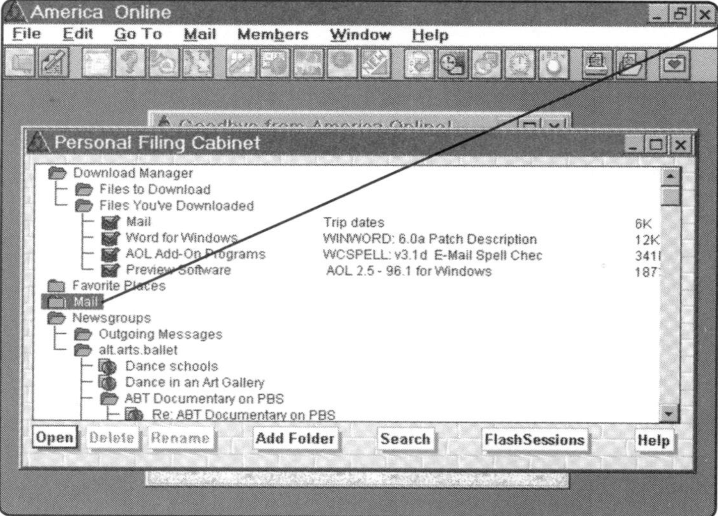

3. **Click twice** on **Mail**, if needed, to open the Mail folder.

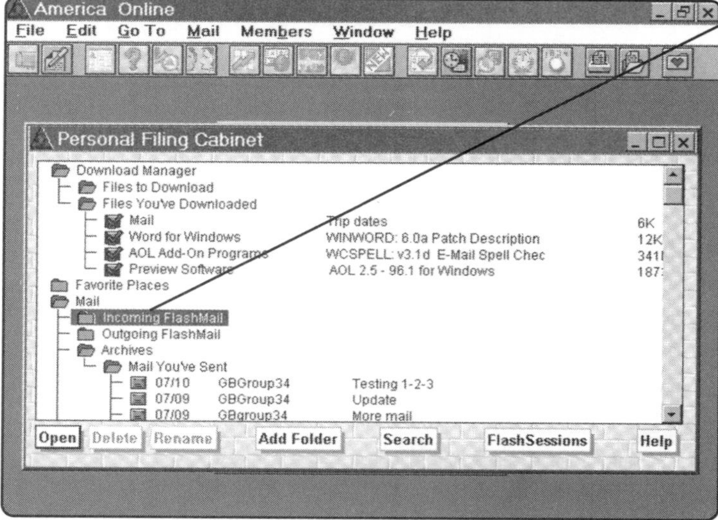

4. **Click twice** on **Incoming FlashMail**. A list of the mail messages you have received will appear.

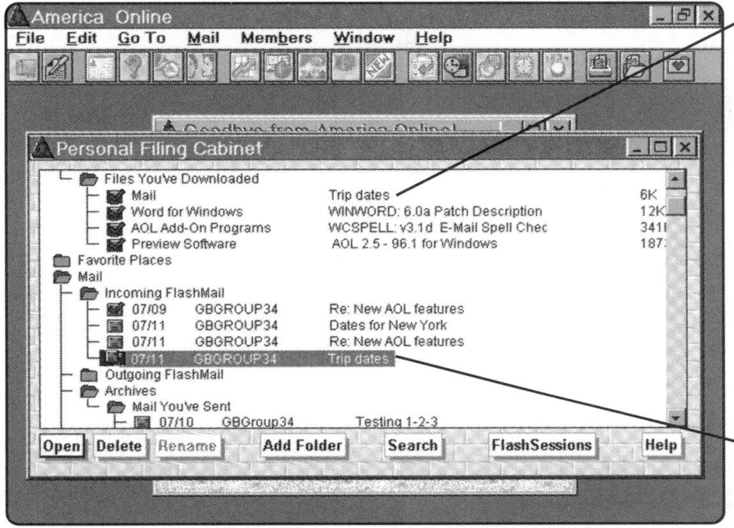

In this example, the letter "Trip dates" had an attached file. (See Chapter 8 to learn how to send and receive attached files). Notice that the file was automatically downloaded in the FlashSession and is located in the c:\aol25\download directory.

5. **Click twice** on a **letter** to read it. You can save or print the e-mail letter using the Save and Print icons. After you have finished responding to your mail, **click** on the **Close button** (☒) in the right corner of the title bar to close the letter.

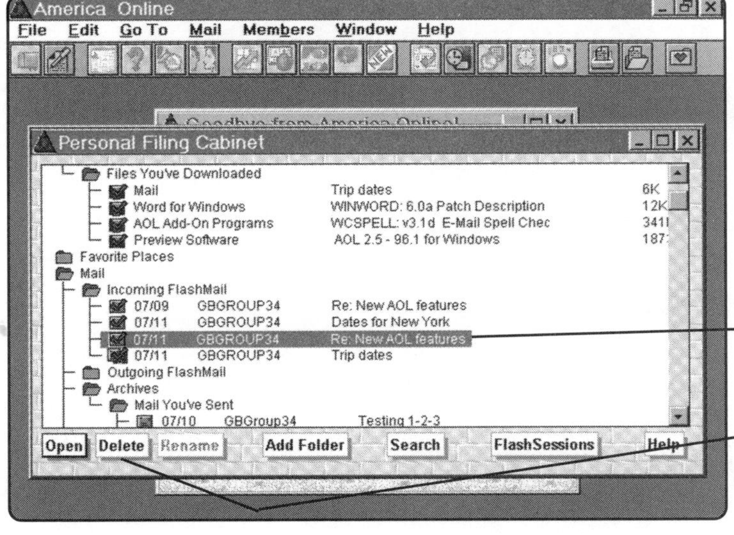

Deleting Mail

If you receive lots of e-mail, you may want to delete letters after you have read them. The letters will, however, remain on your Old Mail list.

1. **Click** on the **letter** you want to delete to highlight it.

2. **Click** on **Delete**. An America Online dialog box will appear.

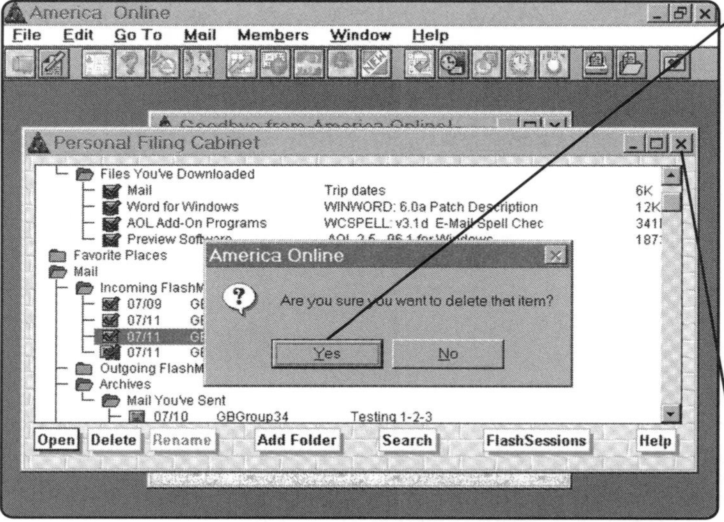

3. **Click** on **Yes.** The dialog box will close, and the file will be deleted from the Personal Filing Cabinet.

Note: Even though you have deleted the file from the Personal Filing cabinet, the original will remain in your Old Mail dialog box when you go back online the next time.

4. **Click** on the **Close buttons** to close the Personal Filing Cabinet and the Goodbye from America Online dialog box.

SCHEDULING A SESSION

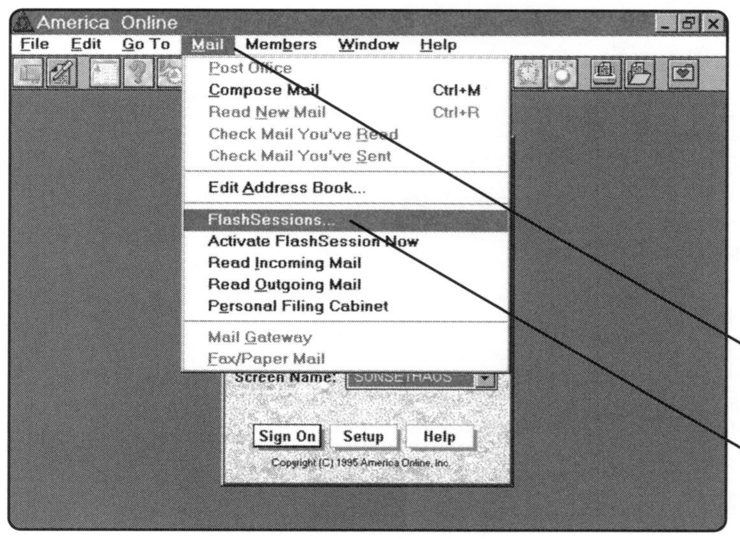

You can set up AOL to run a FlashSession at specific times on specific days for one or more of your screen names. In this section, you will set up AOL to run FlashSessions once a day on Monday through Friday at 11p.m.

1. **Click** on **Mail** in the menu bar. A menu will appear.

2. **Click** on **FlashSessions**. The FlashSessions dialog box will appear.

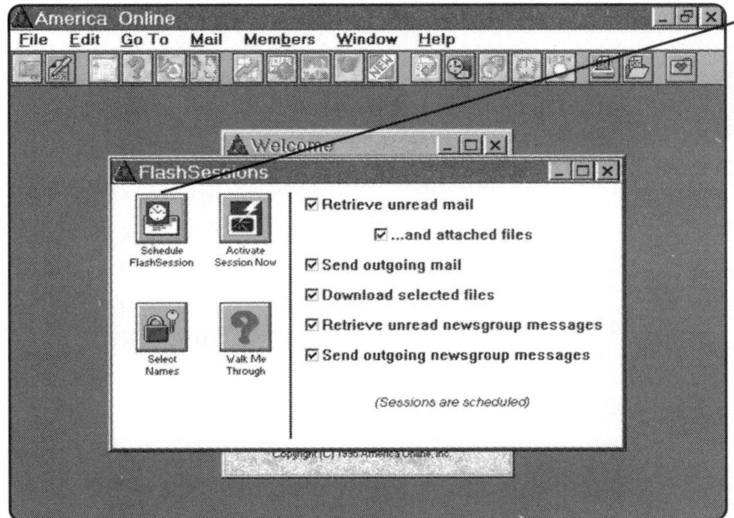

3. **Click** on **Schedule FlashSession**. The Schedule FlashSessions dialog box will appear.

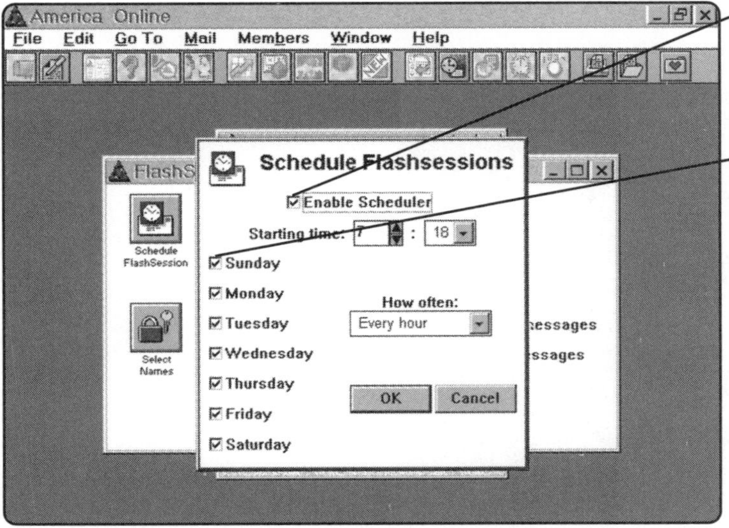

4. **Click** on **Enable Scheduler** to put a ✔ in the box.

5. **Click** on the **days** you do *not* want to run a FlashSession to remove the ✔'s from those boxes.

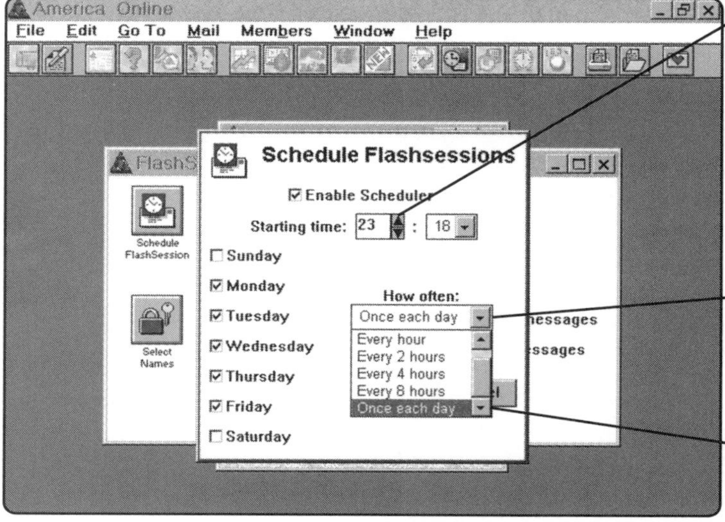

6. **Click repeatedly** on the ▲ to the right of the Starting time box until 23 appears in the box.

Note: In computer time, 23:00 is 11p.m.

7. **Click** on the ▼ to the right of the How Often box. A list will appear.

8. **Click** on **Once each day**. The list will close and "Once each day" will appear in the box.

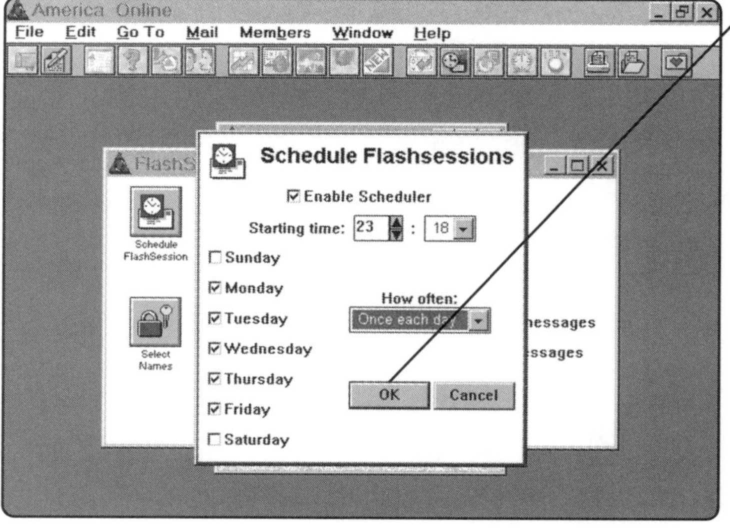

9. **Click** on **OK**. The Schedule FlashSessions dialog box will close.

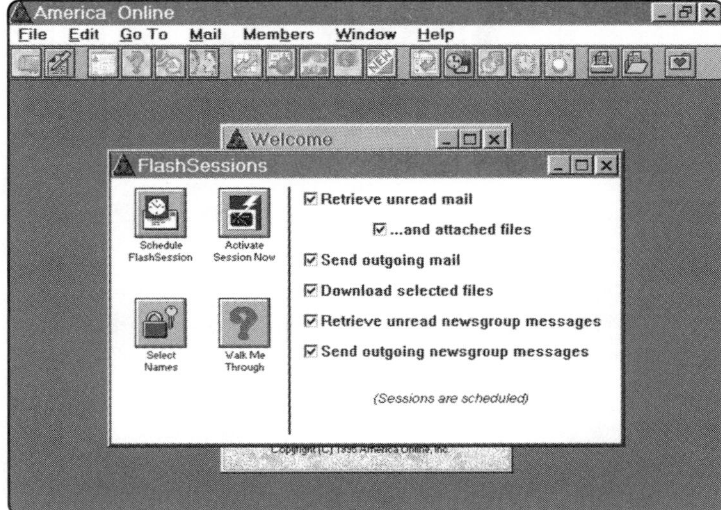

Congratulations! You have just scheduled a FlashSession. In order for the scheduled session to work, you must leave your computer turned on and the America Online program open, but not signed on.

To "unschedule" the FlashSession, repeat steps 1-4 to remove the ✔ in the box next to "Enable Scheduler."

RECAPPING

✔ Use FlashSessions to save money by quickly sending and receiving mail and files.

✔ Schedule FlashSessions to run when it's most convenient for you.

Sending and Receiving files

In "tech talk," sending a file to someone is called *uploading a file* and receiving a file is called *downloading a file*. It's as if the computer you are connecting to were above you in a helicopter. Sending large files is very time consuming and can be expensive, so it is a good idea to *compress* a file, or make it smaller. We'll teach you how to get a shareware compression program and how to use it to compress, or *zip*, a file. In this chapter, you will do the following:

- ✔ Send a file to another AOL member
- ✔ Receive a file from another AOL member
- ✔ Get a compression program
- ✔ Compress, or zip, a file
- ✔ Decompress, or unzip, a file

SENDING A FILE

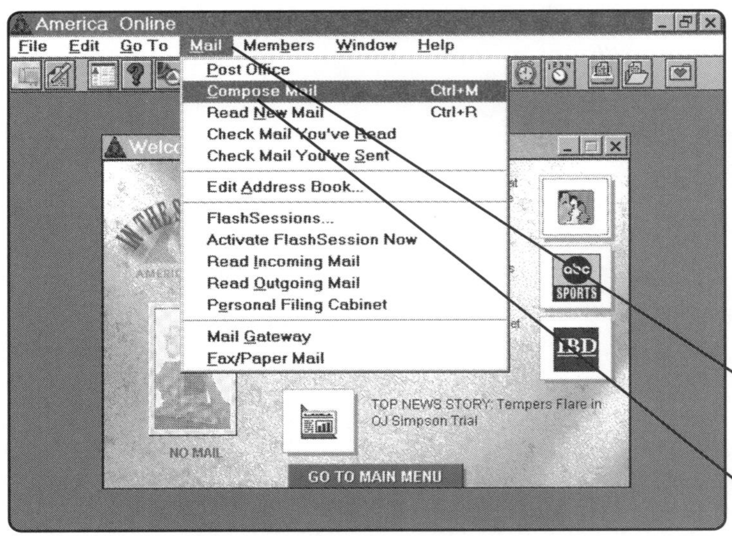

1. **Sign on** to **America Online**. You can compose mail and attach a file before you sign on to AOL, but you must sign on to actually send mail. See Chapter 1, "Sending E-Mail," to review how to compose mail offline.

2. **Click** on **Mail** in the menu bar. A menu will appear.

3. **Click** on **Compose Mail**. The Compose Mail dialog box will appear.

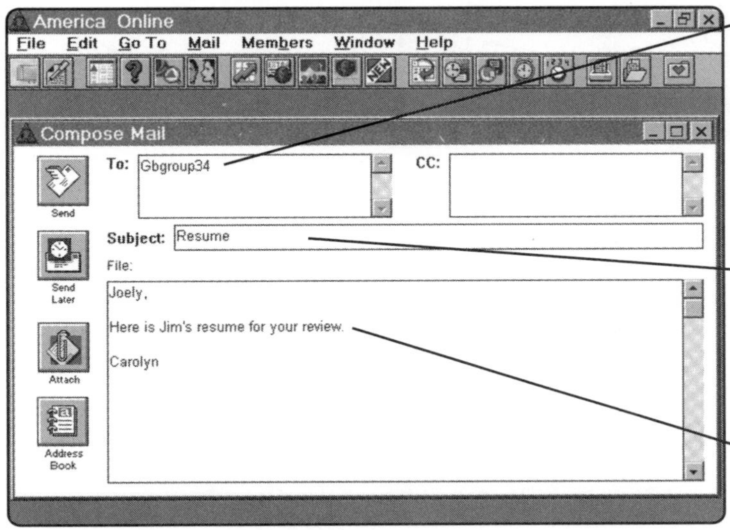

4. **Type** the **screen name** of the person to whom you are sending the file and **press** the **Tab key twice**. The cursor will move to the Subject text box.

5. **Type** a **subject** and **press** the **Tab key**. The cursor will move to the message text box.

6. **Type** a **message**.

Attaching the File

To send a file you must attach it to your e-mail letter.

1. **Click** on **Attach**. The Attach file dialog box will appear.

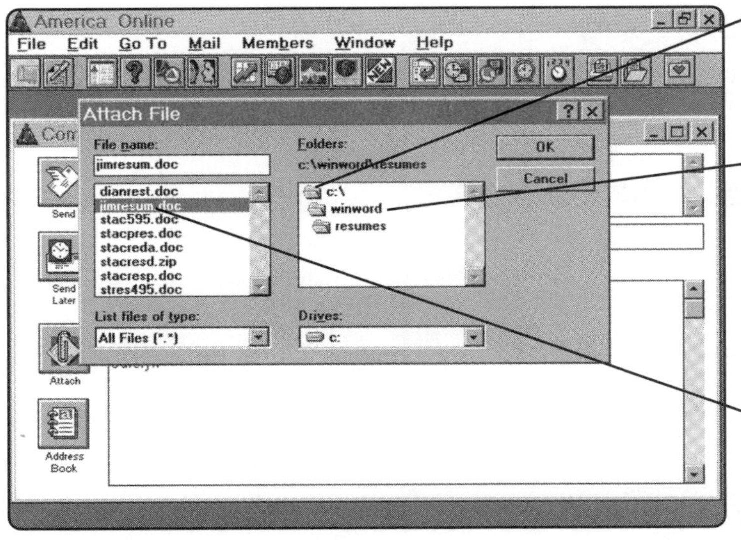

2. **Click twice** on **c:** to bring up a list of all directories on your C drive.

3. **Click twice** on the **directory** that contains the file you want to send. A list of all files in that directory will appear in the File Name list box.

4. **Click** on the **file** you want **to send**.

5. **Click** on **OK**. The dialog box will disappear.

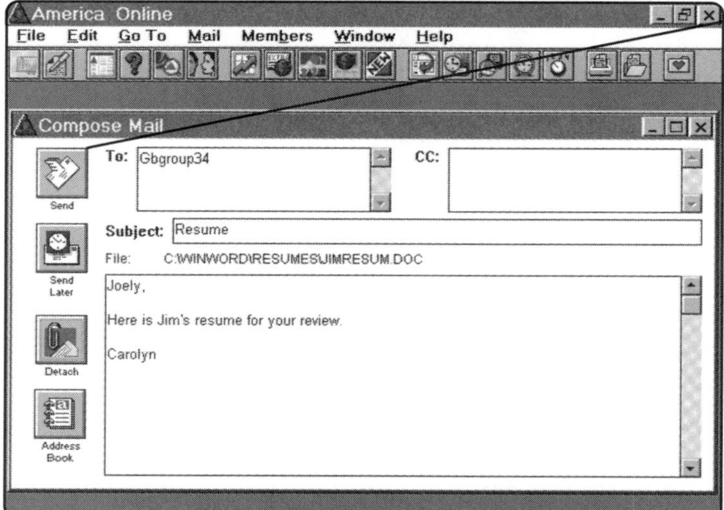

6. **Click** on **Send**. The File Transfer dialog box will appear. When the process is complete, a second dialog box will appear. It is shown at the top of the next page.

Notice that the location and name of the file (*path*) being sent is shown here.

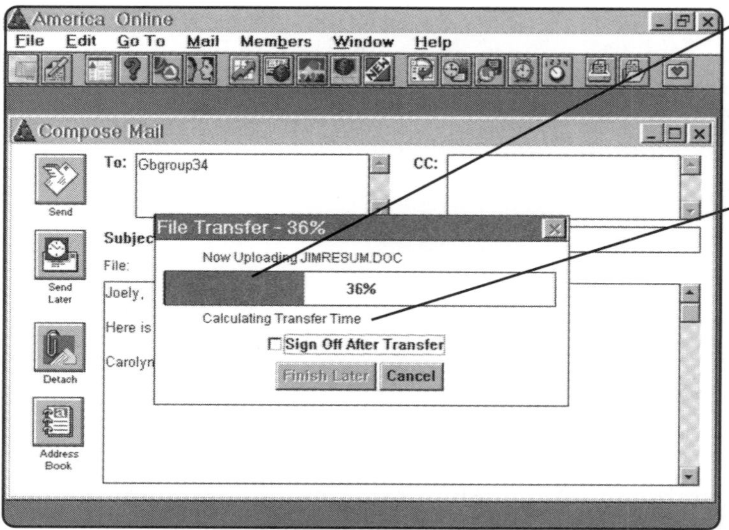

Notice that the File Transfer dialog box keeps you posted on the upload (send) progress.

Notice that first the upload time is being calculated. Then, moments later, the estimated upload time will appear on your screen. In this example, the file was so small that it took less than a minute to upload. When the transfer is complete, the dialog box will close and a message box will appear.

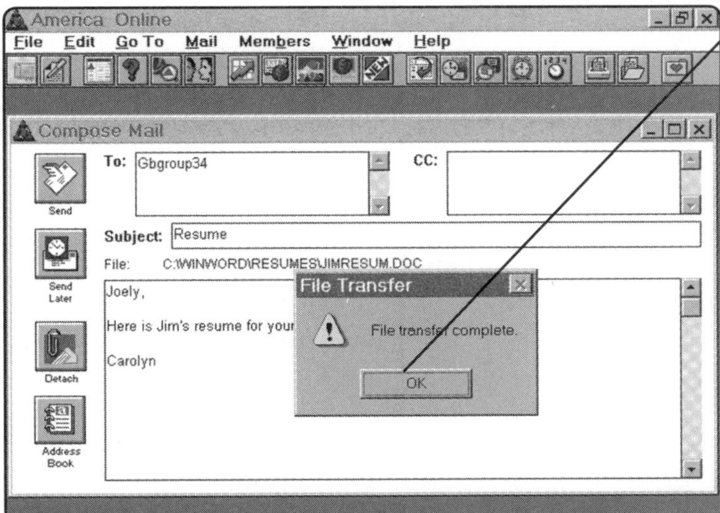

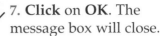

7. **Click** on **OK**. The message box will close.

RECEIVING A FILE

Guess what? You can't receive a file (*download a file*) unless someone has sent you a file! In this section, let's assume you have just connected to AOL and found a "You Have Mail" message on the Mail icon.

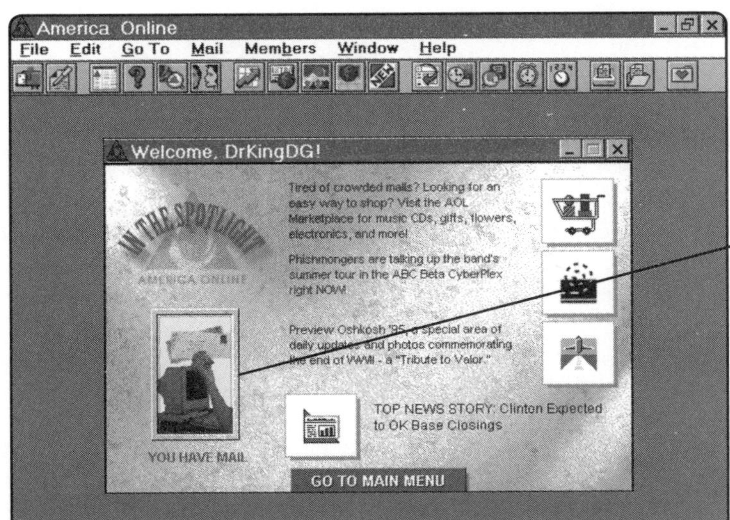

In this example, you will download a file sent to you by a fellow AOL member that he attached to his e-mail

1. **Click** on the **Mail icon**. The New Mail dialog box will appear.

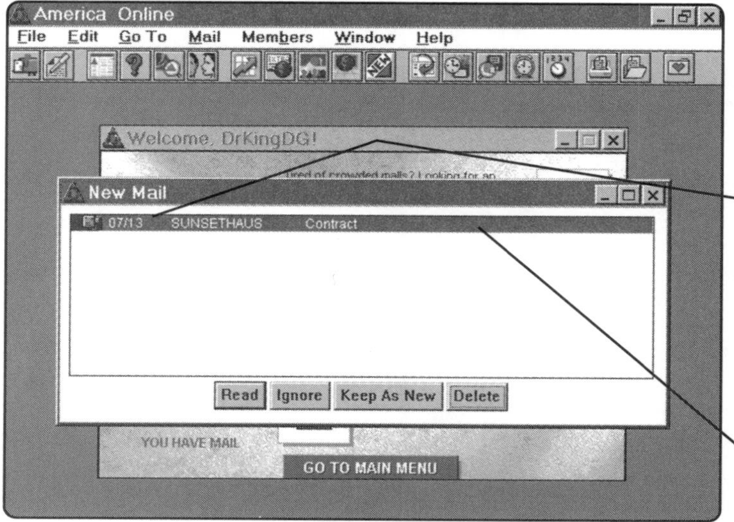

Of course, to download a file, there must be one attached to the letter you open.

Notice the icon that looks like a letter in front of a floppy disk, to the left of the date. This means that there is a downloadable file attached to this letter.

2. **Click twice** on the **letter** with the attached file to open it.

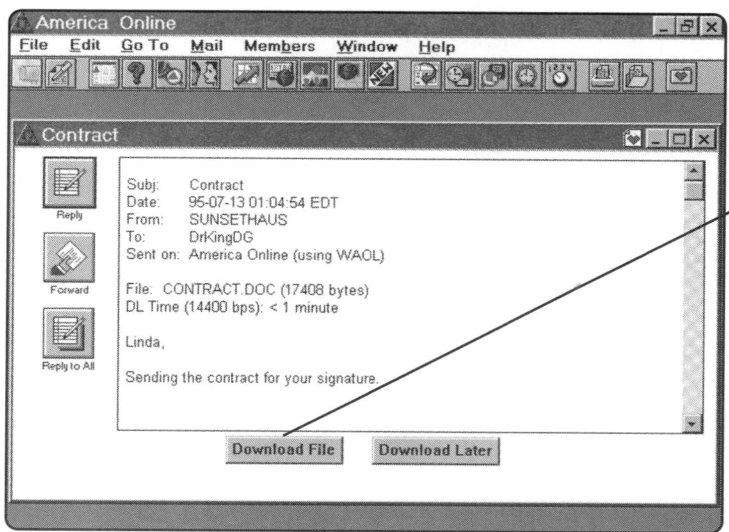

AOL knows there is a file attached to this letter, so the Download buttons will appear with this letter.

3. **Click** on **Download File**. The Download Manager dialog box will appear.

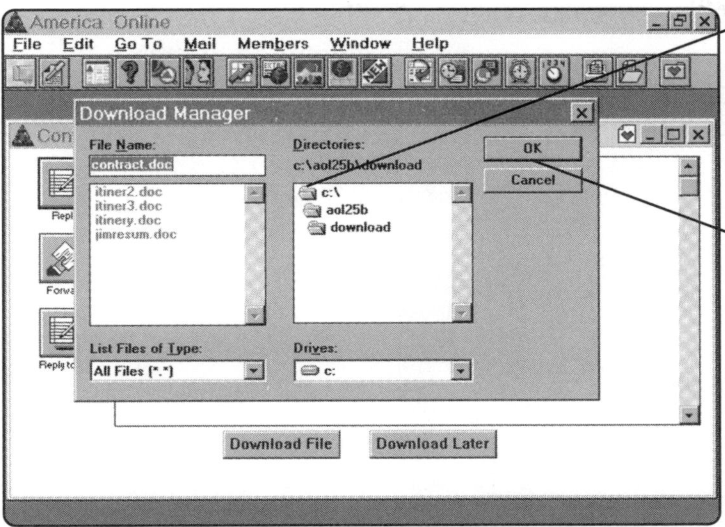

4. **Confirm** that the drive, directory, and folder into which you want your file to download are showing in the dialog box.

5. **Click** on **OK**. The File Transfer dialog box will appear.

Notice that the File Transfer dialog box keeps you posted on the download (receive) progress.

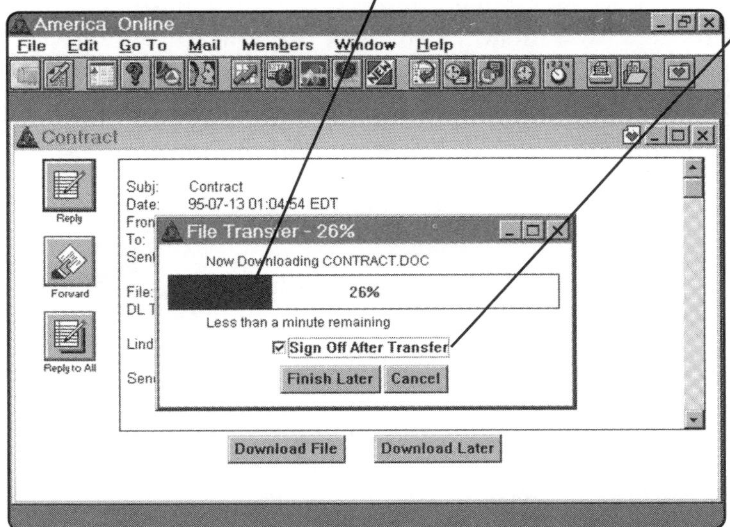

6. **Click** on **Sign Off After Transfer** to put a ✔ in the box. When the transfer is complete, AOL will close the connection and the Goodbye from America Online dialog box will appear. Layered behind it will be the File Transfer Status box. (Of course, you don't have to sign off after transfer if you want to stay online. If you're following along with this chapter, however, it will be easier if you do sign off.)

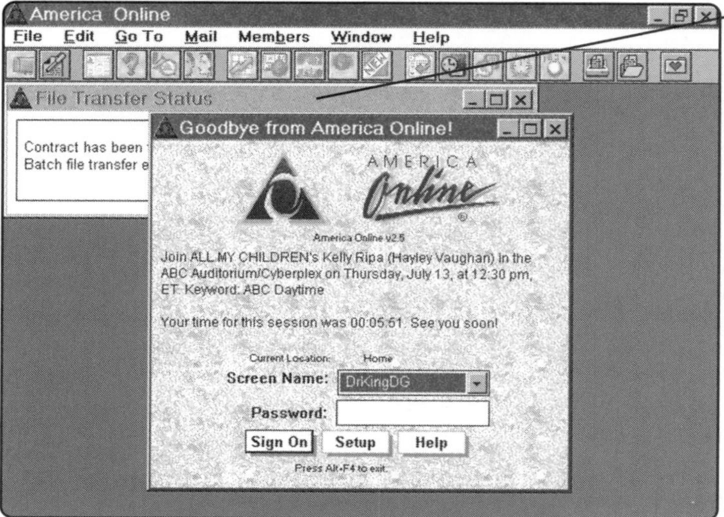

Notice that AOL automatically creates a log of the files you have received (downloaded).

You can read the log by clicking on the log's title bar. It will appear in the foreground.

HANDLING LARGE FILES

In the examples in this chapter we used small files that took less than a minute to send (upload) or receive (download). However, if you want to send a larger file, it's a good idea to compress it first. When you compress a file (often called *zipping a file*), you make it smaller. Compressing files that you send will save both online time and money.

To do this, you need a compression program. The most popular program for compressing files on a PC is called PKZip. It is a *shareware program*. This means you can try it free and pay for it later.

In this section, you will learn how to get PKZip Version 2.04G. You will also learn how to zip (compress) and unzip (decompress) a file. AOL can be set to automatically unzip files for you when you download, but you may have to unzip a file yourself.

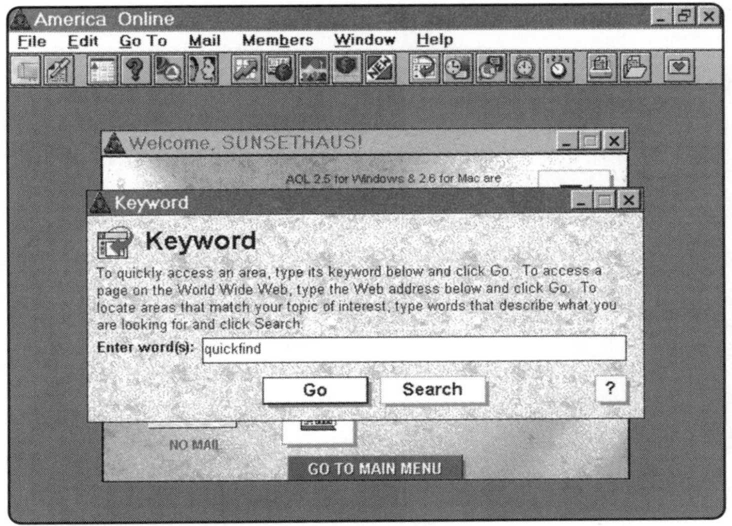
America Online
File Edit Go To Mail Members Window Help
Welcome, SUNSETHAUS!
Keyword
Keyword
To quickly access an area, type its keyword below and click Go. To access a page on the World Wide Web, type the Web address below and click Go. To locate areas that match your topic of interest, type words that describe what you are looking for and click Search.
Enter word(s): quickfind
Go
Search
?
NO MAIL
GO TO MAIN MENU

Getting a Zip Program

1. **Repeat** the **steps** in the first part of Chapter 6 to locate and download PKZip Version 2.04G. (Use the Keyword quickfind to search for PKZ204G.EXE.) Save the file to your Windows directory when you download it. Close AOL after the file has been downloaded. Remember that this program is shareware, so if you like it, register it!

Extracting the PKZip Files

1. **Open File Manager**. If you're using Windows 95, you may have to use the "Start" button, select "Run," type in "winfile" and click on "OK" to open File Manager. Windows 95's Windows Explorer program will not work for the "Zipping a File" section that follows this one.

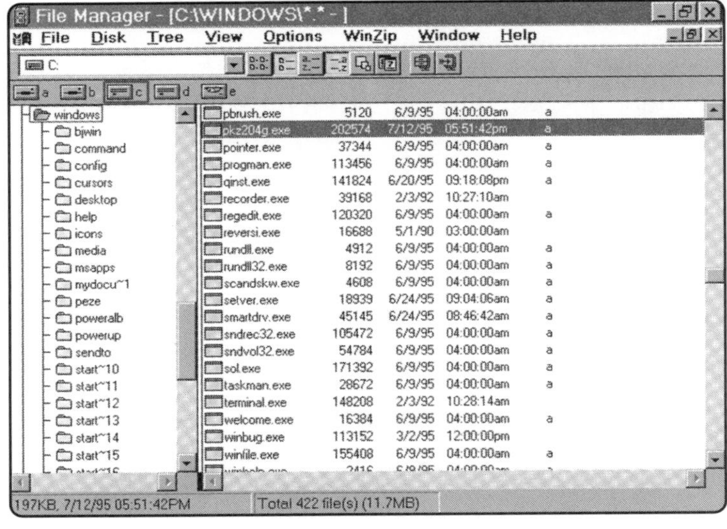
File Manager - [C:\WINDOWS*.* -]
File Disk Tree View Options WinZip Window Help
197KB, 7/12/95 05:51:42PM
Total 422 file(s) (11.7MB)

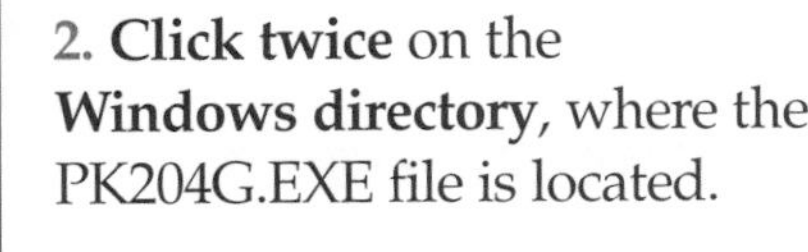

2. **Click twice** on the **Windows directory**, where the PK204G.EXE file is located.

3. **Click** on the ▼ to scroll down the list of files until you see PK204G.EXE.

4. **Click twice** on **PKZ204G.EXE**. A DOS window will appear and the files will be extracted.

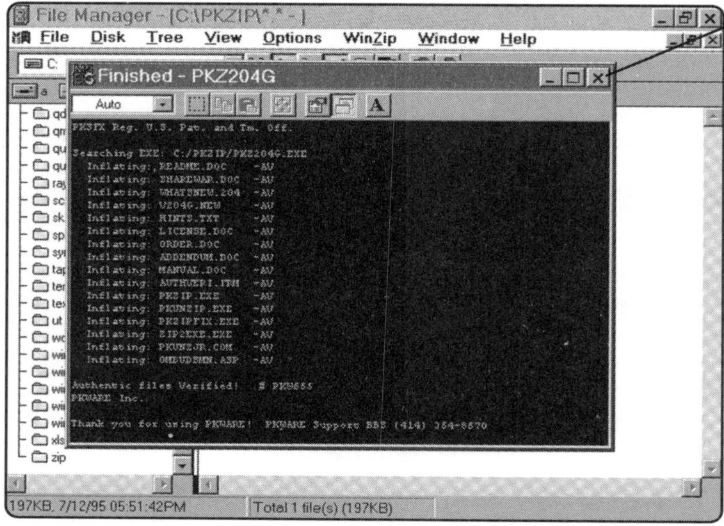

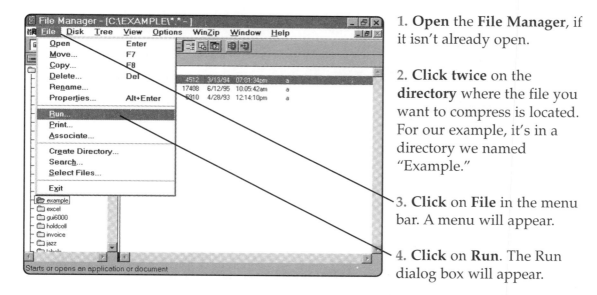

5. Once the files are extracted, **click** on the **Close button** (☒), or (Windows 3.1) click twice on the Control menu box to close the Finished—PKZ204G window and return to File Manager. We will only give the Windows 95 step for closing dialog boxes in the rest of this chapter.

ZIPPING (COMPRESSING) A FILE

In this section, you will compress a file *without going to the DOS prompt!*

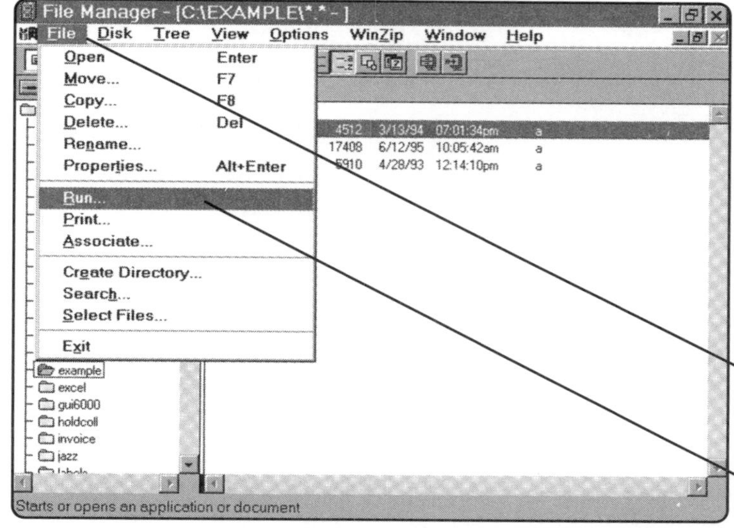

1. **Open** the **File Manager**, if it isn't already open.
2. **Click twice** on the **directory** where the file you want to compress is located. For our example, it's in a directory we named "Example."
3. **Click** on **File** in the menu bar. A menu will appear.
4. **Click** on **Run**. The Run dialog box will appear.

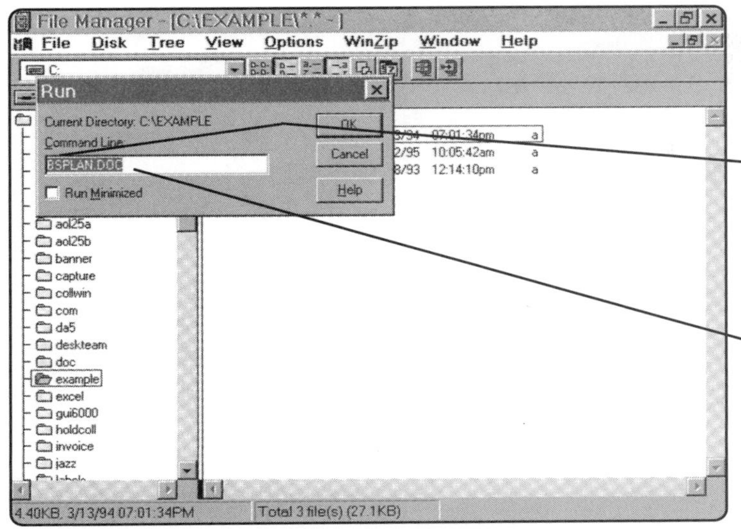

The directory name will be highlighted in the Command line text box.

5. **Type pkzip** and **press** the **spacebar once**. As you start to type, the directory name will disappear.

6. **Type** a **name** for the compressed file and **press** the **spacebar once**. (In this example, the name is "bsplan.zip.") The name may have up to eight characters before the period. *It must always have the extension "zip"* after the period, as shown here.

7. **Type** the **name** of the file you want to compress. In this example it's "bsplan.doc."

Note: If you want to compress all of the files in the directory, type *.* instead of the file names. (The "*" character is a "wild card" that stands for any string of characters in a file name.)

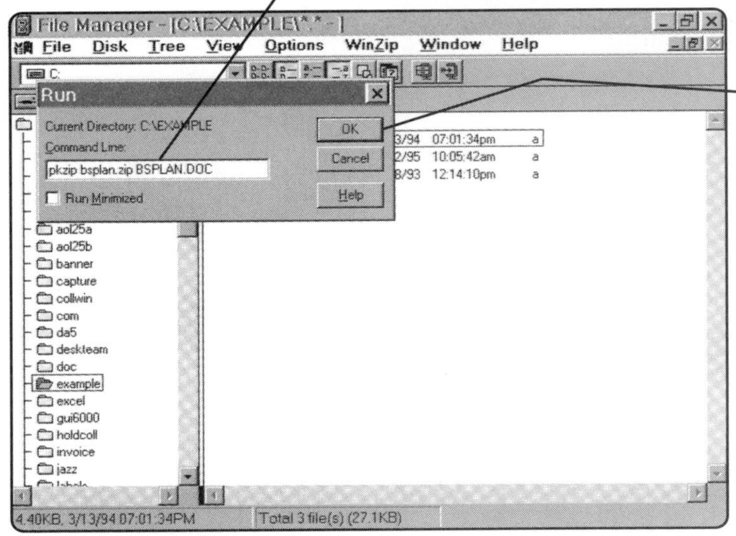

8. **Click** on **OK**. A black-and-white DOS screen with text whizzing by will appear showing the zipping operation. When it's done, click on the Close Button (X). The File Manager window will reappear.

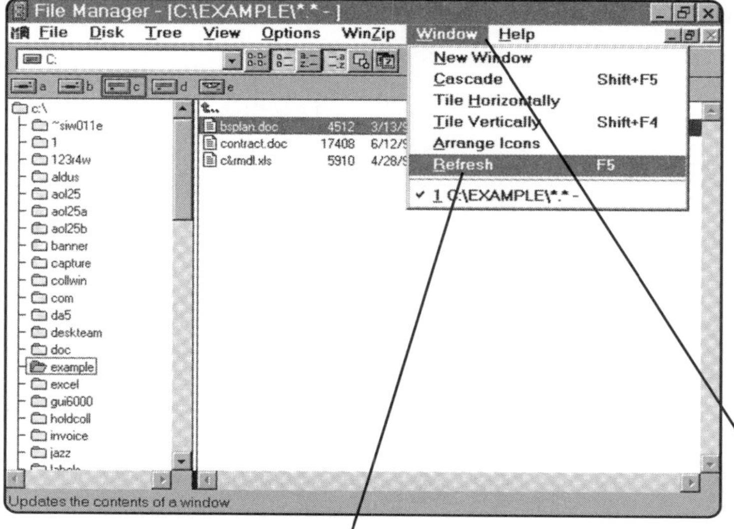

Finding the Zipped File

When you look in the directory where you expect to find the zipped file you just created, you won't see it. That's because File Manager doesn't automatically update its screen. This situation is easily remedied.

1. **Click** on **Window** in the menu bar. A menu will appear.

2. **Click** on **Refresh**. The menu will close. And, lo and behold, the zipped file will be in the list of files in the directory where you put it!

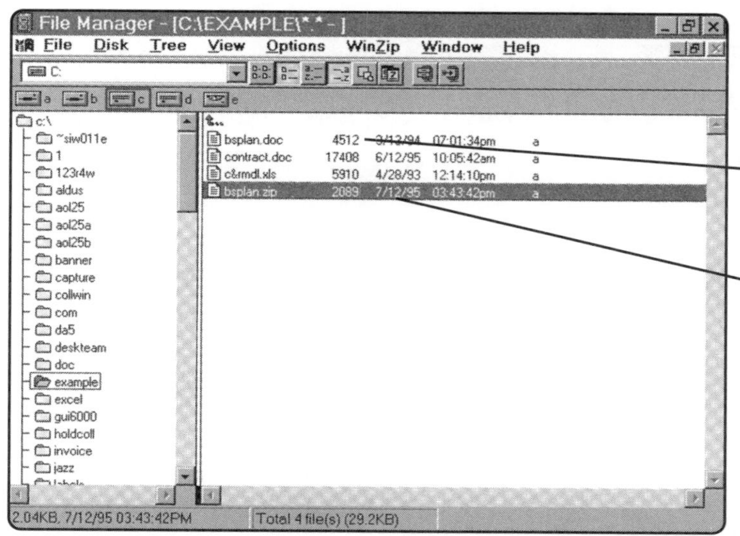

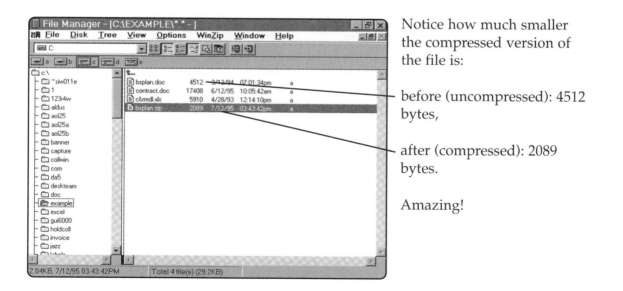

Notice how much smaller the compressed version of the file is:

before (uncompressed): 4512 bytes,

after (compressed): 2089 bytes.

Amazing!

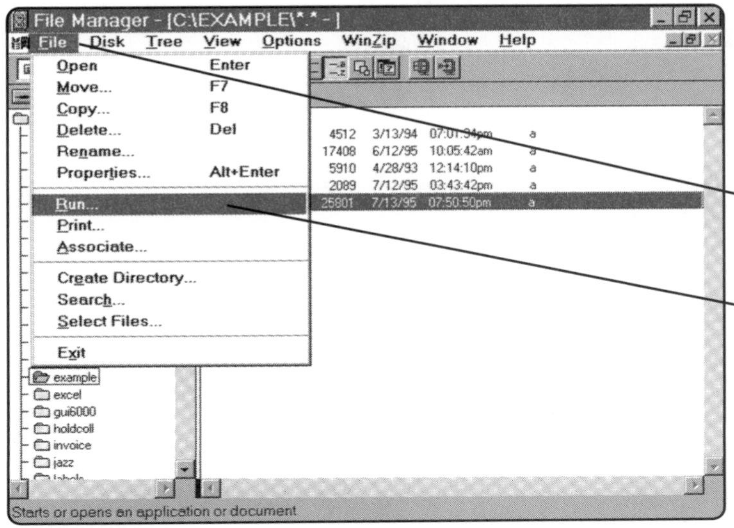

Unzipping a File

1. **Click** on a **zipped file** to highlight it.

2. **Click** on **File** in the menu bar. A menu will appear.

3. **Click** on **Run**. The Run dialog box will appear.

Notice that the file you want to unzip is highlighted in the Command Line box in the screen below.

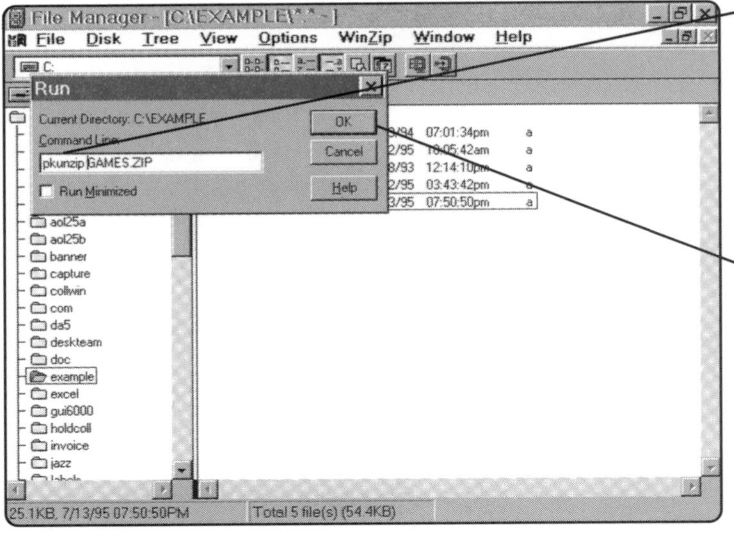

4. **Click** to the **left** of the **first letter** of the **file name** to set the cursor.

5. **Type pkunzip** and **press** the **spacebar once**.

6. **Click** on **OK**. The file will begin unzipping. Once the file is finished, close the PKZip window to return to File Manager, and refresh the window as we did on the previous page.

RECAPPING

✔ Attach and send files with your e-mail letters.

✔ Use PKZip to compress and uncompress files.

PART II: HAVING FUN

CHAPTER

CHAPTER 9

Finding Cool Games

There's a time to work and a time to play, and right now it's play time! AOL gives you access to one of the staples of human social life in the 90's: computer games. AOL has hundreds of games, and we'll show you how to find them. Kick back and get ready to have some fun. In this chapter, you will do the following:

✔ Search for a game on AOL using the Games Forum
✔ Read a game description to see if your computer can handle the game
✔ Use the Download Manager to get a game

SEARCHING FOR A GAME

1. **Sign on** to **America Online** if you haven't already done so.

2. **Click** on the **Keyword icon** in the Flash Bar. The Keyword dialog box will appear.

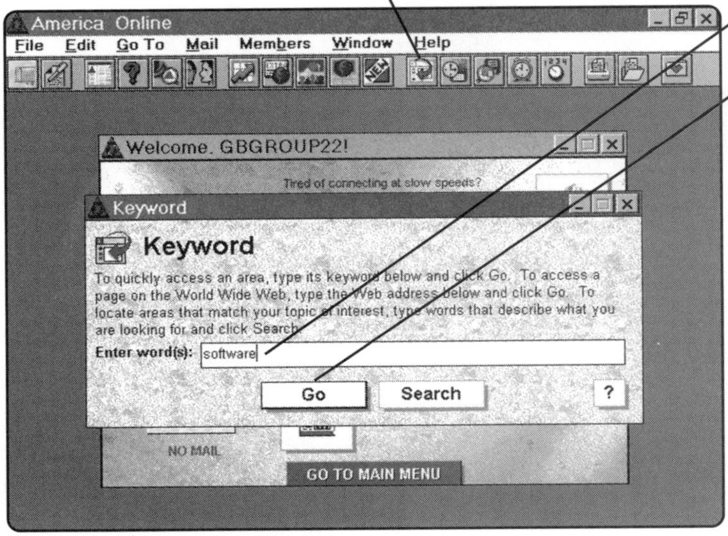

3. **Type software**.

4. **Click** on **Go.** The Software Center dialog box will appear.

5. **Click** on **Forum Libraries**. The Forum libraries dialog box will appear.

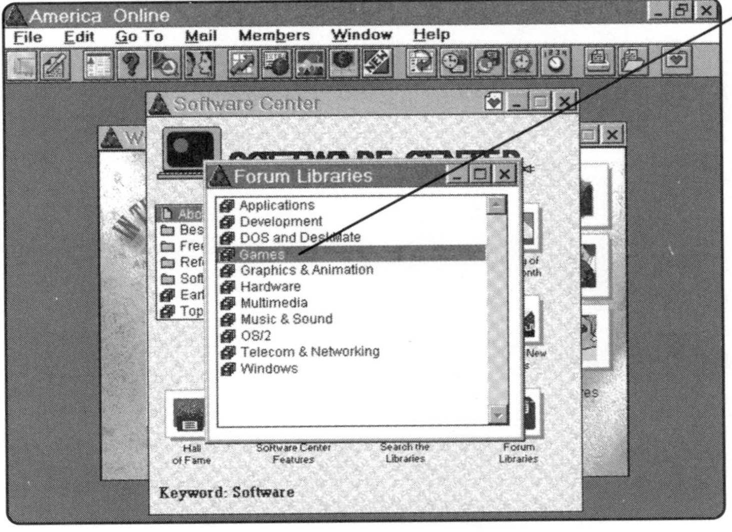

6. **Click twice** on **Games.** The Games Software Libraries dialog box will appear.

Notice the extensive list of game categories. In this example, we'll use the Top Picks category.

7. **Click** on the **Top Picks** icon. A Top Picks dialog box will appear.

Notice that the Top Picks menu contains two listings.

In Download the Top Picks, there's a list of currently popular games. Each game has a description and requirements list.

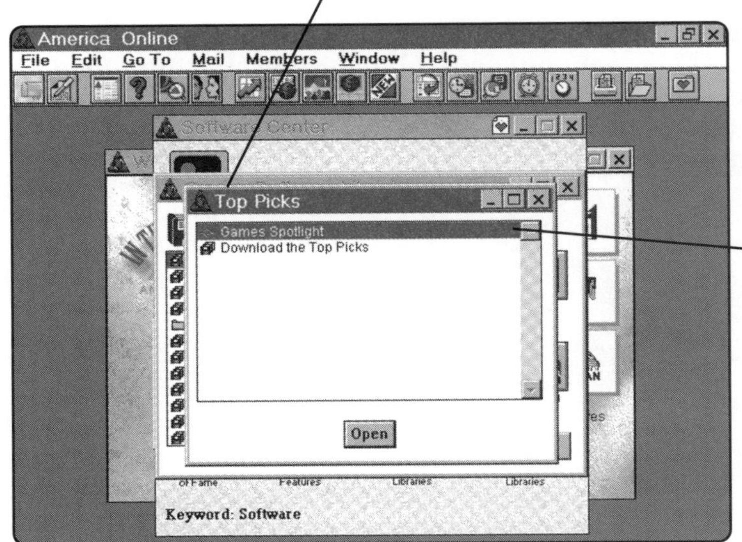

In Games Spotlight, only a few games are listed. But, along with a description, you also get to see a small preview of the graphics.

8. **Click twice** on **Games Spotlight**. The Games Spotlight dialog box will appear.

READING GAME DESCRIPTIONS

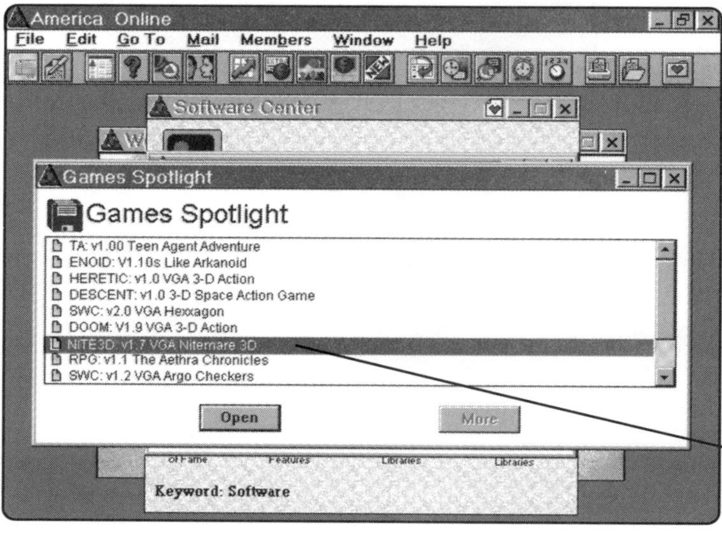

It's extremely important that you read the game description. It tells you the hardware and software requirements of the game. If you don't have the minimum requirements, there's no point in getting the game because you won't be able to play it. In this section, we'll look at the game Nitemare 3D.

1. **Click twice** on **NITE3D: v1.7 VGA Nitemare 3D** to open the game description.

Notice that the graphic takes a little time to appear.

The first part of the description has the file name plus ".ZIP." Most of the games on AOL are *zipped*, or compressed, to reduce the size of the files. AOL contains a program that will automatically unzip most games after you download them to your computer.

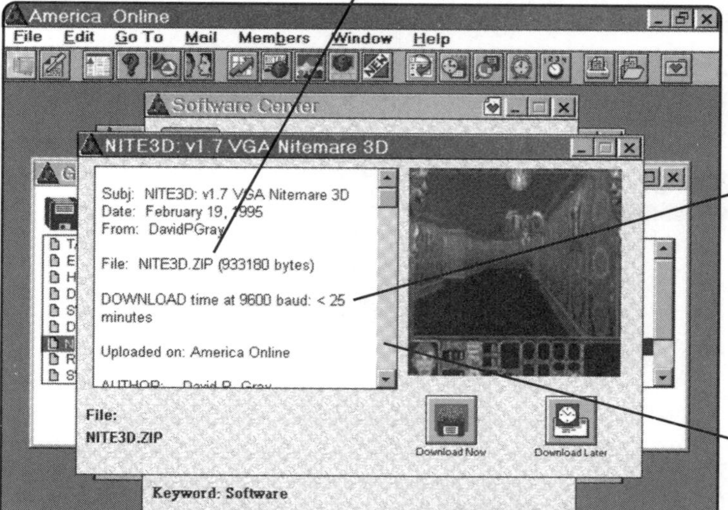

Notice the download time and the baud rate. This is how long it will take to download, or transfer, the game to your computer at the specified baud rate.

2. **Click** on the **scroll bar** to read more of the description.

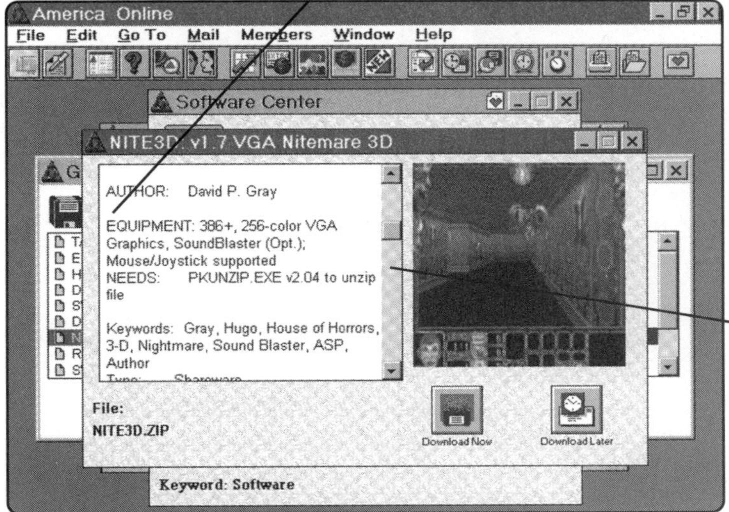

Note: The most important part of this description is the computer equipment that you must have to play the game. If you don't have this equipment, you can't play the game! (You will, of course, immediately run out and purchase what you don't have...that's understood!) Make sure you check this section first before continuing to read the rest of the description.

3. **Click** on the **scroll bar** to read more of the description.

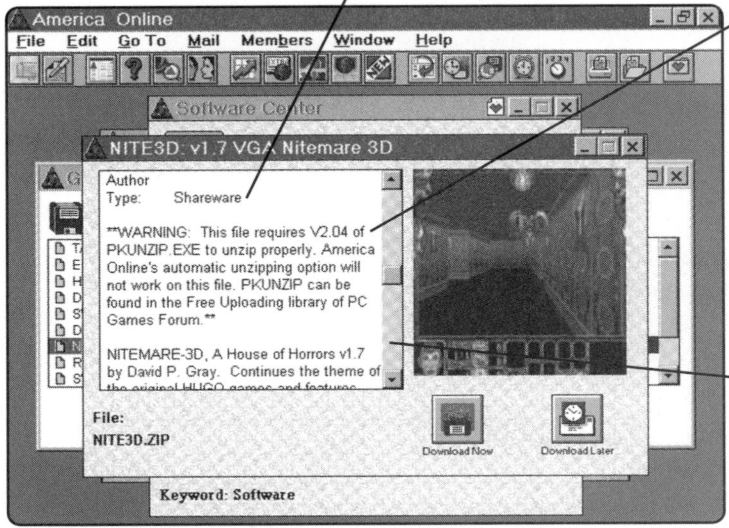

Notice that this game is shareware. This means you may try the game for free but you must pay a registration fee to keep it.

Notice the warning that AOL's automatic unzipping option won't work with this particular game file. Follow the steps in the section entitled "Handling Large Files," in Chapter 8, for help in getting the 2.4 version of PKUNZIP.

4. **Click** on the **scroll bar** to read more of the description.

Be aware that some AOL games portray graphic violence. This particular game "contains no gratuitous violence or nasties."

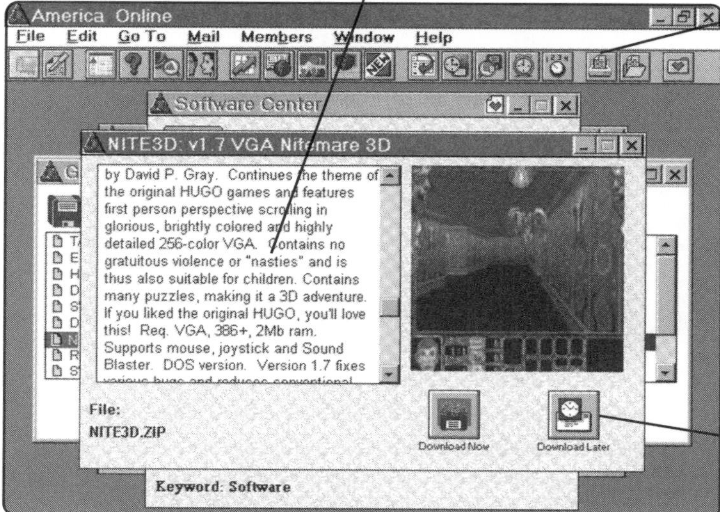

5. If you want this game, **click** on the **Print icon** in the toolbar to get the installation instructions. **Click** on **OK** in the Print dialog box when it appears.

DOWNLOADING A GAME FILE

1. **Click** on **Download Later**. A message box will appear saying the file has been added to your download list.

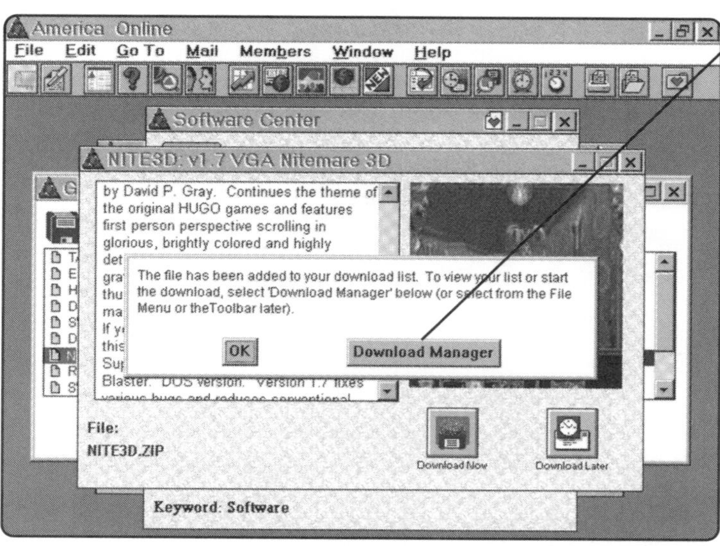

2. **Click** on **Download Manager**. The Download Manager dialog box will appear.

Customizing the Download Manager

The Download Manager lets you specify how you want files downloaded onto your computer.

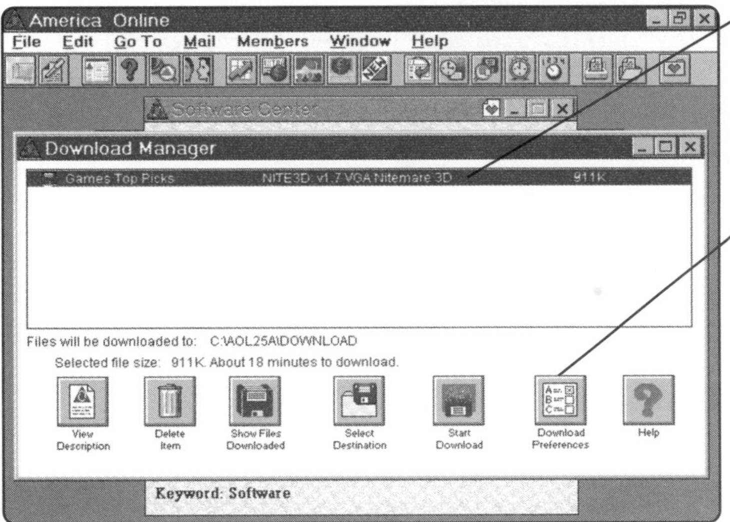

Notice that the game you placed on the Download Later list appears in the Download Manager dialog box.

1. **Click** on **Download Preferences**. The Download Preferences dialog box will appear.

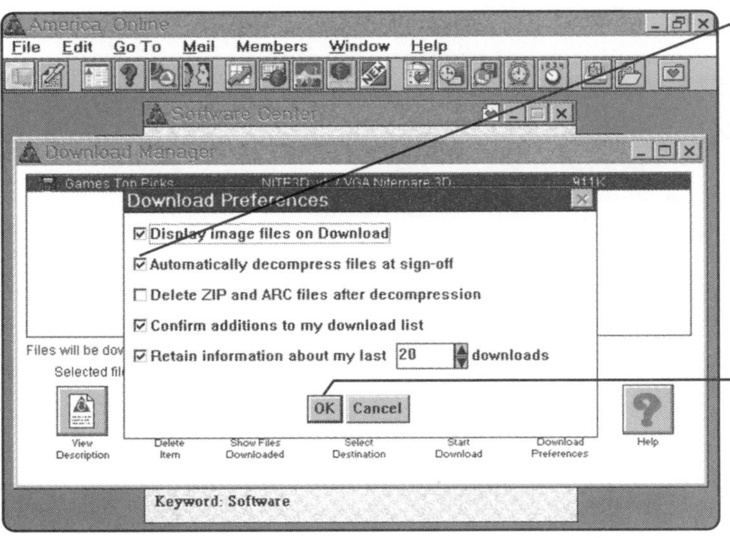

Notice that "Automatically decompress files at sign-off" is selected (has a ✔ in the box). You can customize the download preferences by putting a ✔ in a box to enable a specific option or clicking to take the ✔ out and turn the option off.

2. **Click** on **OK** when you have finished customizing your Download Manager.

Specifying the Download Directory

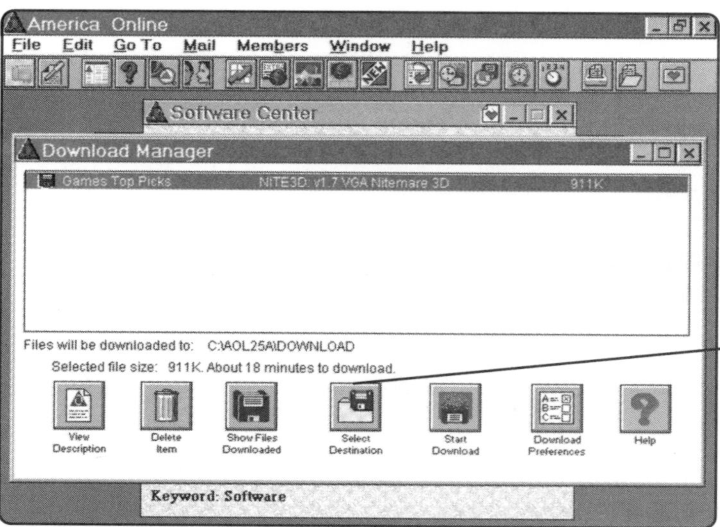

In this example, the compressed game file will be downloaded to the following directory: aol25A\DOWNLOAD. You can copy the files to a different directory if you like.

1. **Click** on **Select Destination**. The Select Path dialog box will appear.

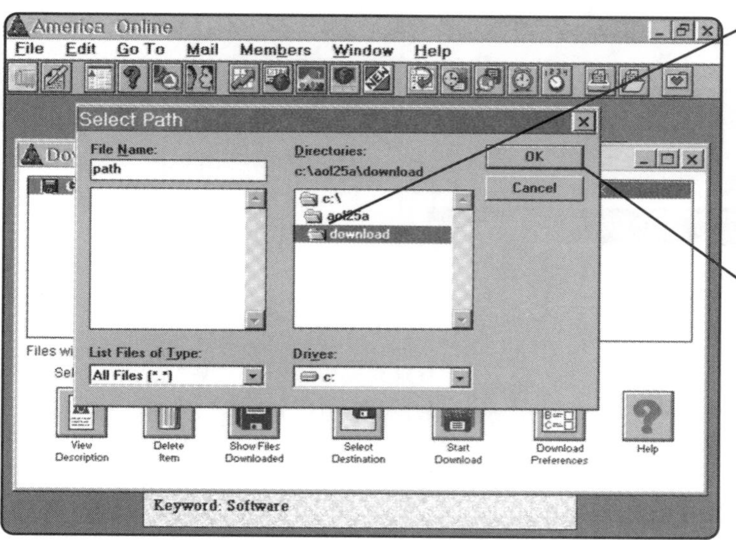

2. **Click twice** on the **directory** where you want to send the file. If you prefer, you can make a separate directory called Games and download the file to it.

3. **Click** on **OK**.

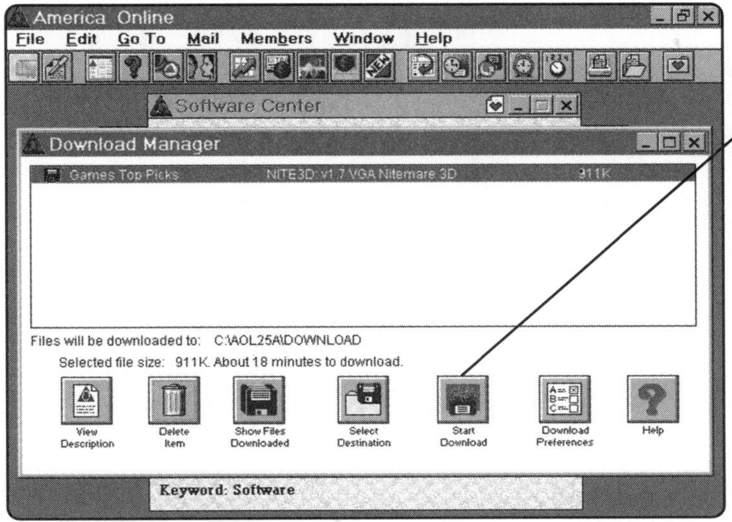

Starting the Download

1. **Click** on **Start Download** to begin copying the game to your computer. The File Transfer dialog box will appear.

Notice that the File Transfer dialog box keeps you up to date on the progress of the downloading process.

2. **Click** on **Sign Off After Transfer** to put a ✔ in the box. When the file has been downloaded, AOL will close. The Goodbye from America Online window will appear. The File Transfer Status box will appear in the upper left-hand corner of the AOL window.

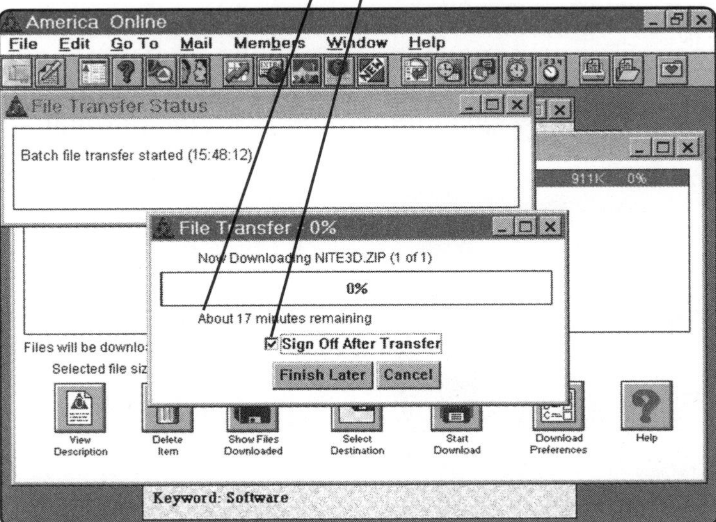

Most games will be automatically unzipped before AOL signs off. However, if you downloaded one of those huge 3D games, you'll need to use the 2.04 version of PKUNZIP to unzip it. Refer to the directions in Chapter 8 if you need help unzipping your game.

CHAPTER
10

Shopping on America Online

Shopping at home on America Online can save you time, money, and miles of walking at the mall. With AOL's shopping service you can compare new or used automobile prices, shop for computer hardware and software, send roses to a friend, order a book, buy a greeting card, or browse a list of department store items, to name a very few. In this chapter, you will do the following:

- ✔ Access AOL's shopping services
- ✔ Shop at the Online Bookstore
- ✔ Add the Marketplace to your Favorite Places List

GOING SHOPPING

As with most AOL features, there's more than one way to open the Shopping mall. You can go to the Main Menu and then click on Marketplace. Or, as in this example, you can use a keyword.

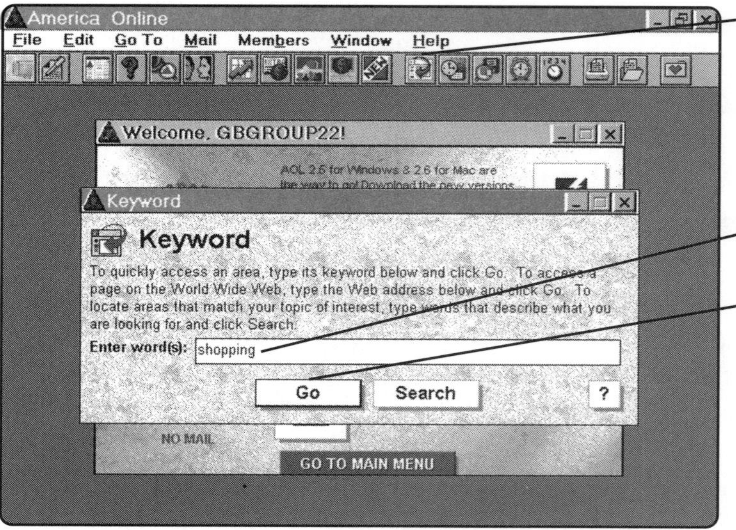
America Online
File
Edit
Go To
Mail
Members
Window
Help
Welcome, GBGROUP22!
Keyword
Keyword
To quickly access an area, type its keyword below and click Go. To access a page on the World Wide Web, type the Web address below and click Go. To locate areas that match your topic of interest, type words that describe what you are looking for and click Search.
Enter word(s):
shopping
Go
Search
?
NO MAIL
GO TO MAIN MENU

1. **Click** on the **Keyword icon** in the tool bar. It's the eighth from the right. The Keyword dialog box will appear.

2. **Type shopping**.

3. **Click** on **Go** (or press Enter). The Marketplace window will appear.

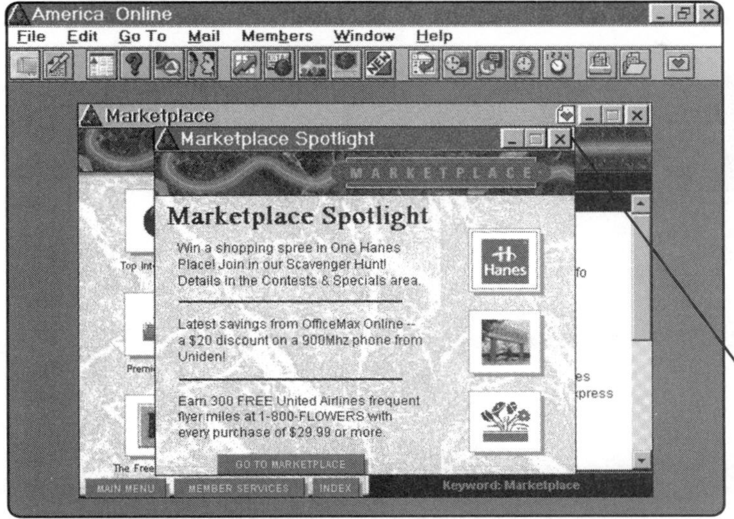

AOL treats you to a Marketplace Spotlight. These featured services and products will change periodically. You can check them out by clicking on the icon. In this example, we'll go to the main Marketplace window.

4. **Click** on the **Close button** (☒) in the right corner of the title bar, or, if you're using Windows 3.1, click twice on the Control menu box in the left corner of the title bar. The Marketplace Spotlight dialog box will close. We will only give the Windows 95 step for closing dialog boxes and windows in the rest of this chapter.

SHOPPING IN THE ONLINE BOOKSTORE

The bookstore is an example of just one of the many fun places to shop on AOL. You can browse through a list of books, place an order, and have the merchandise delivered to your home (in 2 to 5 business days) without ever having to leave your computer.

1. **Click** on the light grey part of the **scroll bar** to see more of the list.

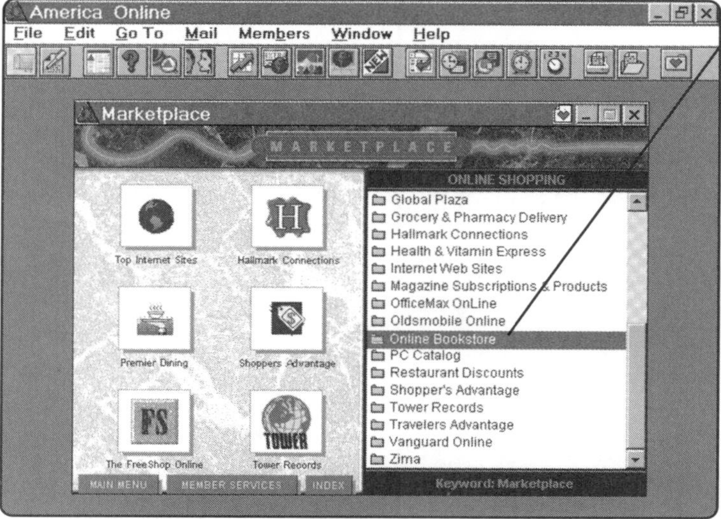

2. **Click twice** on **Online Bookstore**. The Online Bookstore dialog box will appear. Notice the variety of choices!

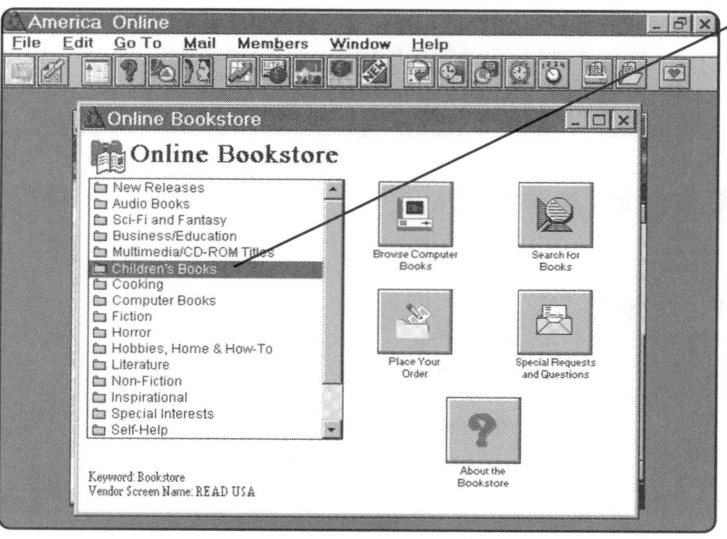

3. **Click twice** on **Children's Books** or the subject matter of your choice. (We found the children's books to be a great bargain.) The Children's Section dialog box will appear.

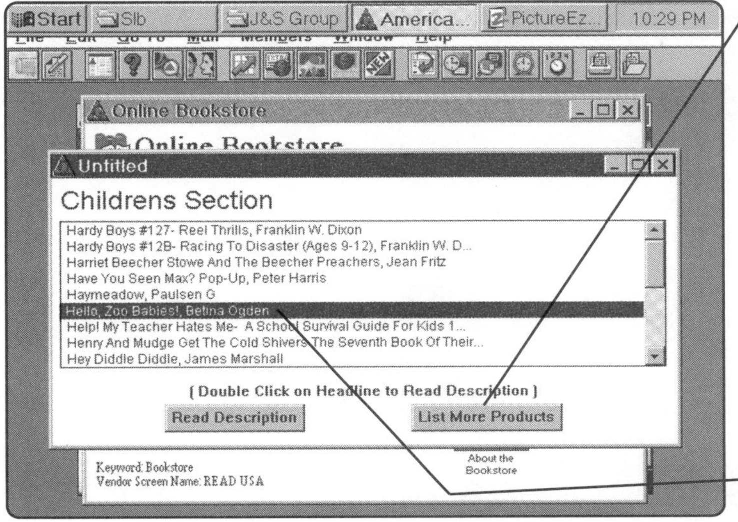

If you want to see more titles, **click repeatedly** on the **List More Products button** on the bottom of the screen until the button "greys out." This tells you that you have the entire list of books.

In this example, we have chosen one of the titles on the first list.

4. Click twice on the **name of the book**. A description of the book will appear.

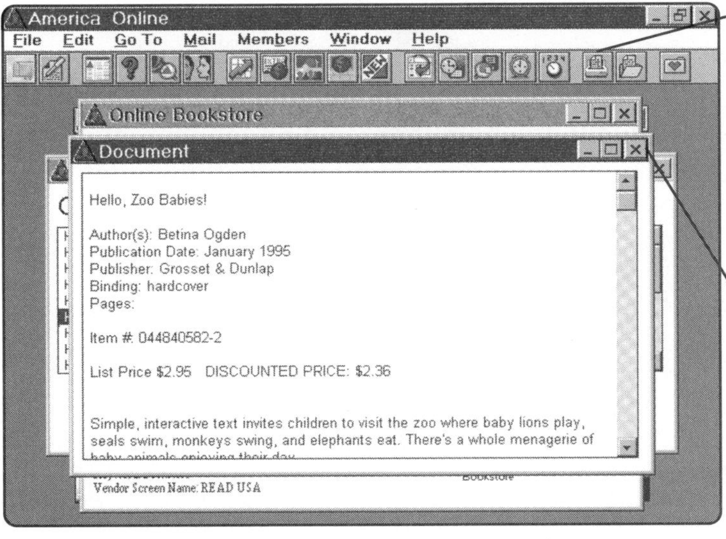

5. If you're interested in ordering the book, **click** on the **Print icon** in the toolbar to get a copy of the information on this screen. It will help you complete the order form later.

6. Click on the **Close box** (☒) in the right corner of the title bar. The Children's Section dialog box will reappear.

7. Click on the **Close box** (☒) in the right corner of the Children's Section title bar to close the dialog box. The Online Bookstore dialog box will reappear.

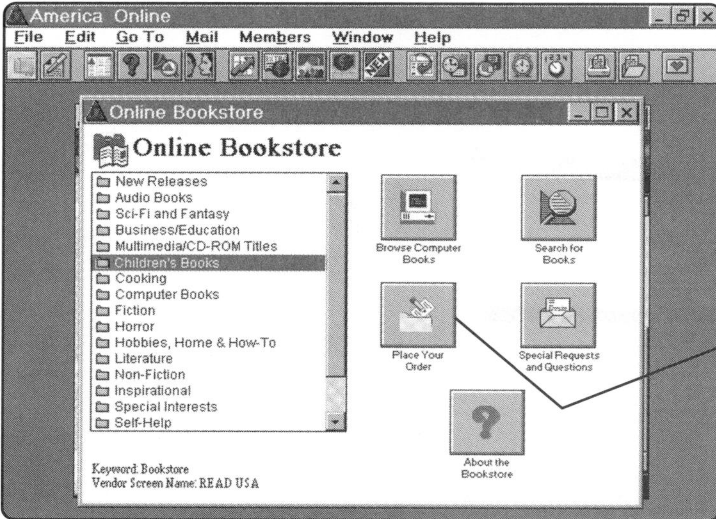

Placing an Order

To get current shipping, pricing, and payment information, take a moment to click on the "About the Bookstore" icon, then print the information.

1. **Click** on the **Place Your Order button**. An order form will appear.

2. **Click** on the **Maximize button** (❐, or ▲ in Windows 3.1) on the title bar to maximize the order form.

3. **Type** your **name,** then **press** the **Tab key**. The cursor will move to the next section.

America Online - [READ USA]
File Edit Go To Mail Members Window Help

Ordering Info:

Full Name: Ms. Barbara Books Phone: 213-555-1234
Street Address: 97 Library Lane
City/State/Zip: My Town, MI 12345

	Item	Product Number	QTY	Price
Product #1:	Book Title	ISBN	1	2.80
Product #2:				
Product #3:				

Method of Payment: mc (MC, VISA, AMEX) Exp.Date: 9/99
Credit Card Number: XXXX-XXXXXX-XXXX
Cancel Send Order

4. **Type** your **address, phone number,** and information regarding the **item, product number** (the ISBN)**, quantity**, and **price**. Refer to your printed copy of the book description if needed.

5. **Complete** the application with **payment method** and **credit card information**.

6. **Click** on the **Send Order button**. A message box (not shown here) will appear saying that your mail has been sent.

7. **Click** on **OK**. The message box will close.

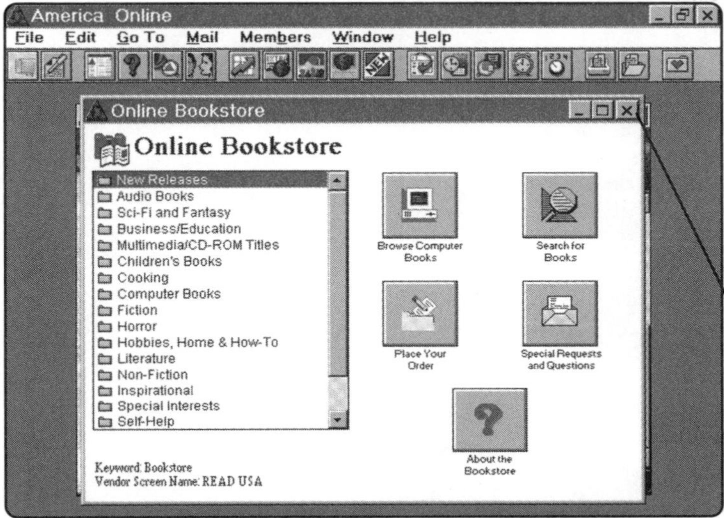

You can check your mailbox in a few days for a confirmation of the order and shipping costs.

Closing the Shopping Service

1. **Click** on the **Close box** ([X]) in the right corner of the Online Bookstore title bar to close this window. The Marketplace window will appear.

ADDING THE MARKETPLACE TO YOUR FAVORITE PLACES LIST

AOL allows you to list all your favorite places in an index for instant access. In this example, you'll add the Marketplace to the Favorite Places list.

1. **Click** on the **Favorite Places icon** (heart) on the Marketplace title bar. A dialog box will appear.

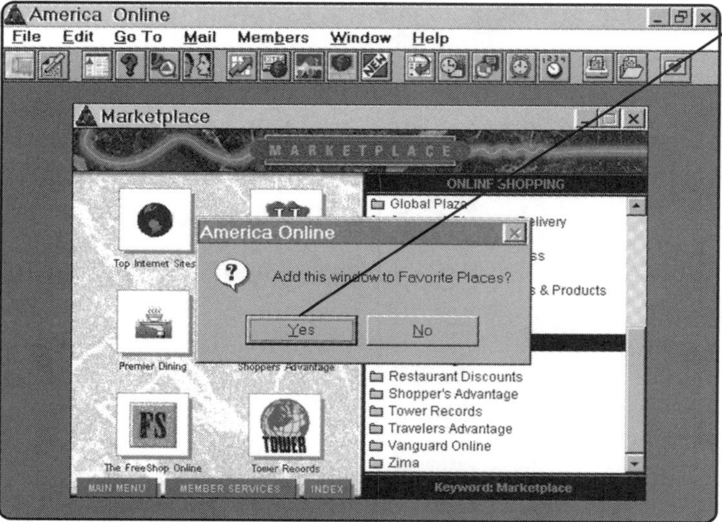

2. **Click** on **Yes.** The dialog box will close, and you'll hear a "beep" that tells you the service has been added to the list.

MANAGING YOUR FAVORITE PLACES LIST

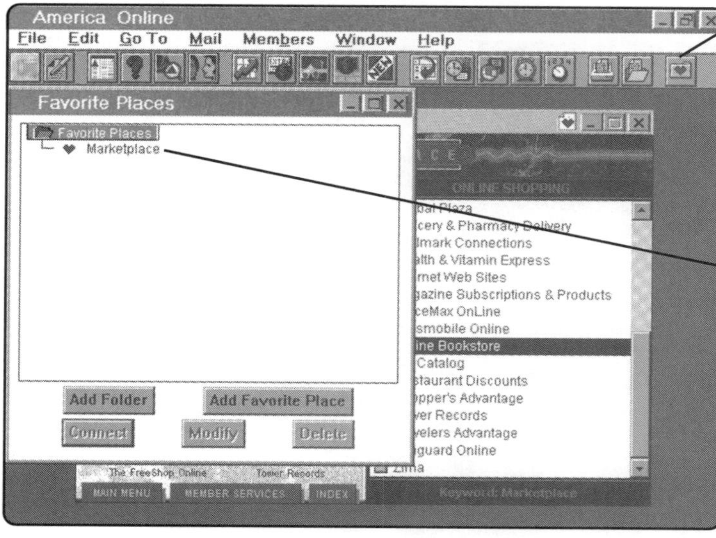

1. **Click** on the **Favorite Places icon** on the toolbar. It's the "heart folder" at the far right on the toolbar. A window will appear, as you see in this example.

Notice that Marketplace is now on the list.

In this example, you'll create a folder in which to organize your favorite places.

2. **Click** on **Favorite Places** to highlight it, if necessary.

3. **Click** on **Add Folder**. A dialog box will appear.

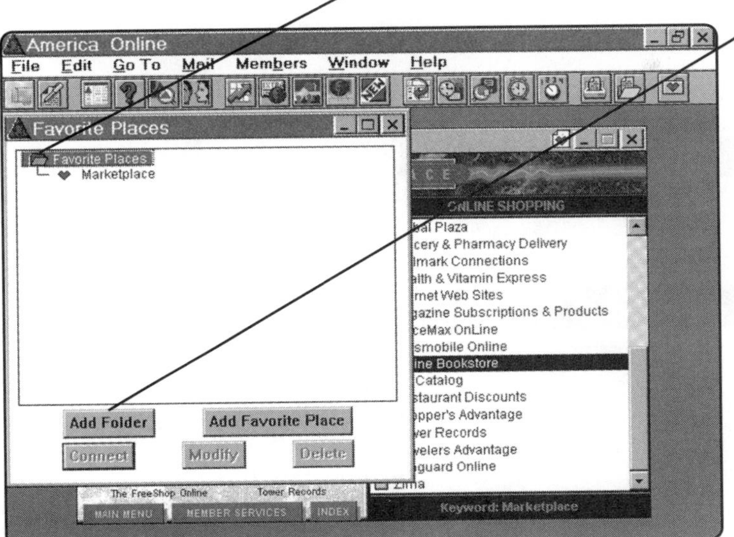

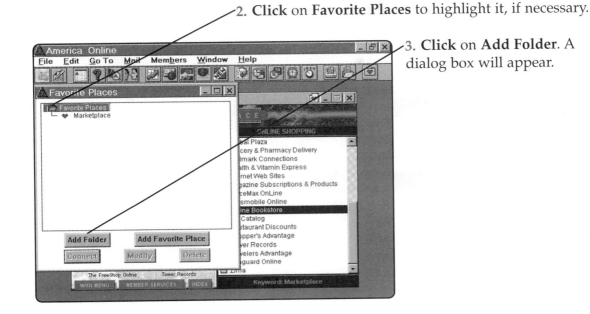

4. **Type** the **name** for your new **folder**. In this example, it's Linda.

5. **Click** on **OK**. The dialog box will close and the new folder will appear in the list.

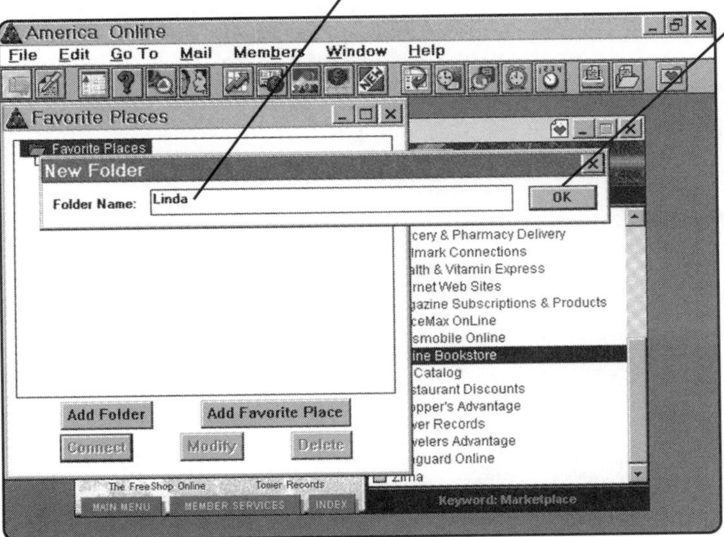

"Filing" Your Favorite Place

The Favorite Places window allows you to organize your choices with the "drag-and-drop" feature.

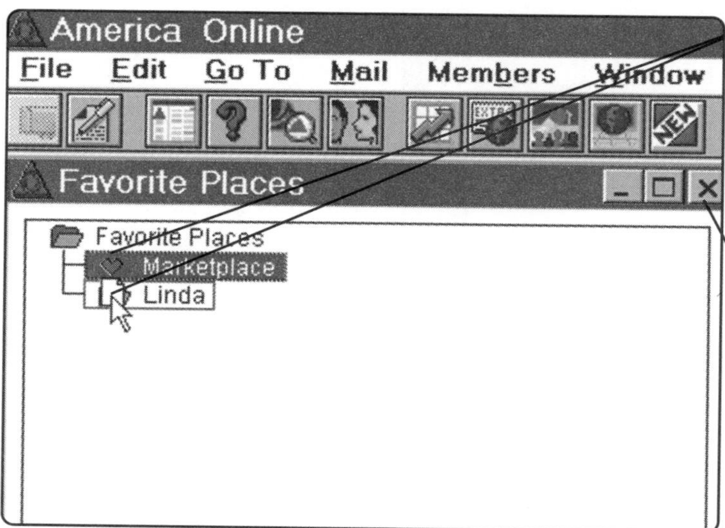

1. **Press and hold** on **Marketplace** as you **drag** the icon onto the new folder **icon**, then **release** the **mouse button**. Marketplace is now placed within the folder.

2. **Click** on the **Close box** (☒) to **close** the **Favorite Places** window.

3. **Click** on the **Close box** (☒) on the Marketplace title bar to **close** the **Marketplace**.

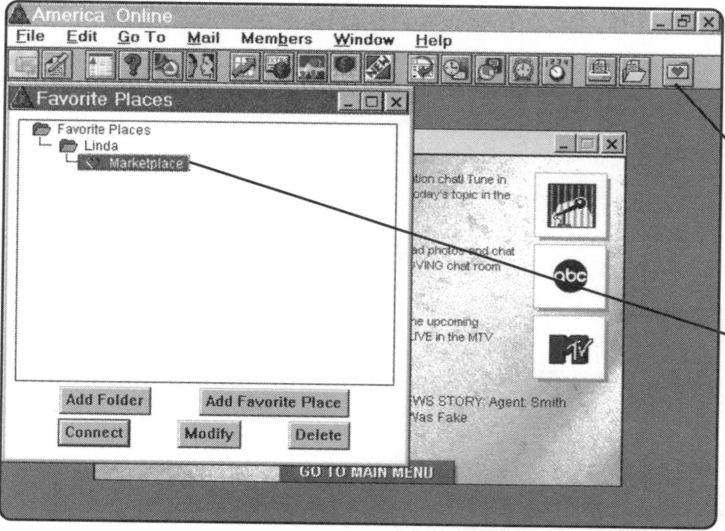

USING FAVORITE PLACES

1. **Click** on the **Favorite Places icon**. The Favorite Places window will appear as you see in this example.

2. **Click twice** on the **service** you want to open. The service window will appear.

Now, get your suitcase packed! In the next chapter, you'll use AOL's Travel section to check bargain fares to Hawaii.

Finding Bargain Airfares

Now you can become your own travel agent and make hotel reservations, reserve rental cars, and even book your own airline flights. If you don't want to give up the services of your travel agent, you can use America Online to shop airline prices and check flight schedules. All of these services are available to you on EAASY SABRE, an American Airlines program. You can shop for prices through EAASY SABRE without joining, but you must be a member to actually make reservations. Joining is free, however, and only requires that you spend a little time filling out the application. In this chapter you will do the following:

✔ Shop for bargain airfares

GETTING TRAVEL INFORMATION

In this chapter, you'll go through the process of finding bargain airfares.

1. **Sign on** to **AOL** if you haven't already done so.

2. **Click** on the **Main Menu icon** on the title bar to open the Main Menu as you see in this example.

3. **Click** on the **Travel & Shopping icon**. The Travel & Shopping dialog box will appear.

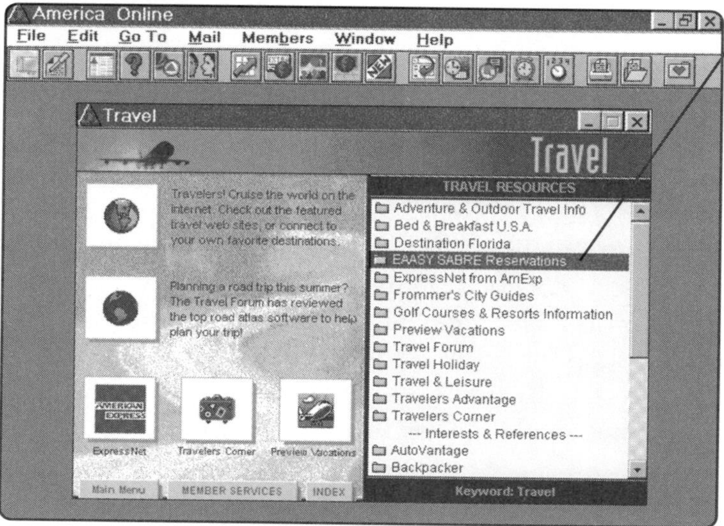

4. **Click twice** on **EAAsy Sabre**. The EAAsy Sabre dialog box will appear.

USING EAASY SABRE

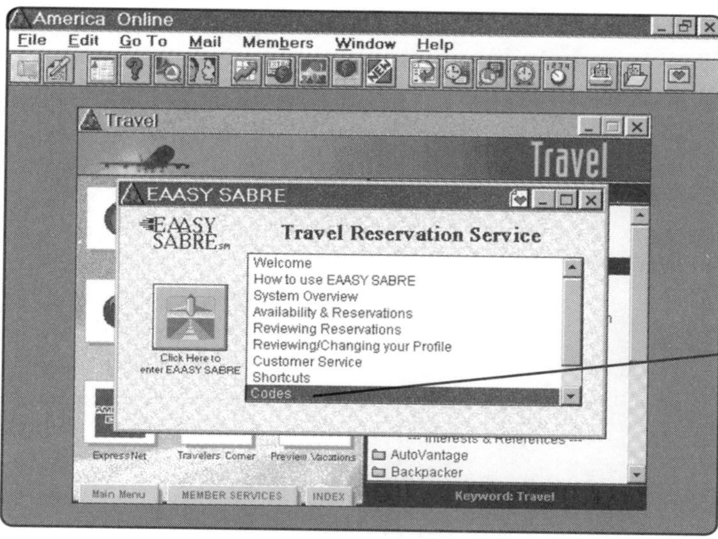

Unless you are familiar with airline, hotel, and rental car codes (and there are a lot of codes), we suggest you take a few minutes to print them so that you'll more easily understand what you see on your screen.

1. **Click twice** on **Codes**. The Codes dialog box will appear with a list of topics relating to EAASY SABRE.

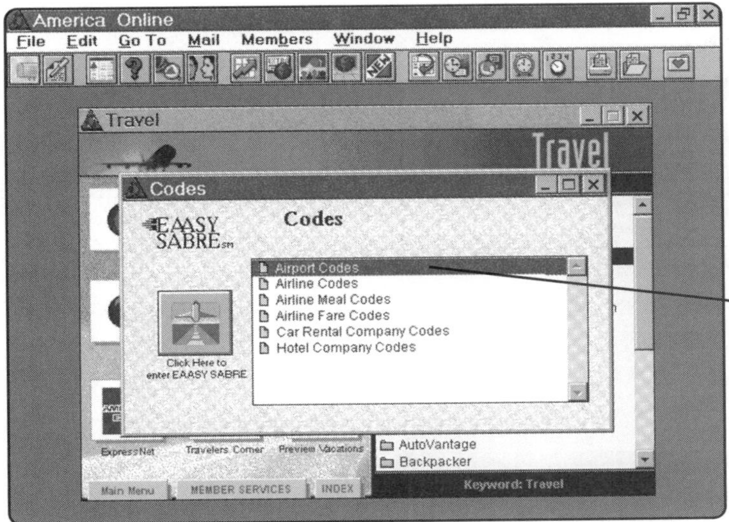

Printing Codes

A document icon (🗋) beside a topic means that clicking twice on the item will bring a document on to your screen.

1. **Click twice** on **Airport Codes**. The Airport Codes dialog box will appear.

2. **Click** on the **Print icon** in the Flash Bar, then **click** on **OK** in the Print dialog box when it appears.

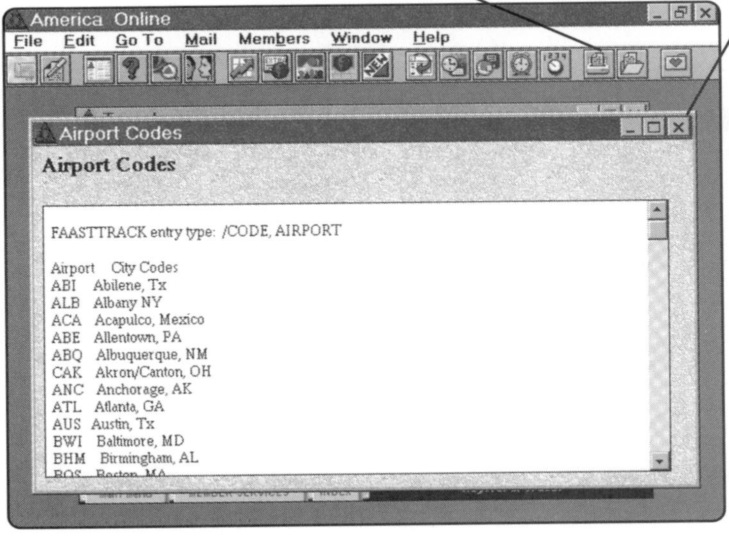

3. **Click** on the **Close box** ([X]) in the right corner of the title bar, or, if you're using Windows 3.1, click twice on the Control menu box in the left corner of the title bar, to close the Airport Codes dialog box. We will only give the Windows 95 step for closing dialog boxes in the rest of this chapter.

4. **Repeat steps 1-3** to print any other codes you might need.

5. **Click** on the **Close box** ([X]) of the Codes window to close it.

Entering EAASY SABRE

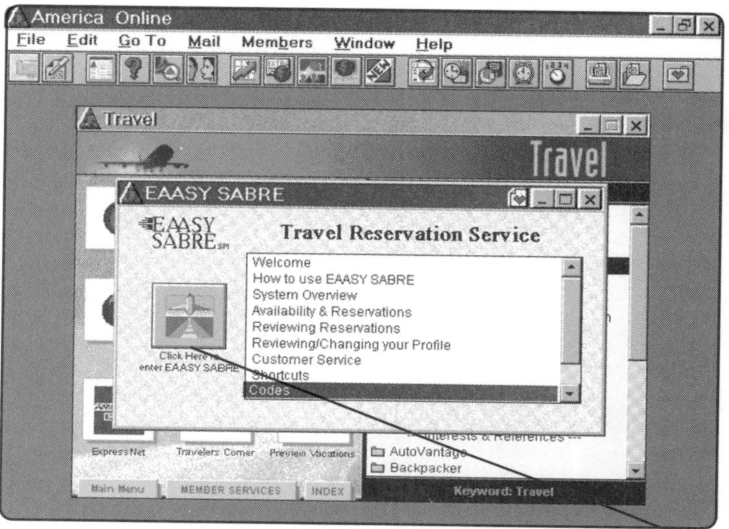

Although EAASY SABRE is an American Airlines program, you can use it to get flight information for any airline. It's an older program, and doesn't work like a Windows-based program. It presents you with numbered choices in menus. You have to type the number corresponding to your choice, sort of like the multiple choice tests you took in school.

1. **Click** on the **Enter EAASY SABRE icon**. The Gateway Host window will appear.

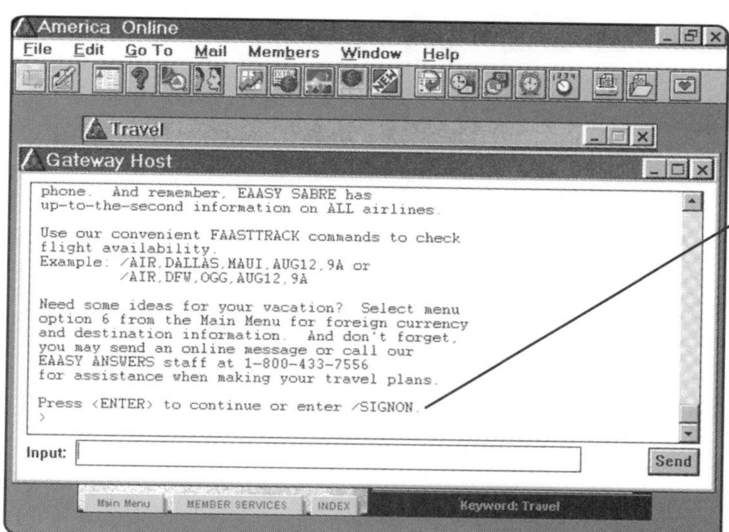

The wording of the information on your screen may be different from what you see in this example.

You receive information screen by screen in EAASY SABRE. You'll be given numbered choices (or specific directions) with each screen.

2. **Press Enter** on your keyboard to continue. The EAASY SABRE Main Menu will appear.

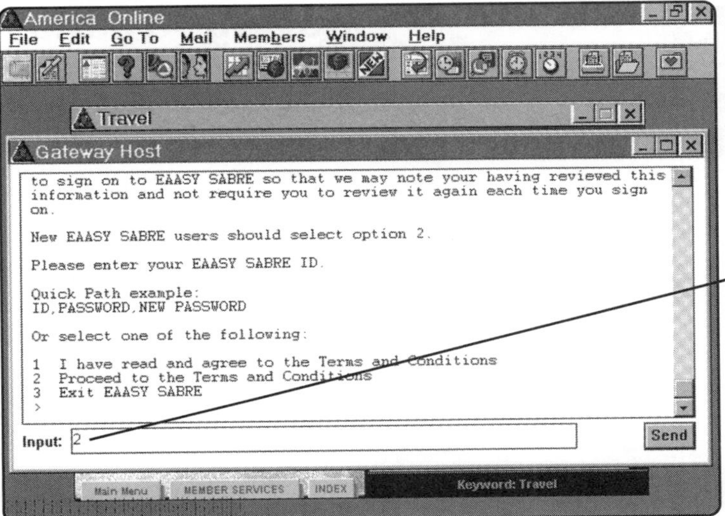

Reviewing Terms and Conditions

EAASY SABRE requires that you review the terms and conditions of use.

1. **Type 2** and **press Enter** to bring up the first screen in the "Terms and Conditions" series.

You'll have to press Enter through five more screens to go through all the terms and conditions.

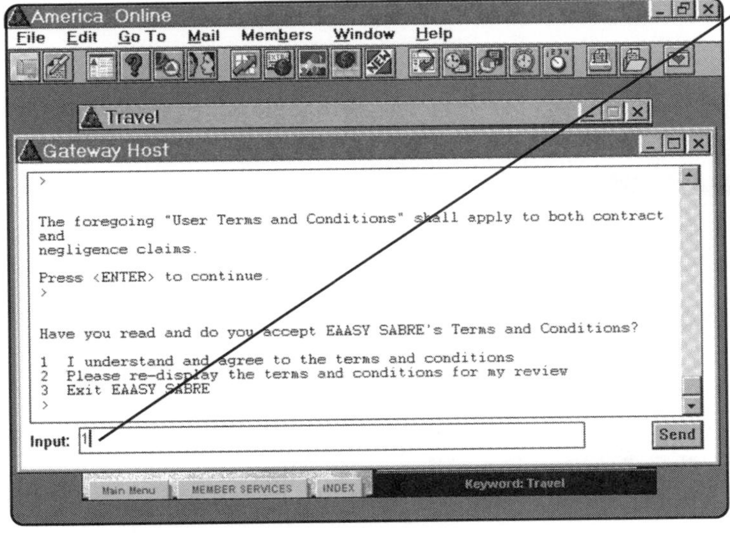

The last screen will give you the same numbered choices. **Type 1**, then **press Enter**. When you're through, you'll see the EAASY SABRE MAIN MENU you see in the next example.

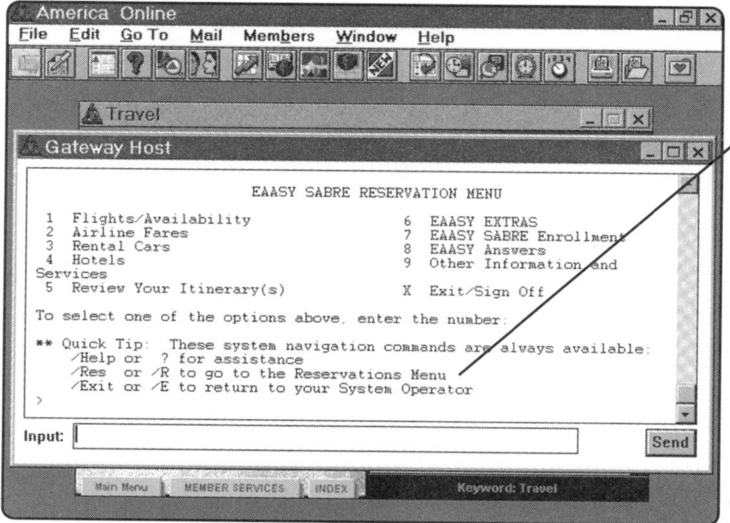

Moving Around in EAASY SABRE

It's easy to get lost in this program, so make note of the system navigation commands to move around in EAASY SABRE. Especially helpful are:

/R to come back to this Reservation menu

/E to return to the EAASY SABRE menu.

GETTING TRAVEL INFORMATION

In this section, you'll look for the least expensive airfare between Boston and Honolulu. Because EAASY SABRE is what is called a *text-based* program, you can't use your mouse to select a choice. You have to type your response. (How quaint!)

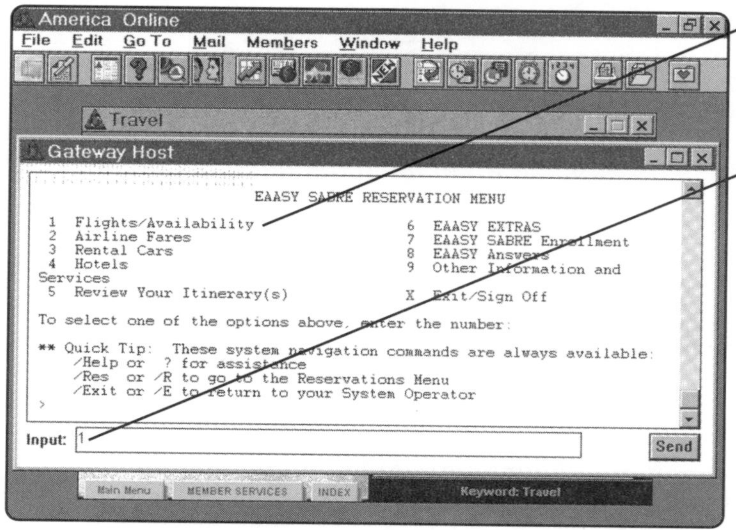

Notice the numbered choices at the top of the screen.

1. The cursor is already flashing in the Input box at the bottom of your screen, so **type 1** to indicate that you want to go to Flights/Availability.

2. Press Enter.

Using Quick Path

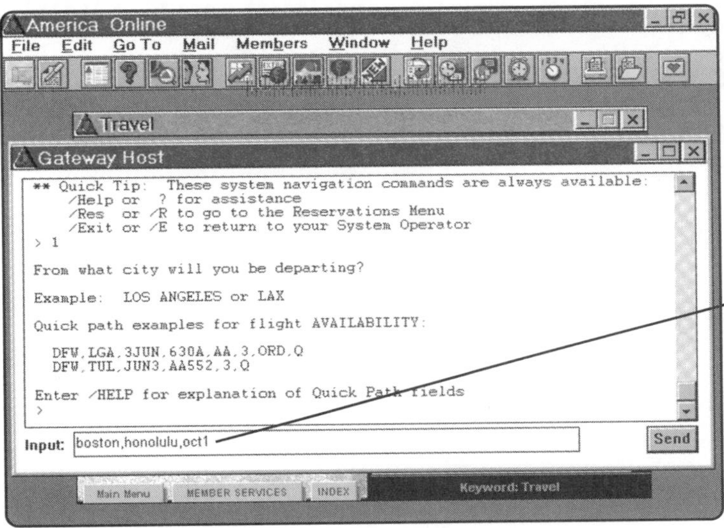

Answering questions screen by screen can become very tedious. EAASY SABRE lets you string information together in a *Quick Path* to answer several questions at once.

1. **Type** the following to indicate the departure city, the destination city, and the departure date in a single entry: **boston,honolulu,oct1**.
2. **Press Enter**.

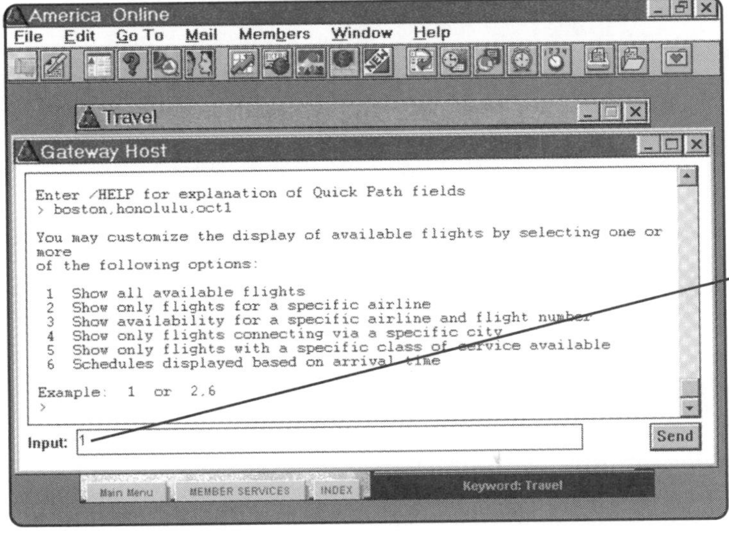

Showing All Available Flights

You can choose to see all available flights or specific flights.

1. **Type 1** to show all available flights from Boston to Honolulu.
2. **Press Enter**.

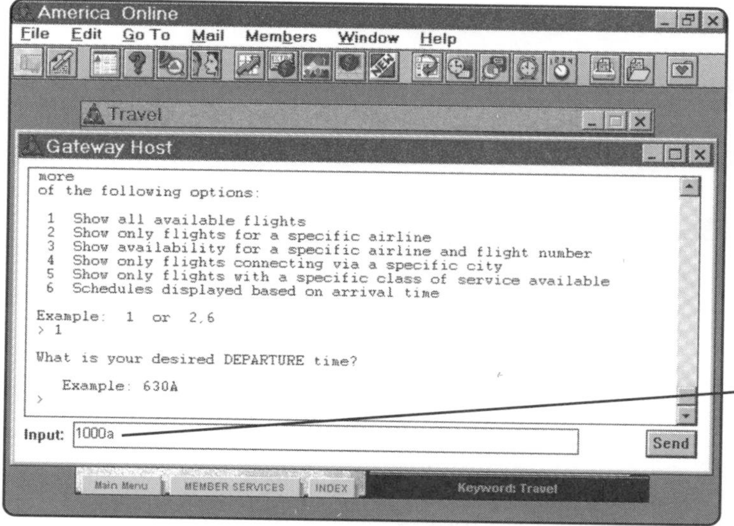

America Online
File Edit Go To Mail Members Window Help
Travel
Gateway Host
more
of the following options:
1 Show all available flights
2 Show only flights for a specific airline
3 Show availability for a specific airline and flight number
4 Show only flights connecting via a specific city
5 Show only flights with a specific class of service available
6 Schedules displayed based on arrival time
Example: 1 or 2,6
> 1
What is your desired DEPARTURE time?
Example: 630A
>
Input: 1000a
Send
Main Menu
MEMBER SERVICES
INDEX
Keyword: Travel

Indicating Departure Time

You don't have to be absolutely certain about your departure time. EAASY SABRE will give you flights within two hours of the time you indicate.

1. **Type** the **estimated departure time**. In this example it is 1000a (for 10:00 a.m.).

2. **Press Enter**.

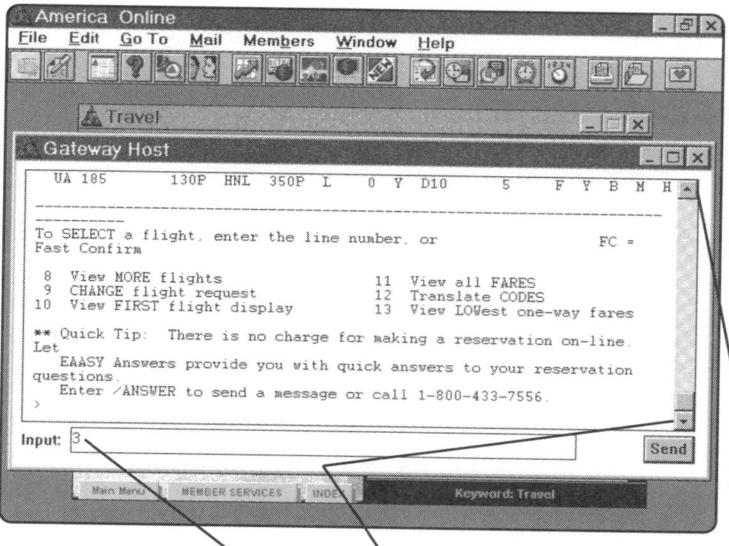

America Online
File Edit Go To Mail Members Window Help
Travel
Gateway Host
UA 185 130P HNL 350P L 0 Y D10 5 F Y B M H
To SELECT a flight, enter the line number, or FC =
Fast Confirm
8 View MORE flights
9 CHANGE flight request
10 View FIRST flight display
11 View all FARES
12 Translate CODES
13 View LOWest one-way fares
** Quick Tip: There is no charge for making a reservation on-line. Let
EAASY Answers provide you with quick answers to your reservation questions.
Enter /ANSWER to send a message or call 1-800-433-7556.
>
Input: 3
Send
Main Menu
MEMBER SERVICES
Keyword: Travel

Scrolling to See Information

This screen asks you to select a flight. However, the window scrolled past the flight information. You can scroll back to see any information that has been on your screen.

1. **Click repeatedly** on the ▲ to scroll back up to the flight information to get the line number of your flight.

2. **Click repeatedly** on the ▼ to scroll down to the bottom of the information.

3. **Type** the **line number** of the flight in which you are interested, then **press Enter**. In this example, the flight was in line #3.

Notice that you can show more flights by typing 8.

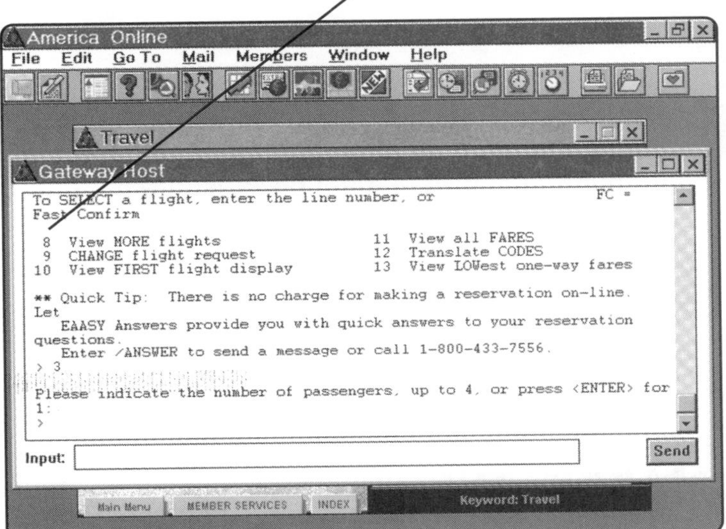

Now that you're familiar with the way this service works, we'll let you fly solo through the rest of the flight information screens. You'll enter the number of passengers and the return date and flight, and then view fares.

Once you have viewed the fare information, **type /R** to go to the screen you see below.

APPLYING FOR EAASY SABRE MEMBERSHIP

If you want to join, you can do so now. You'll get an American AAdvantage number as part of the process. If you already have one, have it handy.

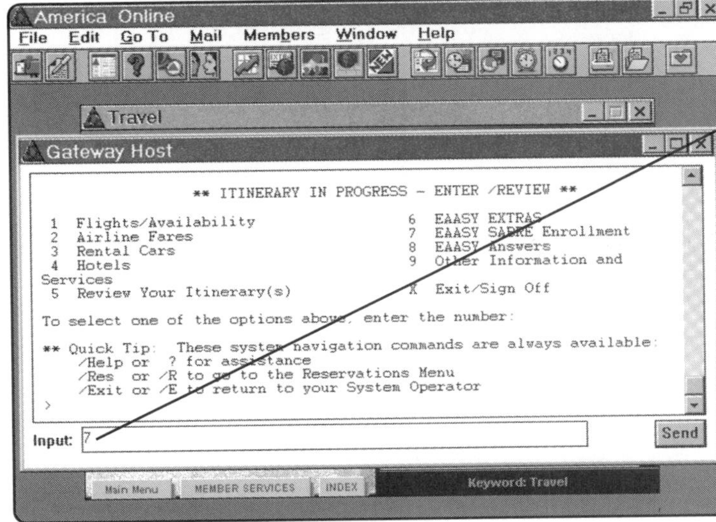

America Online
File Edit Go To Mail Members Window Help
Travel
Gateway Host
** ITINERARY IN PROGRESS - ENTER /REVIEW **
1 Flights/Availability
2 Airline Fares
3 Rental Cars
4 Hotels
Services
5 Review Your Itinerary(s)
6 EAASY EXTRAS
7 EAASY SABRE Enrollment
8 EAASY Answers
9 Other Information and
X Exit/Sign Off
To select one of the options above, enter the number:
** Quick Tip: These system navigation commands are always available:
/Help or ? for assistance
/Res or /R to go to the Reservations Menu
/Exit or /E to return to your System Operator
>
Input: 7
Send
Main Menu
MEMBER SERVICES
INDEX
Keyword: Travel

1. Type 7 and **press Enter** to go to the EAASY SABRE membership application.

The process of filling out the application and then completing a reservation is similar to what you've done in this chapter. If you need help, call American Airlines at 1-800-331-2690. Bon voyage!

CHAPTER

12

Meeting People

You've probably heard about couples who meet online and end up dating and eventually marrying. Even if you've already found the love of your life and aren't interested in a romance connection, America Online is a great place to meet interesting people. In this chapter you will do the following:

✔ Look for interesting discussions
✔ Join a discussion
✔ Set chat preferences
✔ Create a private chat room

MAKING THE PEOPLE CONNECTION

When you first enter the People Connection, you enter what is called the *Lobby*. From the Lobby, you can go to a room on almost any topic you can think of.

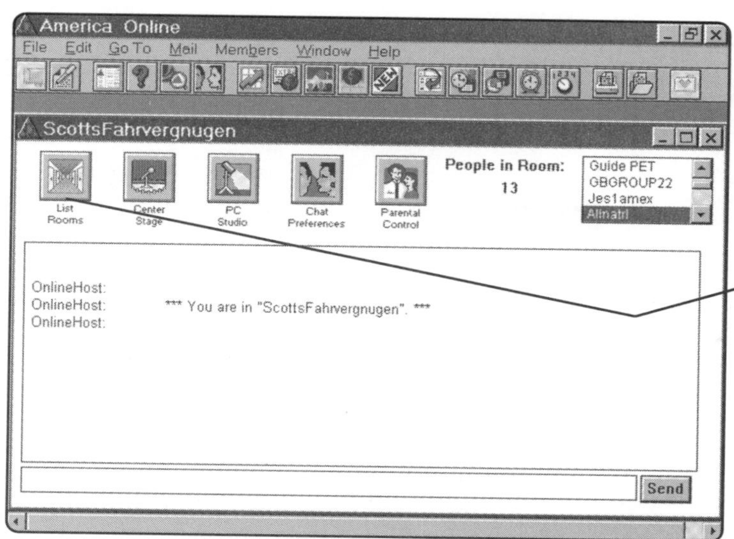

1. **Click** on the **People Connection icon** in the toolbar. It's the sixth icon from the left. A dialog box like the one you see here will appear.

2. **Click** on **List Rooms**. The Active Public Rooms dialog box will appear.

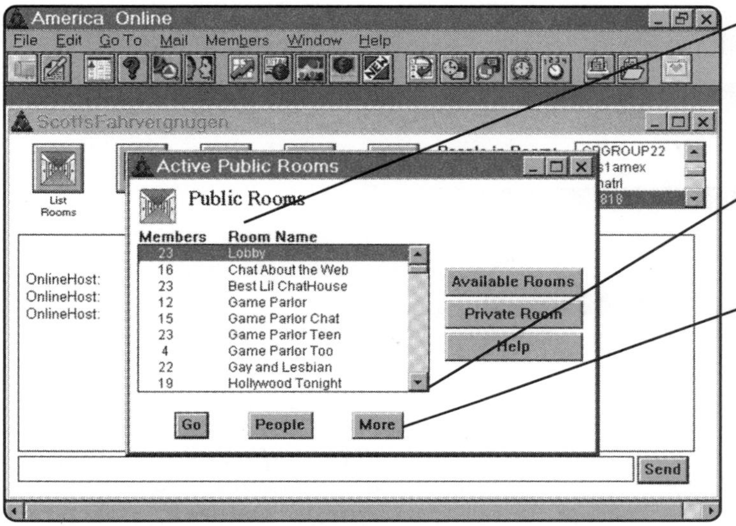

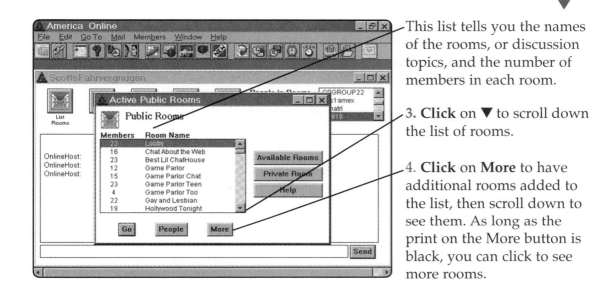

This list tells you the names of the rooms, or discussion topics, and the number of members in each room.

3. **Click** on ▼ to scroll down the list of rooms.

4. **Click** on **More** to have additional rooms added to the list, then scroll down to see them. As long as the print on the More button is black, you can click to see more rooms.

ENTERING A CHAT ROOM

Once you decide on a room that you'd like to join, just go in.

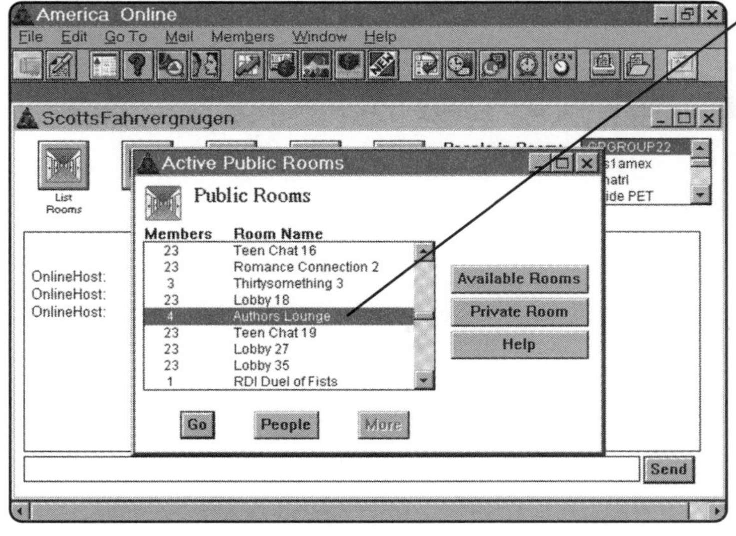

1. **Click twice** on the **room** of your choice. A dialog box will open on your screen as you see in the next example. (You can also click once on the room, then click on Go.)

There's a limit of 23 people allowed in a typical chat room. If the room you selected has too many people in it, you will be asked if you want to join a room like it. Click on Yes to go to a similar room.

It may take a moment for the new room to register. When it does, you'll see a message from the Online Host saying you are in the selected room. (Gossip on AOL has it that Online Host is a distant relative of R2D2.)

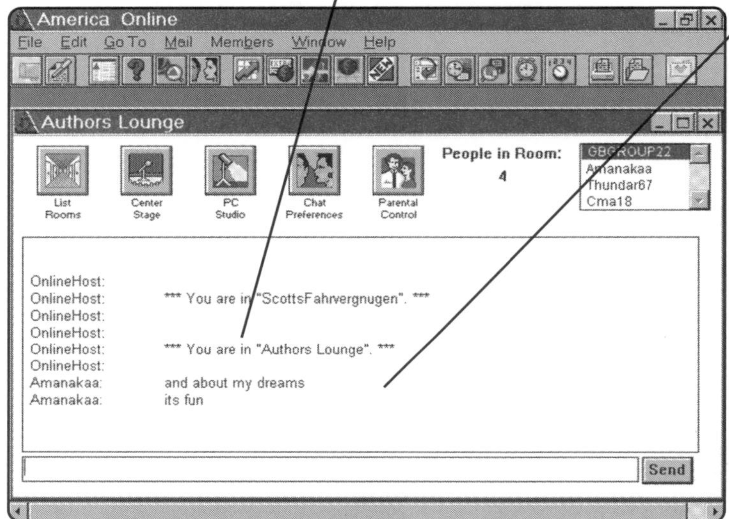

Pretty soon you'll start to see conversations on your screen between the people already in the room.

JOINING THE CONVERSATION

You need reasonable typing skills and the ability to say what you want in one line or less if you want to participate effectively in chat rooms.

1. The cursor will already be flashing in the message box, so **type** your **message**. Remember, you have only one line.

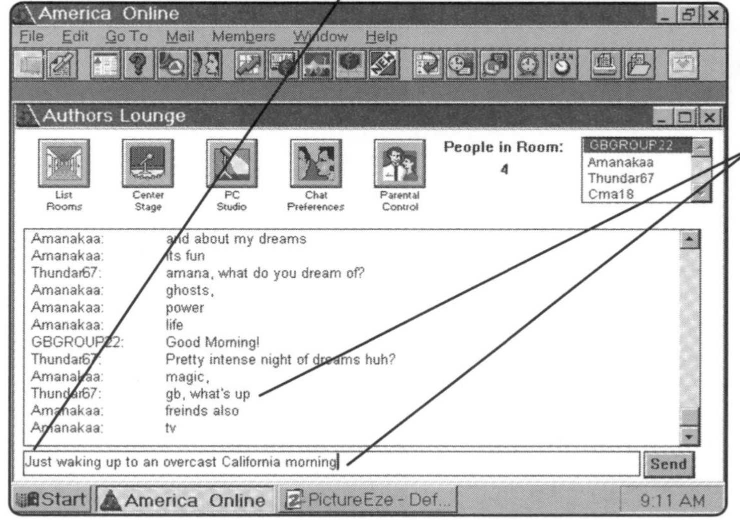

2. Press Enter on your keyboard (or click on Send).

This screen shows a question to me and a statement from me waiting to be sent.

Many conversations can be going on at once, so your message may not appear directly after the comment to which you wanted to reply.

Checking People Out

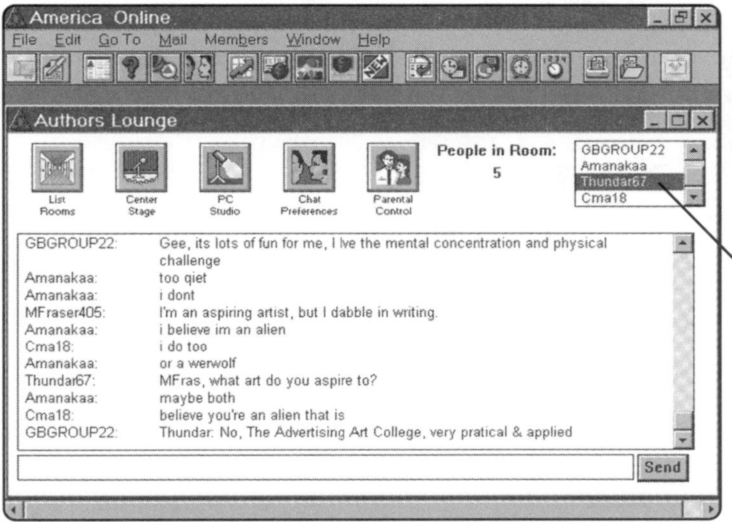

If you want to know something about the people in a room, you can look at each person's profile (if he or she completed an AOL member profile).

1. **Click twice** on the person's **screen name** in the list in the upper right corner of the window. An Information About window will appear.

Notice that the person's screen name appears in the title bar.

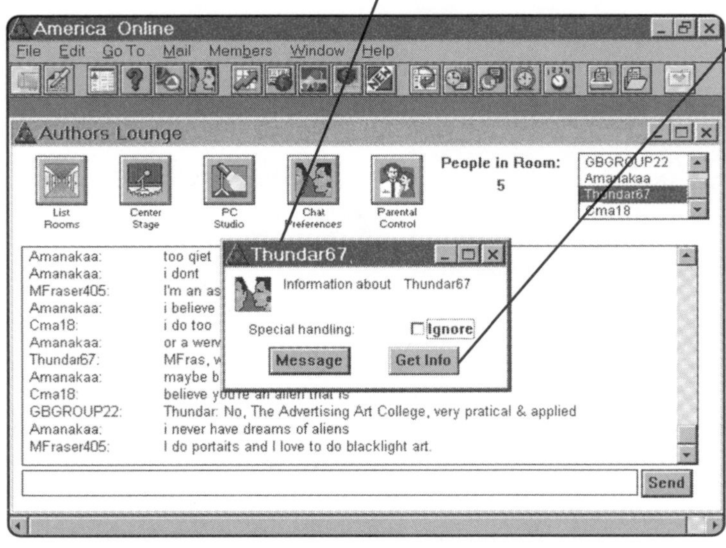

2. **Click** on **Get Info**. If the person has filled out a profile, the information will appear on your screen. (An example is not shown here.)

Chatting Directly with a Member

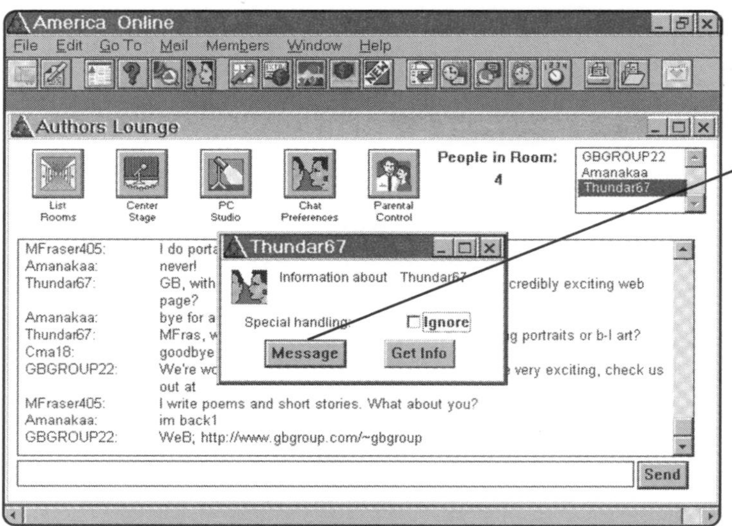

You can send an Instant Message to any member of a chat room.

1. **Click** on **Message.** The Instant Message dialog box will appear. (See Chapter 5, "Sending and Receiving Instant Messages," if you need help).

Ignoring the Ignorant

Unfortunately, not all members are charming chat companions. If someone is being obnoxious and/or offensive, you can stop their messages from appearing on your screen. (Please note: Thundar67 was *not* being obnoxious, but kindly assented to allow us to use her/his screen name).

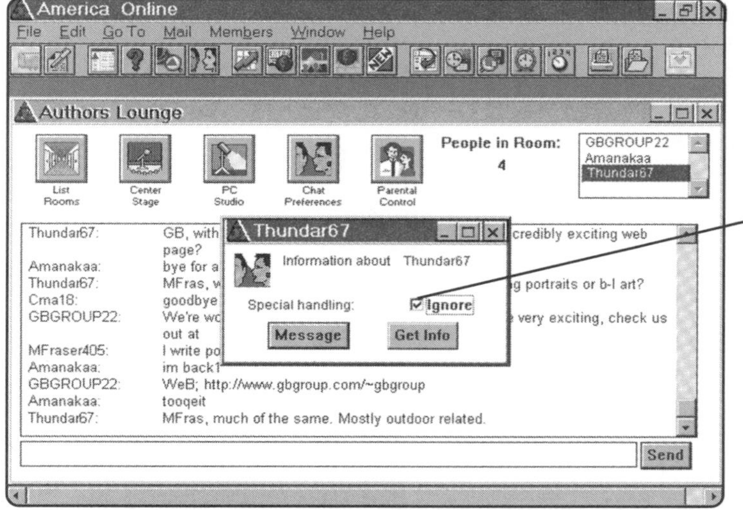

1. **Click** on **Ignore** to place a ✔ in the box. That person's messages will no longer appear on your screen.

2. **Click** on the **Close box** (☒) to close this window and return to the chat room.

Leaving a Room

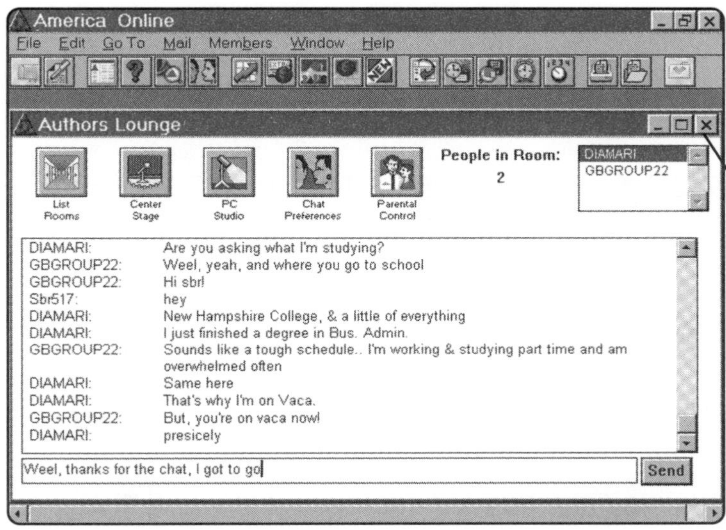

If you have actually been involved in the Conversation, it's polite to tell people you're leaving the room.

1. **Click** on the **Close box** (☒) to close the chat room. The Welcome window will reappear.

SETTING CHAT PREFERENCES

To control the environment in a chat room, go back to the Lobby.

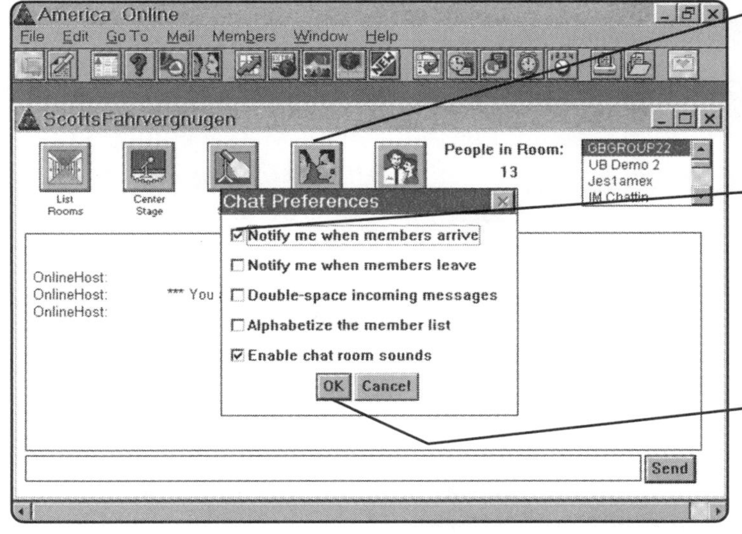

1. **Click** on **Chat Preferences**. The Chat Preferences dialog box you see here will appear.
2. **Click** on an **option** to put a ✔ in the box. This will enable, or activate, the option. (Click on a ✔ that's already there to *remove* it.)
3. **Click** on **OK**.

FINDING A MEMBER ROOM

Members can create a room with the topic of their choice. These differ from private rooms in that anyone is able to join in.

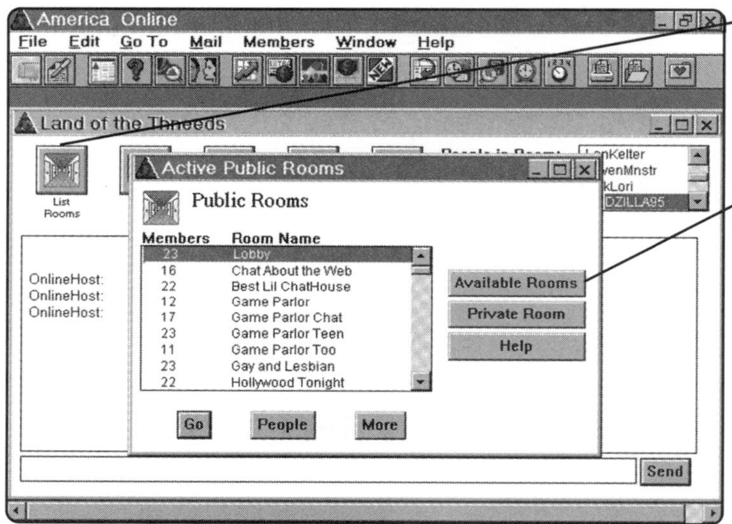

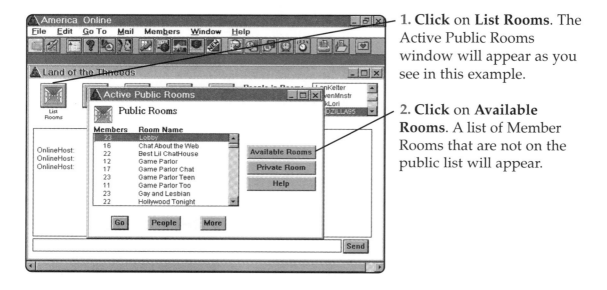

1. **Click** on **List Rooms**. The Active Public Rooms window will appear as you see in this example.

2. **Click** on **Available Rooms**. A list of Member Rooms that are not on the public list will appear.

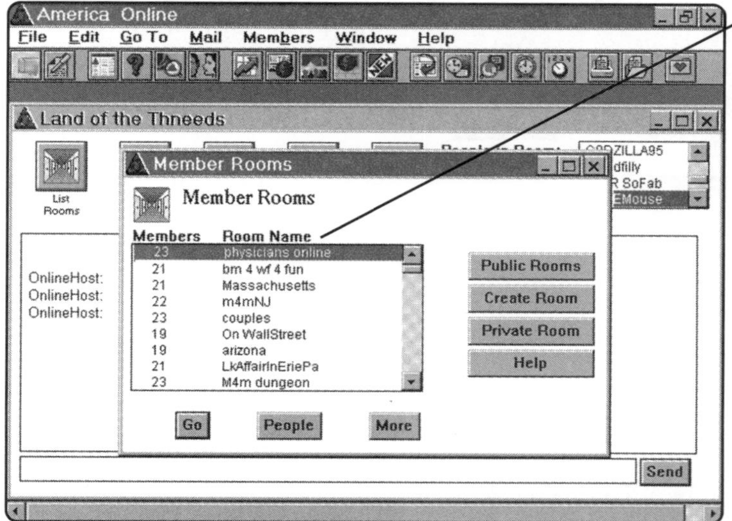

Member Rooms are terrific if you want to have a group conversation. Send an Instant Message inviting all parties concerned and telling them the name of the room. They can find the room listed in the Member Rooms list.

ENTERING OR CREATING A PRIVATE ROOM

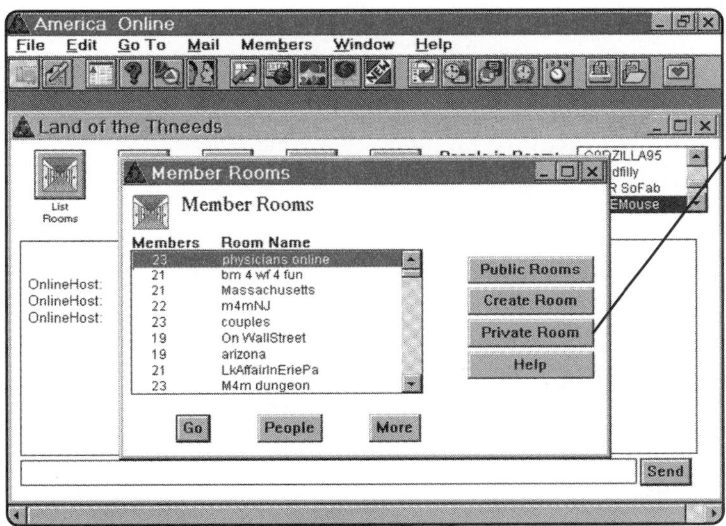

You can create a room for strictly private chats.

1. **Click** on **Private Room**. A dialog box will appear.

2. **Type** a **name** for the private room in the text box.

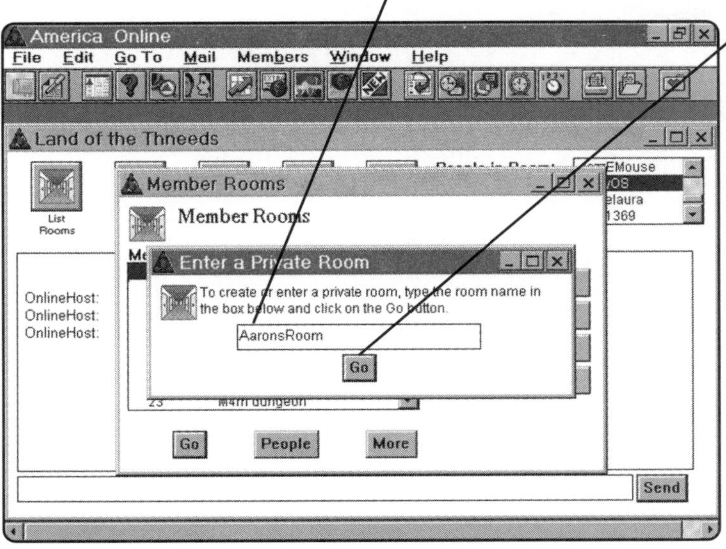

3. **Click** on **GO**. If the name is already in use, you'll enter that room. If this is a new name, you'll create a private room with that name. Private rooms are not listed on any of the room lists. You can invite people to join you with an Instant Message (or e-mail).

4. **Repeat steps 1-3** to **join** a **Private Room**.

One comment about chatting online—it can be very addictive. Have fun!

Using Forums

An AOL Forum combines online chatting, bulletin boards, database searches, information in documents, and files all in one place. Forums are set up around specific topics. These topics include Photography, Genealogy, Ethics and Religion, Trivia, and many more. In this chapter, you will do the following:

✔ Learn how to use Forums

FINDING A FORUM

The Main Menu will take you to the Clubs & Interests window where you'll find a list of forum topics.

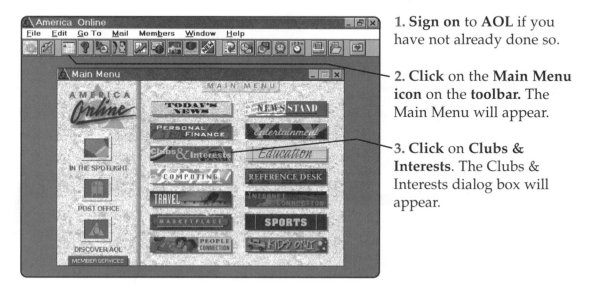

1. **Sign on** to **AOL** if you have not already done so.
2. **Click** on the **Main Menu icon** on the **toolbar.** The Main Menu will appear.
3. **Click** on **Clubs & Interests**. The Clubs & Interests dialog box will appear.

GOING TO THE BETTER HEALTH & MEDICAL FORUM

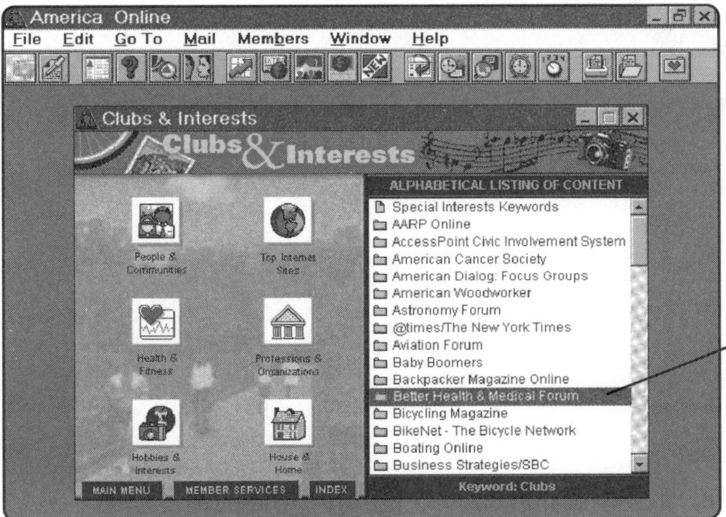

If the forum you want is featured on one of the icons in the Clubs & Interests dialog box, then simply click on the icon. If not, there is an alphabetical listing of forums in the right half of the dialog box.

1. **Click twice** on **Better Health & Medical Forum**. The Better Health & Medical Forum dialog box will appear.

GETTING INFORMATION

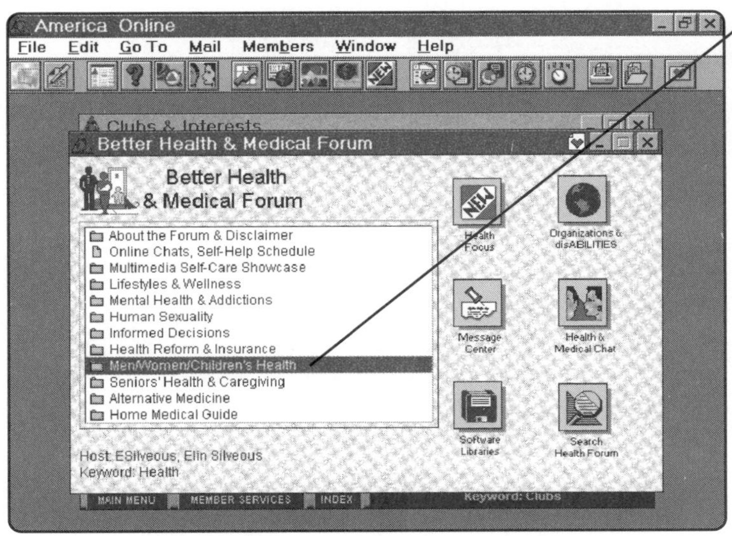

1. **Click twice** on a **topic** that interests you in the list on the left. In this example, it's Men\Women\Children's Health.

The folder icon (□) beside this item indicates that clicking on it will bring up another menu of items that are more specific aspects of the general topic.

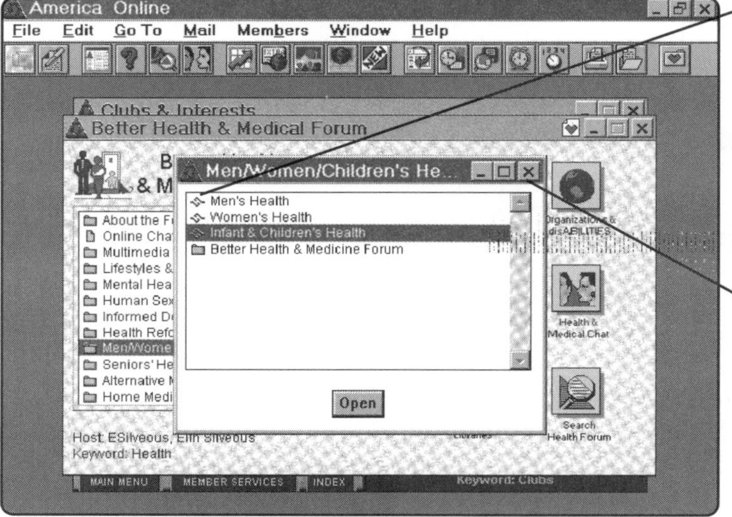

The Action item symbol (-◇-) beside some of these choices indicates that the choice will lead to another dialog box with additional choices. We'll let you explore these additional choices on your own.

2. **Click** on the **Close button** ([X]) in the right corner of the title bar, or, if using Windows 3.1, click twice on the Control menu box in the left corner of the title bar to close the dialog box.

USING THE MESSAGE CENTER

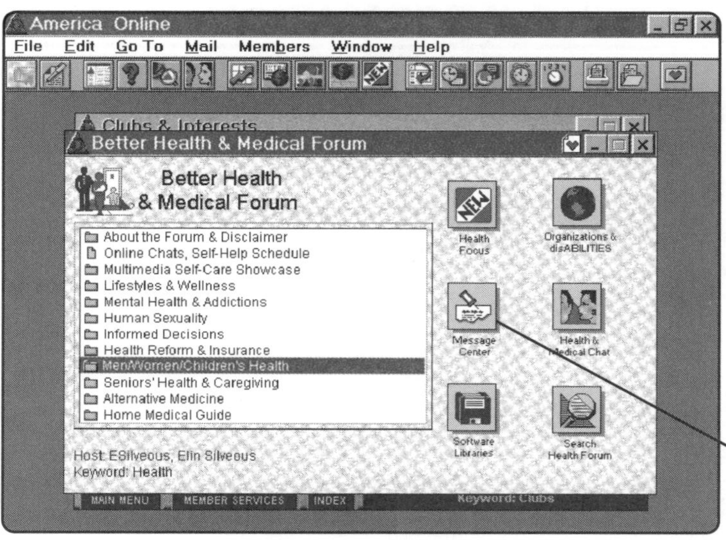

The message center in a forum is a *bulletin board*, or a place where you can ask questions and receive answers from other AOL members on specific topics.

It doesn't matter what topic is highlighted on the left. The Message Center applies to the whole Forum.

1. **Click** on the **Message Center icon**. In this example, the Health Message Center dialog box will appear.

Choosing a Category

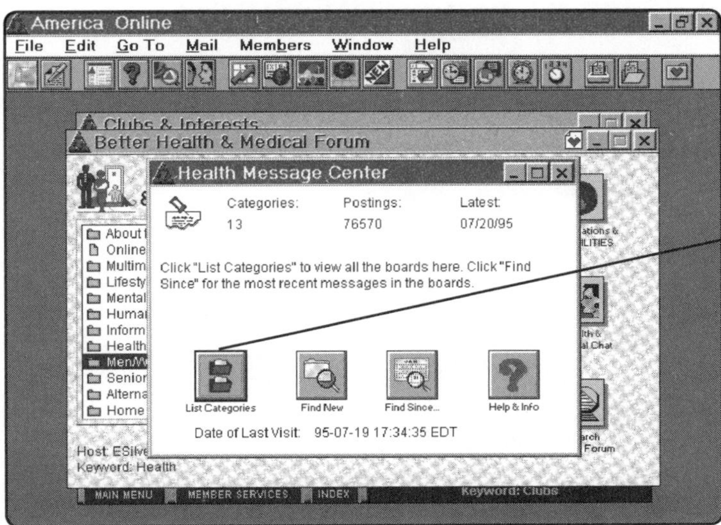

In this example, the Health Message Center has 13 different categories with over 76,000 messages, or *postings*.

1. **Click** on **List Categories**. A dialog box will appear with all categories listed.

Choosing a Topic

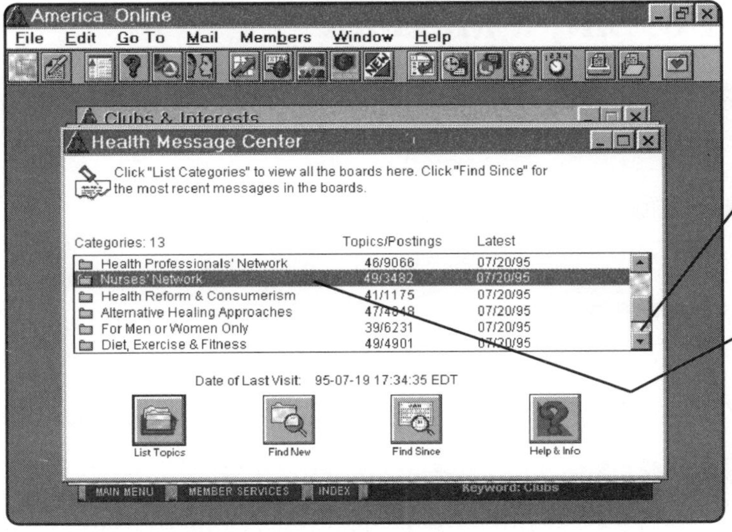

Once you select a broad category, you can choose from a variety of specific topics.

1. **Click** on the ▼ to scroll through the list of Categories.

2. **Click twice** on a **Category** that interests you. In this example it's "Nurses' Network." The Nurses' Network dialog box will appear.

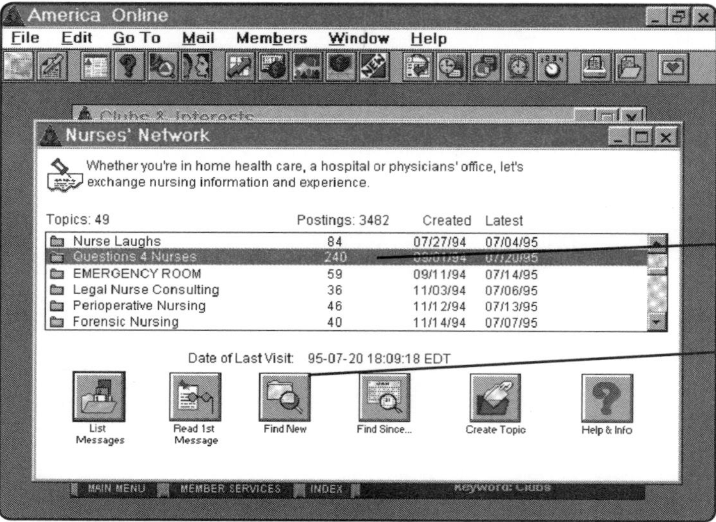

Reading Messages

1. **Click** on the ▼ to scroll through the list of topics.
2. **Click** on a **topic** that interests you.
3. **Click** on **Find New** to see all messages since you were here last. If this is your first visit, you'll see all the messages.

The messages will be listed as shown in the next screen. You can click twice on a message that you want to read to open it.

Posting a Message

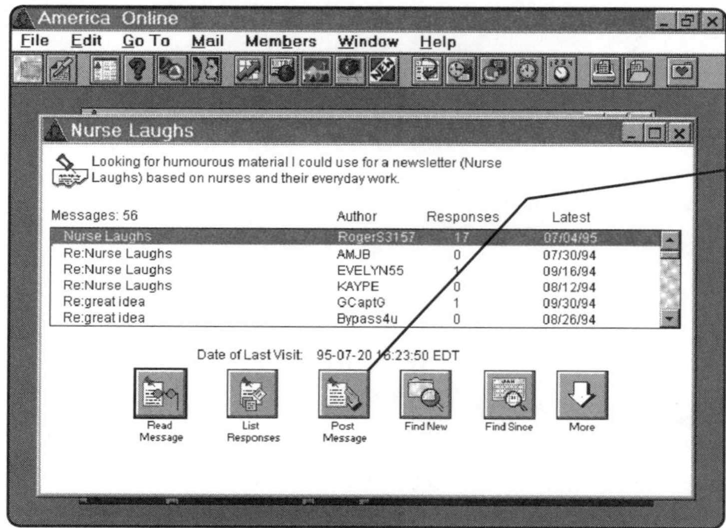

You can reply to a specific message or to a general topic.

1. **Click** on **Post Message**. The Add A Message dialog box will appear. If you click on this icon while you have a message open on your screen, the subject of the open message will automatically be entered in the Subject line of the dialog box.

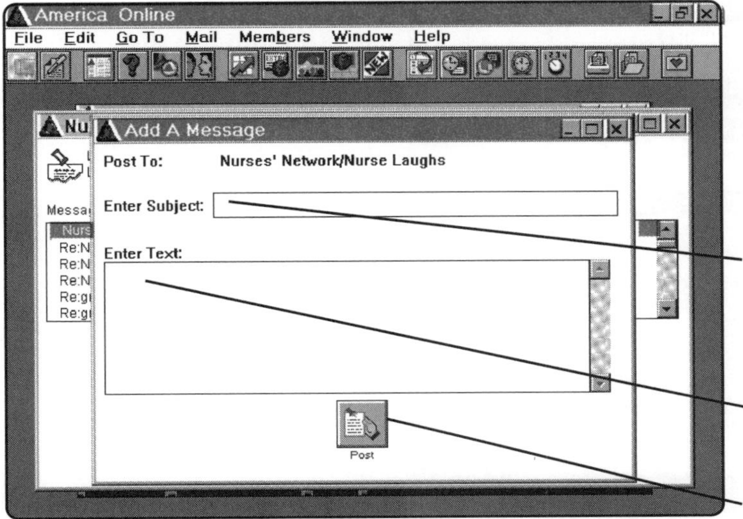

In this example, we clicked on Post Message without having a specific message open. Therefore, the Add a Message dialog box you see here will appear.

2. **Type** a **subject** in the Enter Subject box and **press** the **Tab** key.

3. **Type** your **message** in the Enter Text box.

4. **Click** on **Post** to send the message. A message box will appear stating, "Your message has been added to the folder." **Click** on **OK** to close the message box.

Finding Postings Since a Particular Date

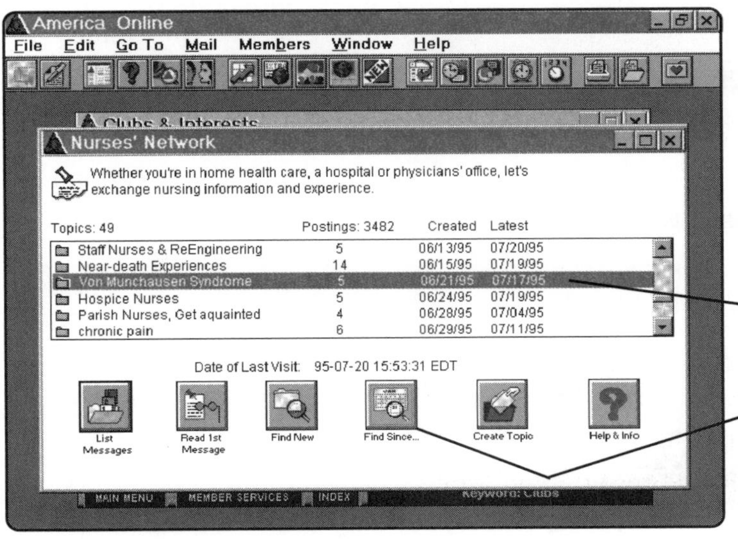

You can check postings as of a certain date.

1. **Close dialog boxes** as needed until you're back at the Nurses' Network dialog box.

2. **Click** on the **topic** you want to check.

3. **Click** on the **Find Since icon**. A dialog box will appear.

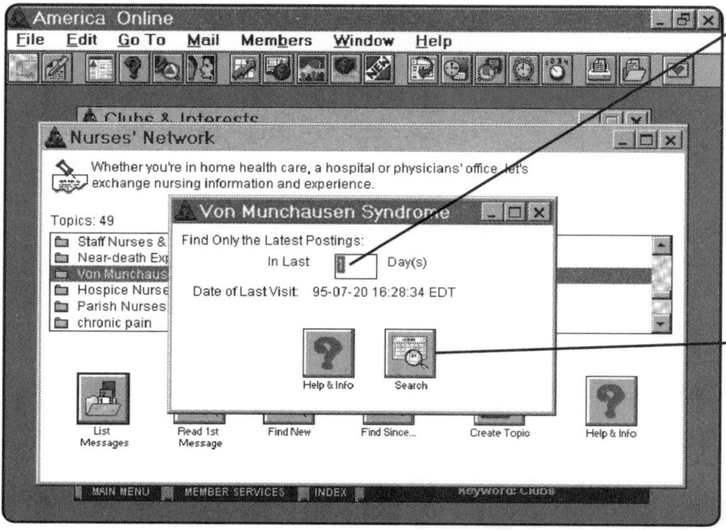

4. **Click twice** in the **Days box** to highlight the 1.

5. **Type** a **number** to indicate how many days' postings you want to display. It will replace the highlighted 1.

6. **Click** on **Search**. If there are any new postings in that period, they will appear on your screen.

7. After you've read the postings, **close** the **dialog box** and go back to the Nurses' Network dialog box.

CREATING A NEW TOPIC

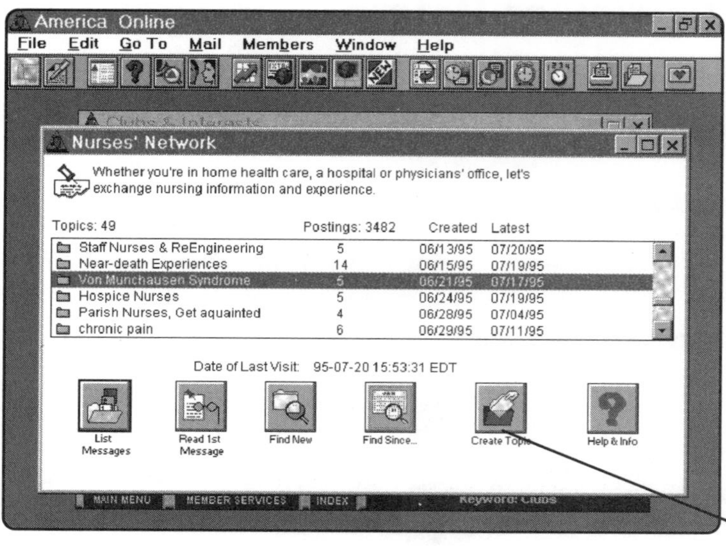

If you don't see a topic folder that matches your interests, you can create one and add a message to it.

Note: Many forums are so popular that they run out of room for new topics. If this happens to you, send a friendly e-mail note to the Forum host, letting him or her know so that the problem can be dealt with.

1. **Click** on **Create Topic**. A dialog box will appear.

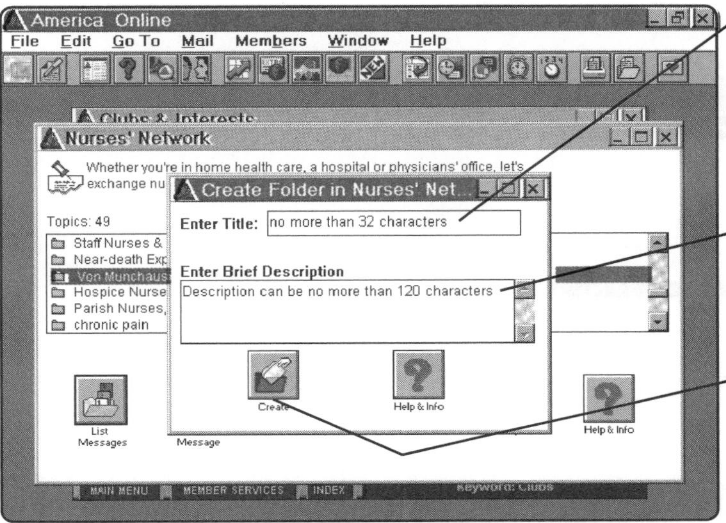

2. **Type** a **title** for the folder (it can have up to 32 characters) and **press** the **Tab key**. The cursor will move to the Description box.

3. **Type** a brief **description** (it can have up to 120 characters).

4. **Click** on **Create**. The new folder will be added to the list of topics.

An AOL message box (not shown here) will then ask if you want to "Add a Message" or "Cancel." Click on "Add a Message" and follow the steps in the "Posting a Message" section a few pages back.

SEARCHING FOR INFORMATION THROUGH A FORUM

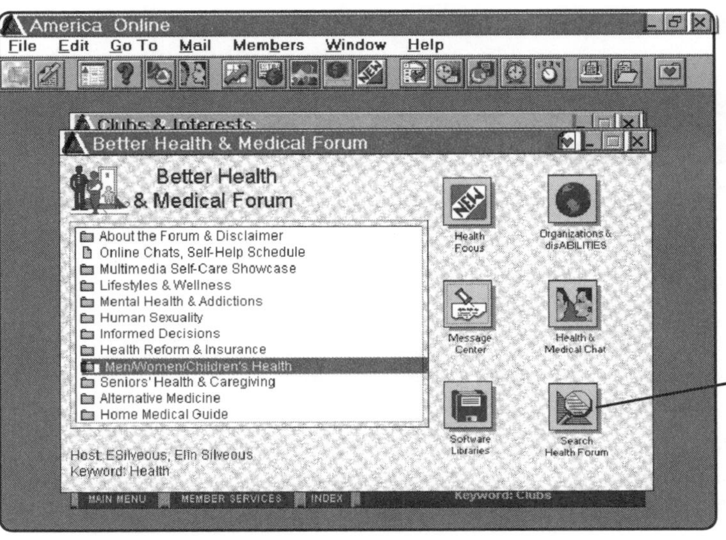

You can search through the Forum library for a specific topic. For our example we have returned to the Better Health & Medical Forum dialog box by closing the Nurses' Network and Health Message Center dialog boxes.

1. **Click** on the **Search Health Forum icon** in the opening screen. A dialog box will appear.

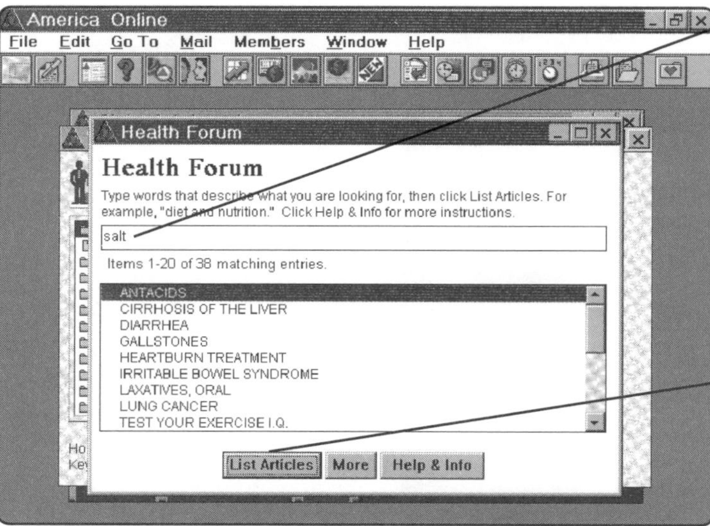

2. Type a **word** or words that you expect will appear in articles on the topic in which you are interested. AOL will then search through the database connected with this forum for any article that has the word(s) in it.

3. Click on **List Articles**. A list of articles that contain the specified word or words will appear, as shown in this example.

4. Click twice on an **article** that interests you. A document dialog box containing the article will appear.

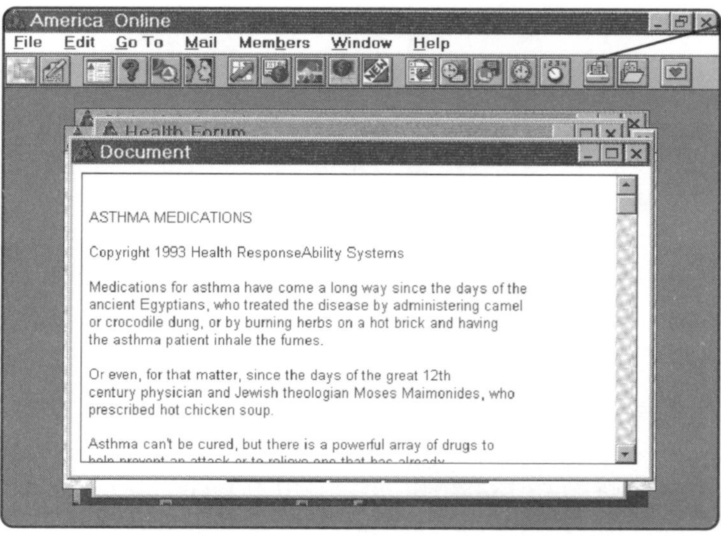

5. Click on the **Print icon** in the toolbar to print the article. A Print document dialog box (not shown here) will appear. **Click** on **OK** and the document will be printed.

You can also save the article on your computer. Simply **click** on the **Save icon** (second from the right on the Flash Bar). A Save file as dialog box will appear. Give the file a name, and **click** on **OK**.

SWITCHING BETWEEN OPEN WINDOWS

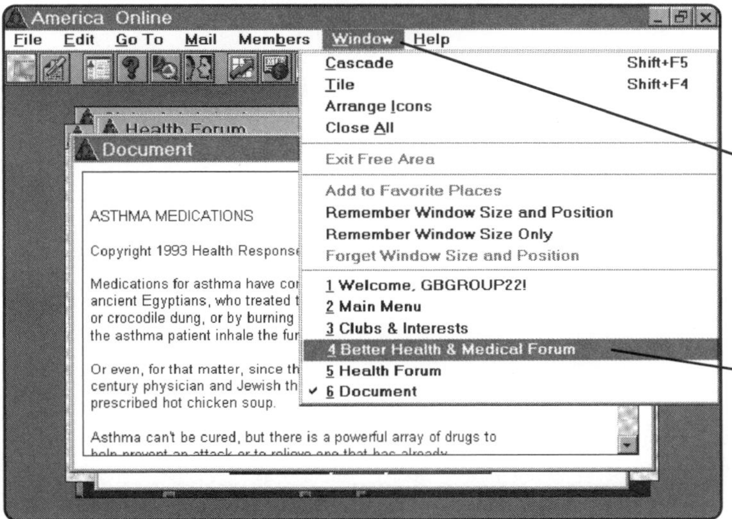

It's easy to switch to the dialog box you want using the Window menu.

1. **Click** on **Window** in the menu bar. A menu will appear. A a list of open dialog boxes will be at the bottom of it.

2. **Click** on **Better Health & Medical Forum** to return to the opening dialog box for this forum.

LEAVING THE FORUM

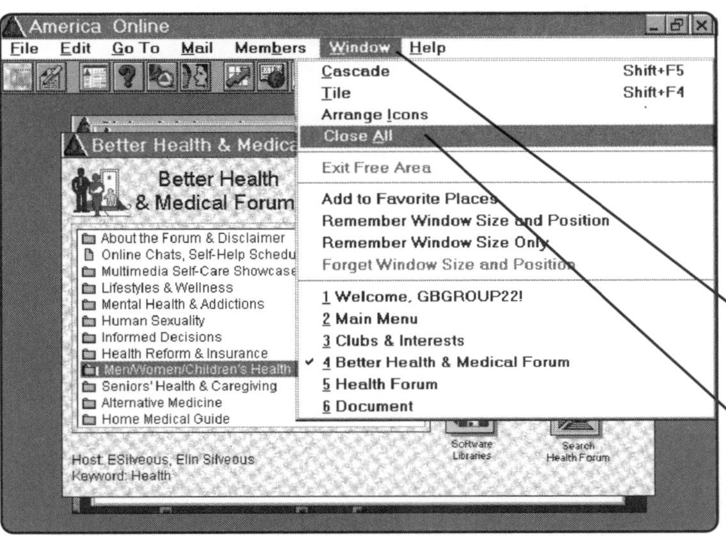

If there are lots of windows and dialog boxes open on your screen, you can close them all and leave the forum in one "swell foop," as Inspector Clousseau used to say.

1. **Click** on **Window** in the menu bar. A menu will appear.

2. **Click** on **Close All**. All windows will close and the Welcome window will be reduced to an icon at the bottom of your screen.

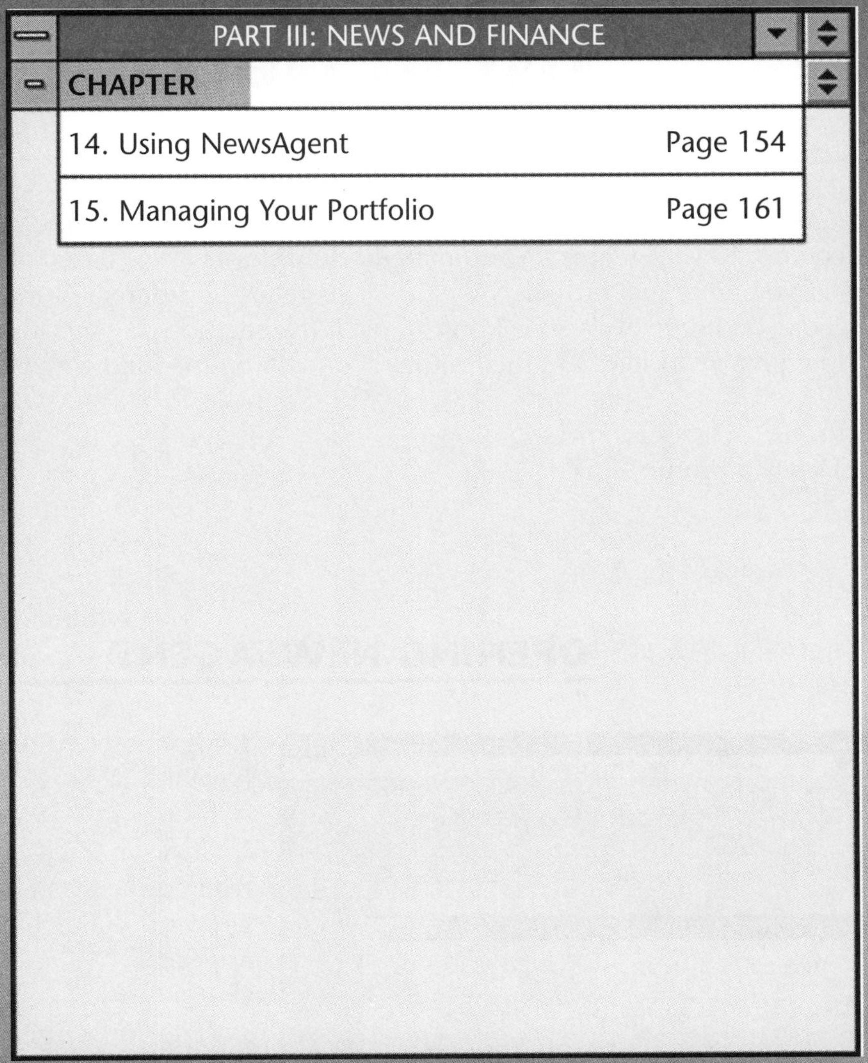

PART III: NEWS AND FINANCE

CHAPTER

CHAPTER
14

Using NewsAgent

Whether you're a student, researcher, or just plain "news junkie," this free feature will really turn you on. NewsAgent is an automated "clipping service." Based on the keywords that you enter in a profile, NewsAgent searches 12 different news sources daily and sends you the relevant articles via e-mail. (Depending on your topic, you could end up with a *lot* of mail!) In this chapter, you will do the following:

✔ Create a Profile
✔ Edit and Delete a Profile

OPENING NEWSAGENT

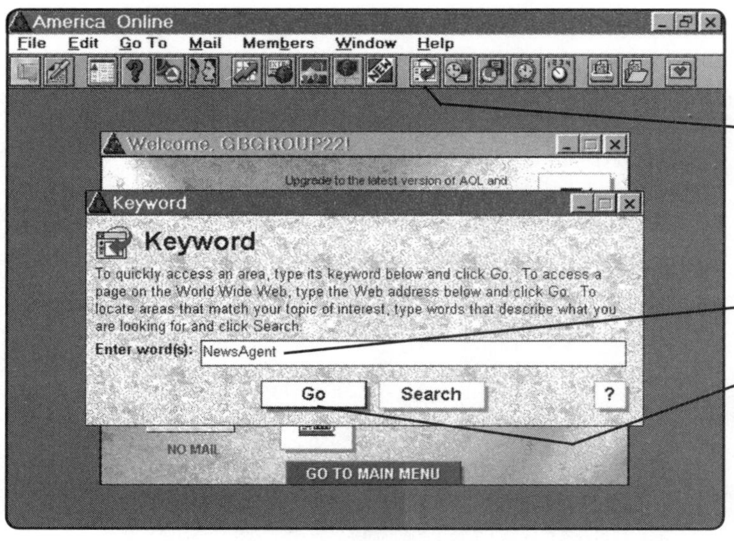
America Online
File Edit Go To Mail Members Window Help
Welcome, GBGROUP22!
Upgrade to the latest version of AOL and
Keyword
Keyword
To quickly access an area, type its keyword below and click Go. To access a page on the World Wide Web, type the Web address below and click Go. To locate areas that match your topic of interest, type words that describe what you are looking for and click Search.
Enter word(s): NewsAgent
Go
Search
?
NO MAIL
GO TO MAIN MENU

1. **Sign on** to **AOL** if you have not already done so.
2. **Click** on the **Keyword icon** on the Flash Bar. The keyword dialog box will appear.
3. **Type NewsAgent.**
4. **Click** on **Go**. The News-Agent window will appear.

CREATING A PROFILE

Take a moment to read the information about Profiles on the left side of the window. You will find it very helpful if you're new to conducting data searches. Just click twice on a topic to open it.

1. **Click** on **Create Your Profile**. If it's your first visit to the NewsAgent, a NewsAgent dialog box will appear.

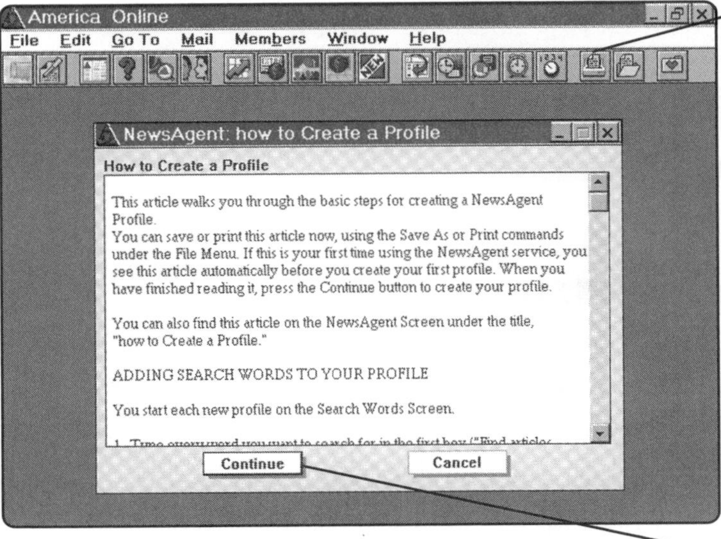

2. **Click** on the **Print icon** on the tool bar. The Print document dialog box (not shown here) will appear. Click on OK and the "How to Create a Profile" instructions will print.

In this chapter, we'll be taking you step by step through creating and editing a profile. However, you may find this additional reference helpful.

3. **Click** on **Continue**. The News Profile dialog box will appear.

4. **Type all of the words** that you want NewsAgent to search for.

In this example, we're looking for news stories on some fishing-related activities of Greenpeace. We've also included words, separated by commas, that *may* appear in such an article.

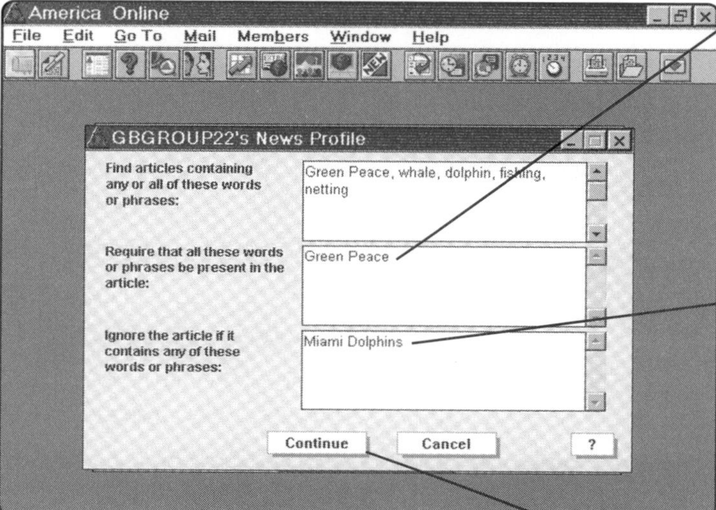

5. **Click** in the **middle box** to place the cursor.

6. **Type** the **required word(s)**. Required words are those that *must* appear in the article.

7. **Click** in the **bottom box** to place the cursor.

8. **Type every word** that you want NewsAgent to ***ignore***. The "ignore" words are important for eliminating articles that are not useful.

9. **Click** on **Continue**. A second News Profile window will appear.

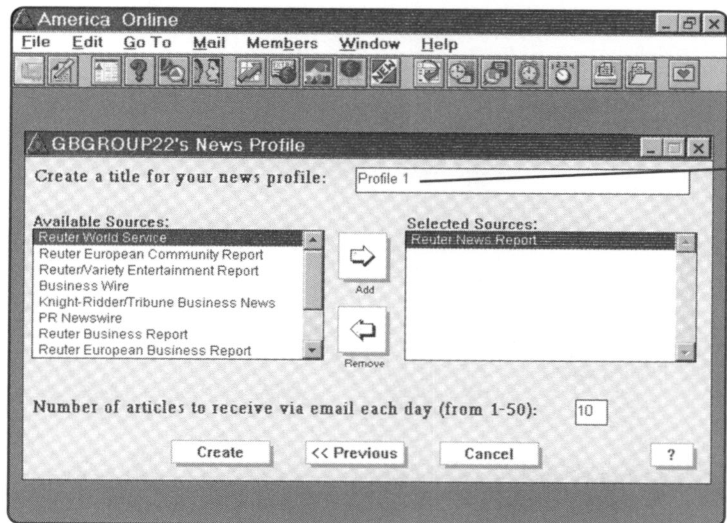

Notice that NewsAgent has automatically named your profile as Profile 1. If you want a different name, press and hold the mouse button as you drag the cursor to the left to highlight "Profile 1," then type a different name for your Profile.

Specifying Sources

NewsAgent will automatically search the Reuter News Report. You can remove it from your list of sources if you want, and add any of the other eleven news sources available.

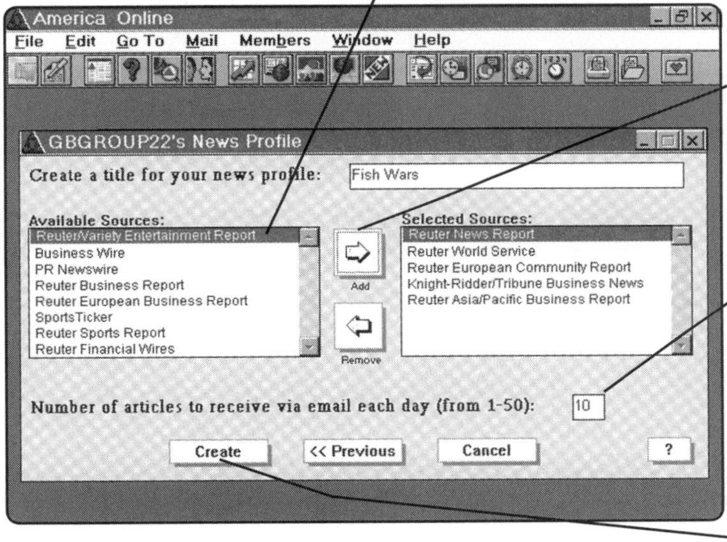

1. **Click** on the **news service** you want to add (or remove) to highlight it.

2. **Click** on **Add** (or Remove). The news service will move to the Selected Sources list or the Available Sources list.

Notice that you can change the maximum number of articles you receive each day. Click twice on the number to highlight it, then type the new number.

3. When you are satisfied with your list, **click** on **Create**. A dialog box will appear.

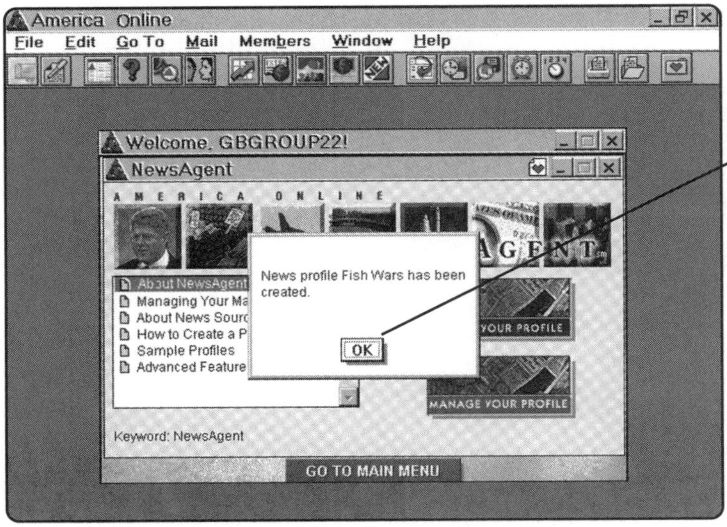

4. **Click** on **OK**. The dialog box will close. Soon NewsAgent will be sending clippings to your mailbox.

EDITING, DELETING, AND PUTTING A PROFILE ON HOLD

If you find that your profile resulted in too wide or too narrow a search, you can change it. You can enlarge or reduce the search parameters, or delete the entire profile. You can also put the search on hold while you're on vacation.

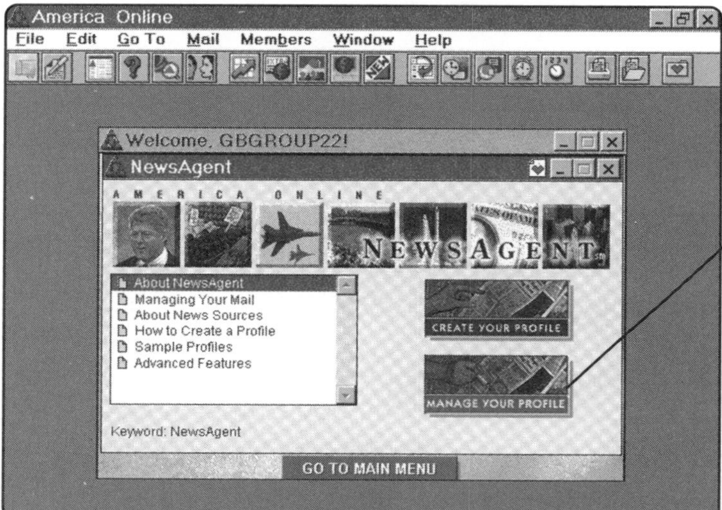

1. **Click** on **Manage Your Profile**. The News Profiles dialog box will appear.

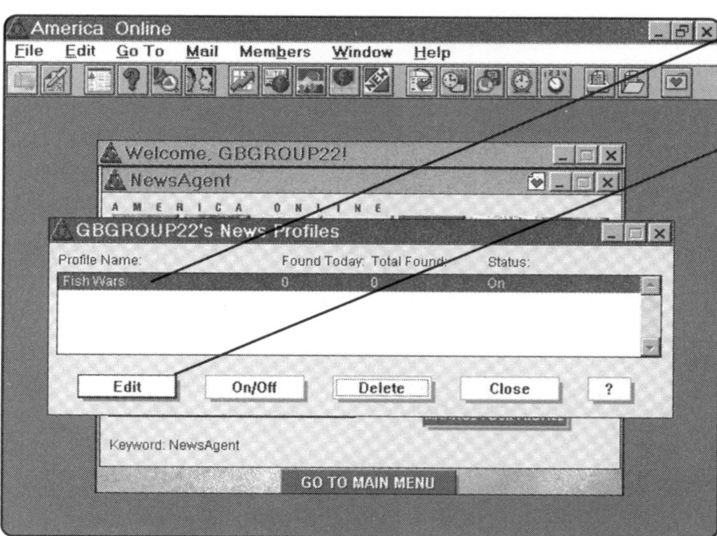

2. **Click** on the **profile** you want to edit to highlight it.

3. **Click** on **Edit**. The News Profiles dialog box will appear.

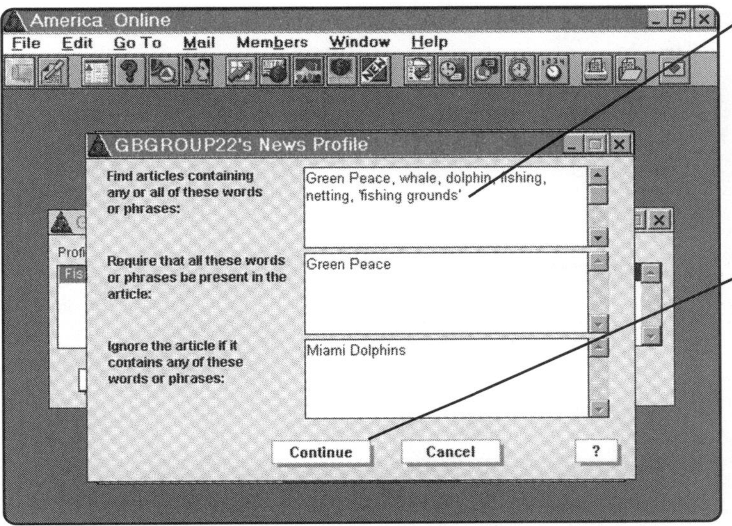

4. **Click** in the **text box** you want to change to place the cursor.

5. **Type** the additional or correct **words**.

6. **Click** on **Continue**. A second window will appear.

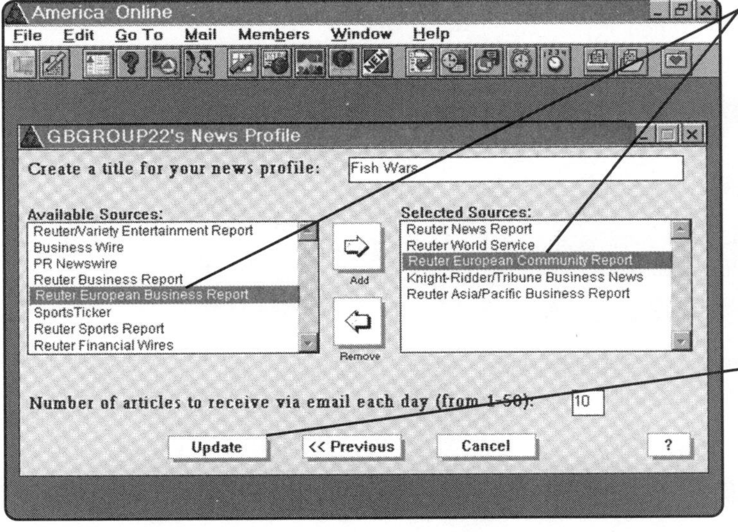

7. **Click** on the **service** you want to add to or remove from your profile to highlight it.

8. **Click** on **Add** or **Remove** to add the service to or remove it from your Selected Sources list.

9. **Click** on **Update**. A dialog box will appear.

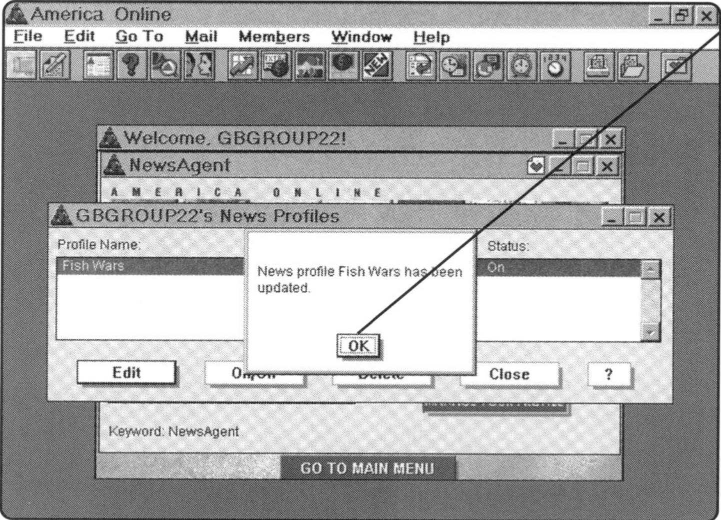

10. Click on **OK**. The dialog box will close.

Putting a Profile on Hold

If you are away from your computer for a long time, you don't have to come back to a stuffed mailbox.

1. Click on the **profile** to highlight it.

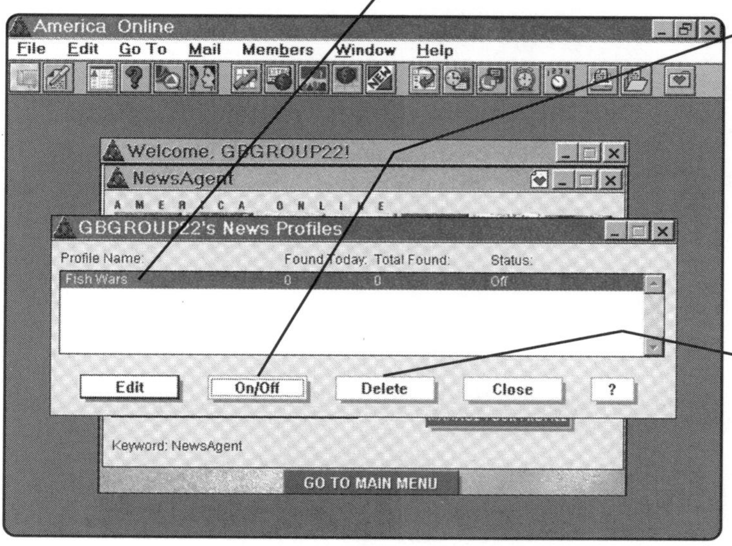

2. Click on **On/Off**. Notice that the profile's status chages from On to Off.

Deleting a Profile

1. Repeat step 1, above.

2. Click on **Delete**. A dialog box (not shown here) will appear.

3. Click on **OK**. The profile will be deleted.

Managing Your Portfolio

America Online will help you manage your investment portfolio. You can check stocks, mutual funds, and money market mutual funds on the NYSE, AMEX, and NASDAQ exchanges and track their performance. The prices you get in AOL will be within 15 to 20 minutes of the latest prices, and you can have up to 100 stocks and funds in your portfolio. In this chapter, you will do the following:

✔ Check on the latest price of a stock
✔ Add stocks to your portfolio and check their value
✔ Research a company through Hoover's Business Resources

GOING TO PERSONAL FINANCE

The Personal Finance gateway puts a wealth of information at your fingertips.

1. **Sign on** to **AOL** if you have not already done so.

2. **Click** on the **Main Menu icon** on the Flash Bar if needed to open the Main Menu.

3. **Click** on the **Personal Finance icon**. The Personal Finance dialog box will appear. If you have not visited this area before, you will be asked if you want to download all of the art for the area at once. We recommend that you follow the instructions on your screen to do so.

GETTING A STOCK QUOTATION

If you need to look up a security symbol before getting a quote, see the section titled "Looking Up a Symbol," a few pages forward in this chapter.

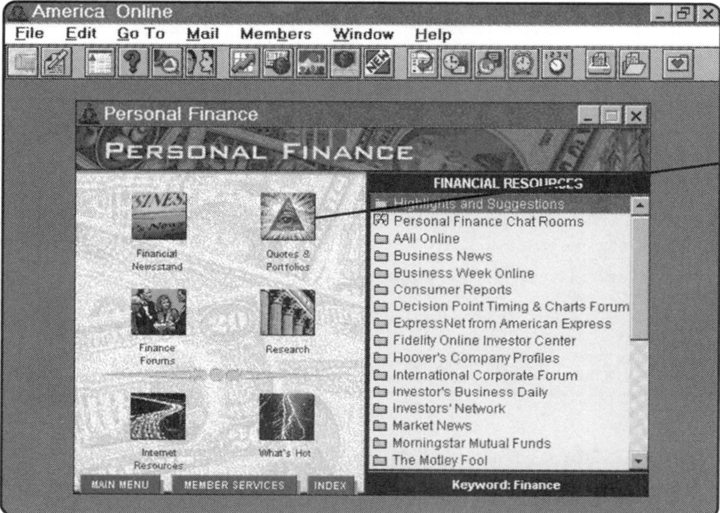

Stock quotations are accurate within 15 to 20 minutes.

1. **Click** on the **Quotes & Portfolios icon**. The dialog box will appear.

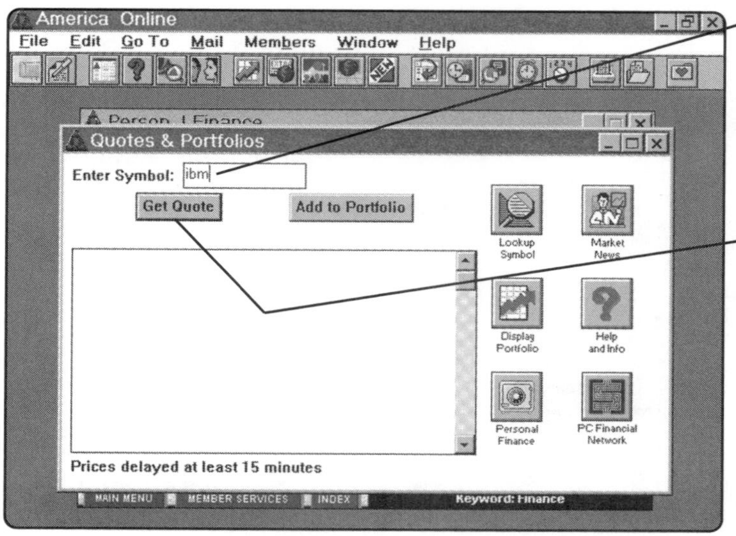

2. **Type** the **security symbol**. It doesn't matter whether you use capital or small letters. The search function is not case sensitive.

3. **Click** on the **Get Quote** button. The quote will appear on your screen.

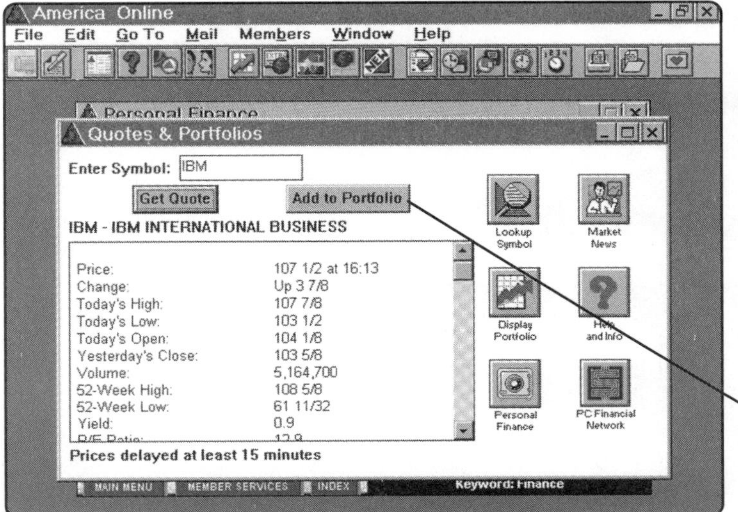

ADDING A STOCK TO YOUR PORTFOLIO

America Online will keep track of a portfolio for you. You can add securities you actually own to it, or ones that you just want to track.

1. **Click** on **Add to Portfolio**. The Portfolio Information dialog box will appear.

2. **Type** the **number** of shares you own. You can also type the number of shares you have just purchased if you want to use the portfolio to keep track of the value of individual *tax lots*, or purchases.

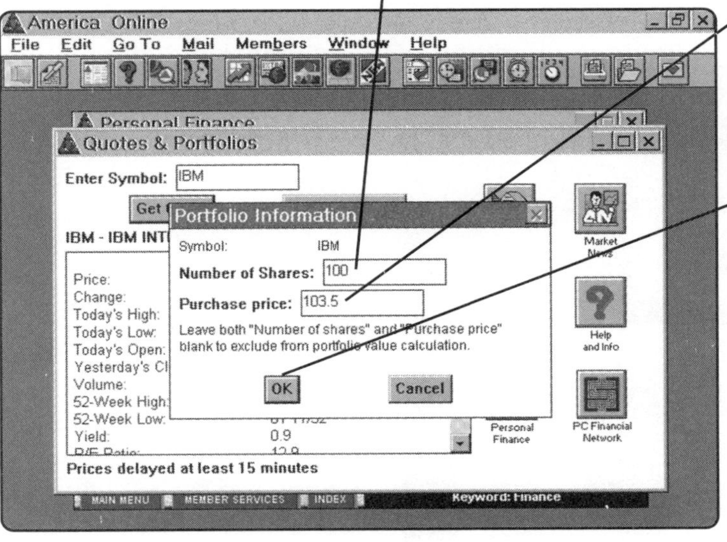

3. **Type** the **purchase price**. The price can be typed as a fraction (103 1/2) or as a decimal (103.5).

4. **Click** on **OK**. You'll see a message saying the stock has been added to your portfolio.

5. **Click** on **OK**. The message dialog box will close.

LOOKING UP A SYMBOL

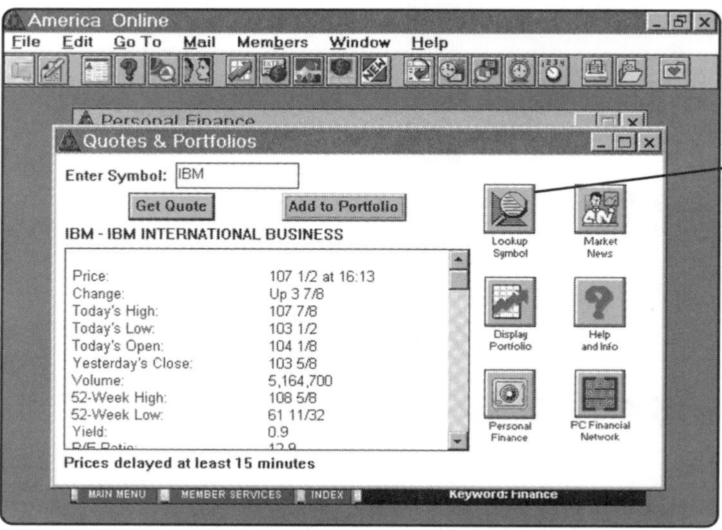

If you don't know the symbol for a specific security, you can look it up.

1. **Click** on **Lookup Symbol** in the Quotes & Portfolios dialog box. The Search Symbols dialog box will appear.

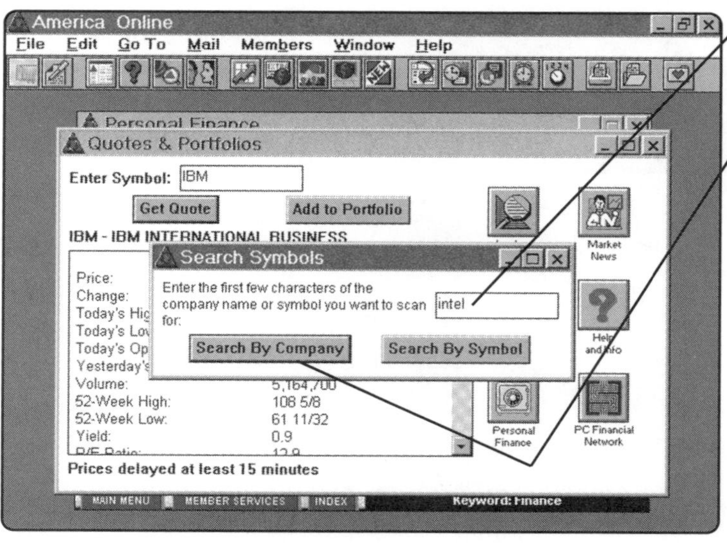

2. **Type** the **name** of the company.

3. **Click** on **Search By Company**.

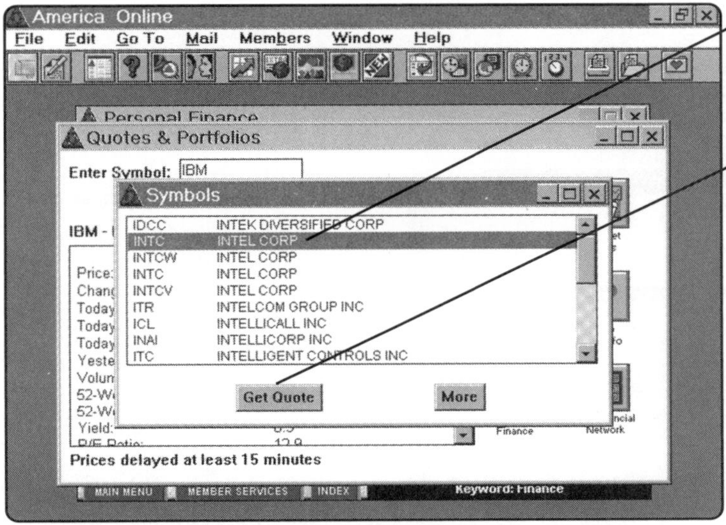

4. **Click** on the **name** of the company in which you are interested.

5. **Click** on **Get Quote**. The stock quote will appear on your screen.

6. **Repeat** the **steps** in "Adding a Stock to Your Portfolio" if you want to add it to your portfolio.

CHECKING YOUR PORTFOLIO

Your portfolio will keep track of the total value of your securities and the gain or loss for each tax lot.

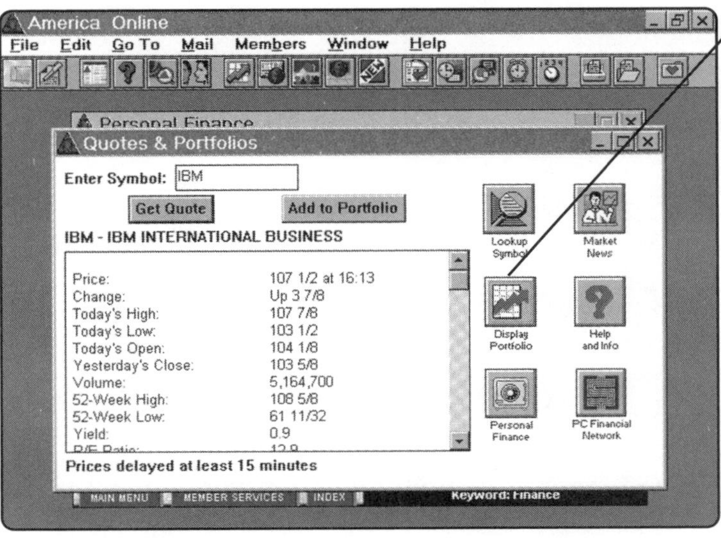

1. **Click** on the **Display Portfolio icon** in the Quotes & Portfolios dialog box.

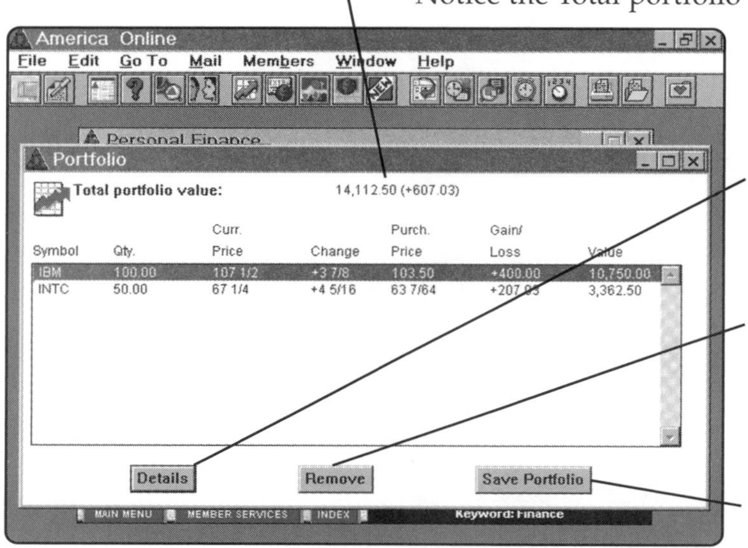

Notice the Total portfolio value. For each security you see a variety of information that allows you to track its performance

2. **Click** on **Details** to show the latest quote for the highlighted item.

3. **Click** on **Remove** if you want to remove the highlighted item from your portfolio.

4. **Click** on **Save Portfolio** to save a copy of your portfolio. The Save to File dialog box will appear.

5. Use standard Windows techniques to **go to** the **directory** in which you want to save the file.

6. **Type** a **name** for the file.

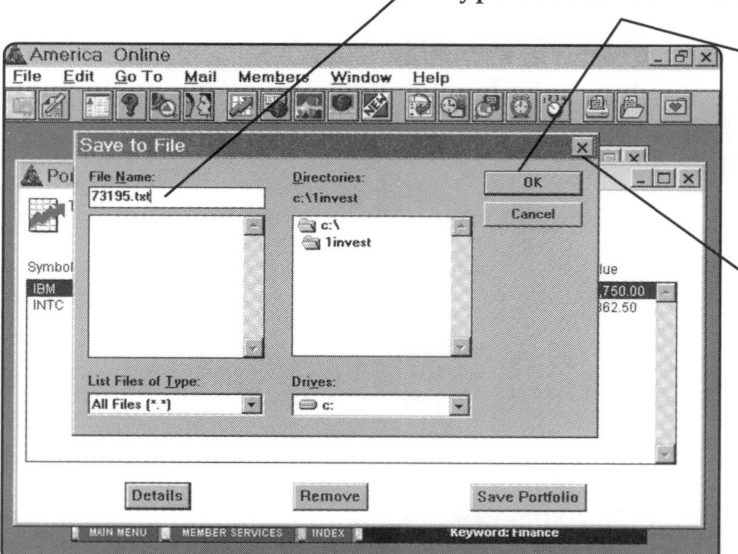

7. **Click** on **OK**. The file will be saved. You can print it later using your word processor and/or use it in a spreadsheet program.

8. **Click** on the **Close box** (☒) in the right corner of the title bar, or (Windows 3.1) click twice on the Control menu box in the left corner to close the Portfolio dialog box. We'll show only the Windows 95 step for closing dialog boxes in the rest of the chapter.

RESEARCHING A COMPANY

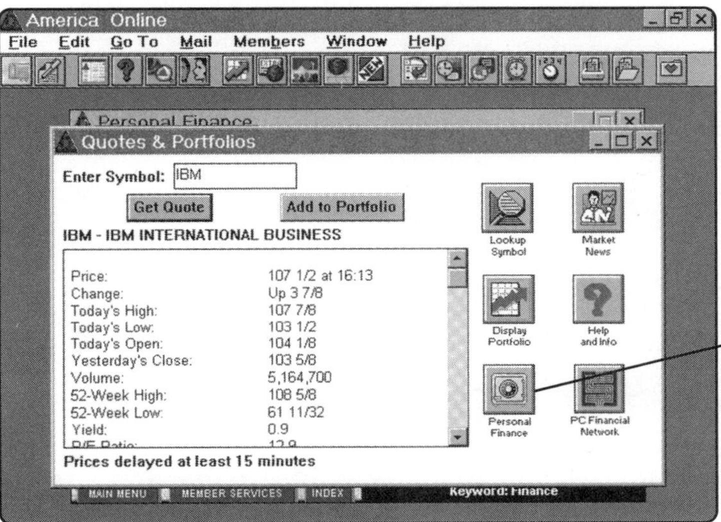

AOL gives you access to the Hoover's Handbook database, which contains profiles of over 900 of the largest and fastest-growing public and private companies in the U.S. and abroad.

1. **Click** on the **Personal Finance icon**. The Personal Finance dialog box will reappear.

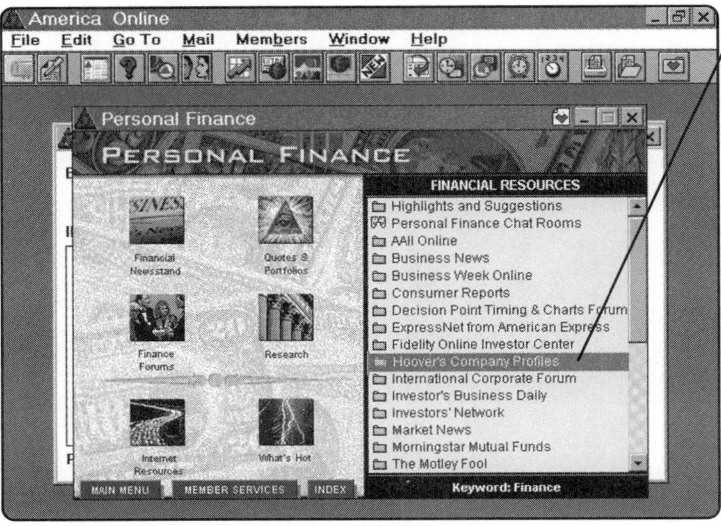

2. **Click twice** on **Hoover's Company Profiles** in the Financial Resources list. The Hoover's Business Resources dialog box will appear.

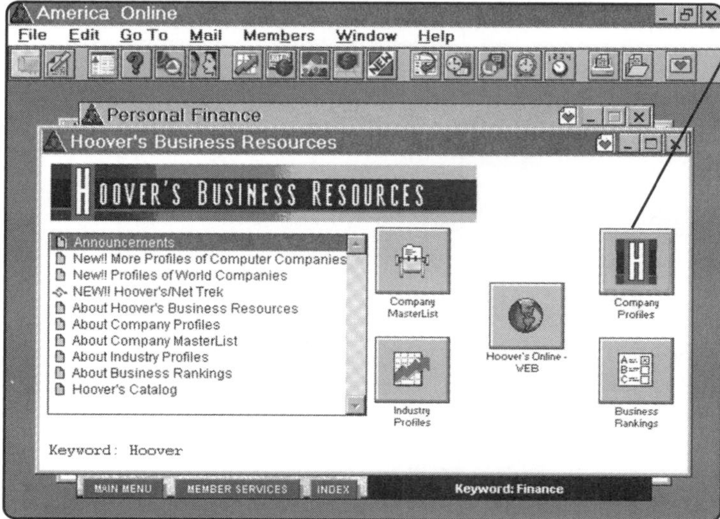

3. **Click** on the **Company Profiles icon**. The Hoover's Company Profiles dialog box will appear.

Notice that you can use the icons in this dialog box to search by industry or by geographic location. In this example, we want to look up Intel Corporation, so we'll use the alphabetical listings.

4. **Click twice** on **I thru K Companies.** A dialog box will appear with companies beginning with I through K.

5. **Click** on the **More button** if needed to add more companies to the listing.

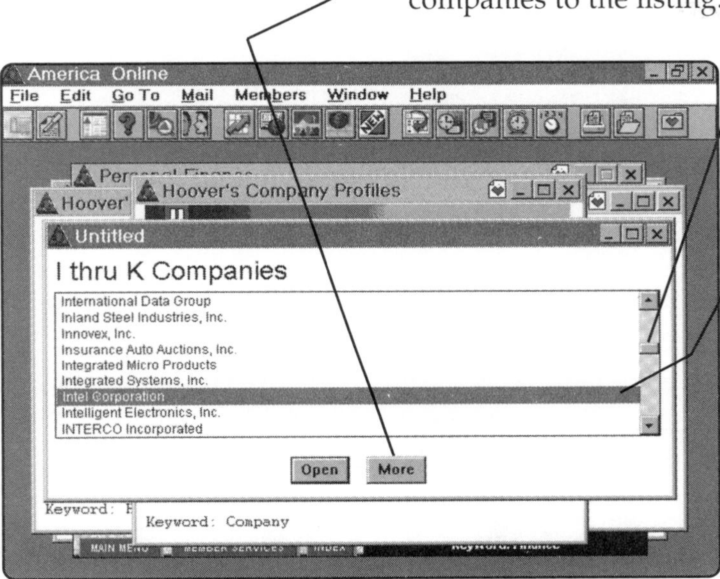

6. **Press and hold** on the **scroll button** and **drag** it down the scroll bar until you see Intel Corporation.

7. **Click twice** on **Intel Corporation**. A dialog box will appear with the Intel information.

Each company profile contains information about company history, operations and strategy, and products and services by division and brand name.

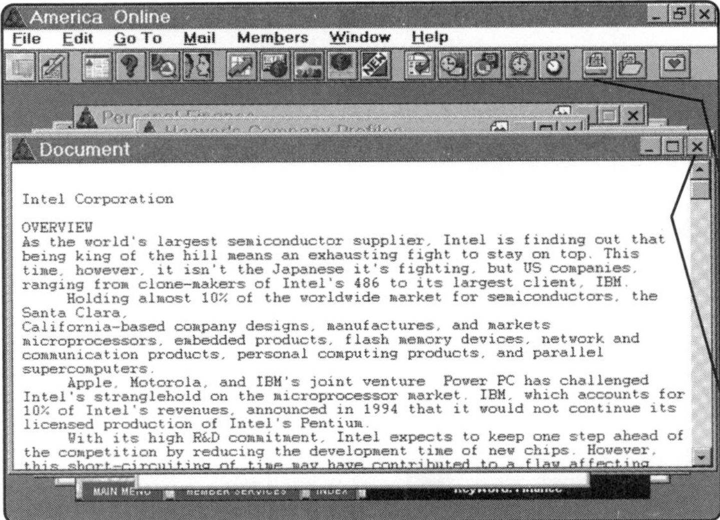

8. **Click** on the ▼ at the bottom of the scroll bar to scroll through the profile. You'll notice that the profile contains the names, ages, and salaries of key officers.

9. **Click** on the **Print icon** in the toolbar if you want to print this profile. **Click** on **OK** in the Print document dialog box when it appears.

10. **Click** on the **Close buttons** (☒) of all the open windows until you return to the Personal Finance window.

EXPLORING OTHER FEATURES

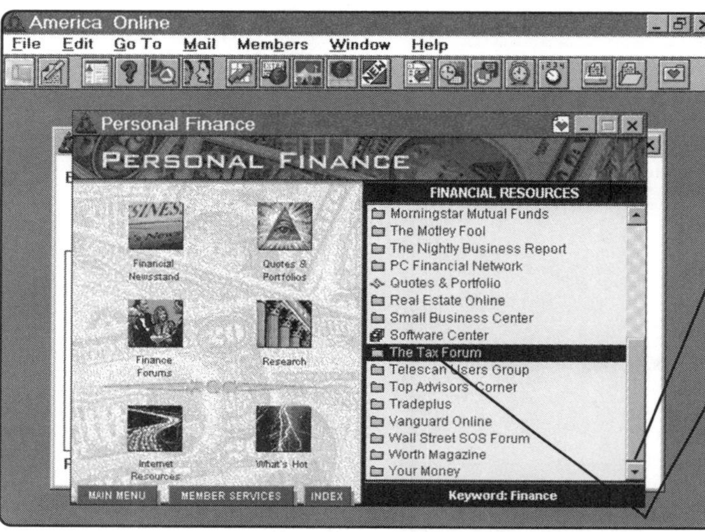

The Personal Finance window has many more valuable features to help you manage your money.

1. **Click** repeatedly on the ▼ on the **scroll bar** to view the list of Financial Resources.

2. **Click twice** on the **Tax Forum**. The Tax Forum will appear.

It has been said that there are only two certain things in life. AOL has created a comprehensive resource center to help you with one of these: taxes.

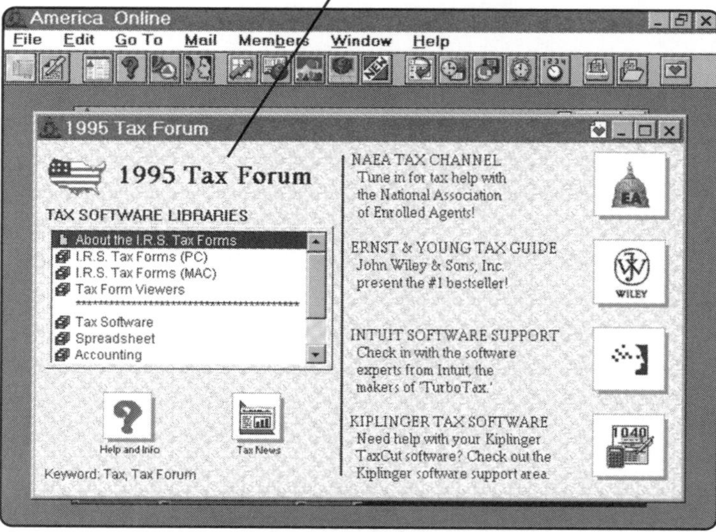

You'll find all sorts of information, instruction, software, message boards, and chat lines.We encourage you to explore this area on your own. (We're off to an appointment with our CPA.)

PART IV: COMPUTERS AND SOFTWARE

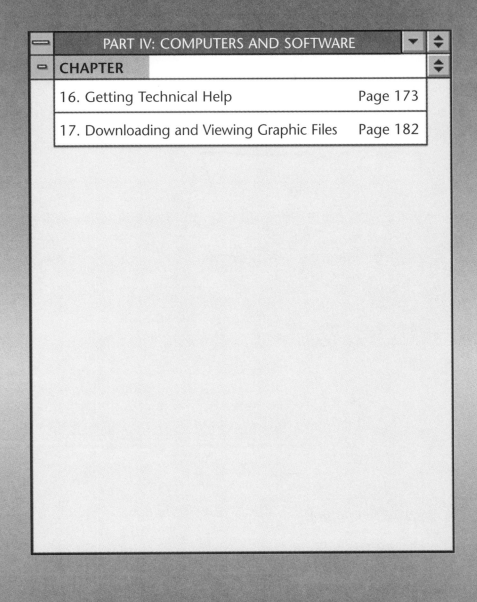

CHAPTER

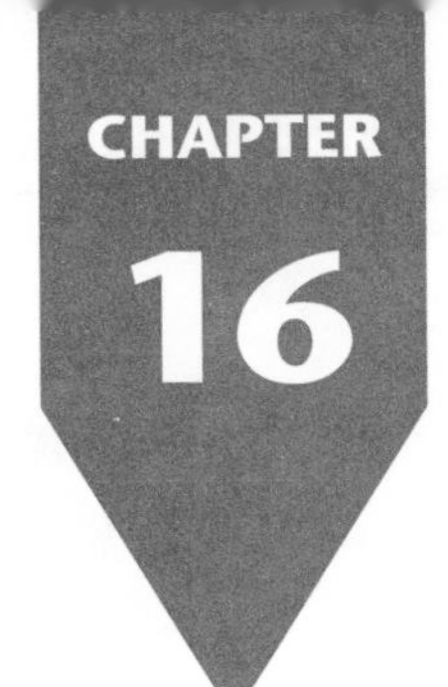

Getting Technical Help

You can get online technical help for AOL problems from the Members' Online Support department. The type of online technical help runs the gamut from reviewing answers to common problems, to actually chatting live with a technical representative online. In this chapter, you will do the following:

✔ Go to the Members' Online Support department
✔ Get instant answers
✔ Get online technical help for common problems
✔ Get online, live technical help
✔ Get help from other members
✔ Get telephone support

OPENING MEMBERS' ONLINE SUPPORT DIALOG BOX

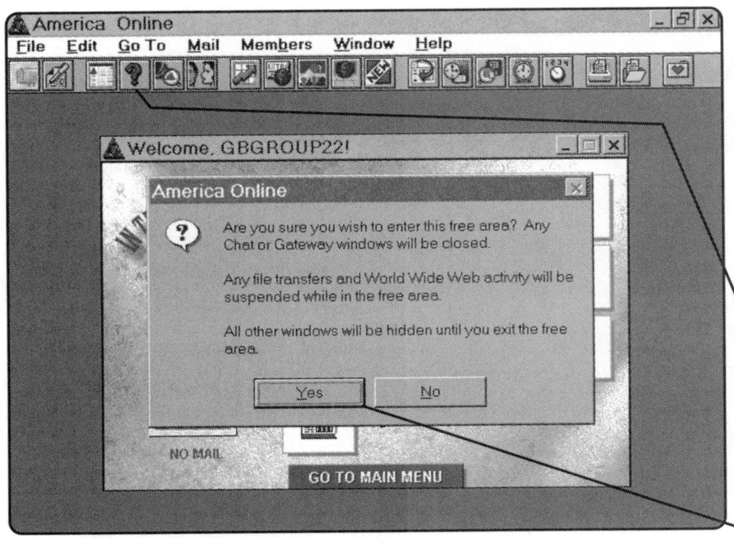

In order to get technical support, you must open the Members' Online Support dialog box.

1. **Sign on** to **America Online** if you haven't already done so.

2. **Click** on the **Member Services icon** on the Flash Bar (the red question mark). An America Online dialog box will appear.

3. **Click** on **Yes**. The Free Online Help dialog box will appear.

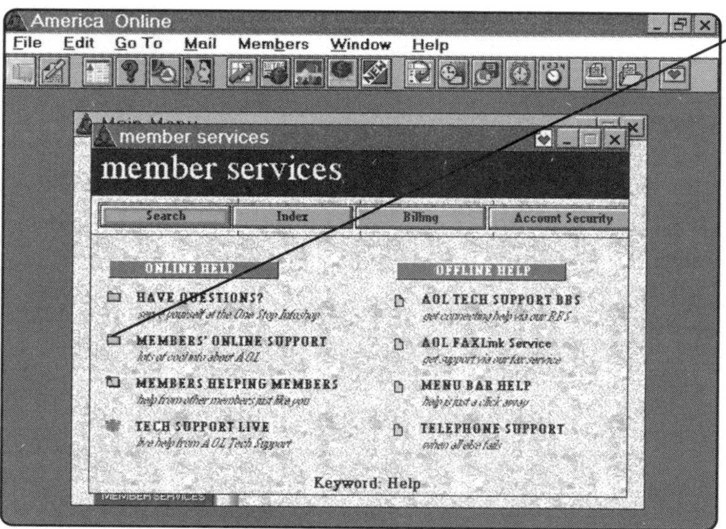

4. **Click** on **Members' Online Support**. The Your FREE Online Help Center (Members' Online Support) dialog box will appear.

GETTING INSTANT ANSWERS

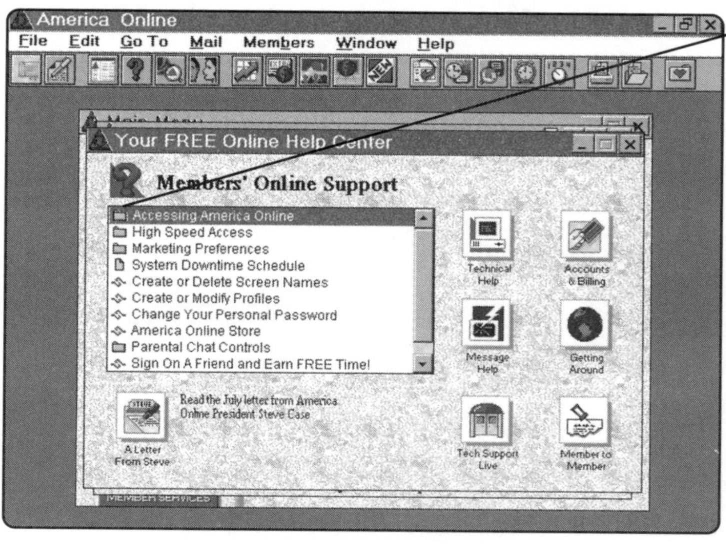

❖ This is a list of topics and services that allow you to find answers and/or accomplish a goal. You can use the ▼ at the bottom of the scroll bar to scroll down the list of choices. The items on the list of choices range from getting 9600 baud telephone numbers to an opportunity to earn free hours. Informational choices and options change periodically, so if the list of items on your screen is different from this one, don't be surprised. You are in the right place!

GETTING TECHNICAL HELP

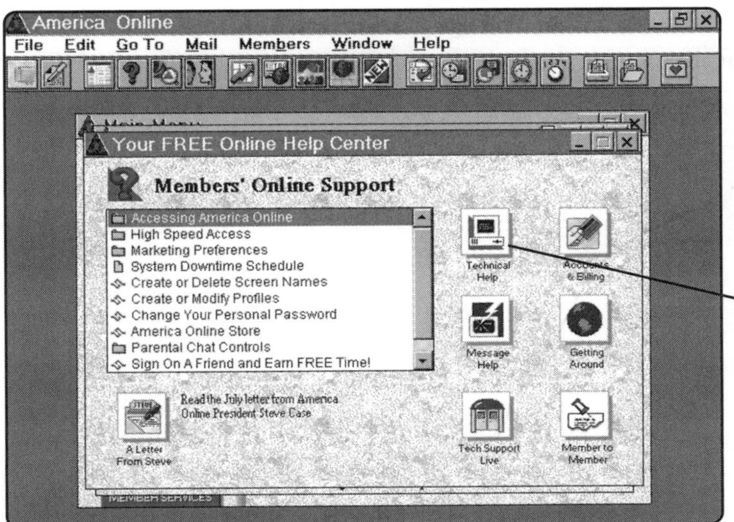

Online technical help for many common problems is a just a mouse-click away.

1. **Click** on **Technical Help**. The Technical Help dialog box will appear.

❖ This list of technical information ranges from instructions on how to report error messages and problems to tips on making AOL run better on your computer. Just click twice on any topic to begin getting instant information on the topics.

❖ Clicking on any of the five buttons in this part of the dialog box will open a list of help files related to the button's label. For example, clicking on High Speed Access will bring up a list of modem topics.

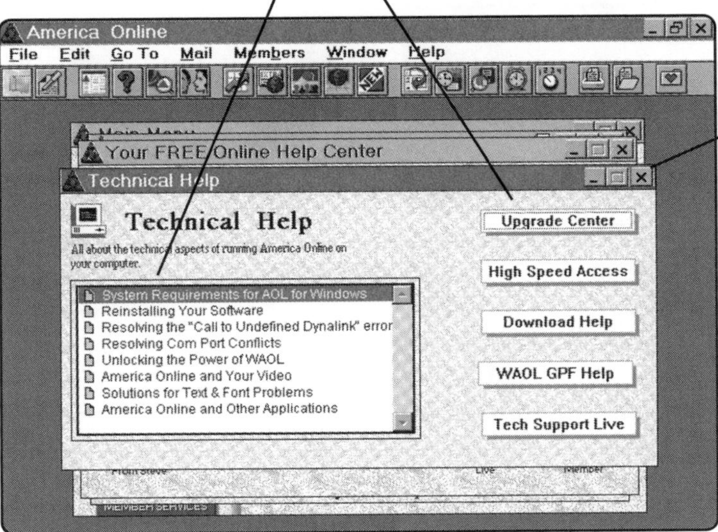

2. **Click** on the **Close button** (☒) in the right corner of the title bar, or, if you're using Windows 3.1, click twice on the Control menu box in the left corner of the title bar to close the dialog box. We will only give the Windows 95 step for closing dialog boxes in the rest of the chapter.

GETTING LIVE TECHNICAL HELP

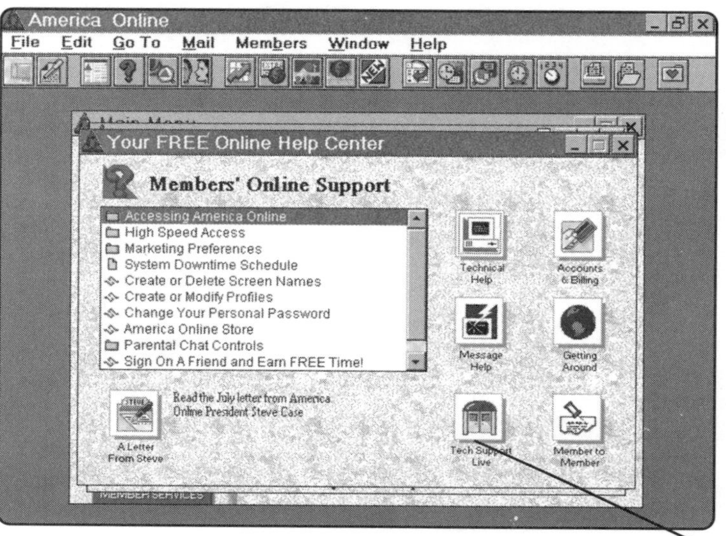

Those who have the patience to search through folders and read a lot of text will probably find the answers to their technical questions by following the steps in the previous section (eventually). However, if you tend to be a less patient type online, you can get instant answers in a conversation with a live technical representative.

1. **Click** on **Tech Support Live**. A Tech Support Live dialog box will appear.

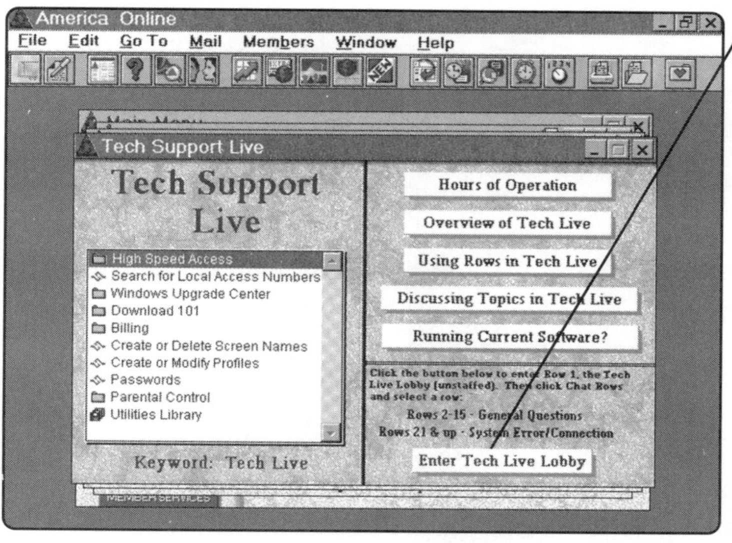

2. **Click** on **Enter Tech Live Lobby**. The Tech Live Lobby dialog box will appear.

Going Live!

In this example you will enter a technical chat room, ask a technical question, and receive an answer.

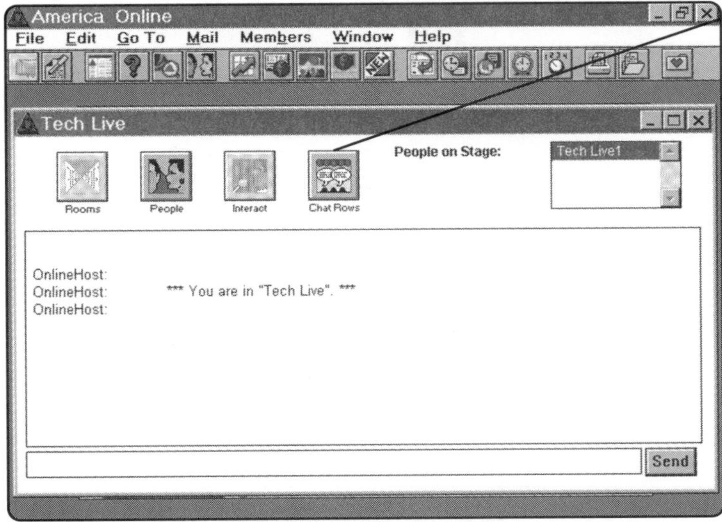

1. Click on **Chat Rows**. The Chat Rows dialog box will appear.

AOL has separated live technical service into small "rooms," or "rows." Each set of rows accepts technical questions on specific topics:

❖ Rows 2-15 are for service-related questions (e.g., How do I find...?).

❖ Rows 21 and up are for connecting problems or system errors.

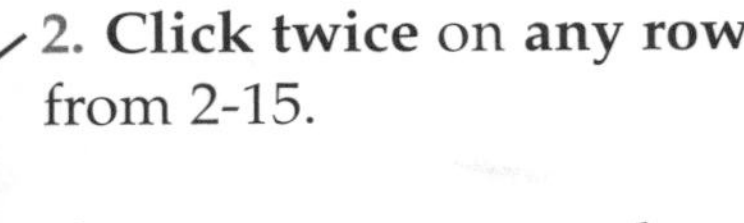

2. Click twice on **any row** from 2-15.

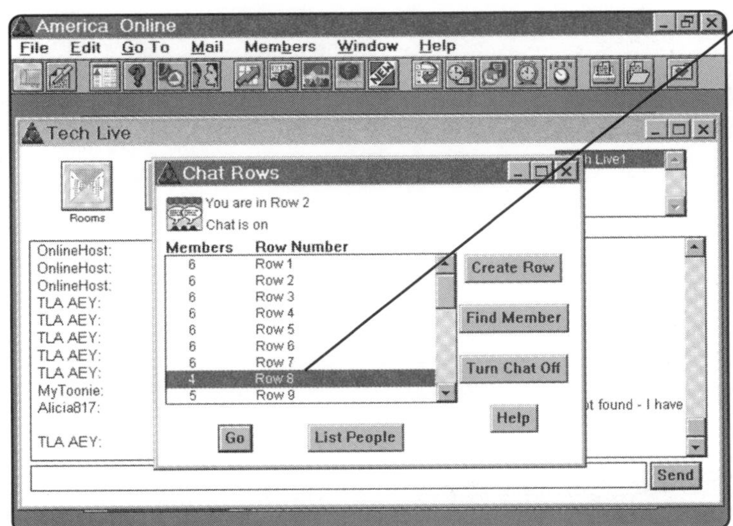

If you get a message that the row is "full," click on a row with fewer members in it. Or, click on "Create Row." A message box confirming your row choice will appear. **Click** on **OK**. The message box will close, and you will be in the row you selected.

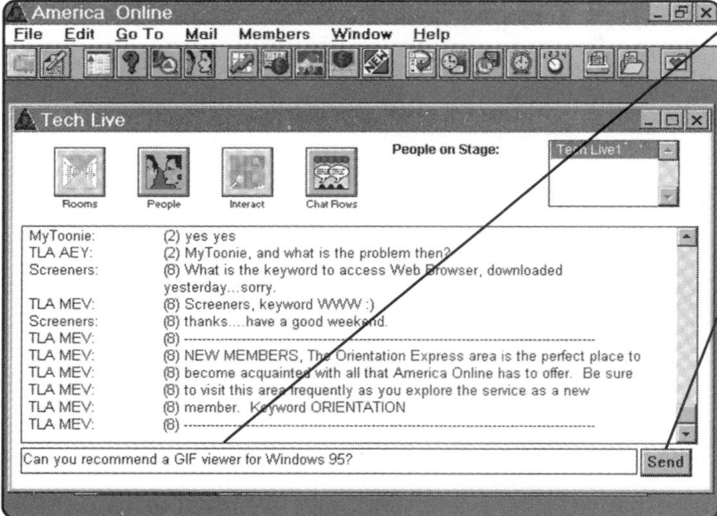

3. **Type** your **question** in the Send text box. (Your screen may differ from this one. There may be no "conversation" as you see here).

4. **Click** on **Send**. Your question will show up in the chat screen.

❖ Your question will be answered in a first come, first served sequence.

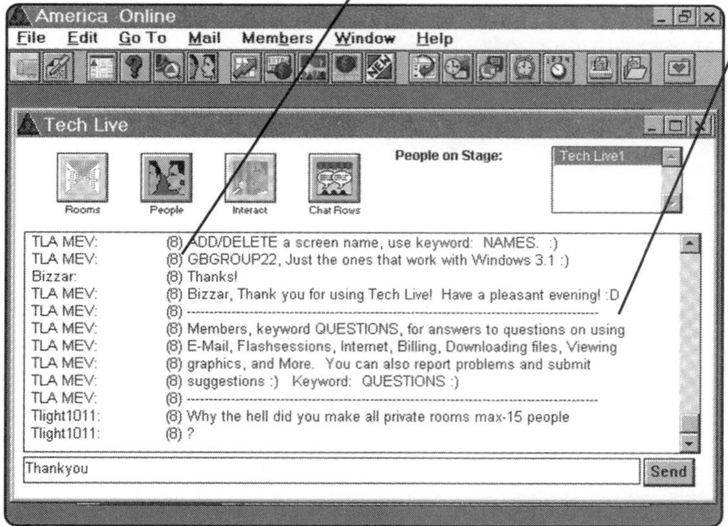

❖ Notice that some answers consisting of many rows of text.

❖ Before you leave, it's a nice idea to type a "Thanks" and/or a "Goodbye" message as shown here.

We believe that AOL's online live tech service is the greatest. We've had nothing but positive experiences!

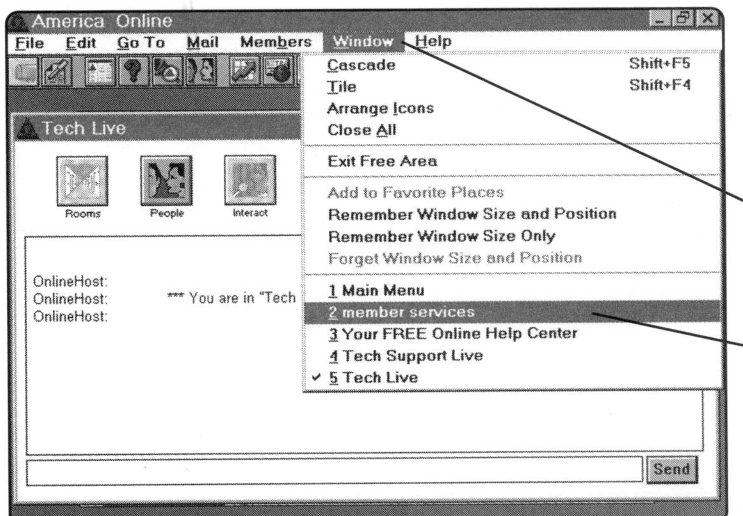

RETURNING TO MEMBER SERVICES

1. **Click** on **Window** in the menu bar. A menu will appear.
2. **Click** on **Member Services**. The Member Services dialog box will appear.

GETTING OTHER MEMBERS' HELP

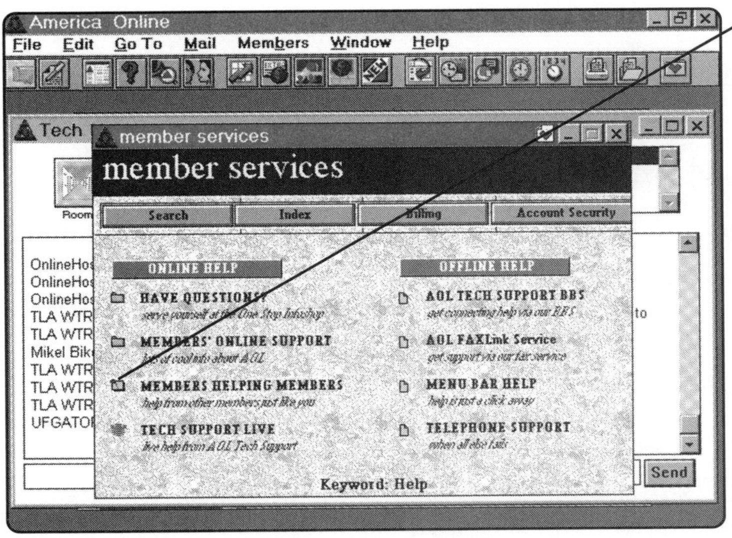

❖ By clicking on Members Helping Members, you can browse through a list of messages on various AOL-related topics. Members Helping Members is a bulletin board where you can read messages from other members, post your own message, or create a new topic. If you like "browsing," you may eventually find an answer to your problem. If not, there is an e-mail icon available in this area that you can use to send a message directly to AOL's technical staff and get an answer within 24 hours. When time is of the essence, we prefer chatting live with a technical expert!

GETTING TELEPHONE SUPPORT

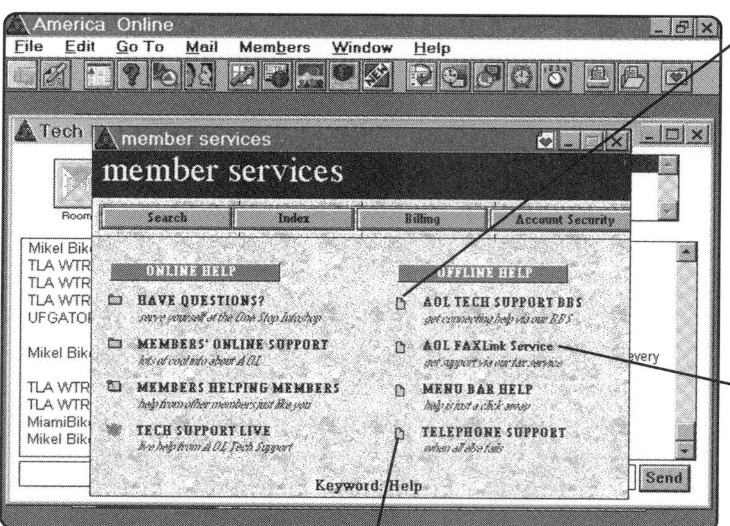

America Online
File Edit Go To Mail Members Window Help
Tech
member services
member services
Search
Index
Billing
Account Security
ONLINE HELP
OFFLINE HELP
HAVE QUESTIONS?
MEMBERS' ONLINE SUPPORT
MEMBERS HELPING MEMBERS
TECH SUPPORT LIVE
AOL TECH SUPPORT BBS
AOL FAXLink Service
MENU BAR HELP
TELEPHONE SUPPORT
Keyword: Help
Send

❖ You can get technical support via a BBS (Bulletin Board Service) by having your modem dial the appropriate telephone number. Click twice to get directions. The BBS telephone number is a toll-free call (1-800-827-5808).

❖ You can get Fax support by calling 1-800-827-5551 from a touch-tone telephone. An automated voice system will guide you through requesting the list of available faxes, and prompt you for your fax number. Click twice on AOL FAXLink Service for complete directions.

1. **Click** on **Telephone Support**. A Phone Support message will appear.

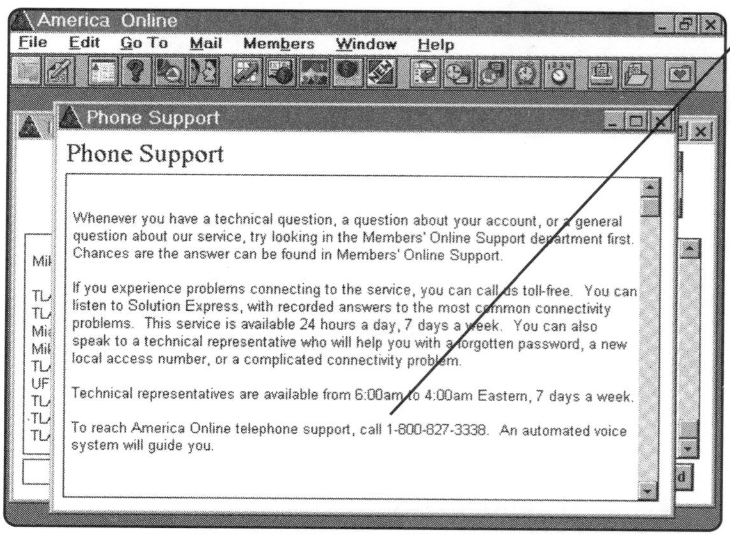

America Online
File Edit Go To Mail Members Window Help
Phone Support
Phone Support
Whenever you have a technical question, a question about your account, or a general question about our service, try looking in the Members' Online Support department first. Chances are the answer can be found in Members' Online Support.
If you experience problems connecting to the service, you can call us toll-free. You can listen to Solution Express, with recorded answers to the most common connectivity problems. This service is available 24 hours a day, 7 days a week. You can also speak to a technical representative who will help you with a forgotten password, a new local access number, or a complicated connectivity problem.
Technical representatives are available from 6:00am to 4:00am Eastern, 7 days a week.
To reach America Online telephone support, call 1-800-827-3338. An automated voice system will guide you.

❖ You can talk directly with an AOL technical representative by dialing 1-800-827-3338. Live, telephone technical help is available from 6:00 am to 4:00 am Eastern, 7 days a week.

EXITING ONLINE HELP

1. **Click** on **Window** in the menu bar. A menu will appear.

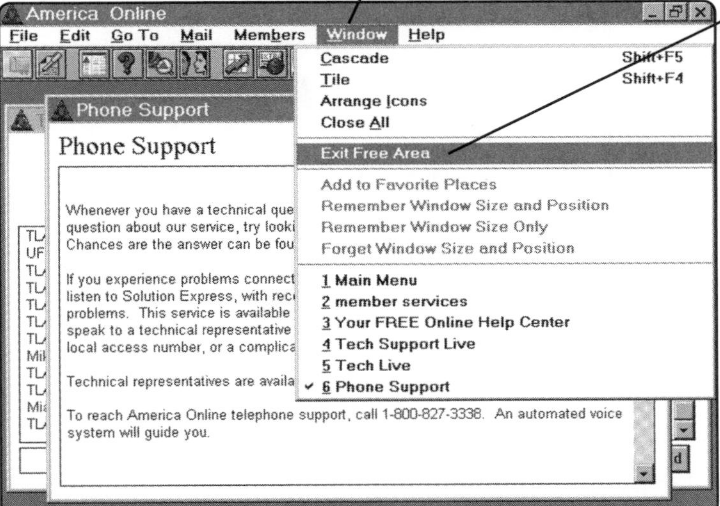
America Online
File Edit Go To Mail Members Window Help
Cascade Shift+F5
Tile Shift+F4
Arrange Icons
Close All
Exit Free Area
Add to Favorite Places
Remember Window Size and Position
Remember Window Size Only
Forget Window Size and Position
1 Main Menu
2 member services
3 Your FREE Online Help Center
4 Tech Support Live
5 Tech Live
6 Phone Support
Phone Support
To reach America Online telephone support, call 1-800-827-3338. An automated voice system will guide you.

2. **Click** on **Exit Free Area**. An America Online dialog box will appear.

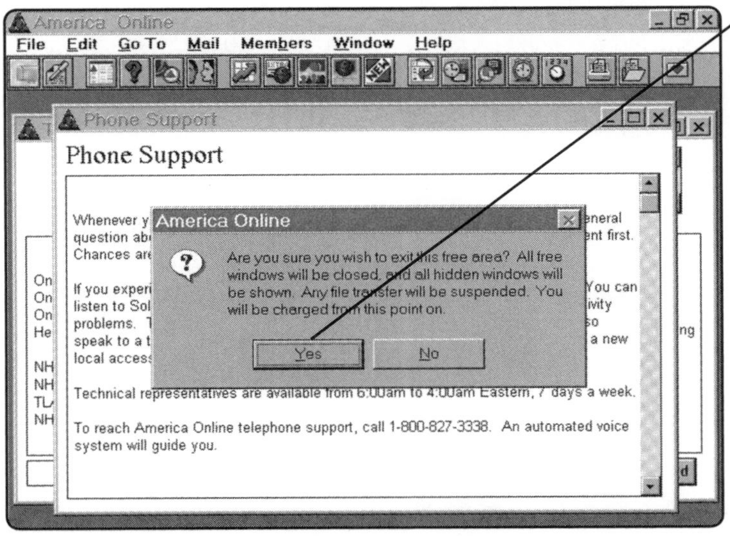
America Online
File Edit Go To Mail Members Window Help
Phone Support
America Online
Are you sure you wish to exit this free area? All free windows will be closed, and all hidden windows will be shown. Any file transfer will be suspended. You will be charged from this point on.
Yes
No
Technical representatives are available from 6:00am to 4:00am Eastern, 7 days a week.
To reach America Online telephone support, call 1-800-827-3338. An automated voice system will guide you.

3. **Click** on **Yes**. The Main Menu will reappear. You can go on with other tasks or sign off/exit AOL by clicking on the close box (☒) in the right corner of the AOL title bar.

Downloading and Viewing Graphic Files

In the old days, before AOL's file-viewing feature, downloading graphics was like buying the proverbial pig in the poke. You couldn't see what you got until after you went through the effort of downloading. Even then, you had to have a separate graphic viewer to see the darned thing. AOL has changed all that. Now, you can view graphic files in a thumbnail view while reading the description. Moreover, you can *see a full-size view of a graphic file as it is downloading*. You can cancel at any time prior to completing the download. Even more exciting is the fact that you do not need a special graphic viewer offline. AOL will now open most graphic formats offline! In this chapter, you will do the following:

✔ Find a graphic file
✔ Read a description of a graphic and look at it in a thumbnail view
✔ Download a graphic file and view it full-size as it downloads
✔ View a graphic file offline with AOL's viewing feature

FINDING A GRAPHIC FILE

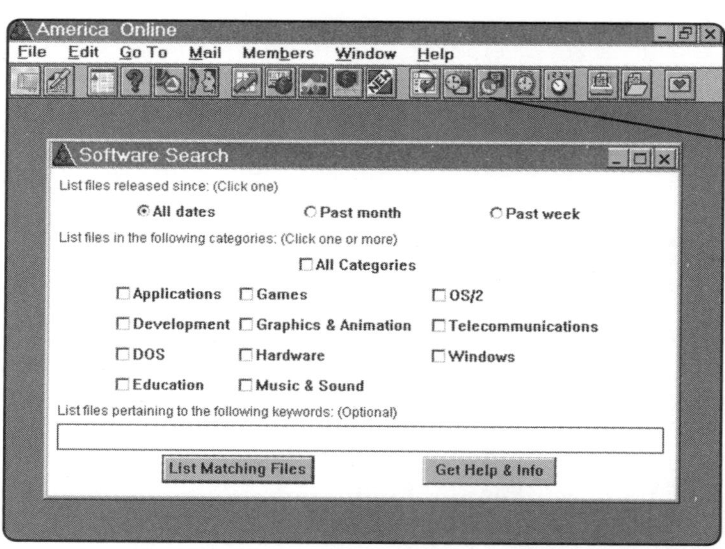

1. **Sign on** to **AOL** if you have not already done so.

2. **Click** on the **File Search icon** in the Flash Bar. The Software Search dialog box will appear as you see in this example.

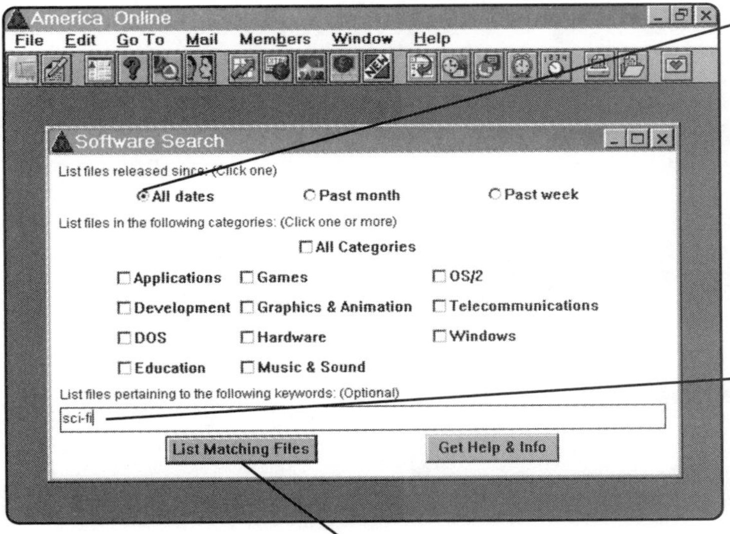

3. **Click** on **All dates** to put a dot in the circle if there isn't one there already. This broadens the search to all files in AOL in the category you will specify below. You can narrow your search by clicking on Past month or Past week.

4. **Type sci-fi**. This means that AOL will only search for files in this category. (Sci-fi stands for science fiction.)

5. **Click** on **List Matching Files**. The File Search Results dialog box will appear.

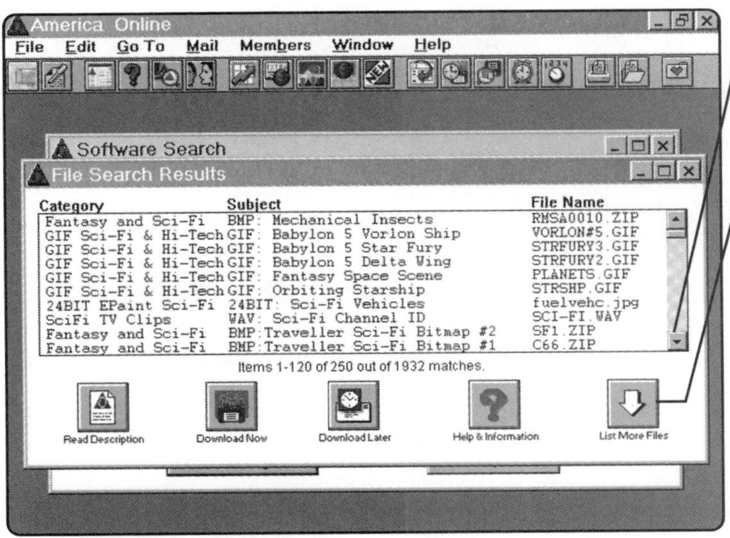

6. **Click repeatedly** on the ▼ to scroll down the list of graphic files.

7. **Click** on the **List More Files icon** to access more files.

8. **Repeat steps 7 and 8** until you find a file you like.

Note: Your screen will differ from the one shown here and the one on the next page simply because the list of uploaded files changes daily.

Reading a Description

You can't always tell whether a graphic is something you want to download unless you read the description first. If the description section also has a thumbnail view, it's even easier to decide whether or not to download it.

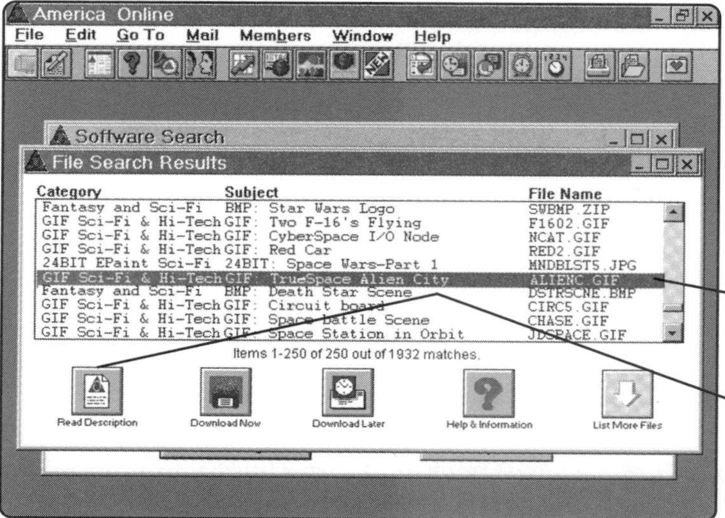

1. **Click** on the **name** of the graphic to highlight it.

2. **Click** on **Read Description**. A dialog box will appear with the name of the graphic in the title bar.

Notice that this dialog box contains a thumbnail view of the graphic. Not all graphics will offer this feature.

Notice also that the description says you need a GIF Viewer. Don't worry, AOL includes a GIF viewer.

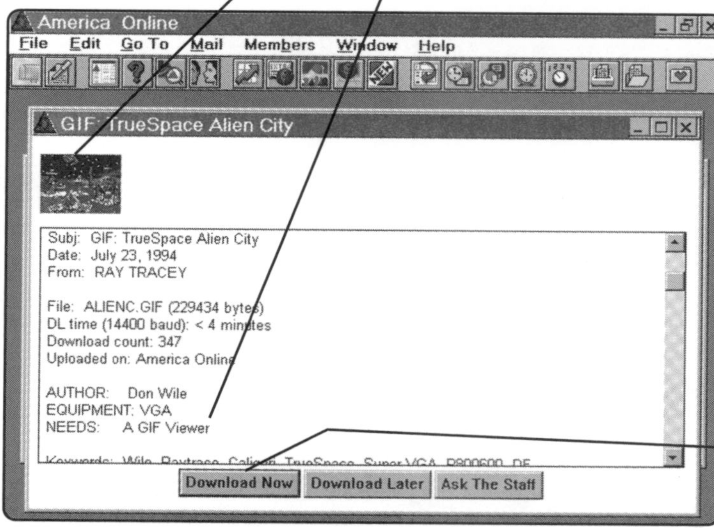

3. **Click repeatedly** on the ▼ to scroll down the file to read all of the description.

DOWNLOADING A FILE

In this section, you'll download a file and view it at the same time.

1. **Click** on **Download Now**. The Download Manager dialog box will appear.

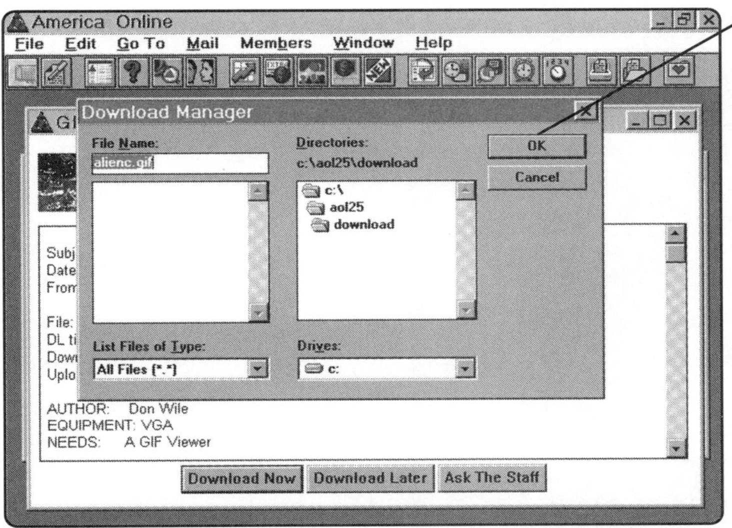

2. **Click** on **OK**. The Image Transfer dialog box will appear and a full-size view of the graphic will appear shortly thereafter (in stages, a little at a time).

3. **Click** on the **File Transfer title bar** to bring it to the front, if necessary. The moving bar shows the rate of transfer.

❖ You can delay the download until later by clicking on Finish Later.

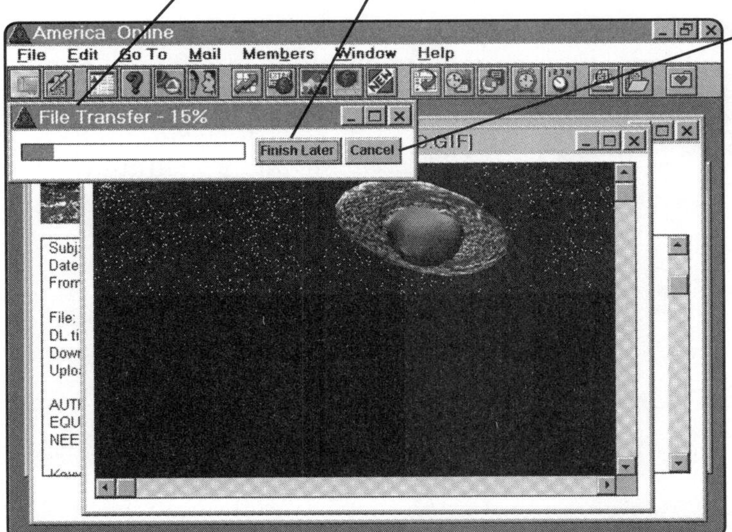

❖ You can stop the download by clicking on Cancel at any time until just before the process is completed.

SIGNING OFF AFTER TRANSFER

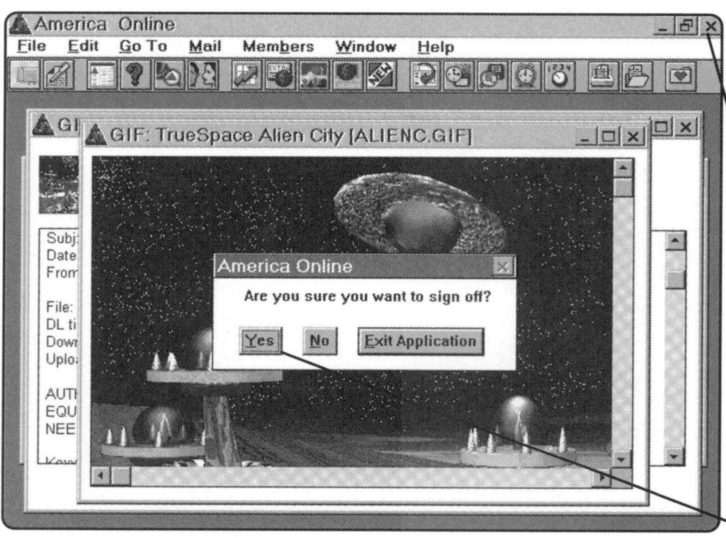

In the next section you will view a graphic file offline. So, let's sign off now.

1. **Click** on the**Close box** (☒) in the right corner of the America Online title bar, or, if you're using Windows 3.1, click twice on the Control menu box in the left corner of the title bar to exit AOL. An America Online dialog box will appear.

2. **Click** on **Yes**. The Goodbye from America Online dialog box will appear.

VIEWING A GRAPHIC OFFLINE

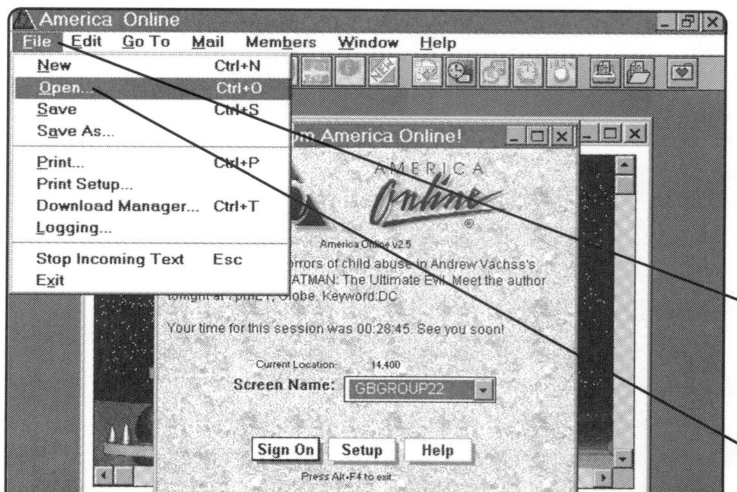

With just a few clicks of the mouse you can view almost any type of graphic file offline using AOL's software. We tested the process with *bmp, pcx, jpeg, gif, tiff,* and *wmf* graphic files. We were able read them all except *wmf* files.

1. **Click** on **File** in the menu bar. A pull-down menu will appear.

2. **Click** on **Open**. The Open a file dialog box will appear.

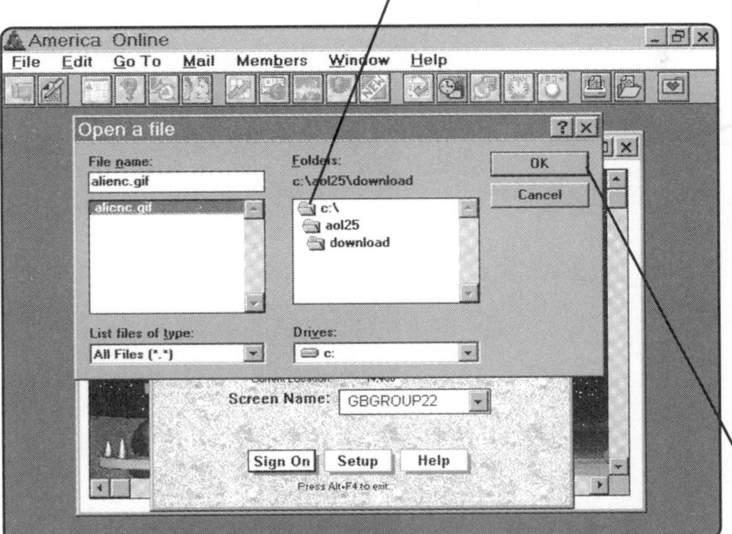

3. **Click twice** on **c:** to bring up a list of files located on the c drive.

4. **Scroll** to the **directory** where the graphic file you downloaded is located, then **click twice** on the **directory name** to open it.

5. **Click twice** on the **name** of the graphic file you want to view. It will move to the File Name text box.

6. **Click** on **OK**.

❖ Voilà! The file will open as easy as pie.

CLOSING AOL

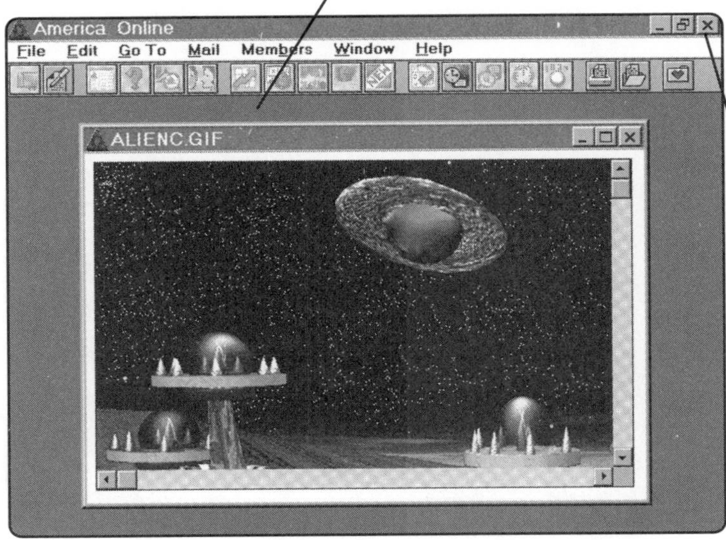

You may want to view some of your clip art and scanned images before closing AOL.

1. **Click** on the **Close box** (☒) in the right corner of the AOL title bar, or, if you're using Windows 3.1, click twice on the Control menu box in the left corner of the title bar. AOL will close.

PART V: INFORMATION CENTRAL

CHAPTER

CHAPTER 18

Getting Online Help with Research and Homework

AOL's Reference Desk is a collection of services and databases that contain information on a huge spectrum of topics. Magazines, newspapers, and electronic libraries are available 24 hours a day as invaluable resources for any school paper or research project. You can also join chat rooms and forums with real live teachers for instant assistance. In this chapter, you will do the following:

- ✔ Search Compton's Encyclopedia
- ✔ Search AskEric
- ✔ Get expert guidance with Reference Help
- ✔ Use the Teacher Pager Service
- ✔ Sign up for individual instruction

OPENING THE REFERENCE DESK

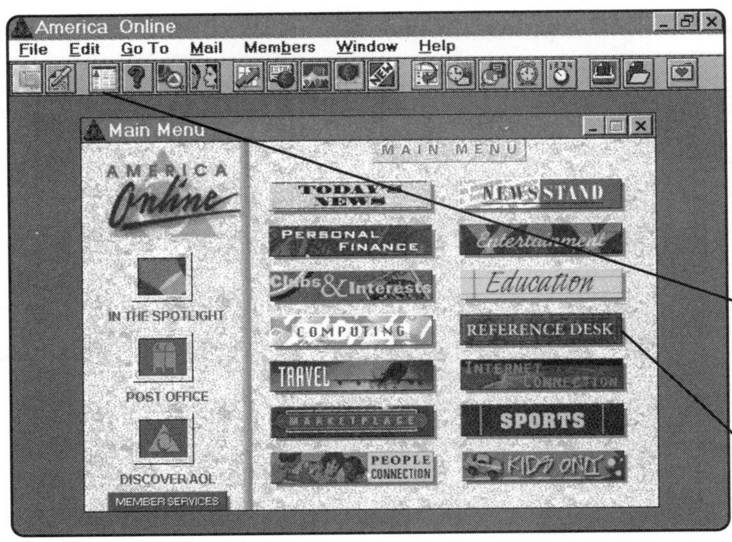

The Reference Desk gives you easy access to a variety of searchable databases.

1. **Sign** on to **America Online** if you haven't already done so.

2. **Click** on the **Main Menu icon**. The Main Menu will appear.

3. **Click** on **Reference Desk**. The Reference Desk window will appear.

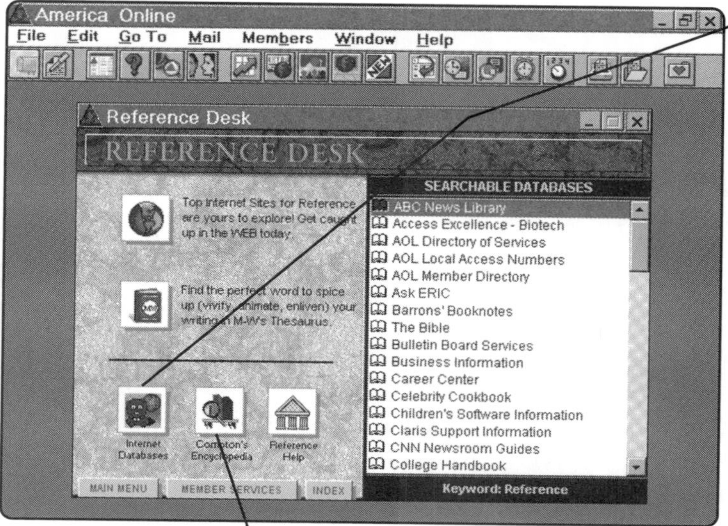

Notice the Internet Databases icon. See Chapter 21 for an introduction to the Internet gateway. Gopher & WAIS are covered in step-by-step detail in our book, "Internet for Windows: The America Online Edition." Access to the Internet expands the capabilities of America Online exponentially. It's worth checking out.

SEARCHING COMPTON'S ENCYCLOPEDIA

1. **Click** on the **Compton's Encyclopedia icon**. The Compton's Encyclopedia window will appear. If you have not visited Compton's Encyclopedia before, you will be prompted to download the art for this area at no charge. We recommend that you follow the instructions on the screen to do so at this time.

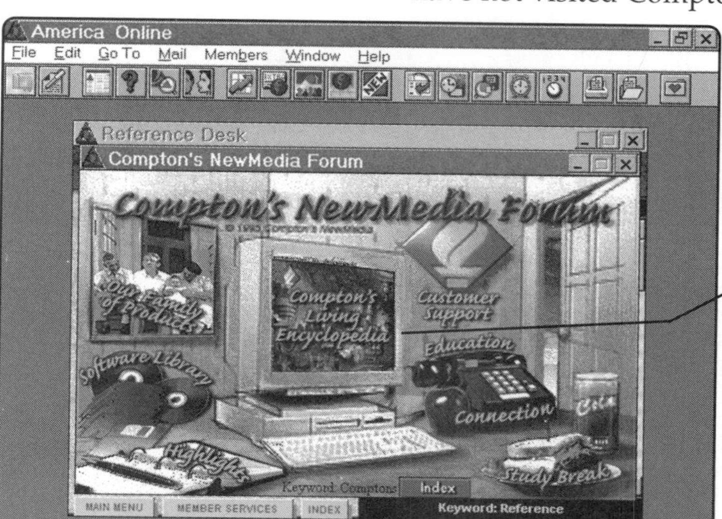

2. **Click** on **Compton's Living Encyclopedia**. The Compton's Living Encyclopedia dialog box will appear.

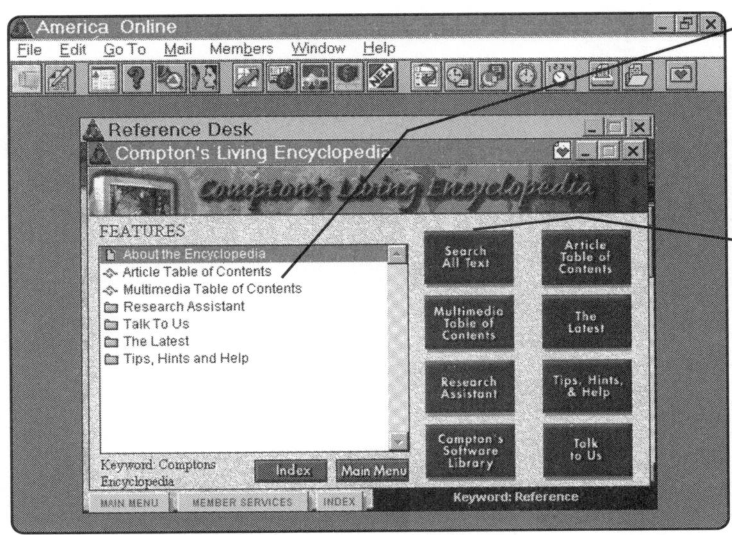

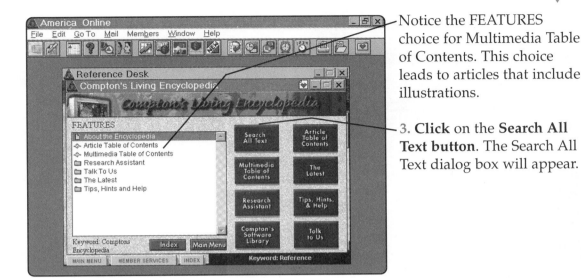

Notice the FEATURES choice for Multimedia Table of Contents. This choice leads to articles that include illustrations.

3. **Click** on the **Search All Text button**. The Search All Text dialog box will appear.

4. **Type** the **word(s)** that describe your research topic. In this example it's "academic excellence."

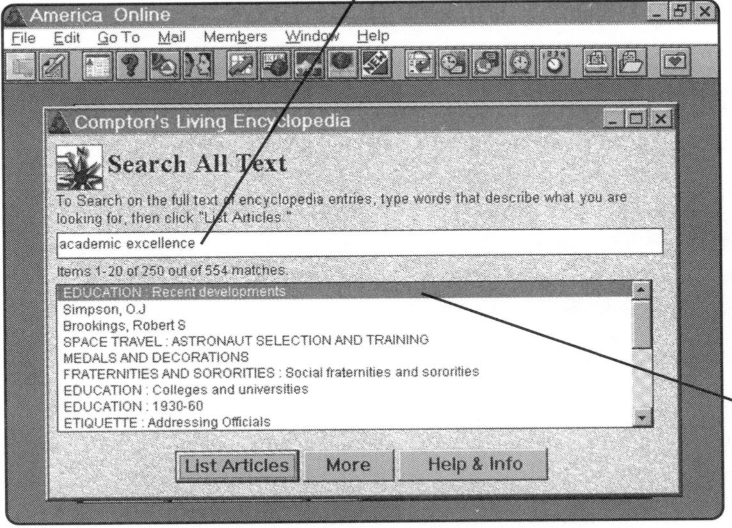

5. **Click** on the **List Articles button**. A list of articles will appear in the lower box.

Although some of the items listed may not appear to be related to your topic, the phrase "academic excellence" occurs somewhere in each article.

6. **Click twice** on any **article** that you want to read. The article will appear, as shown in the example at the top of the next page.

7. When you've read or printed the article, **click** on the **Close box** (☒) (or, in Windows 3.1, click twice on the ☒) of the open dialog boxes until you return to the Compton's Living Encyclopedia dialog box.

Finding Research Pointers

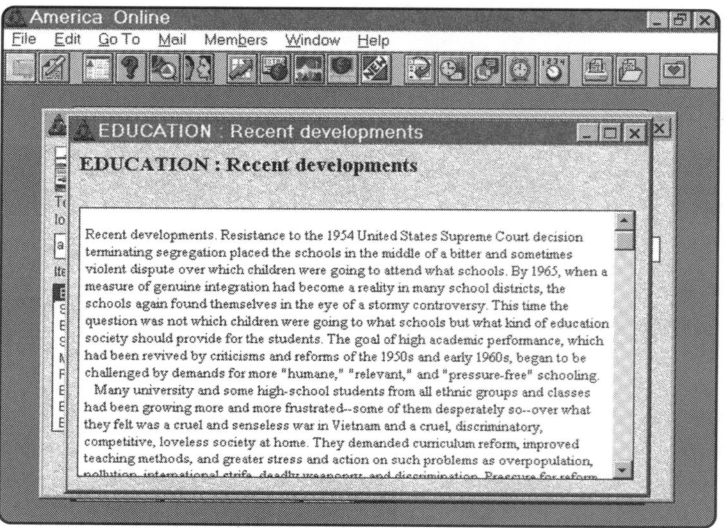

Compton's Forum also contains many good tips on doing research. We'll quickly navigate to an important one.

1. At the Compton's Living Encyclopedia dialog box (not shown here), **click twice** on the FEATURES choice, **"Research Assistant."** The Research Assistant dialog box (not shown here) will appear.

2. In the Research Assistnat dialog box, **click twice** on the choice, **"The Research Process."** The Research Process dialog box (not shown here) will appear.

3. In the Research Process dialog box, **click twice** on the choice, **"Cite Your Research Sources."** The Cite Your Research Sources dialog box will appear.

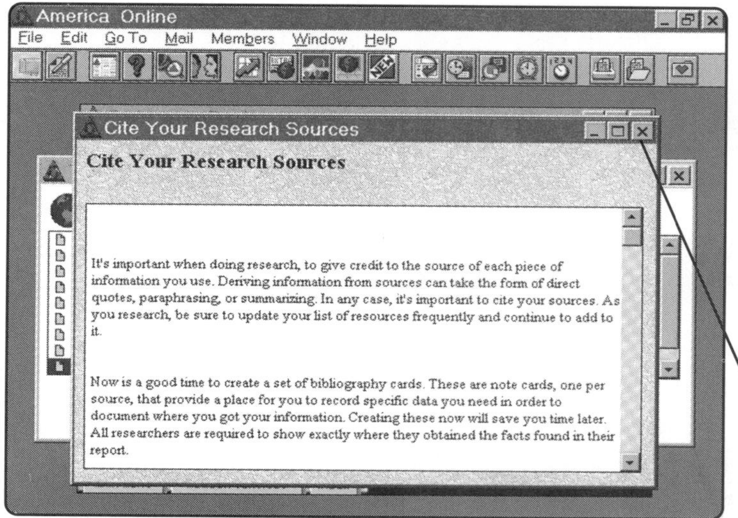

Citing Sources

It's very important to cite the sources for the information that you use.

1. Print or save the **citation information** for use in making your bibliography.

2. Click on the **Close boxes** (☒) of the open dialog boxes to return again to the Reference Desk dialog box.

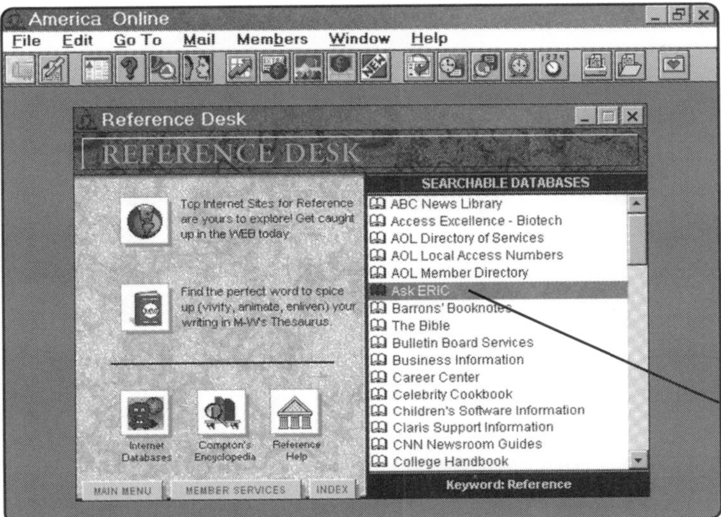

SEARCHING AN ALTERNATIVE SOURCE

In this example, we'll show you how to search for articles not available in a magazine, newspaper, or encyclopedia.

1. **Click twice** on **AskERIC**. The AskEric dialog box will appear.

ERIC (The Educational Resources Information Center) is just one of the many alternative information services available through the Reference Desk. The ERIC system contains a huge range of education-related literature, research summaries, bibliographies, and reference and referral services.

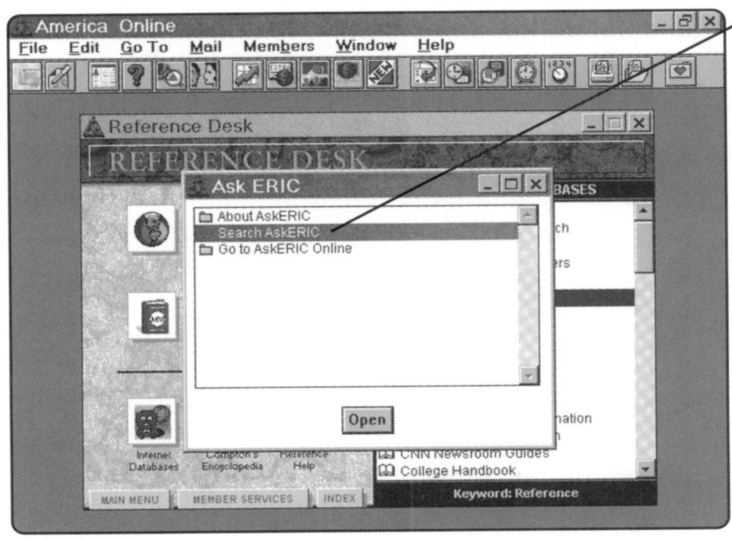

2. **Click twice** on **Search AskERIC**. The Search AskERIC dialog box will appear.

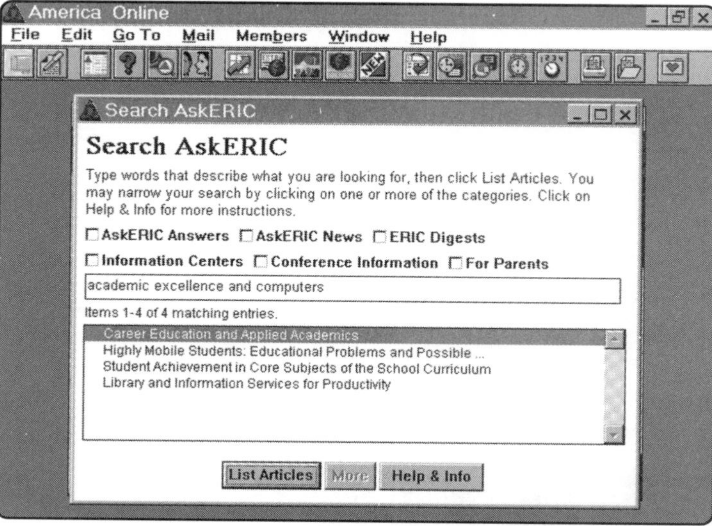

3. **Type** the **keyword(s)** that describe the topic. In this example, it is "academic excellence and computers."

4. **Click** on **List Articles** at the bottom of the Health Forum dialog box. A list of related topics will appear as you see in this example.

5. **Click** on the **Close boxes** ([X]) of all the open dialog boxes to return to the Reference Desk window.

GETTING HELP THROUGH THE ACADEMIC RESEARCH CENTER

The Academic Research Center (ARC) won't do your research for you or upload articles from databases. It will provide you with advice, leads, sources of information, search strategies, individual instruction, and, perhaps, the inspiration to get that paper finished.

1. **Click** on the **Reference Help** icon. The Reference Help dialog box will appear.

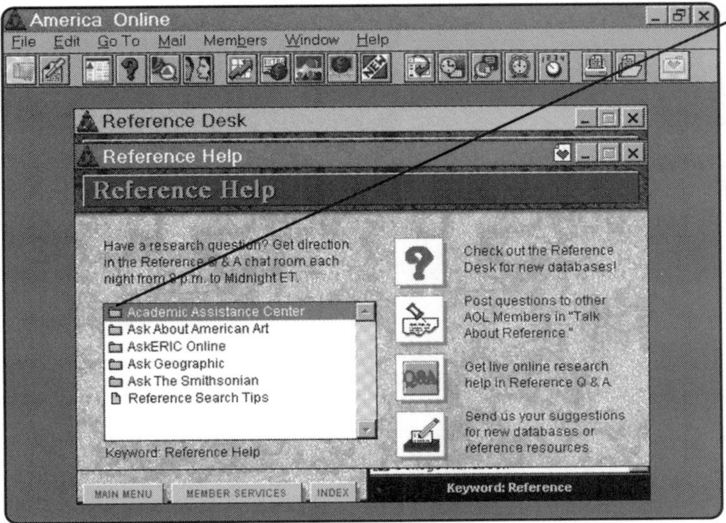

2. **Click twice** on **Academic Assistance Center**. The Academic Assistance Center dialog box will open.

The Academic Assistance Center is a truly wonderful resource for any student of any age. They currently have the largest single remote staff of any online service. And, according to Henry Rosengarten, AAC Coordinator, no question goes unanswered by a true authority in that field of study.

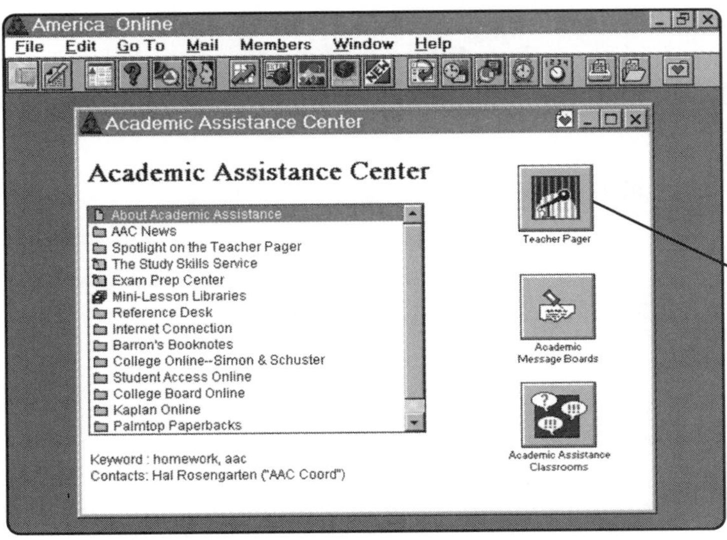

In this example, we'll use the Teacher Pager. The Teacher Pager is an E-mail message that is directed to teachers who specialize in the subject(s) of your topic.

3. **Click** on the **Teacher Pager icon**. The Teacher Pager window will appear.

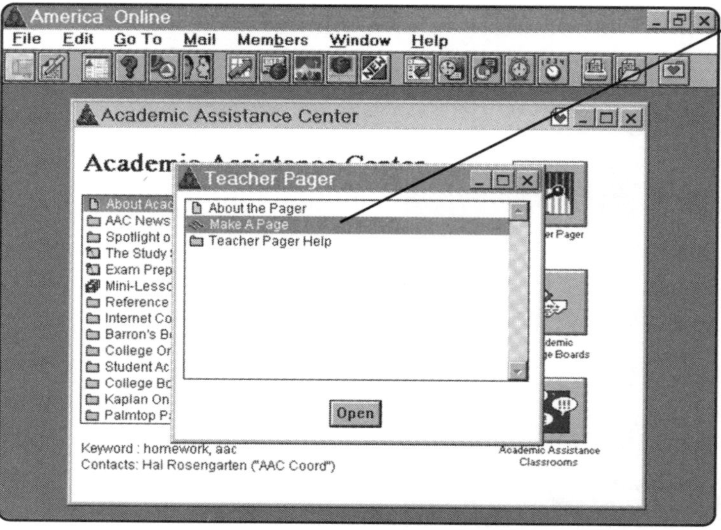

4. **Click twice** on **Make a Page**. The Teacher Pager dialog box will appear.

5. **Type** a **brief description** of your topic, being as specific as possible.

6. **Click** in the **middle box** and **type** your **grade level**.

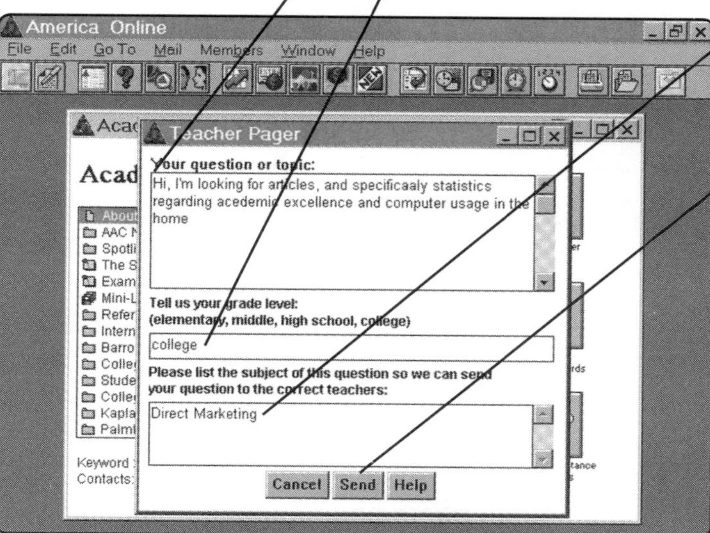

America Online
Teacher Pager
Your question or topic:
Hi, I'm looking for articles, and specificaaly statistics regarding acedemic excellence and computer usage in the home
Tell us your grade level:
(elementary, middle, high school, college)
college
Please list the subject of this question so we can send your question to the correct teachers:
Direct Marketing
Cancel
Send
Help

7. **Click** in the **bottom box** and **type** the general **subject** of your topic.

8. **Click** on **Send**. An AOL dialog box will appear.

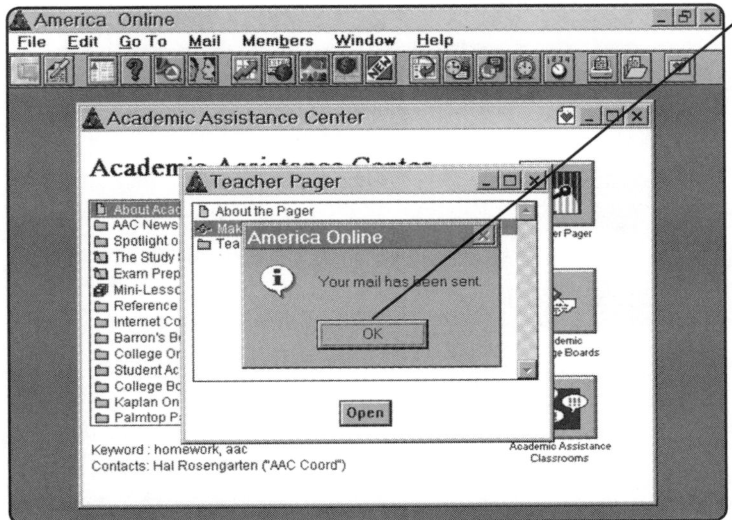

9. **Click** on **OK**. The dialog box will close.

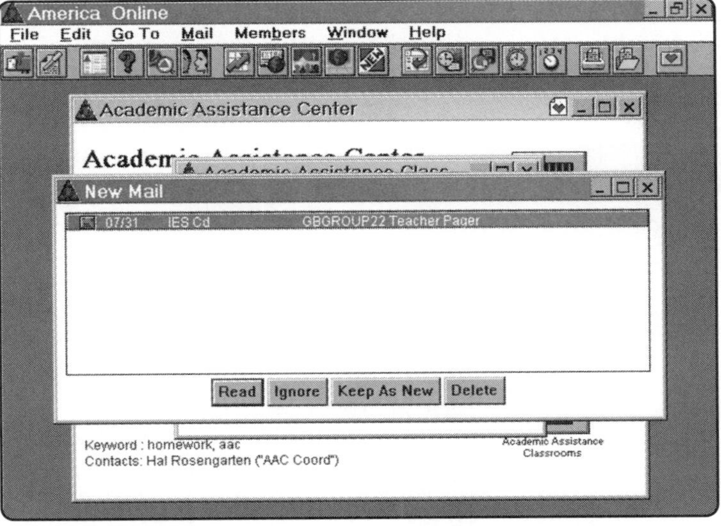

It's entirely possible that you'll receive a reply by e-mail within 2 to 3 minutes. Check your mailbox. In any case, you'll have a reply within 6 to 12 hours.

A Special Note

If you have any trouble posting your message or getting an answer, the AAC Coordinator says you can send e-mail directly to "**AAC Coord**."

GETTING HOMEWORK HELP

There are many different ways to get help in the Academic Assistance Center. Here's another way.

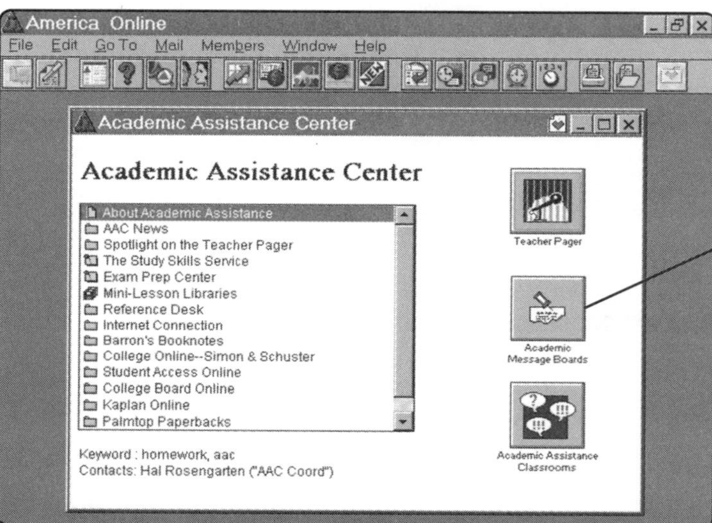

1. **Close** all **open dialog boxes** until you're back at the Academic Assistance Center dialog box you see in this example.
2. **Click** on the **Academic Message Boards icon.** The Academic Message Board dialog box will appear.

Notice the various topics with the stick-pin symbol to the left. These are forums on each of those subjects. See Chapter 13, "Using Forums," for more information about using a forum.

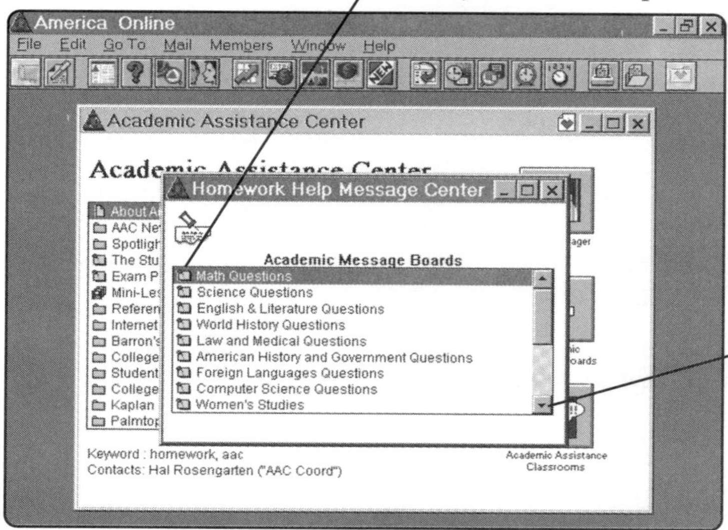

Take a few minutes to explore these forums on your own. You may find the answers to your questions or problems right here.

3. **Click repeatedly** on the ▼ to scroll through to the bottom of the list.

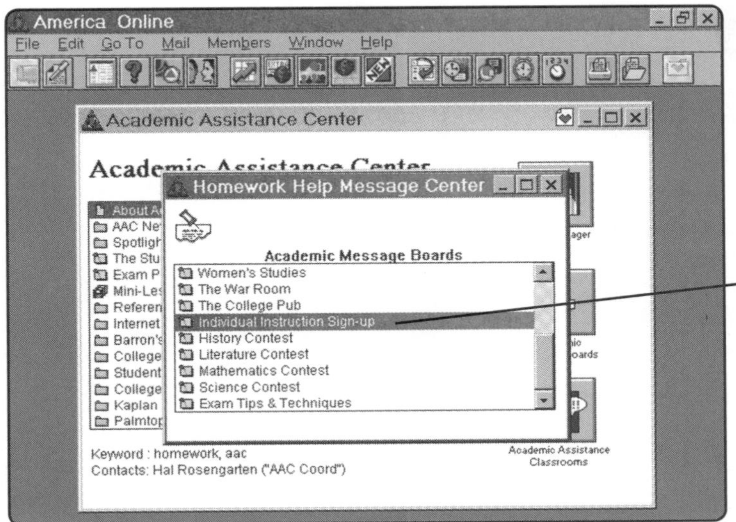

Getting One-On-One Attention

If the forums don't have what you need, you can ask for personal help.

1. **Click twice** on **Individual Instruction Sign-Up**. The Individual Instruction Sign-Up dialog box will appear.

This service is also in a forum format.

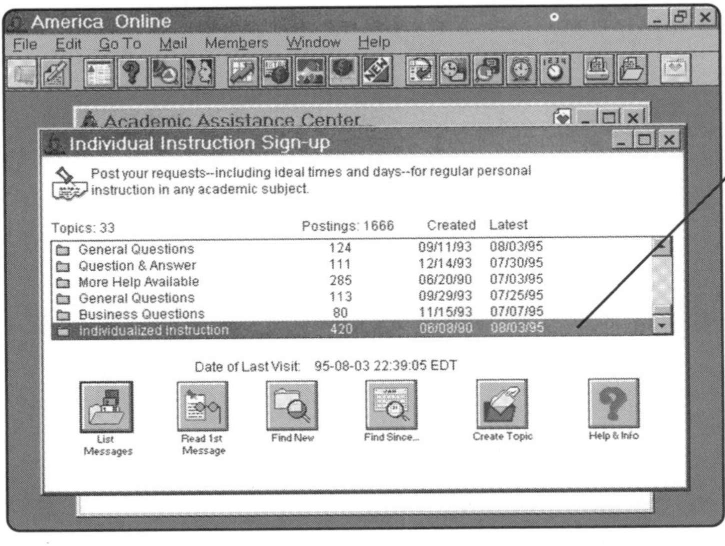

2. **Click repeatedly** on the ▼ to **scroll** to the bottom of the list.

3. **Click twice** on **Individualized Instruction**. The Individualized Instruction forum dialog box will appear.

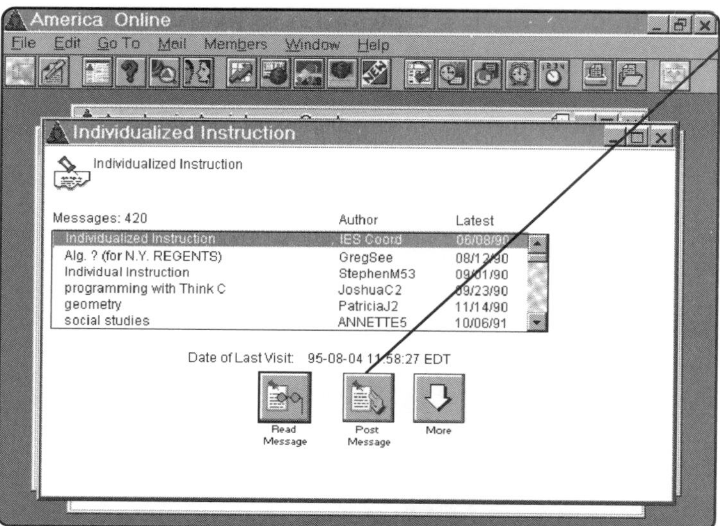

4. **Click on Post Message**. The Add A Message dialog box will appear.

5. **Type** a **brief description** of your topic, being as specific as possible.

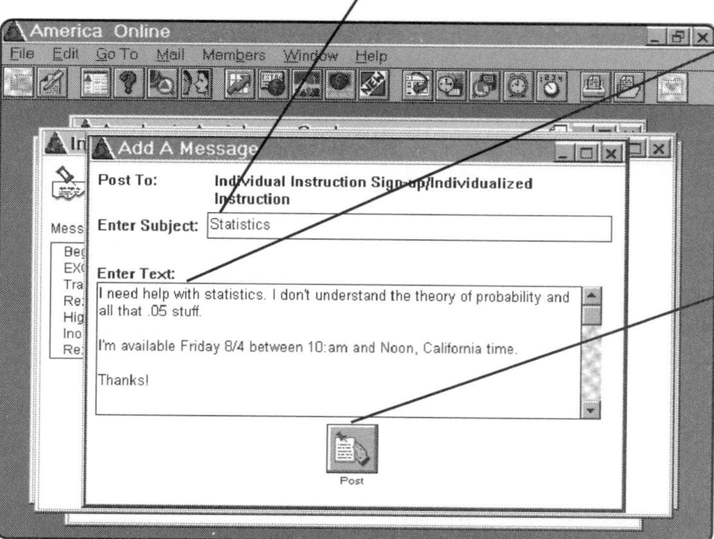

6. **Click** in the **bottom box** and **type** the general **subject** of your topic or question and a convenient time when an instructor can meet with you.

7. **Click** on **Post**. An AOL dialog box will appear.

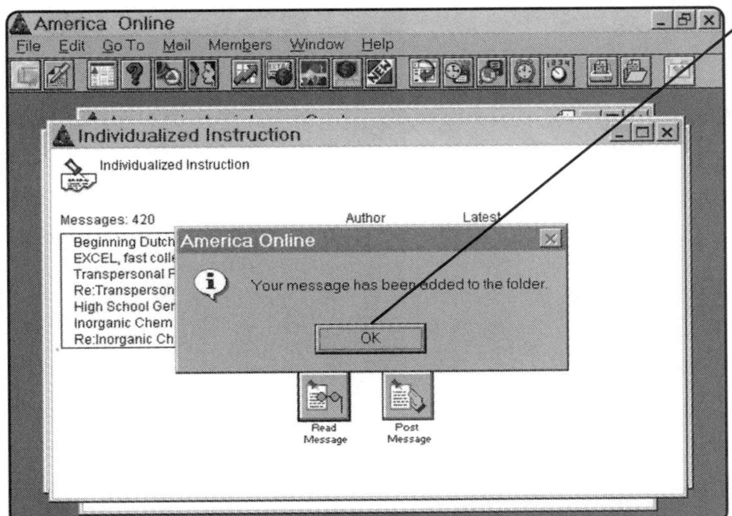

8. **Click** on **OK**. The dialog box will close.

What Happens Now?

The Homework Help Message Center Boards are cleaned out four times a day, and members of the 900+ professional teaching staff browse through several times hourly to see if there are new postings that need answers.

Stay online for a few minutes. You don't have to stay in the Academic Message board, you can do other things in AOL. Then check your e-mail. If you don't have a message right away, you will definitely have one within 6 to 12 hours.

Finding a College or a College Course

Choosing the right college and figuring out how to pay for it can be a daunting task. AOL's Education Center can help. You can also take an impressive array of courses online, for credit or purely for self-enhancement. In this chapter, you will do the following:

✔ Search for a college and get information on financial aid
✔ Investigate online college courses

GOING TO THE EDUCATION CENTER

Opening the door to The Education Center is like opening the door to Aladdin's cave of treasures. We can only introduce you to the incredible array of services available through this center. Once there, explore to your heart's content. A wealth of information is a mouse-click away.

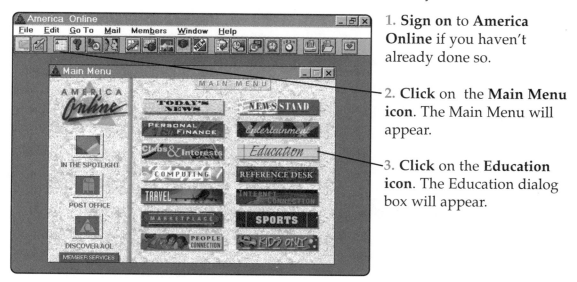

1. **Sign on** to **America Online** if you haven't already done so.

2. **Click** on the **Main Menu icon**. The Main Menu will appear.

3. **Click** on the **Education icon**. The Education dialog box will appear.

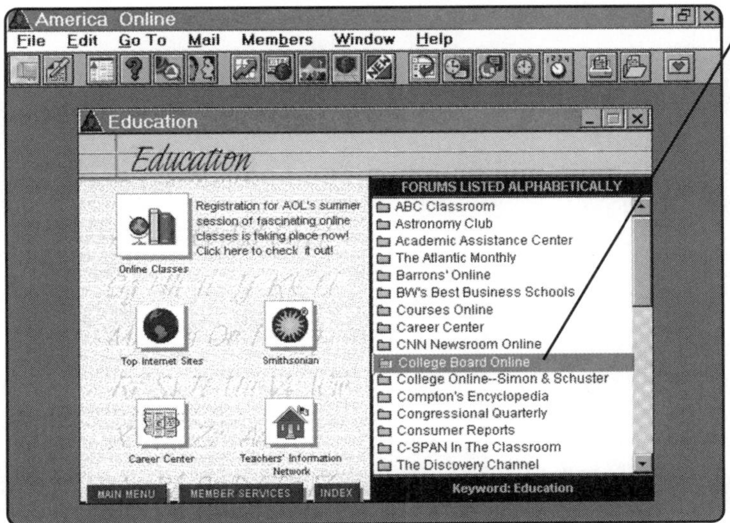

4. **Click twice** on **College Board Online** in the Forums list. The College Board dialog box will appear.

GETTING TIPS ON CHOOSING A COLLEGE

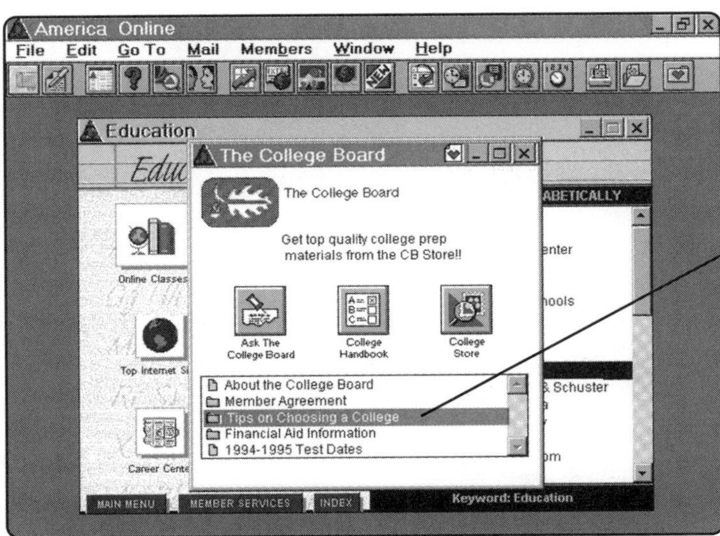

The College Board dialog box gives you access to a wealth of information. This section will introduce you to Tips on Choosing a College.

1. **Click twice** on **Tips on Choosing a College**. The Tips on Choosing a College dialog box will appear.

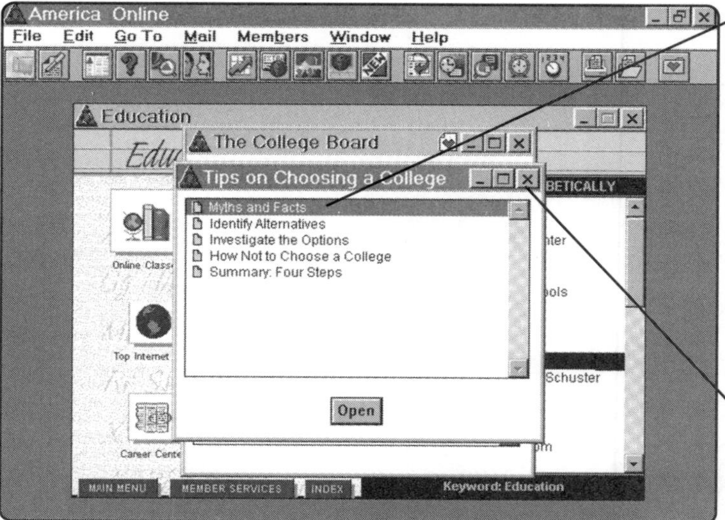

2. **Click twice** on **Myths and Facts**. The document will appear. You can read it now, or print or save it using the steps for printing and saving files that we've shown in earlier chapters. It will be worth your while to look at each document in this list.

3. **Click on** the **Close button** (x) in the right corner of the Tips on Choosing a College title bar, or, if you're using Windows 3.1, click twice on the Control menu box in the left corner of the title bar to close this dialog box and return to The College Board dialog box. We will give only the Windows 95 step for closing dialog boxes in the rest of the chapter.

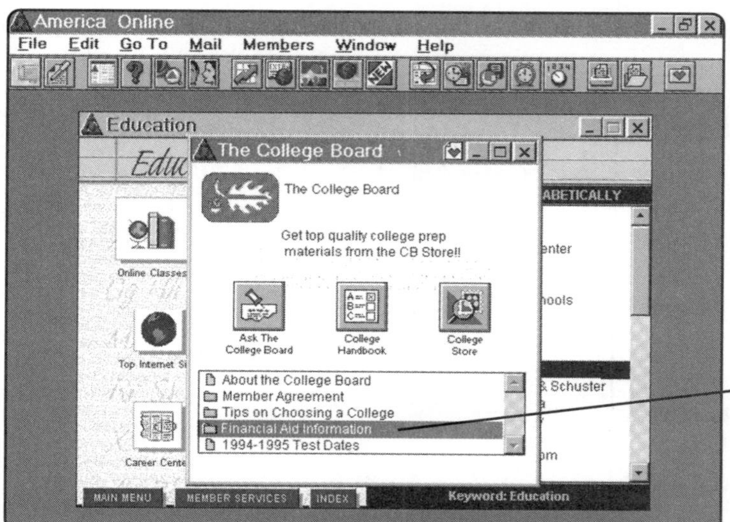

GETTING FINANCIAL AID INFORMATION

The College Board dialog box contains useful information about financial aid.

1. **Click twice** on **Financial Aid Information**. The Financial Aid Information dialog box will appear.

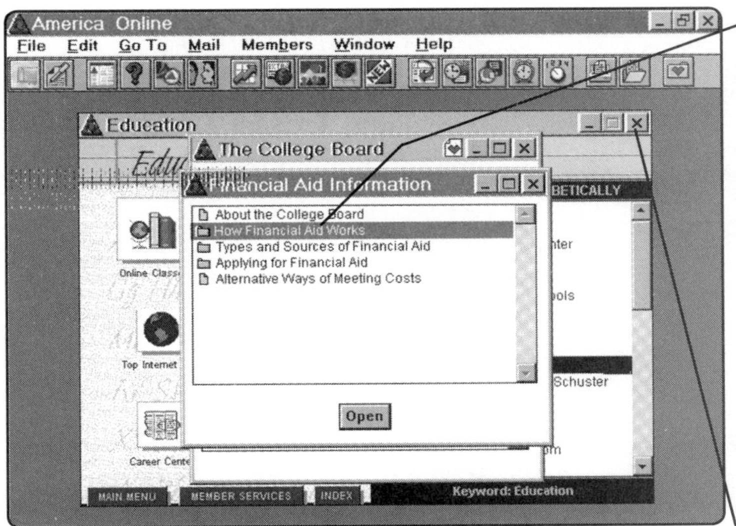

2. **Click twice** on **How Financial Aid Works**. A dialog box will appear with additional choices. Click twice on any of the choices in this new dialog box to open and read, print, or save it, just as we did in the last section.

3. **Repeat step 2** with each of the selections in the Financial Aid Information dialog box.

4. **Click on** the **Close button** (X) in the right corner of the title bar to close open dialog boxes until you're back at the College Board dialog box that you see in the next example.

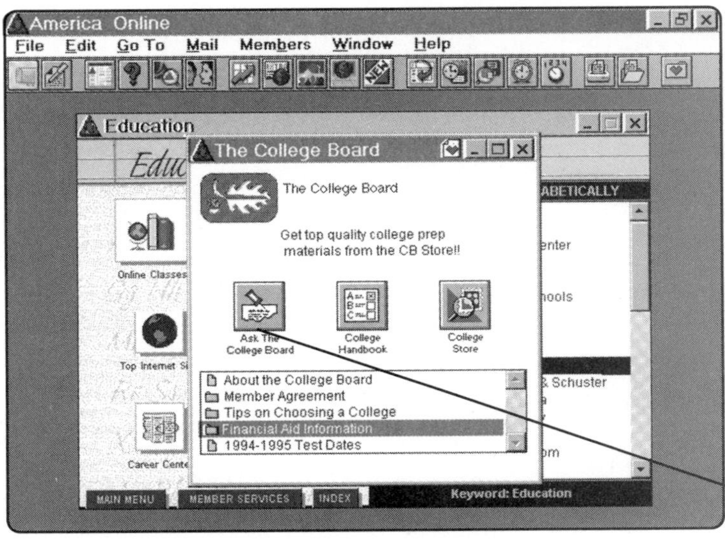

Reading Bulletin Board Messages on College Admissions and Financial Aid

You can post questions and read comments from other AOL members in a bulletin board devoted exclusively to this issue.

1. **Click** on **Ask the College Board**. The Ask the College Board dialog box will appear.

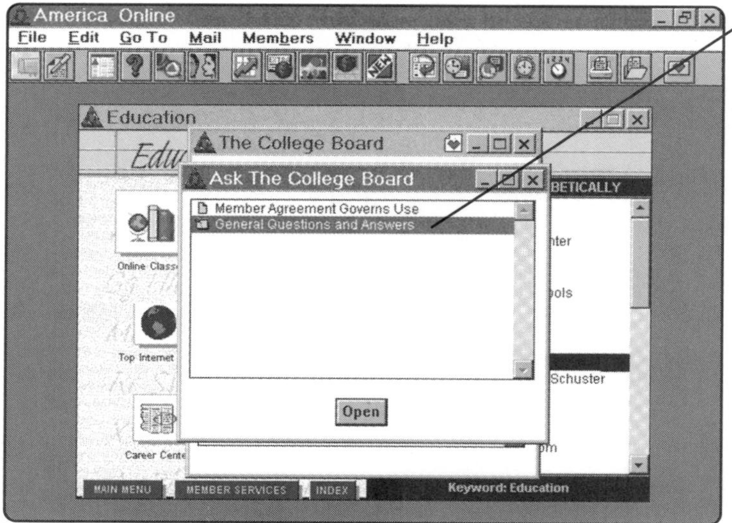

2. **Click twice** on **General Questions and Answers**. The icon that looks like a board with a stick-pin indicates that this choice will bring up a bulletin board.

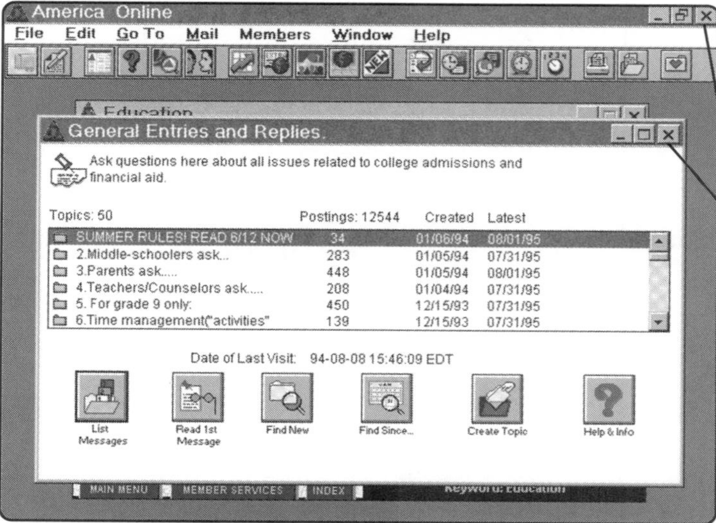

3. **See** Chapter 13, "Using Forums," for step-by-step directions on participating in bulletin board discussions.

4. When you're through exploring this bulletin board, **click** on the **Close buttons** (☒) in the right corners of the title bars to close all open dialog boxes until you're back at the College Board dialog box that you see in the next example.

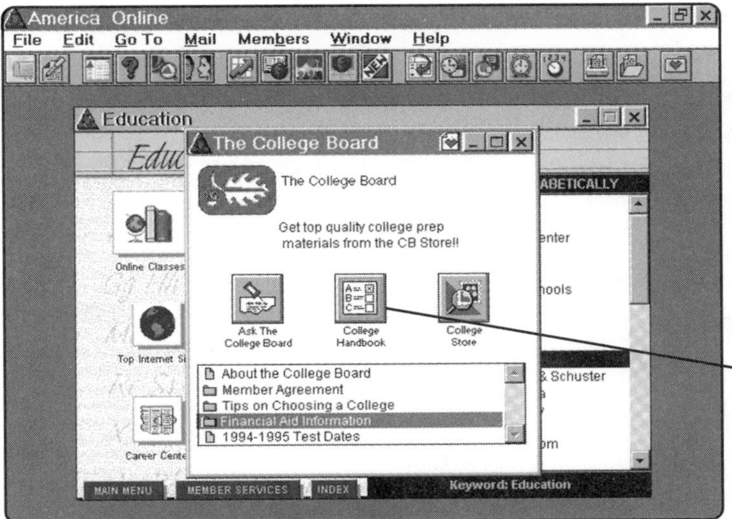

SEARCHING FOR A COLLEGE

AOL has 3,100 colleges and universities in its database. You can search this database to find just the right college for you.

1. **Click** on **College Handbook**. The College Handbook dialog box will appear.

Getting a List of Colleges that Match Your Criteria

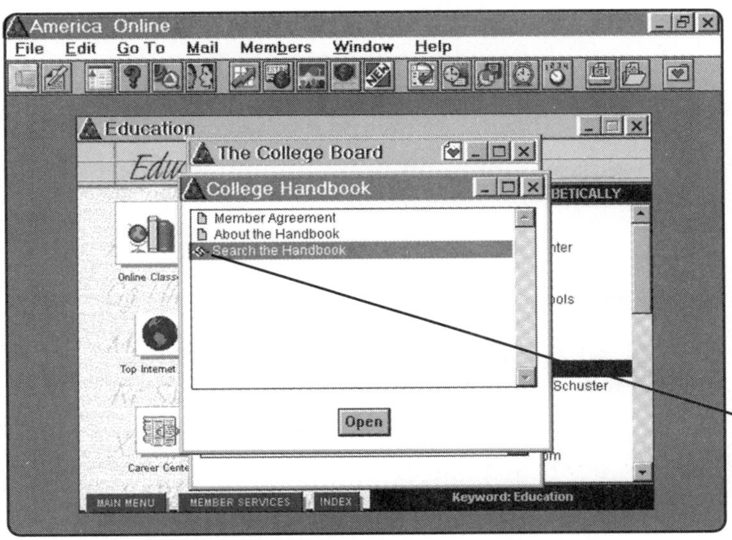

You can use a number of criteria for your college search. For example, you can search for colleges that offer a specific major or are in a particular geographic area. You can even list several criteria in the same search as you'll see in this example.

1. **Click twice** on **Search the Handbook.** The College Board (College Handbook Search) dialog box will appear.

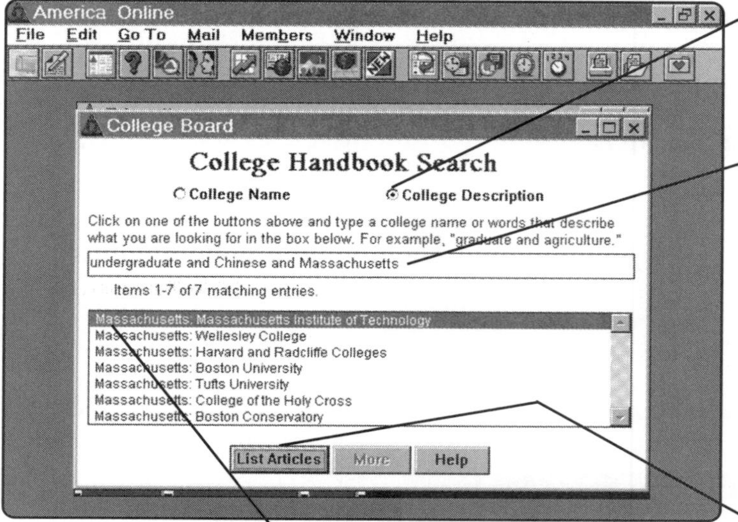

2. **Click** on **College Description** to place a dot in the circle, if necessary.

3. **Click** in the **text box** to place the cursor.

4. **Type** the **word or words** that best describe your interests. In this example, we'll search for undergraduate Chinese programs in Massachusetts.

5. **Click** on **List Articles**. As you see in this example, a list of colleges that match your criteria will appear. Notice that this search identified seven colleges that meet these criteria.

6. **Click twice** on a **school** that interests you. A dialog box containing a description will appear.

7. When you're through searching the College Handbook, **close** all of the open **dialog boxes** until you are back at the College Handbook dialog box that you see in the next example.

TAKING ONLINE SELF-ENRICHMENT COURSES

AOL offers a terrific feature called Interactive Education Services. IES provides online self-enrichment courses on an impressive variety of academic and professional topics. The courses are typically eight weeks long and, although they are not for credit, the courses are taught by top-level professionals from around the country.

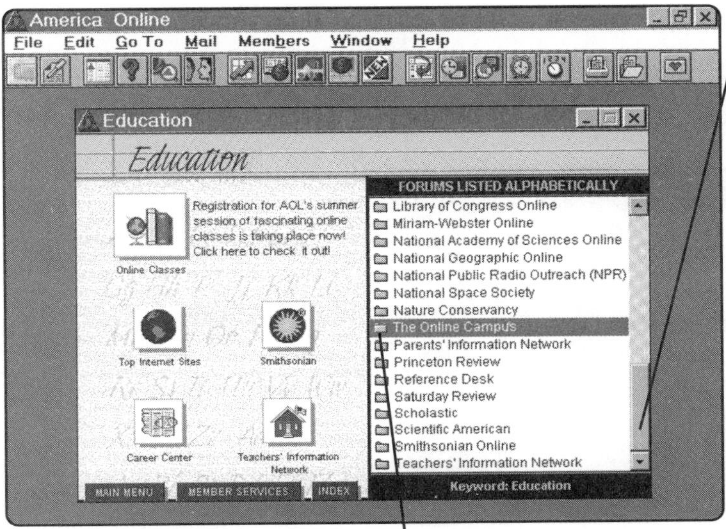

1. **Position** the **mouse arrow** over the scroll box.

2. **Press and hold** the **mouse button** as you **drag** the **scroll button** to the bottom of the bar.

3. **Click twice** on **The Online Campus (IES, EUN, ICS)**. The Interactive Education Services dialog box will appear.

You'll probably want to explore the options in this dialog box more fully on your own. In this example, we'll look at the Professional Studies Department.

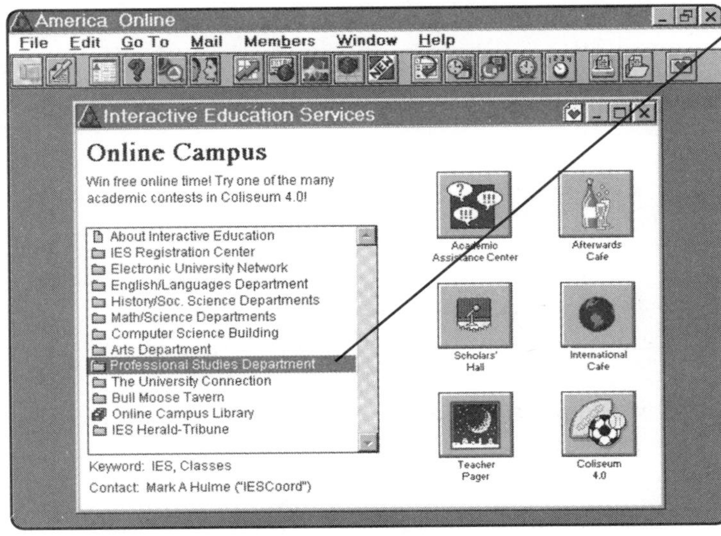

4. **Click twice** on **Professional Studies Department**. The Professional Studies Department dialog box, listing numerous professional topics, will appear.

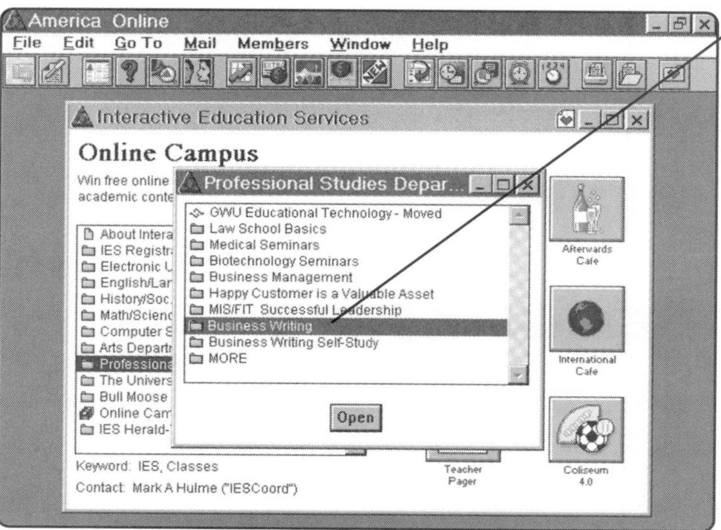

5. **Click twice** on **Business Writing**. A dialog box will appear.

6. **Click twice** on the **Course Description** to see details about the course.

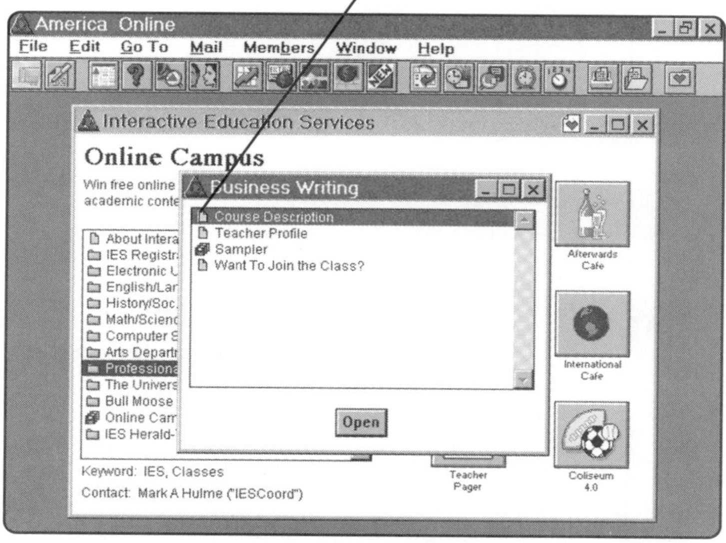

This is just one example of the many excellent courses offered through this service. You should also consider exploring the other choices in this dialog box.

7. When you're through, **close** this **dialog box** and go back to the Interactive Education Services dialog box to see how to register for online courses.

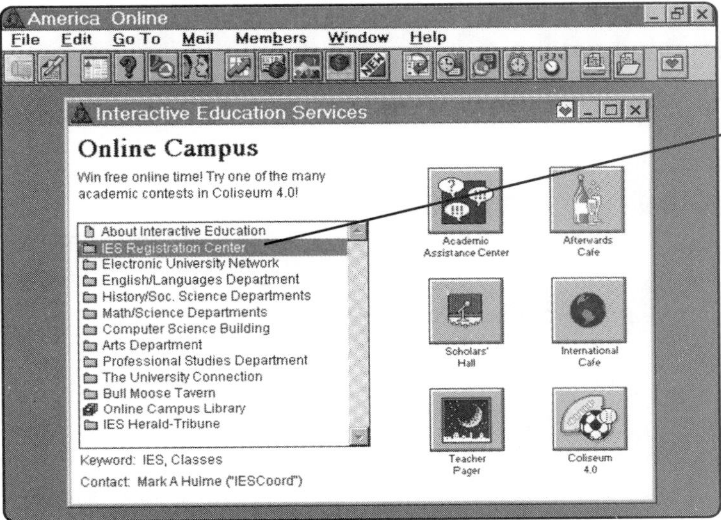

Registering for an Online Course

1. **Click twice** on **IES Registration Center**. A dialog box listing additional information about registering will appear. You can also find information about regular college courses in that dialog box. Return to the Interactive Education Services dialog box when you're done.

TAKING ONLINE COLLEGE COURSES FOR CREDIT

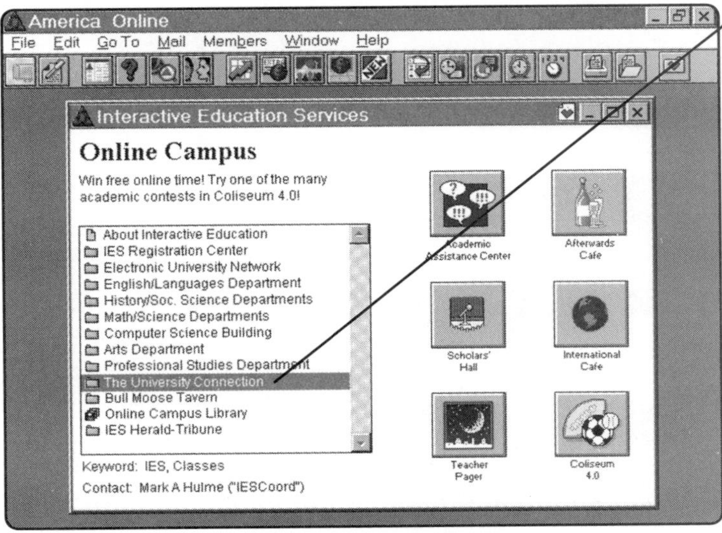

1. **Click twice** on **The University Connection** to see information about colleges and universities that offer online courses for credit. Explore the resources you find there as we have in the sections before this.

Opportunities abound on AOL to learn something new, or to learn more about something you're already familiar with. Remember that your mind needs exercise to keep it fit and healthy, just like your body does.

CHAPTER

20

Finding a Job Online

The Career Center offers a tremendous range of resources and services for a successful job search. Not only are there three job-listing databases, but you can schedule a private career guidance counseling session, search a library for information relevant to your particular career, or explore new career directions. In this chapter, you will do the following:

✔ View the Job Listings Databases
✔ Explore the Employer Contact Database
✔ Review resume styles
✔ Upload your resume to the Resume Library

ENTERING THE CAREER CENTER

1. **Open** and **sign on** to **America Online**, if you haven't already done so.

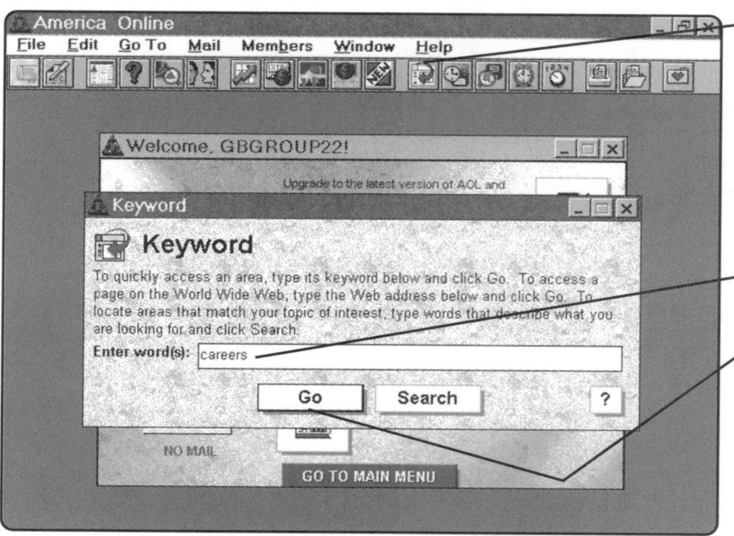

America Online
File Edit Go To Mail Members Window Help
Welcome, GBGROUP22!
Keyword
Keyword
To quickly access an area, type its keyword below and click Go. To access a page on the World Wide Web, type the Web address below and click Go. To locate areas that match your topic of interest, type words that describe what you are looking for and click Search.
Enter word(s): careers
Go
Search
?
NO MAIL
GO TO MAIN MENU

2. **Click** on the **Keyword** icon in the tool bar. It's the eighth icon from the right. The Keyword dialog box will appear, as you see in this example.

3. **Type careers**.

4. **Click** on **Go**. The Career Center dialog box will appear.

READING THE JOB LISTINGS

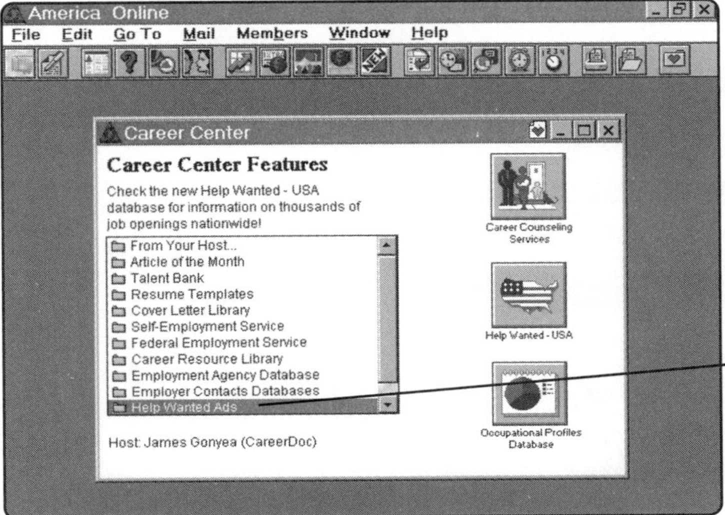

You can access three different databases, listing more than 4,000 jobs nationwide, through the Career Center.

1. **Click twice** on **Help Wanted Ads**. The Help Wanted Ads dialog box will appear.

Notice the action symbol (⟡) and the open-book icon (🕮) beside two of the items in the list. These indicate that you can do a database search when you click on them. The Search Help Wanted-USA and the Search E-Span listings contain thousands of positions that you won't find in traditional help-wanted publications. Notice also the "Go to Classifieds Area," the next-to-last item on the list. The Classifieds contain ads that other AOL members have posted.

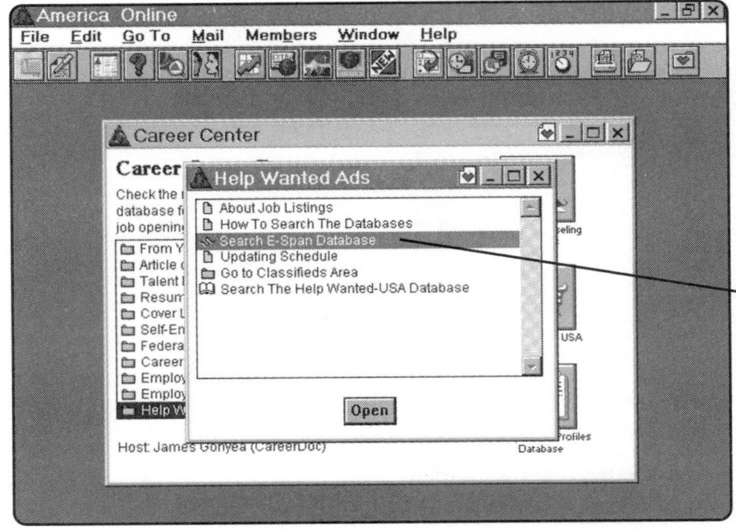

In this example, we'll search E-Span.

2. **Click twice** on **Search E-Span Database**. A Search the Database dialog box will appear.

3. **Type** the **word(s)** that describe your search parameters. In this example, we are using "programming and CA," to search for computer programming jobs in California.

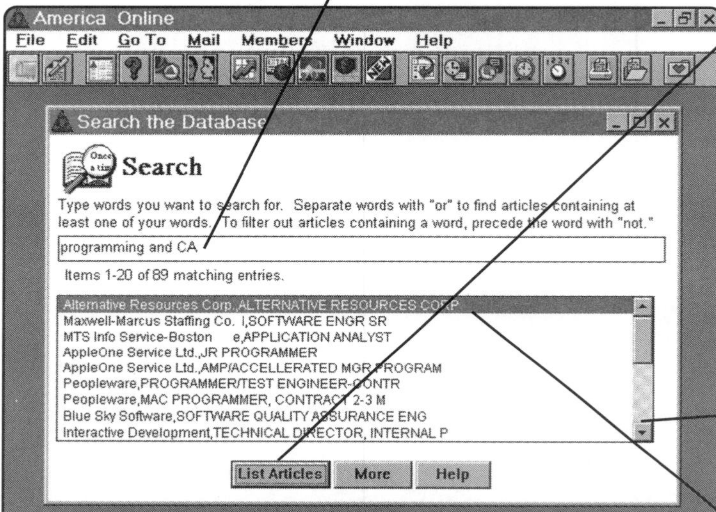

4. **Click** on **List Articles**. A list of articles that fit your parameters will appear.

Notice that this screen shows 20 of 89 entries.

5. **Click repeatedly** on the **More button** until it "greys out" to list all 89 choices.

6. **Click repeatedly** on the ▼ to **scroll** down the list.

7. **Click twice** on any **article** you want to read. The article will open. You can read it now, or print or save it using the steps for printing or saving files that we showed in earlier chapters.

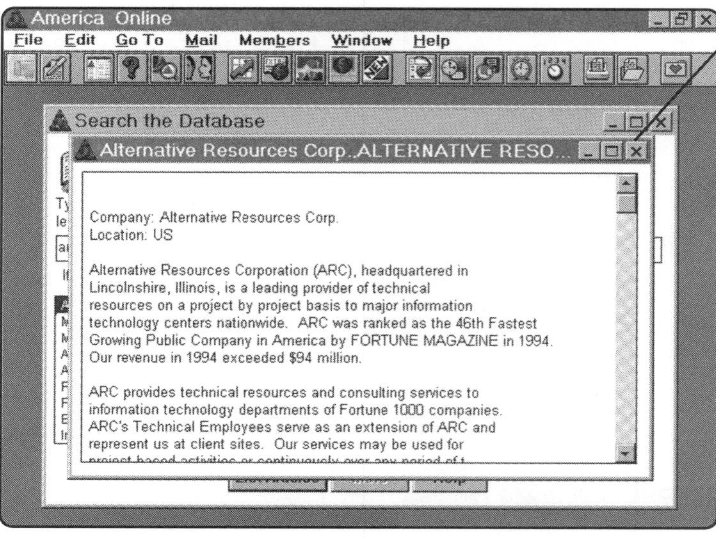

8. **Click** on the **Close buttons** (☒) in the right corners of the title bars, or, if you're using Windows 3.1, click twice on the Control menu boxes in the left corners of the title bars to close all the open dialog boxes and return to the Job Listings Database you see in the example at the top of the next page. We will only give the Windows 95 step for closing dialog boxes in the rest of the chapter.

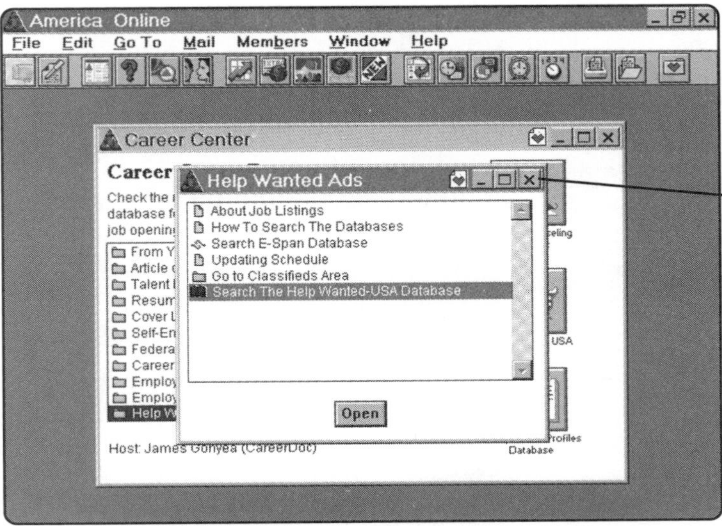

9. **Repeat steps 2-8** to search the Help Wanted-USA database. Also, check out the Classified services.

10. When you're done, **Click** on the **Close button** (X) of the Help Wanted Ads title bar to close the dialog box and return to the Career Center dialog box that you see below.

FINDING EMPLOYER CONTACTS

The Employer Contacts section contains two databases to help you identify and contact the right people at companies that are of interest to you.

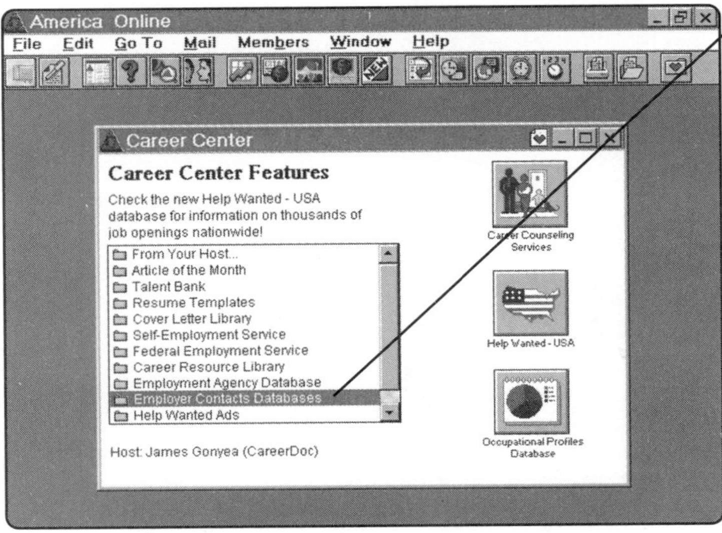

1. **Click twice** on **Employer Contacts Database**. The Employer Contacts Database dialog box will appear.

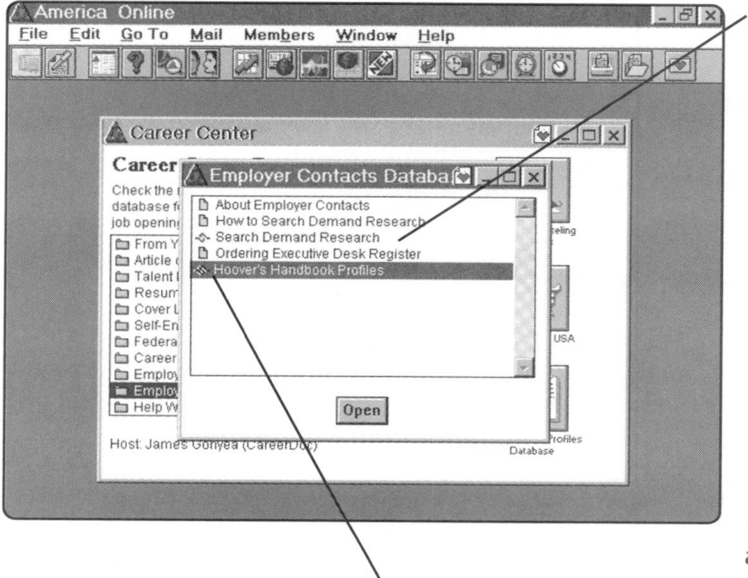

Notice the Search Demand Research choice. This database lists basic information on approximately 5,000 US public companies. It's a good resource that you should search later on your own. In this example, we will access the Hoover's Handbooks Profiles database, which provides an in-depth profile of over 900 of the largest public and private companies in the U.S. and abroad.

2. **Click twice** on **Hoover's Handbook Profiles**. The Hoover's Company Profiles dialog box will appear.

Note that there are three ways to search the Profiles:

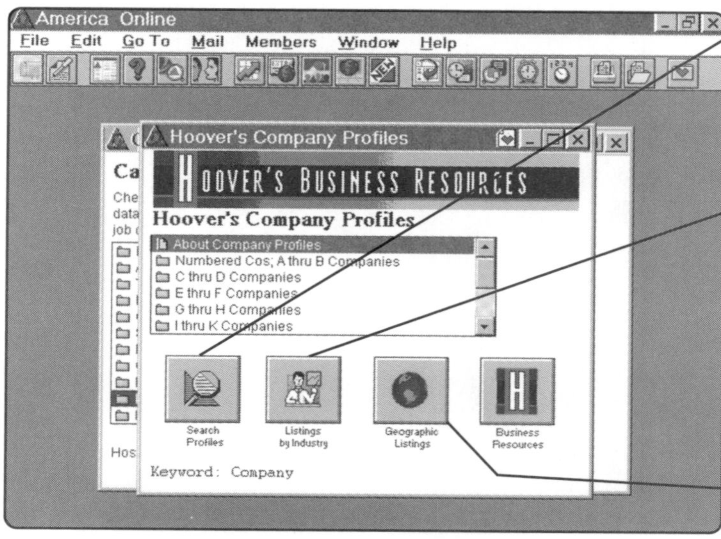

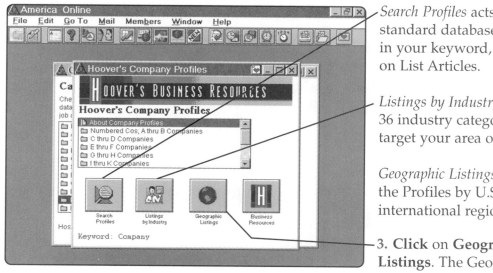

Search Profiles acts like a standard database. Just type in your keyword, then click on List Articles.

Listings by Industry provides 36 industry categories to target your area of interest.

Geographic Listings groups the Profiles by U.S. and international regions.

3. **Click** on **Geographic Listings**. The Geographic Listings dialog box will appear.

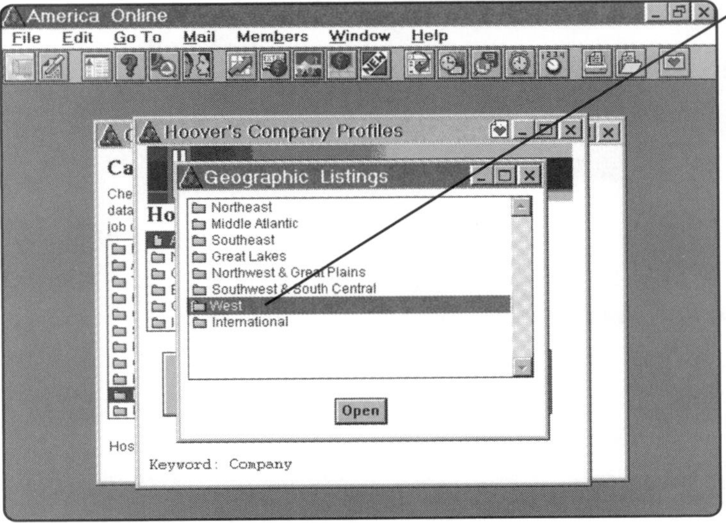

4. **Click twice** on the general **region** you want to explore. In this example, it's West. A dialog box listing states will appear.

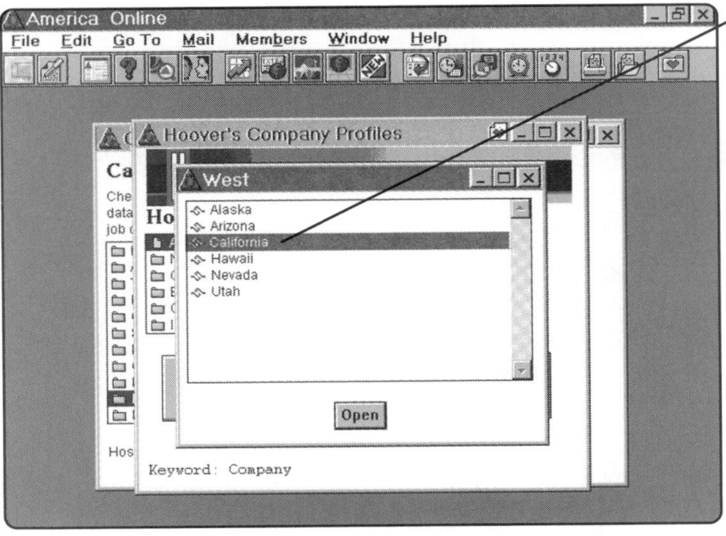

5. **Click twice** on the **state** you want to check. In this example, it's California. A dialog box listing companies will appear.

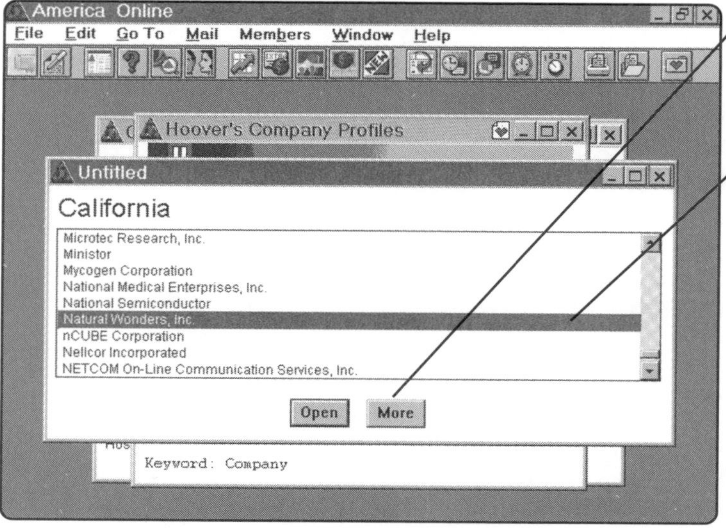

6. **Click repeatedly** on the **More button** until it "greys out" to list all of the choices.

7. **Click twice** on the company **profile** you want to view. The profile will appear on your screen

8. When you've finished reading or printing the profile, **click** on the **Close buttons** (☒) of all the open dialog boxes to return to the Career Center dialog box that you see in the example below.

WORKING ON YOUR RESUME

We don't consider the sample resumes in this section to be outstanding examples. They may, however, give you some ideas for what to include in your resume.

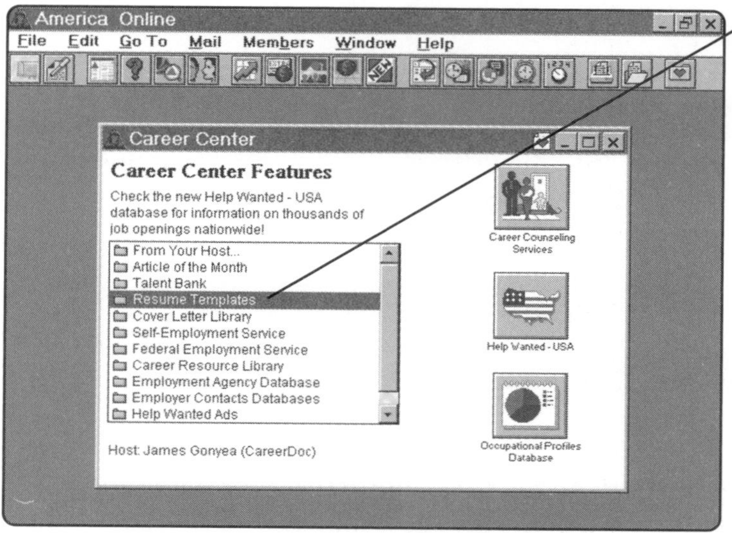

1. **Click twice** on **Resume Templates**. The Resume Template dialog box will appear.

Choosing a Resume Style

Notice the folder icons (🗀) beside four of the items in the list. Each of these folders contains three examples of the most common resume styles.

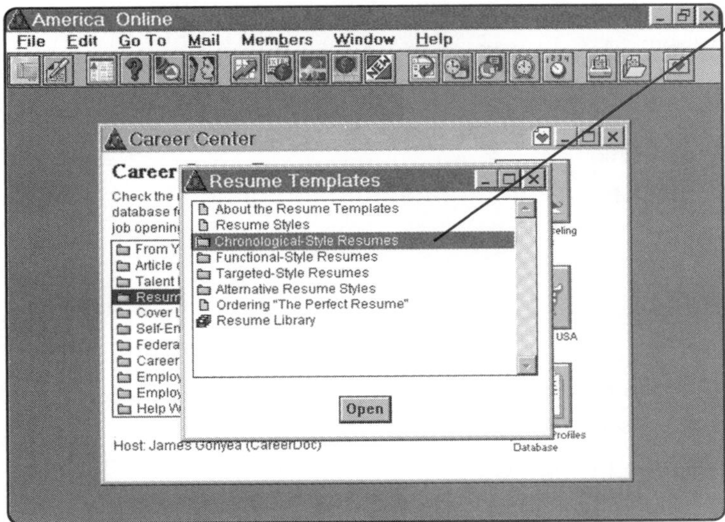

Chronological-Style starts with your most current position and works back in time. It's considered traditional.

Functional-Style emphasizes your areas of expertise and accomplishments.

Targeted-Style uses aspects of both chronological and functional styles and aims your resume at a specific job opportunity.

Alternative-Style is a highly researched letter describing how your talents can benefit a specific company.

If you feel insecure about your current resume, or are looking to create one, there are some excellent guidebooks available. You can order a resume book and software program online in Resume Templates or see Chapter 10, "Shopping on America Online" for directions on using AOL's Bookstore.

1. **Click twice** on the **style** you want to view. The Style window will open, showing you a list of three examples in that style of resume.

2. When you've read or printed the style samples you want, **click** on the **Close buttons** to return to the dialog box you see in the next example.

VIEWING THE RESUME LIBRARY

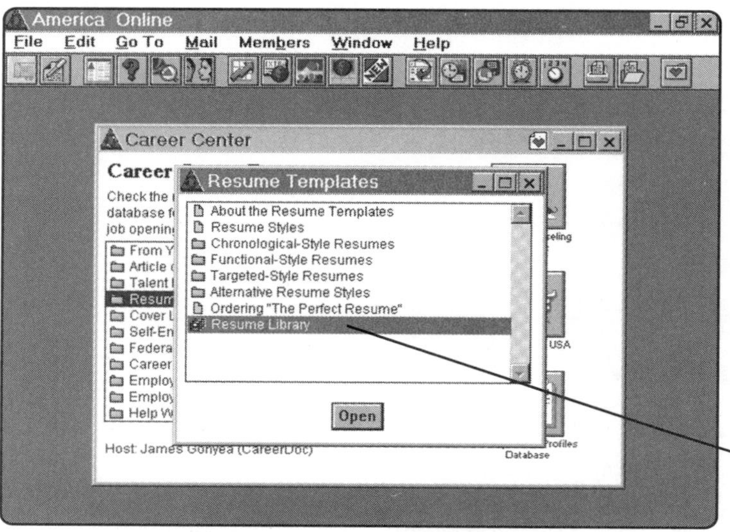

The Resume Library is not a searchable database. It is simply a listing of the resumes that AOL members have added to the library. AOL members may read the descriptions, then download any resumes to their computers. If you need help downloading, see "Getting Spell Check " in Chapter 6.

1. **Click twice** on **Resume Library**. The Resume Library dialog box will appear.

Notice the disk icon (🖫) on the far left of the window. This signifies that there are downloadable files (resumes, in this case) within that file.

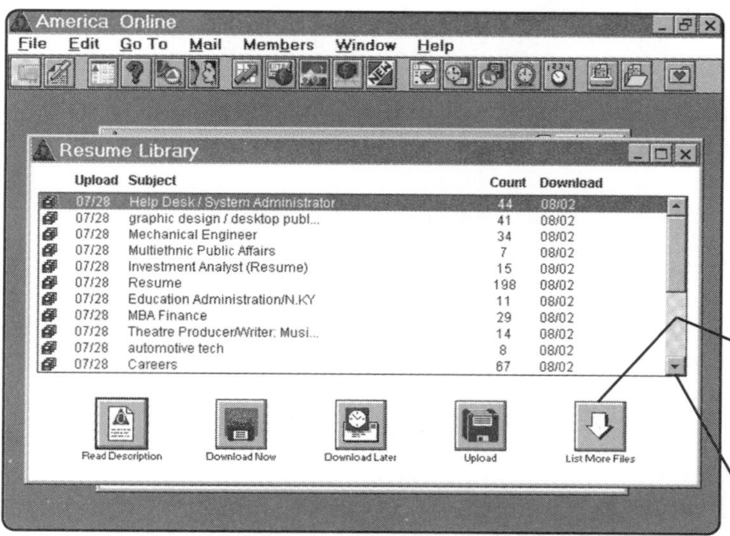

"Upload" shows the date that the file was sent to the library.

"Count" shows the number of times the file has been downloaded.

"Download" shows the date of the last download.

2. **Click repeatedly** on **List More Files** to find them all.

3. **Click** on the ▼ to scroll down the list.

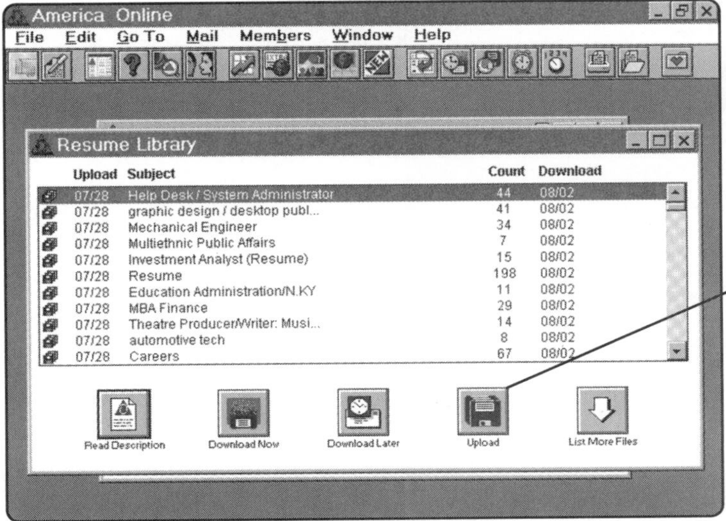

Uploading Your Resume to Resume Library

You can add your resume to this library.

1. **Click** on **Upload**. An Upload File dialog box will appear.

2. **Type** your **information** in the spaces provided. In this example, we are uploading Scott Tiller's resume.

Notice that in the "Subject" area, Scott has listed a brief job description *and* a preferred location. You're allowed 32 characters, including spaces.

In "Equipment," Scott has listed what someone will need in order to receive the file. In this case, a PC.

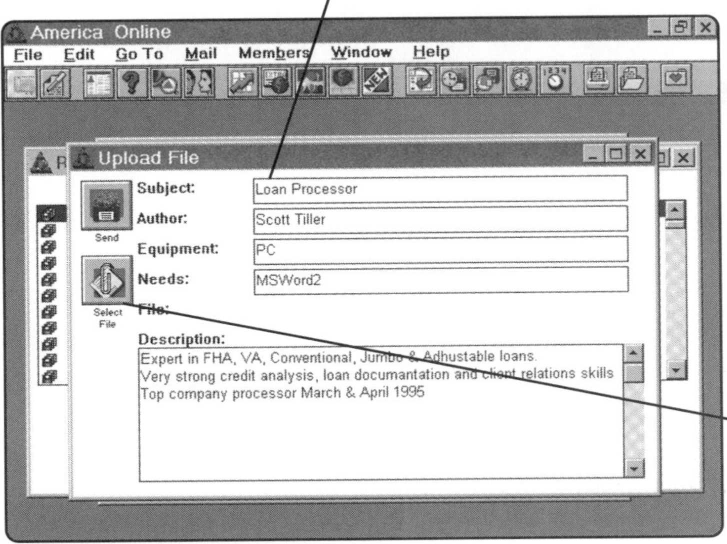

In "Needs," list what program(s) will be needed to read your file. In this case, Microsoft Word2.

In "Description," provide an overview of your resume and pertinent information. Now you're ready to attach your resume.

3. **Click** on **Select File**. An Attach File dialog box will appear.

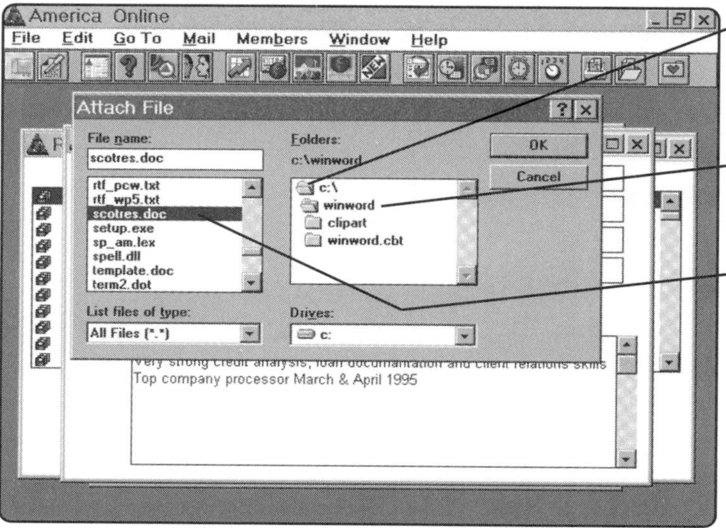

4. **Click twice** on **c:** to bring up a list of all the directories on the C drive.
5. **Click twice** on the **directory** that the file is in.
6. **Click twice** on the appropriate **file** in the File Name list box. The Attach File dialog box will disappear.

Notice that the file is now listed in the Upload File dialog box.

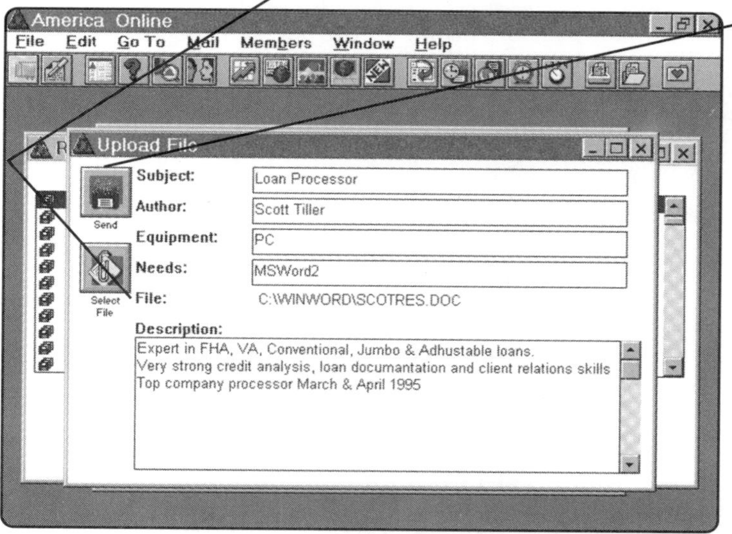

7. **Click** on **Send**. A File Transfer message box will appear briefly, tracking the transfer.

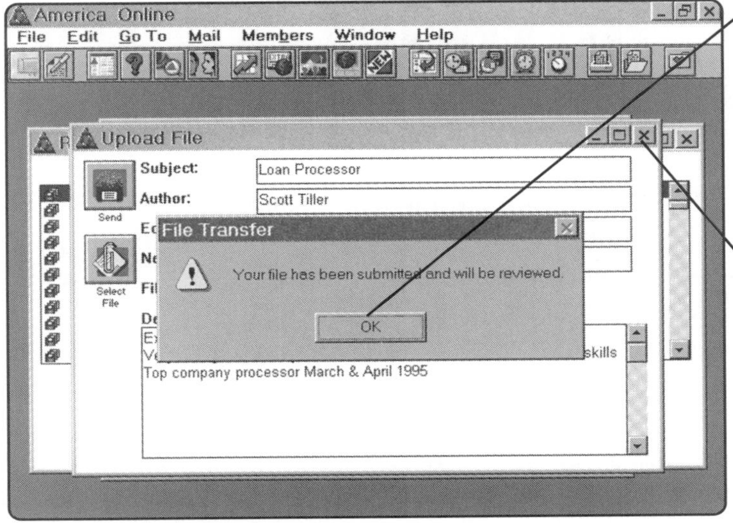

8. When your file has been uploaded, a File Transfer dialog box will appear, saying that your file has been submitted and will be reviewed. **Click** on **OK**.

9. **Click** on the **Close buttons** (☒) of all open dialog boxes to return to the Career Center dialog box that you see below.

Continuing Your Search

The Career Center has so many features to that we don't have space to fit them all into this chapter. There are several we couldn't cover. Notice:

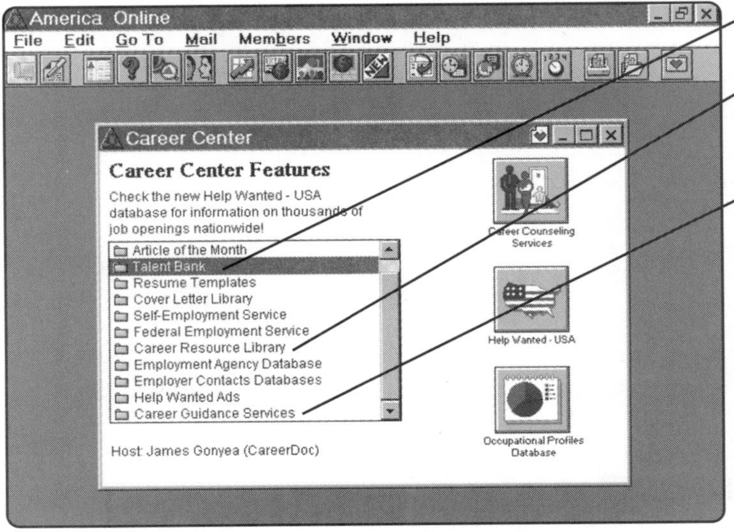

- ❖ Talent Bank,
- ❖ Career Resource Library, and
- ❖ Career Guidance Services.

Take the time to explore each on your own. Be creative in your job search. Consider making a career change, or moving to another state. The resources here show that a variety of opportunities all over the country is available.

Introducing the Internet

The Internet was originally developed by the government as a communication network for universities, research centers, and the military. Most people didn't have access to the Internet. Now, however, members of online services such as AOL have a connection to the Internet that includes all of its most popular features. With this gateway to the Internet, you can communicate with millions of computers around the world. Amazing, isn't it? In this chapter, you will do the following:

✔ Get an overview of the Internet
✔ Take a quick look at access to the Internet through AOL

LOOKING AT THE INTERNET: A SIMPLIFIED VIEW

This diagram is a simplified overview of Internet connections:

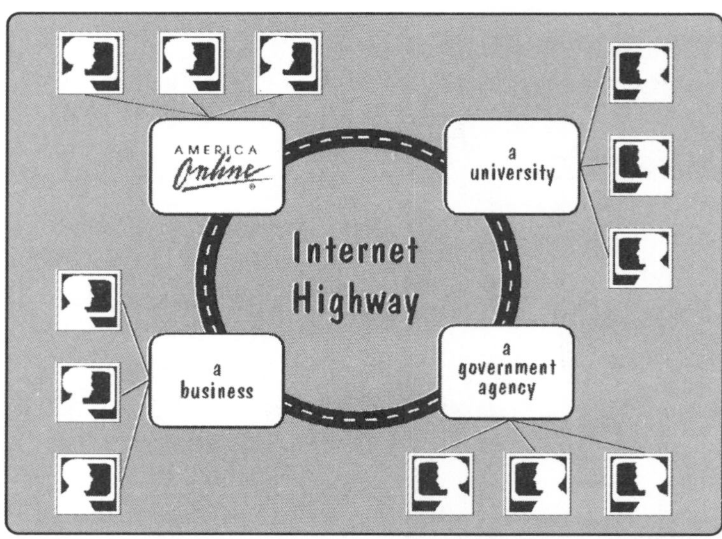

❖ AOL and other online services, universities, and government agencies are just a few examples of organizations that are connected to the Internet.

❖ These organizations (and their members) can communicate with each other over the Internet highway that connects them. This means that you, as a member of AOL, can connect to a university library in Germany, a commercial database in the U.S., or perhaps, in the future, even a spacecraft orbiting the earth.

VISITING INTERNET CONNECTION

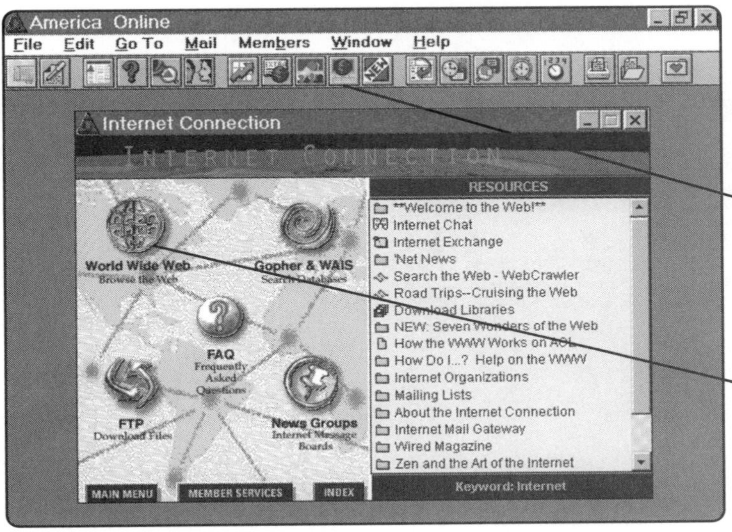

You'll find links to the Internet throughout AOL, but there's also a central access point.

1. **Click** on the **Internet icon** in the Flash Bar. The Internet Connection dialog box will appear.

2. **Click** on **World Wide Web**. The AOL Web browser with AOL's home page will appear. If this is your first visit, you'll be asked if you want to download the browser software. (See Appendix A.)

Getting to Know the Web

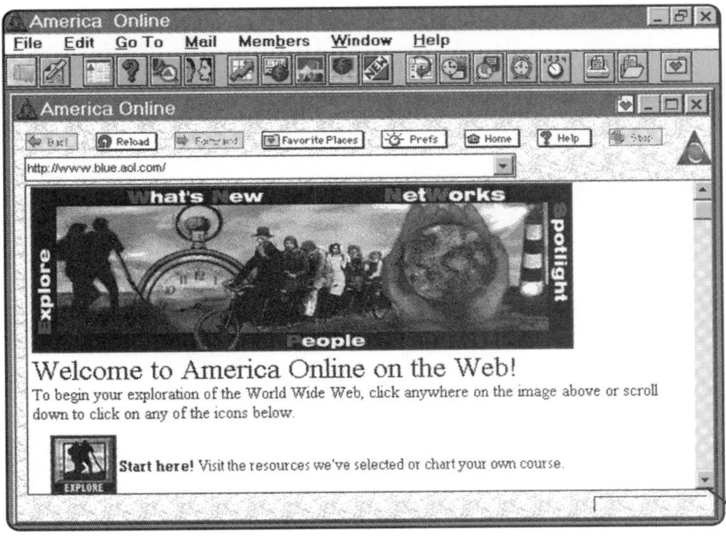

The screens that you see on the Web browser are called *Web Pages*. The main page that a person, organization, or company has on the Web is called their *home page*. A home page will usually lead to other pages with more detailed information about the organization or company, or to pages at other *Web sites* (internet computers that use the Web software).

1. **Click repeatedly** on the ▼. The rest of the AOL home page will appear.

The analogy to printed pages makes sense because when you visit a Web site, you're actually only connected to the site's computer long enough for it to send your computer one Web page. That way you don't tie up the computer you're visiting. When you "browse the Web" or "cruise the Web" (go from one page to another), you're actually requesting different pages that display on your computer after they're received.

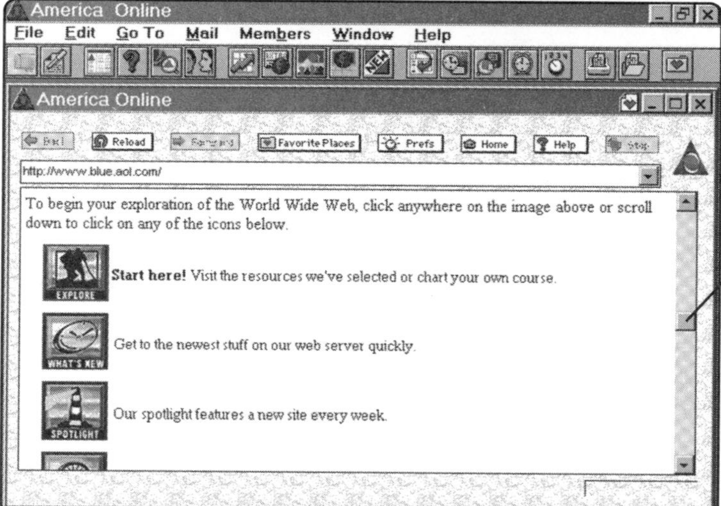

2. **Move** the **mouse arrow** over the **scroll block**.

3. **Press and hold** the **mouse button** and **drag** the **scroll block** to the bottom of the scroll bar. The rest of the Web page will appear.

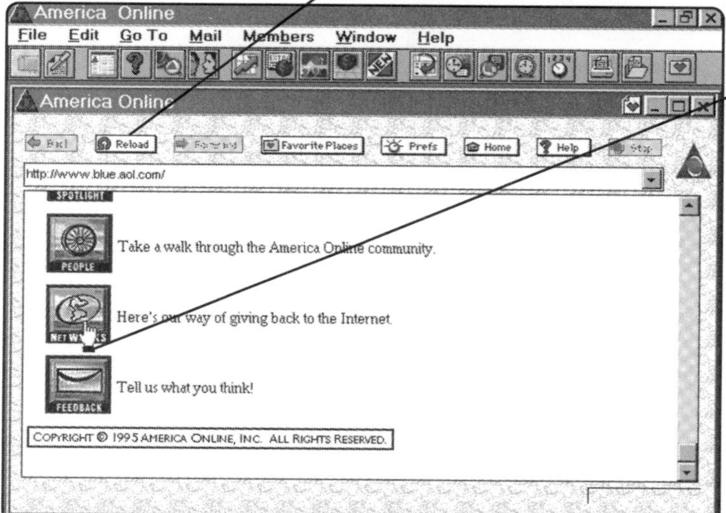

If a Web page doesn't display properly, you can click on the Reload button to receive another copy of the page from the Web site.

If the mouse arrow turns into a small hand as you pass it over a graphic, you can click on the graphic to take you to another page.

4. **Scroll back** up the page until you can see the Explore graphic.

5. **Click** on the **Explore icon**. The Explore page will appear.

Exploring AOL's Pages

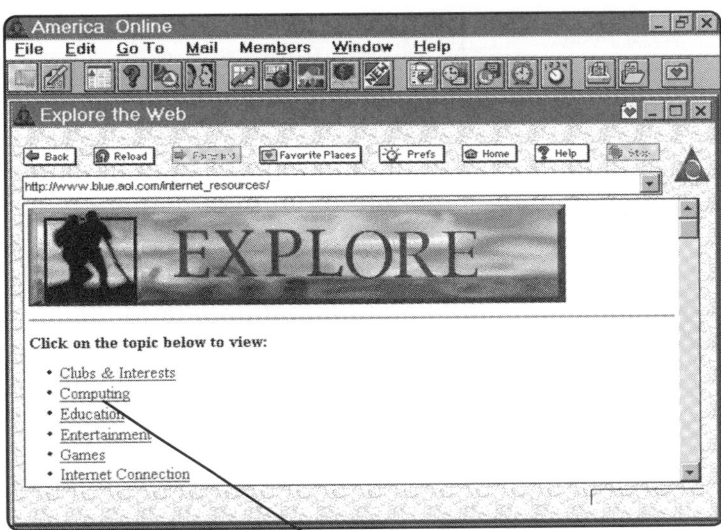

The Explore page lists various topics that you can pursue on the Web.

Notice the Home button. Clicking on this button will return you to the home page if you start feeling lost.

Blue, underlined text can also be clicked on to take you to another page.

1. **Click** on **Computing.** The Computing page will appear.

If a page takes a while to "load" (display), don't worry. The Web is a busy place and sometimes you just have to wait a little while.

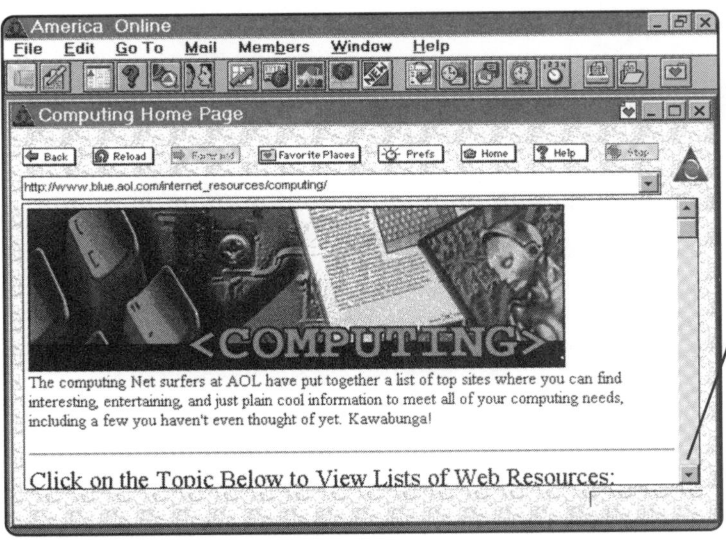

The Computing page breaks the topic down a little more. There are millions of Web pages out there and they change all the time. Trying to keep them organized is a daunting task.

2. **Scroll down** to the bottom of the Computing page.

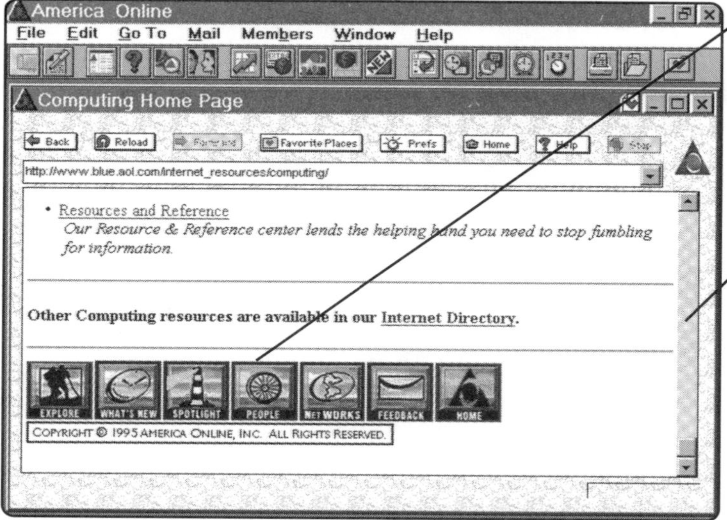

At the bottom of the Computing page are icon buttons that will take you directly to the other major sub-pages of the AOL home page.

3. **Scroll back** up to near the **middle** of the page.

AOL's browser keeps a list of the pages you've visited. It's a list of what are called *universal resource locators*, or URLs. URLs give the location of the page in "Internet-ese." Most that you see in the list will start with "http://" which indicates a *hypertext* resource. Hypertext refers to text that includes "links," like the blue, underlined text on most Web pages.

4. **Click** on the ▼ next to the list box. A list will appear.

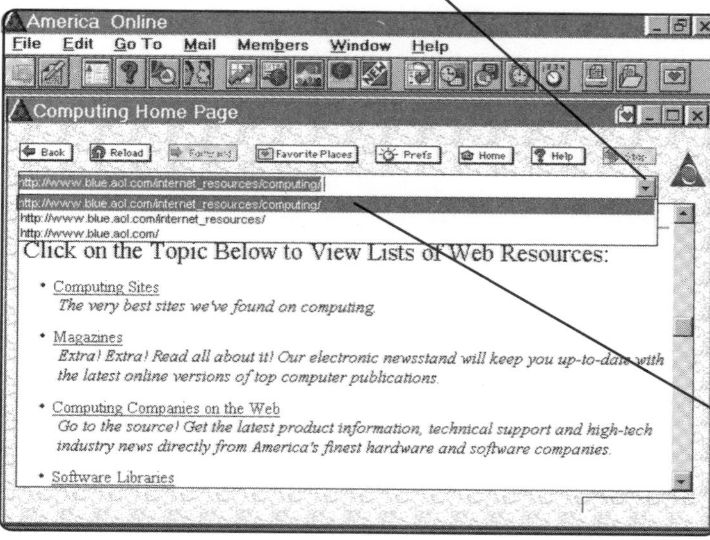

You can click twice on any URL in the list to go back to the page it represents. You can also use this box to go to the URL of your chioce. To do this, click in the box to place the cursor, backspace to delete the old URL, type in a new one, and press the Enter key.

5. **Click** on the **URL** for the Computing page. The list will close.

Printing a Web Page

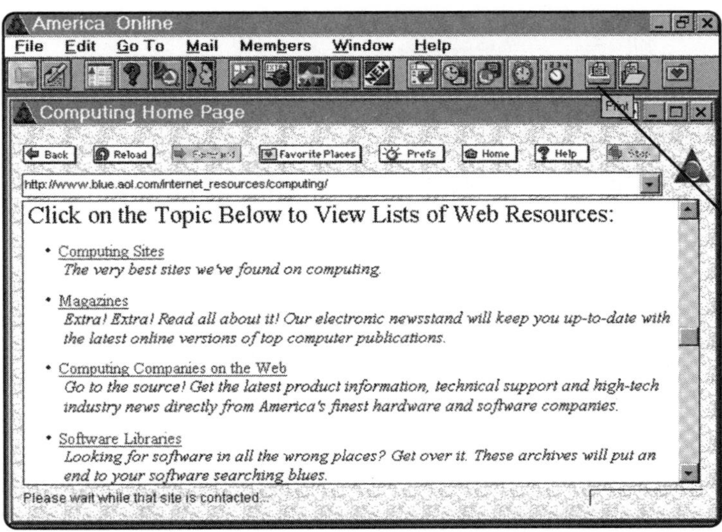

Like other things you find on AOL, Web pages can be printed. Most printers will print the graphics included on the Web page, too.

1. **Click** on the **Print icon** in the Flash Bar. The Print Document dialog box will appear.

2. **Click** on **OK**. The page will print.

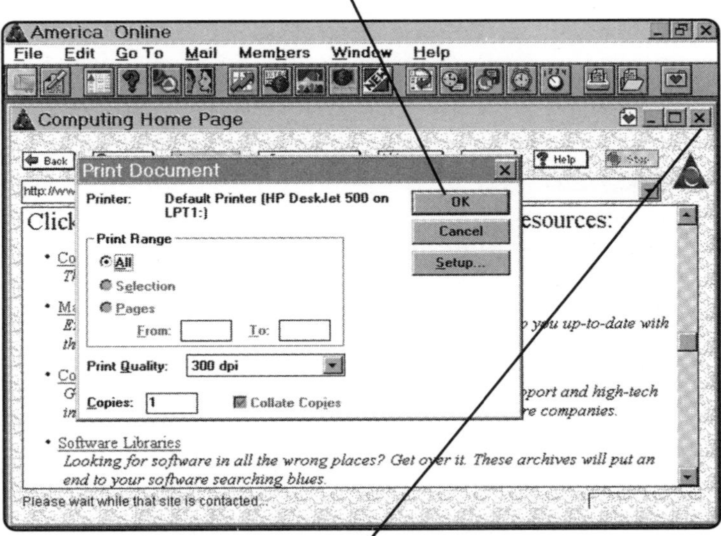

You can save Web pages using the Save icon on the Flash Bar, too. However, the document will be saved in hypertext markup language, or *HTML*. HTML includes special characters that tell the browser how to display the page.

We'll let you explore the Web at your own pace later. Right now we have a couple of unique AOL Internet resources to show you.

3. **Click** on the **Close box** (☒) in the right corner of the title bar, or, if you're using Windows 3.1, **click twice** on the **Control menu box** in the left corner of the title bar to close the browser.

TAKING A ROAD TRIP

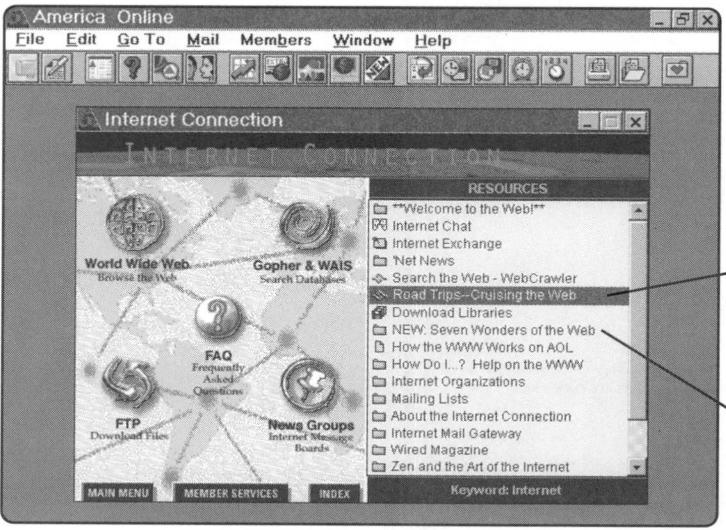

One of AOL's most interesting Internet features is "Road Trips." Road Trips are like a combination of Instant Messages and the Web browser.

1. **Click twice** on **Road Trips**. The AOL Road Trips dialog box will appear.

Note: "Seven Wonders of the Web" is a search-the-web contest that offers free time on AOL as its prize!

You can make up your own Road Trip or take one that someone else has created and filed. You set up a road trip by making a list of Web sites or AOL service areas that you want to visit. Then you give the Road Trip a name and schedule it. Any other AOL member you give the Road Trip name to can go with you. You can use these trips for fun, for Internet training, or to put together a business presentation.

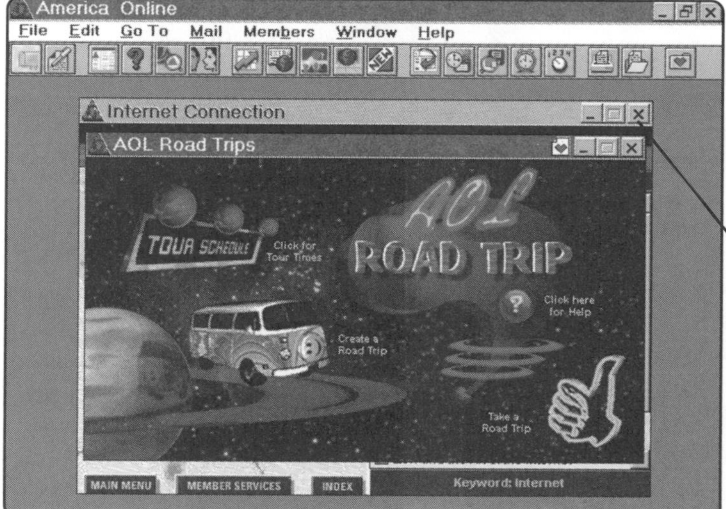

2. **Click** on the **Close box** (☒), or, if you're using Windows 3.1, **click twice** on the **Control menu box** in the title bar to close the Road Trip dialog box and return to the Internet Connection.

GETTING THE FAQS

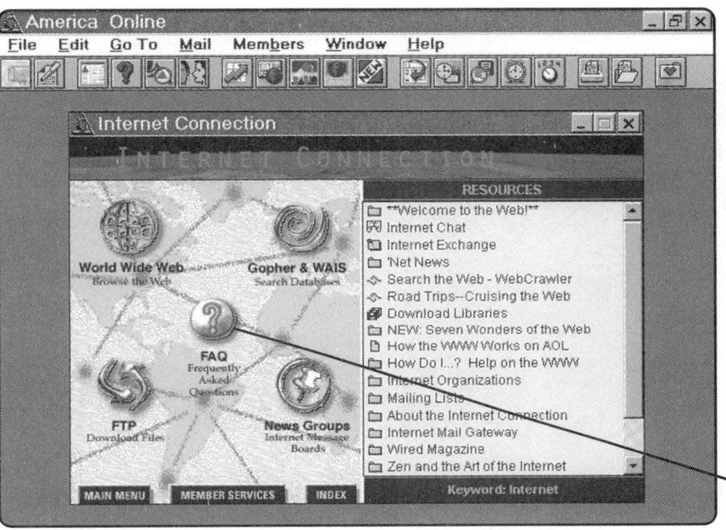

FAQ stands for Frequently Asked Questions. You'll find FAQ files all over the Internet, because experience has shown that most people have the same questions about what they find there. AOL has put together a great collection of FAQ files about the Internet and their Internet services that you can read online, print, or save.

1. **Click** on **FAQ**. A message box will appear.

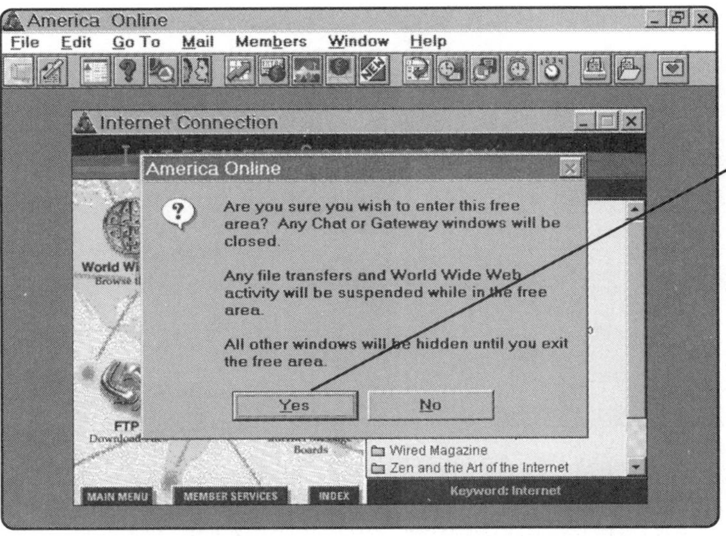

You won't be charged for the time you spend exploring the FAQs.

2. **Click** on **Yes**. The FAQ menu will appear.

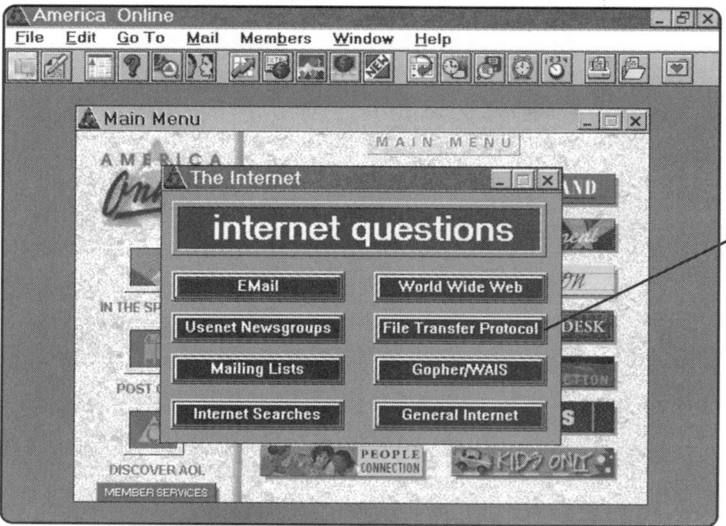

From this menu you can reach information on all aspects of AOL's Internet services. Let's look a little more closely at one.

3. **Click** on **File Transfer Protocol**. The File Transfer Protocol dialog box will appear.

This menu offers detailed information on getting files from other computers using FTP. Each of AOL's Internet services also has online help to guide you.

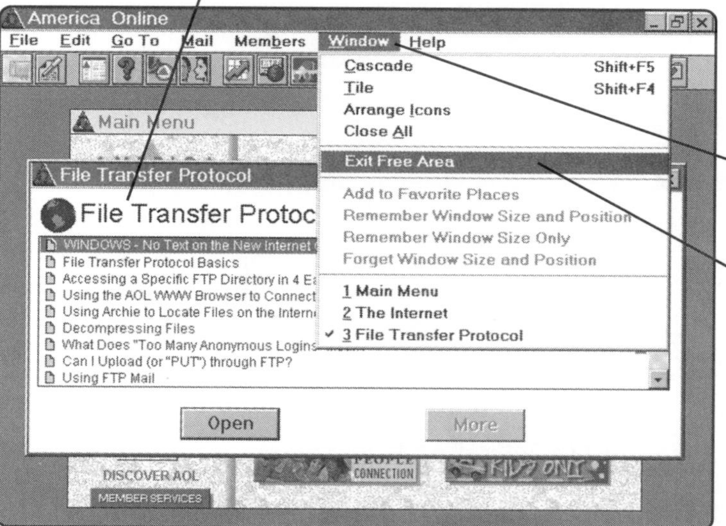

To get back to the Internet Center, you have to leave the "Free Area."

4. **Click** on **Window** in the menu bar. A menu will appear.

5. **Click** on **Exit Free Area**. The File Transfer Protocol menu will disappear and the Internet Center dialog box will reappear.

There are so many ways to use the Internet through America Online that it would take an entire book to explain it. For a thorough, detailed tour of the Internet, we recommend our other book about AOL, ***Internet for Windows: America Online 2.5 Edition***.

APPENDICES

APPENDIX

Installing and Setting Up America Online

Before you can begin your online adventure, you must have America Online installed and set up. In this chapter, you will do the following:

✔ Install America Online
✔ Set Up a variety of program features

GETTING STARTED

1. **Turn off** your **screen saver** if you are using one.

2. **Make** a **backup copy** of your AOL diskette.

3. **Insert** your **backup AOL diskette** into **drive a** (or b).

If you are using Windows 95:

4. **Click** on **Start** on the Taskbar. The Start menu will appear. (Your Taskbar may be located at the bottom or on one side of your screen.)

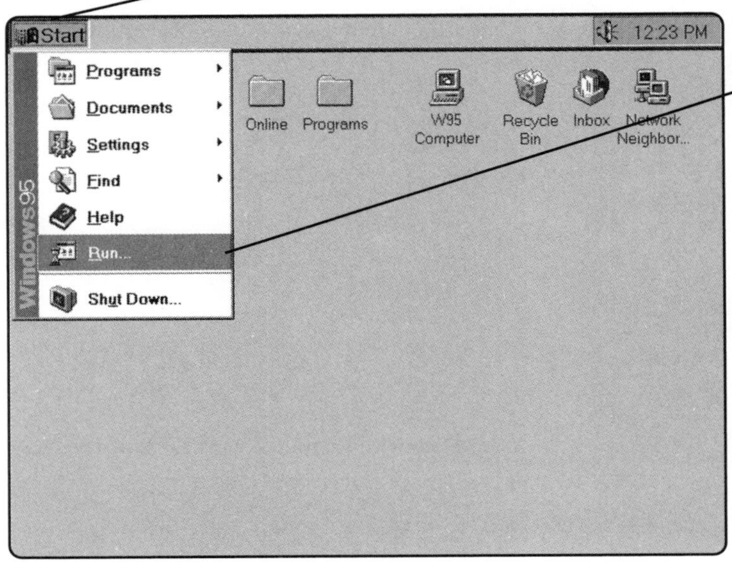

5. **Click** on **Run**. The Run dialog box will appear.

OR, if you are using Windows 3.1:

6. **Open Windows** if it is not already open.

7. **Click** on **File** in the menu bar. A menu will appear.

8. **Click** on **Run**. The Run dialog box will appear.

INSTALLING THE PROGRAM

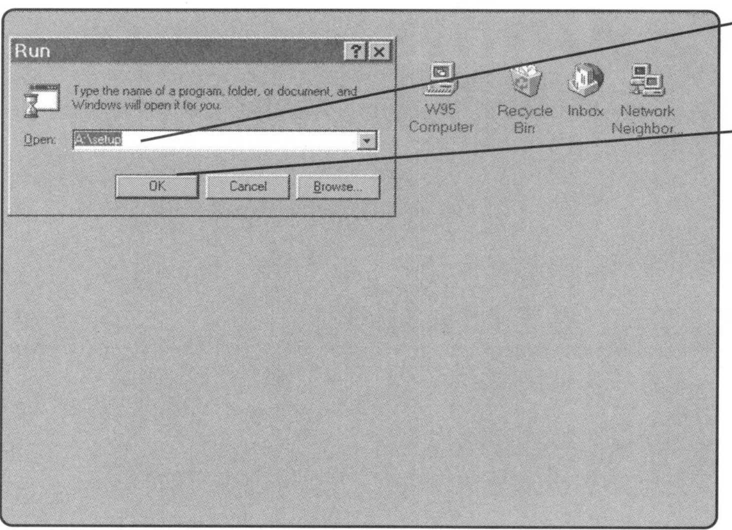

1. **Type a:\setup** (or b:\setup).
2. **Click** on **OK**. An America Online message box will appear.

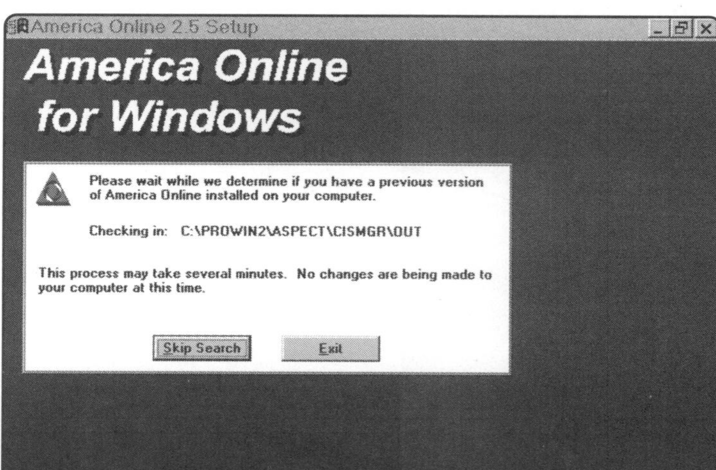

The setup program checks your computer's hard disk for previous versions of the AOL program, and tries to identify your modem. After a few moments, the Welcome dialog box will appear.

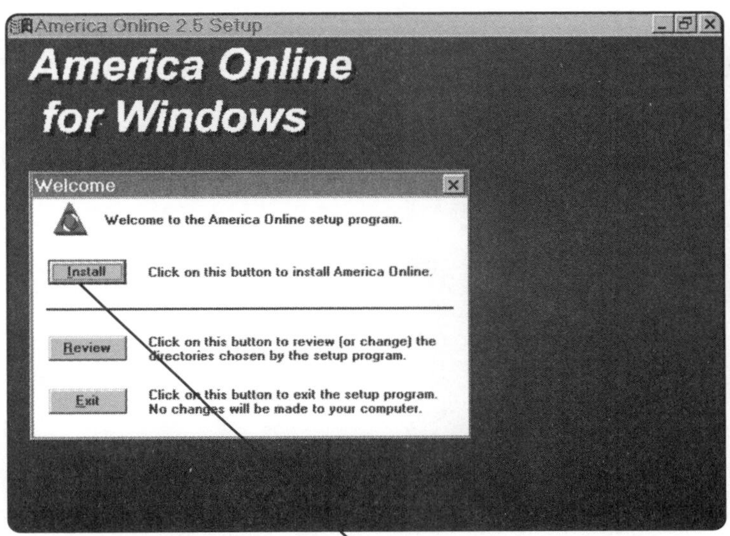

If you have a previous version of America Online installed and DO NOT want to transfer your address book and preferences to the new version, click on Review. Another dialog box will appear with options. Follow the directions on the screen. After following the directions, the dialog box shown below will appear.

3. If you are new to AOL (or you DO want to transfer your address book and preferences to this new version) **click** on **Install**. The dialog box shown below will appear.

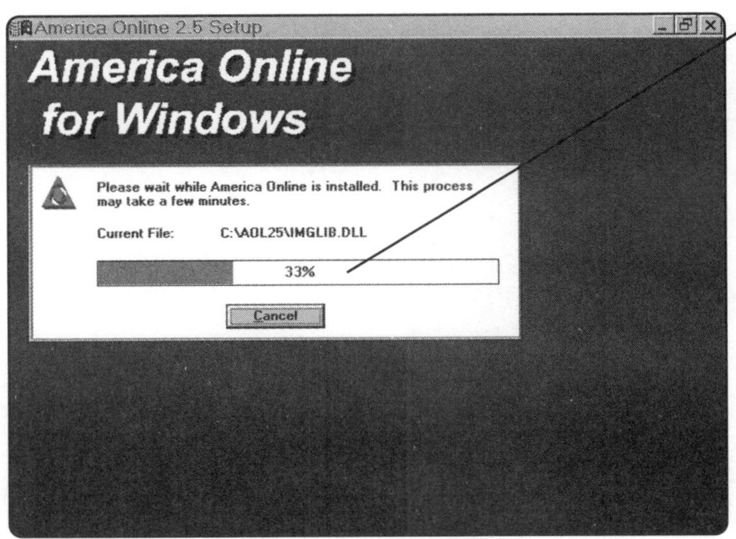

This dialog box will keep you informed of the progress of the installation. Once all the files are copied, the Setup dialog box will appear.

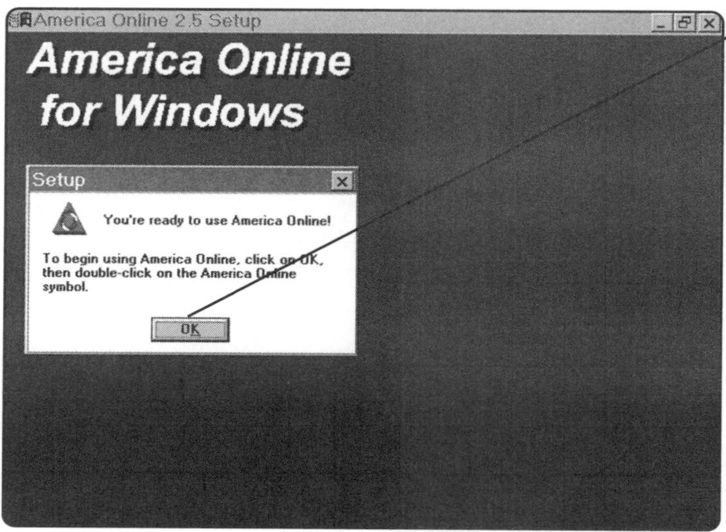

4. **Click** on **OK**. The setup program will close. If you are using Windows 3.1, a new group with the America Online icon will appear. If you are using Windows 95, a window with the AOL icon will appear.

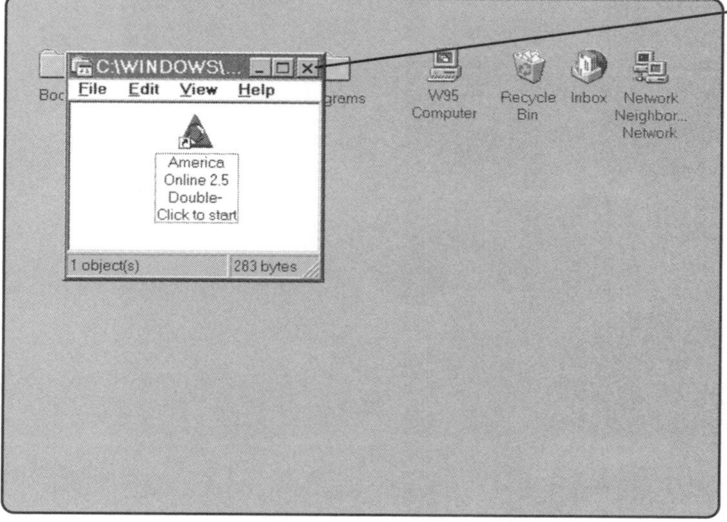

5. **Click** on the ☒ in the right corner of the title bar, or, if you are using Windows 3.1, **click twice** on the **Control menu box** (☒) in the left corner of the title bar to close the window. We will not give the Windows 3.1 step for closing dialog boxes in the rest of this chapter.

The installation is complete. Next, we will connect to America Online for the first time.

STARTING AOL

1. Use the standard technique for the version of Windows you are using (3.1 or 95) to **open** the **AOL** program. (Windows 3.1: open the AOL group and click twice on the AOL icon. Windows 95: use the Start menu to go to Programs, then AOL, and click on the AOL icon.) A Welcome to America Online dialog box will appear.

Checking the Setup

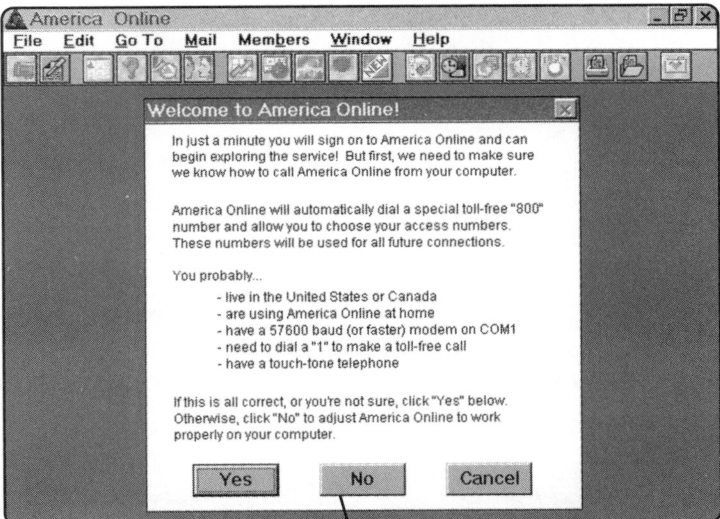

When we first saw this screen we were surprised that the AOL program thought our computer had a 57,600 baud modem! If yours has, you don't need to make any changes. Since most don't, you probably will. If you upgraded from an earlier version of AOL, the program will have filled in your old settings.

1. **Click** on **Yes** *if you match the setup* described on the screen. Another welcome to America Online dialog box, shown on the page after the next, will appear.

OR

2. **Click** on **No** *if you don't match the setup* shown here. The Set up America Online dialog box will appear.

Customizing Dialing Options

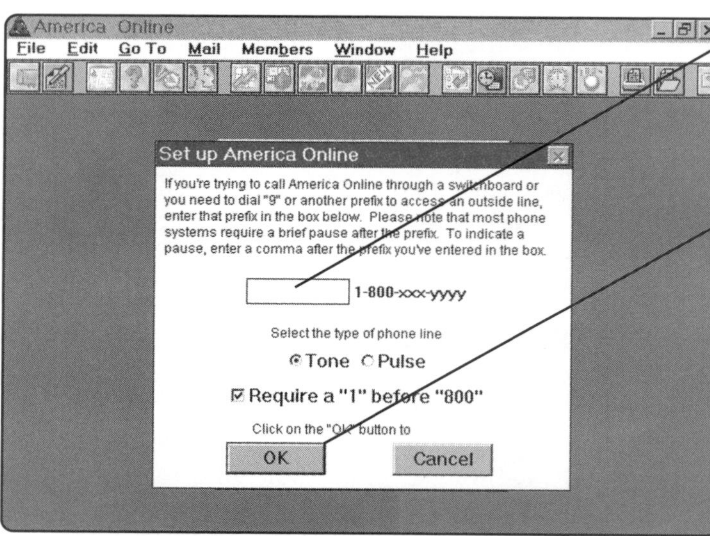

1. **Type** the appropriate **number** (e.g. 9) if you need to dial a number to get an outside line.

2. **Click** on **OK**. Another Set up America Online dialog box will appear.

The program should have detected the correct COM port for your computer, and the speed of your modem. If you are certain that it has not done this correctly, click on the correct settings. In our case we had to change the modem's speed, but not the COM port. Consult your computer and modem owner's manuals for these details.

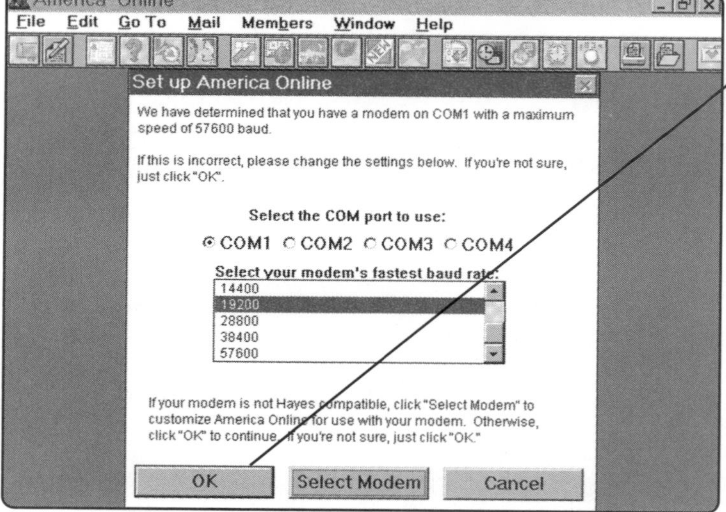

3. **Click** on **OK**. The Network Setup dialog box will appear.

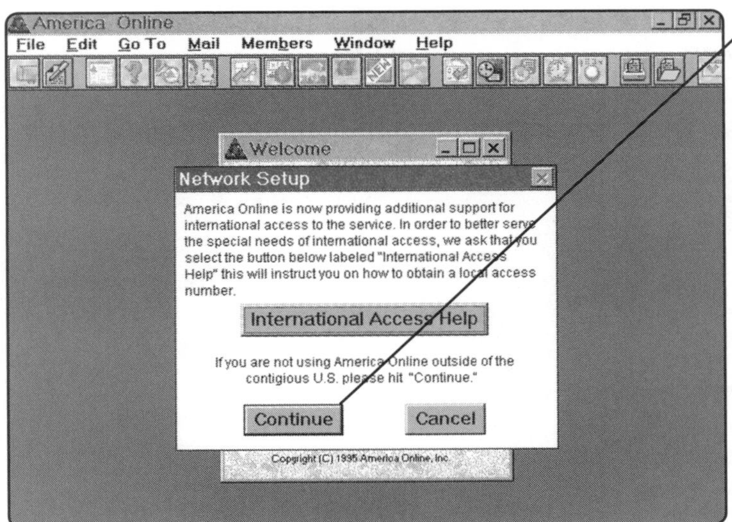

4. **Click** on **Continue** unless you're in Alaska, Hawaii, or outside the United States. The Welcome to America Online dialog box will appear.

At this point, you should stop and assemble some information, as noted in the Welcome to America Online dialog box. If you're upgrading your America Online software, have your screen name and password handy. If you're signing on for the first time, have the registration number and password that came with your AOL diskette handy, plus a credit card to set up billing information for your account.

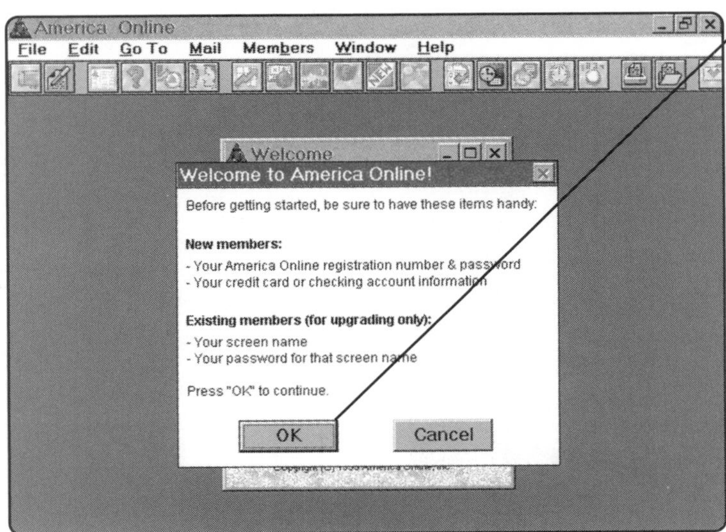

5. **Click** on **OK**. The America Online dialog box will appear.

If you are upgrading from an earlier version of AOL, your local access phone number will have been copied from the earlier version. You may skip to the section titled "Dialing The Local Access Number."

Selecting a Local Number - First Choice

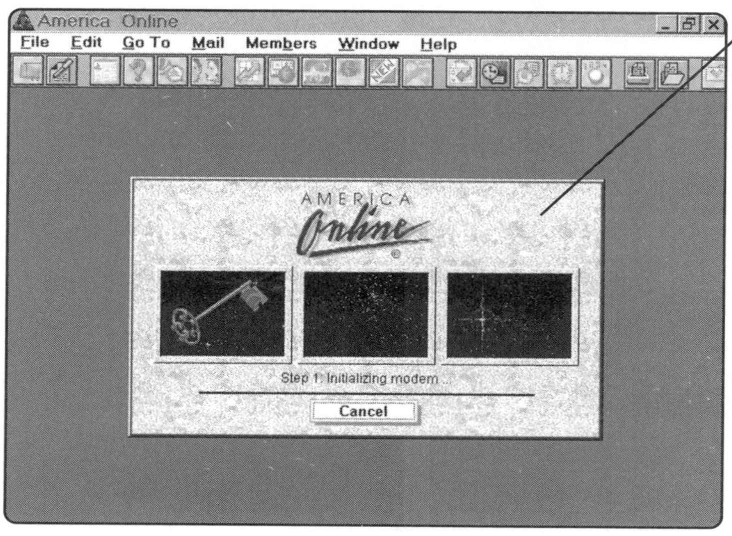

The dialog box shows the progress of connecting to AOL. Once you are connected, a Welcome to America Online dialog box will appear.

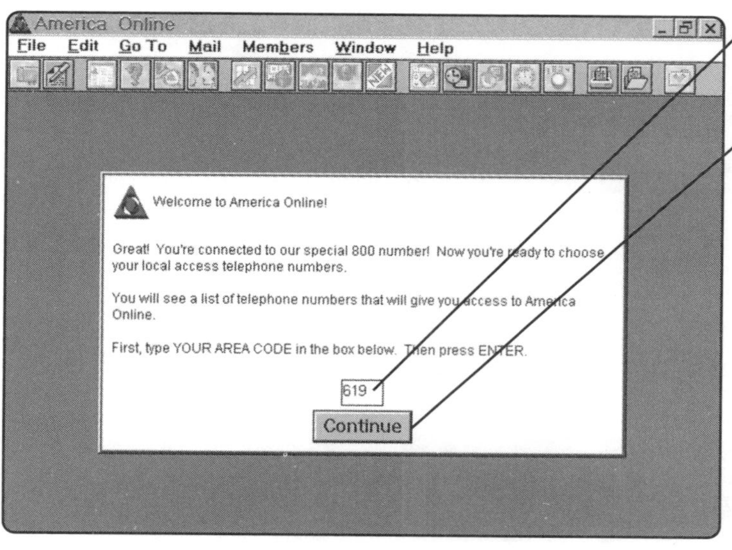

1. **Type** your **area code** in the box.

2. **Click** on **Continue**. The Choose Local Access Telephone Number — First Choice dialog box will appear.

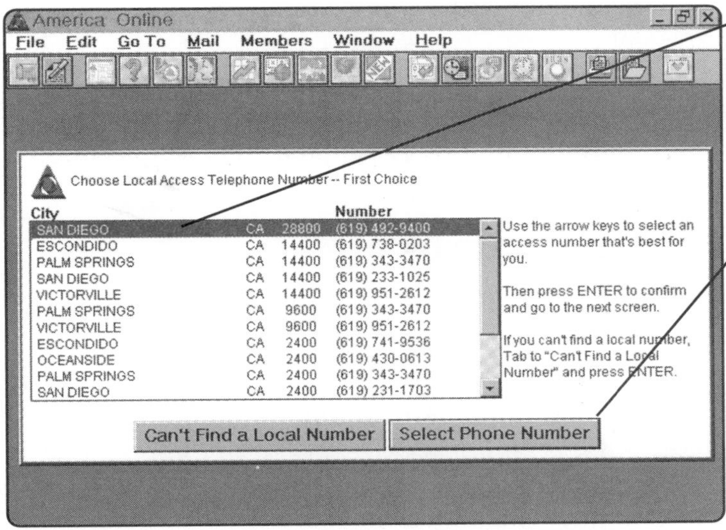

3. **Click** on the appropriate **telephone number** to highlight it. You can change this number if you find a less expensive number later.

4. **Click** on **Select Phone Number**. The Choose Local Access Telephone Number — Second Choice dialog box will appear.

Note: If a local number is not listed, click on Can't Find a Local Number. Special instructions will appear.

Selecting a Local Number—Second Choice

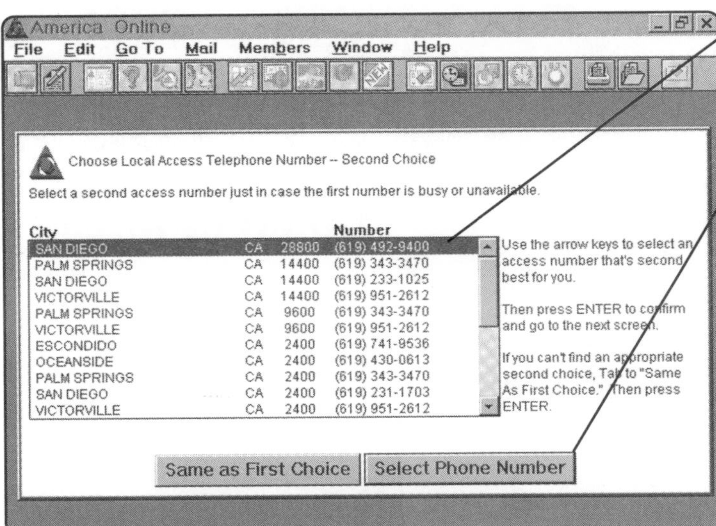

1. **Click** on the **alternate telephone number**, if there is one, to highlight it.

2. **Click** on **Select Phone Number** or **Same As First Choice**. The Confirm Your Access Number Choices dialog box will appear.

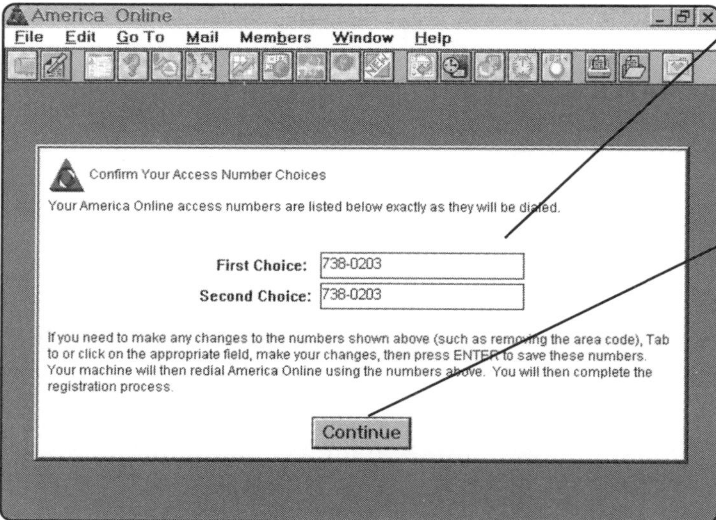

Make certain that these are the telephone numbers you want to use. If they are not, follow the instructions below them.

3. **Click** on **Continue**. The America Online dialog box will appear.

DIALING THE LOCAL ACCESS NUMBER

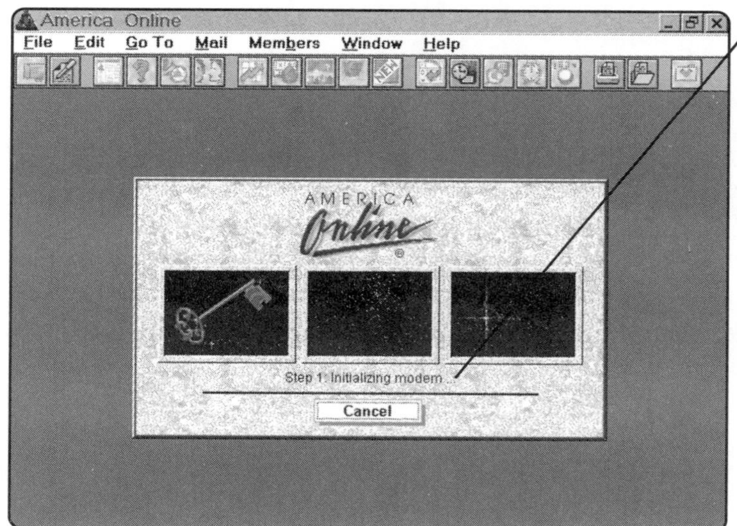

This line will give you a continuous update of the dialing and connecting process. Once the dialing and connecting is complete, the Welcome to America Online dialog box will appear.

Thinking Ahead

If you are new to AOL, you will need:

✔ Your certificate number

✔ A credit card for billing

If you are upgrading from an earlier version of AOL, skip ahead to the section titled "Creating Other Screen Names."

ENTERING THE CERTIFICATE NUMBER AND PASSWORD

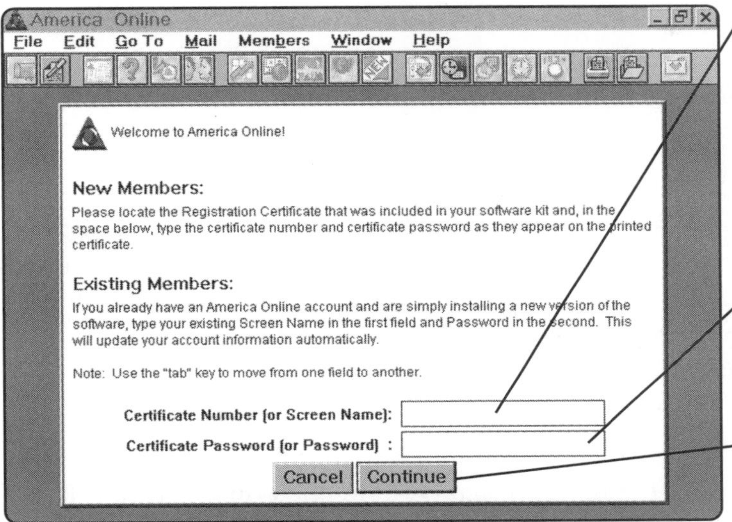

1. **Type** the **certificate number** that came with your software in the Certificate Number box and **press Tab**. The cursor will move to the Certificate Password box.
2. **Type** the **password** that came with your software in the Certificate Password box.
3. **Click** on **Continue**. The Getting Around dialog box will appear.

Note: If you are upgrading from a previous version of AOL, follow the instructions shown for *Existing Members*.

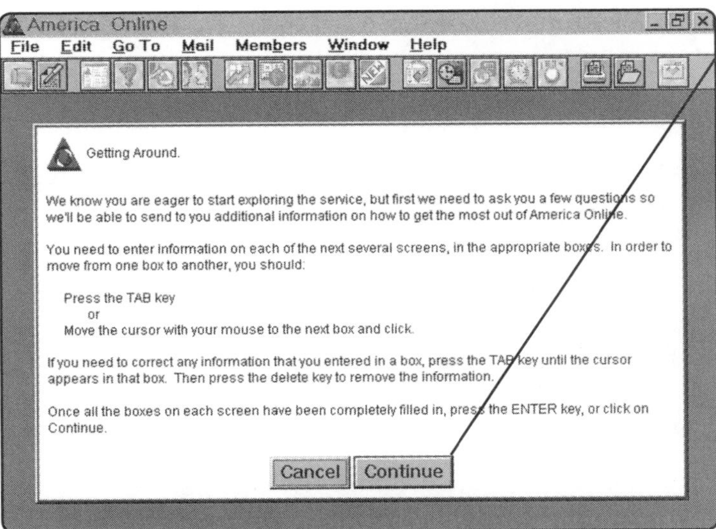

4. **Click** on **Continue**. An information fill-in dialog box will appear. AOL will use fill-in dialog boxes (not shown here) to request personal data and billing information from you. After these are completed, you will receive a few screens of information about AOL and the terms of your account. These are followed by fill-in dialog boxes for choosing a screen name and password.

CHOOSING A SCREEN NAME

You may not be able to get your first choice, so have several ideas. A screen name must have:

- ✔ A letter, not a number, as the first character.
- ✔ A minimum of 3 characters and a maximum of 10.
- ✔ Any combination of letters, numbers, and spaces.

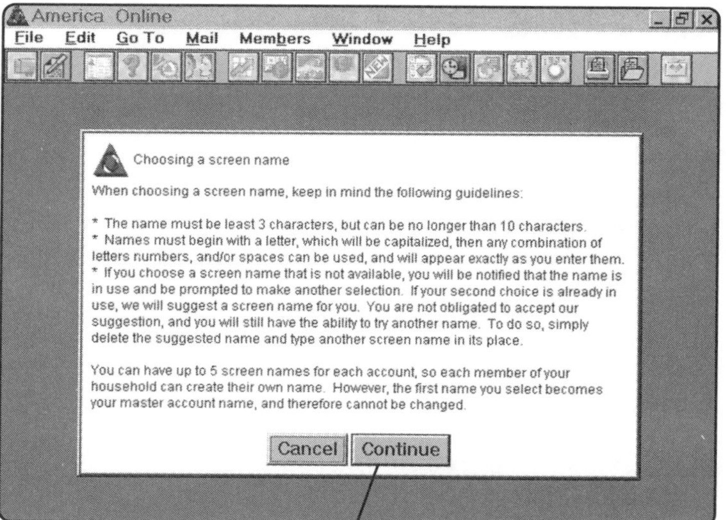

1. **Click** on **Continue**. Another Choosing a screen name dialog box will appear. It will not be shown here. After reading the information in it, **click** on **Continue**. The final Choosing a screen name dialog box will appear.

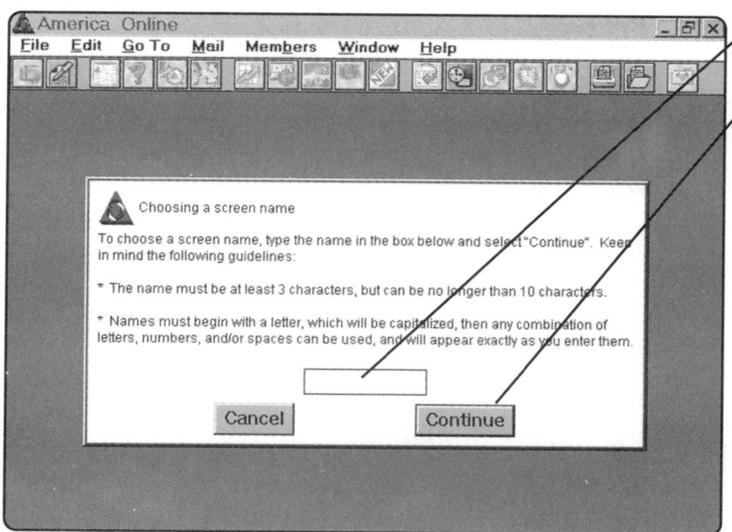

2. **Type** a **screen name**.

3. **Click** on **Continue**. The Choosing a password dialog box will appear.

Note: You may have to repeat this process several times if someone else has already chosen "your" screen name.

CHOOSING A PASSWORD

A password should be:

✔ Easy to remember! (It's a good idea to write it down and hide it somewhere, just in case.)

✔ *Not obvious* to anyone.

✔ At least 4 but no more than 8 characters.

✔ Any combination of letters and numbers.

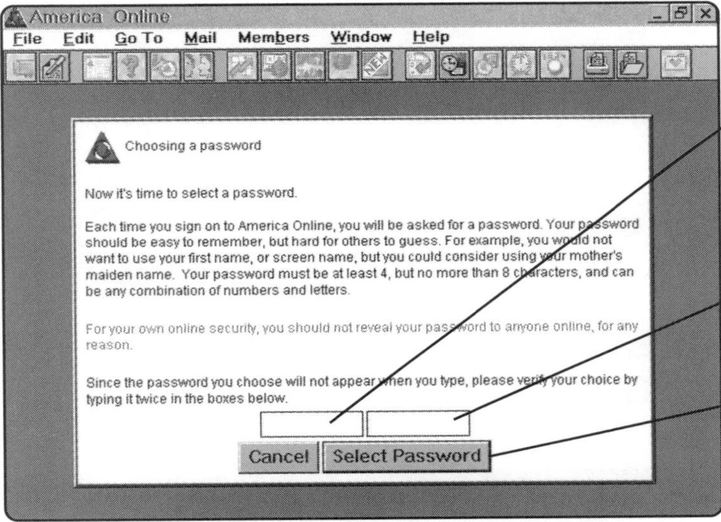
America Online
File Edit Go To Mail Members Window Help
Choosing a password
Now it's time to select a password.
Each time you sign on to America Online, you will be asked for a password. Your password should be easy to remember, but hard for others to guess. For example, you would not want to use your first name, or screen name, but you could consider using your mother's maiden name. Your password must be at least 4, but no more than 8 characters, and can be any combination of numbers and letters.
For your own online security, you should not reveal your password to anyone online, for any reason.
Since the password you choose will not appear when you type, please verify your choice by typing it twice in the boxes below.
Cancel
Select Password

1. **Type** your **password** and **press** the **Tab key**. The cursor will move to the next password box.

2. **Type** the *same* **password** again.

3. **Click** on **Select Password**. The first of two Getting to Know America Online dialog boxes (not shown here) will appear.

4. **Click** on **Continue** on both dialog boxes. A Welcome to America Online dialog box (not shown here) will appear.

ENTERING AMERICA ONLINE

1. **Click** on **Enter America Online**. You may receive a few screens asking, for example, if your computer has a CD-ROM drive, and offering you the AOL printed guide. **Click** on the **button** of your choice on each screen. Eventually, the Welcome dialog box and Main Menu will appear. The Main Menu will display first, then the Welcome dialog box will cover it.

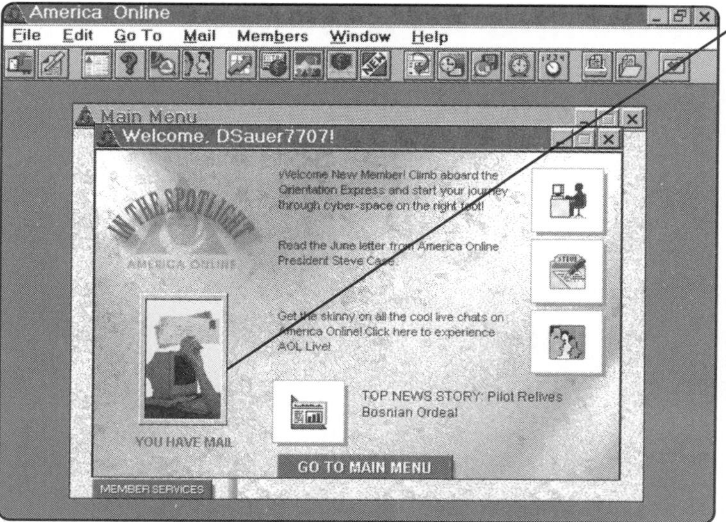

The Mail icon will show that you have *e-mail* (electronic mail) waiting. This will be "welcome" messages from the AOL staff. You can read these later; they won't go away in the meantime. (Consult the chapters on mail for more information about e-mail.) The icons and messages on the right side of the dialog box will change every day.

CREATING OTHER SCREEN NAMES

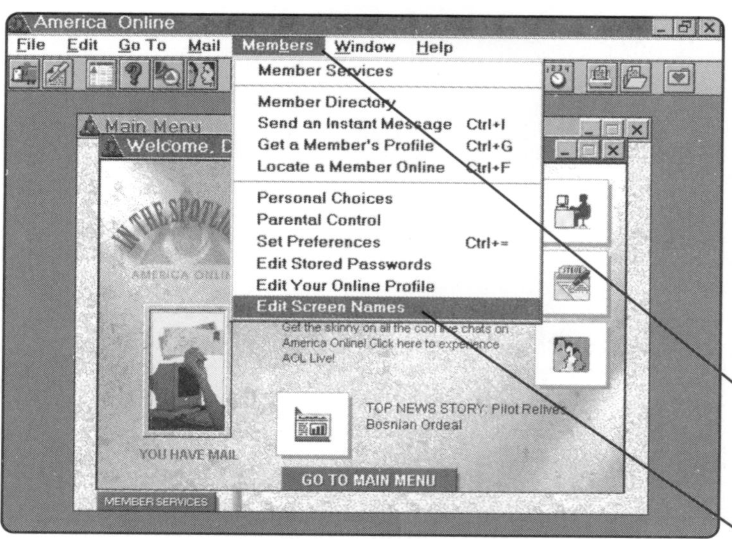

As an AOL member, you can have up to five different screen names under one account. You can create individual screen names for others in your family or create special screen names to use when you participate in chats and newsgroups.

1. **Click** on **Members** in the menu bar. A menu will appear.

2. **Click** on **Edit Screen Names**. The Create or Delete Screen Name dialog box will appear.

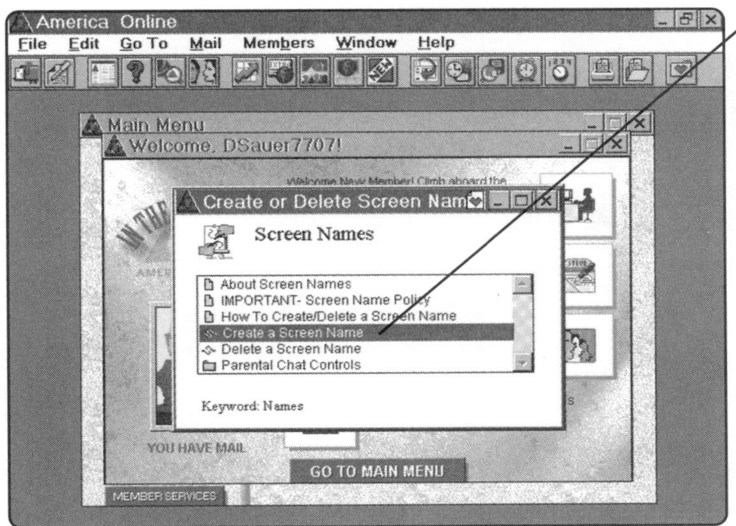

3. **Click twice** on **Create A Screen Name**. A Create A Screen Name dialog box will appear.

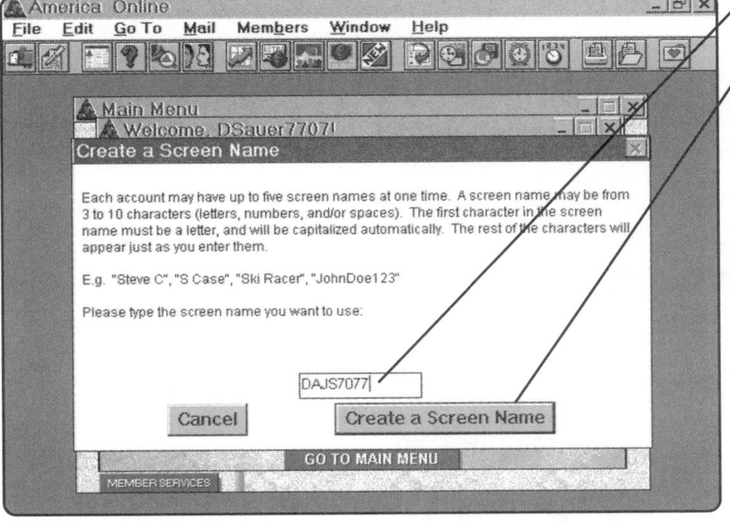

4. **Type** a **screen name**.

5. **Click** on **Create a Screen Name**. A Set Password dialog box will appear.

Note: If a dialog box appears with the message, "The name you requested is already in use. Please try another name," **click** on **OK** and choose a different screen name.

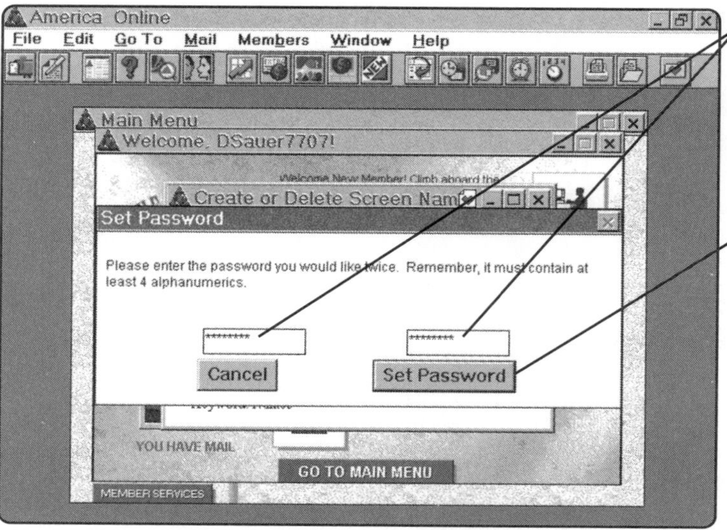

6. **Type** the **password** you want to use in the first text box, then tab to the second text box and type the *same password* there.

7. **Click** on **Set Password**. An America Online dialog box will appear.

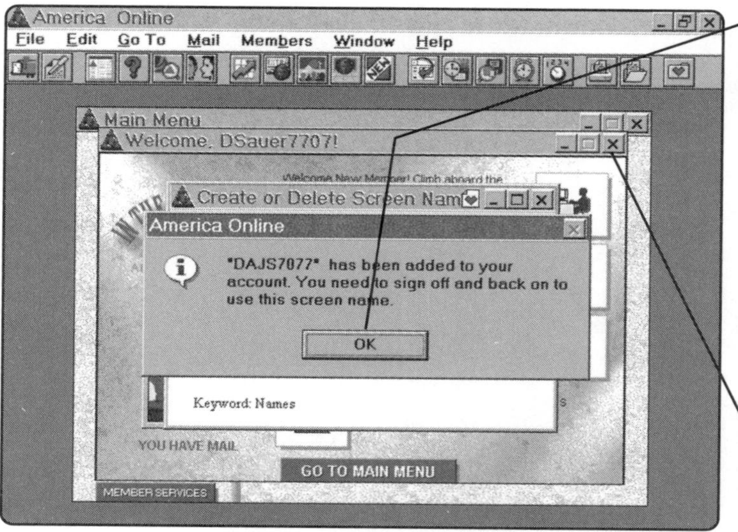

8. **Click** on **OK**. Your new screen name has now been added to the AOL database.

Note: In order to activate this screen name, you will have to sign off and sign back on again under the new name. We'll show you this later.

9. **Click** on the ☒ in the right corner of the Create or Delete Screen Name title bar to close the dialog box.

STORING YOUR PASSWORD

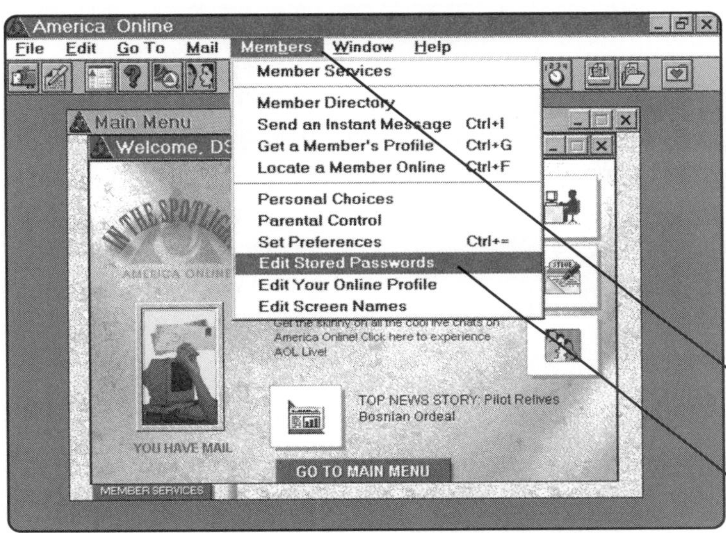

By storing your password, you won't have to type it in each time you connect to AOL. Of course, if you're using AOL in an office or other situation where security and your online charges may be concerns, you may not want to do this.

1. **Click** on **Members** in the menu bar. A menu will appear.

2. **Click** on **Edit Stored Passwords**. The Edit Stored Passwords dialog box will appear.

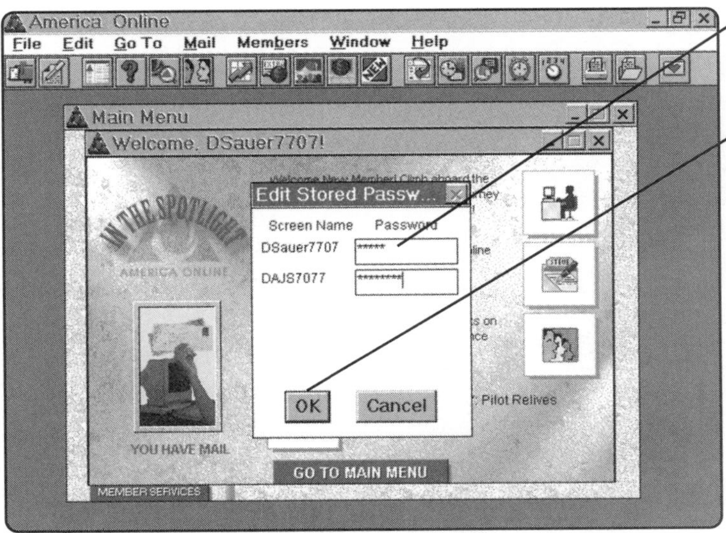

3. **Type** your **password(s)** in the **box(es)**.

4. **Click** on **OK**. Your passwords will be stored and entered automatically whenever you sign on. You can use this procedure to remove a stored password as well, by deleting the password from the box and clicking on OK.

GETTING THE WORLD WIDE WEB BROWSER SOFTWARE

To make distributing the AOL sign-up program as efficient as possible, the *Web browser* software is not included with it. Web browser software lets you use the World Wide Web on the Internet through America Online. The first time you go to the Web, AOL downloads the software to you.

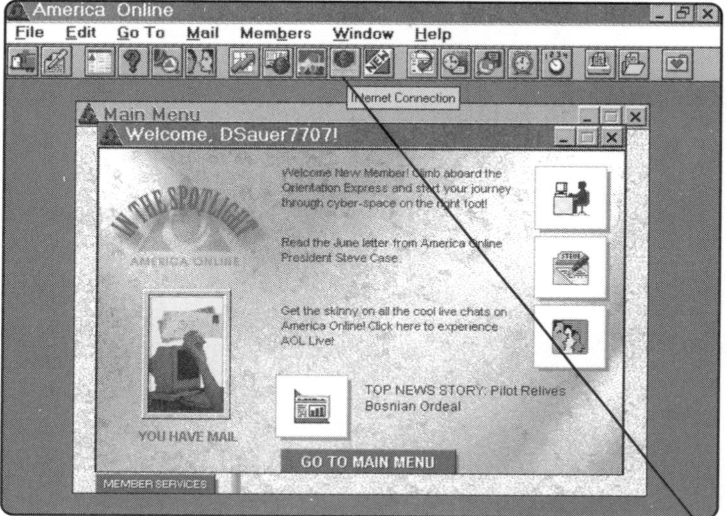

Similarly, the graphic files that make up the colorful "art" on AOL's screens change from time to time. They will automatically download the first time you go to an area in the service, or the first time you go after the art has changed.

America Online
File Edit Go To Mail Members Window Help
New Internet Connection Artwork
INTERNET CONNECTION
Get ALL the New Artwork In One Shot—FREE!
We have designed a colorful new look to make your Internet Connection online experience more fun, easy, and informative. You will receive ALL the new art at once by clicking "Get Artwork Now" below.
You will NOT be charged for the time spent downloading the art to your hard drive.
Approximate Art Download Times:
* 2400 baud 5 minutes
* 9600 baud 3 minutes
* 14400 baud 1 minute
Get Artwork Now

1. **Click** on the **Internet Connection** icon in the Flash Bar. If you're not sure which icon it is, place the mouse arrow over an icon for a moment and look for the label that appears. A dialog box offering to download all the Internet Connection art at once without connect-time charges will appear.

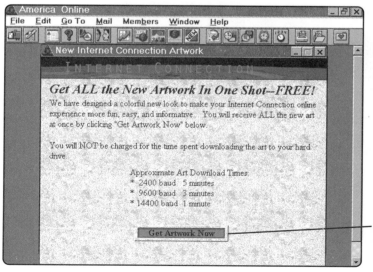

2. **Click** on **Get Artwork Now**. An America Online dialog box will appear.

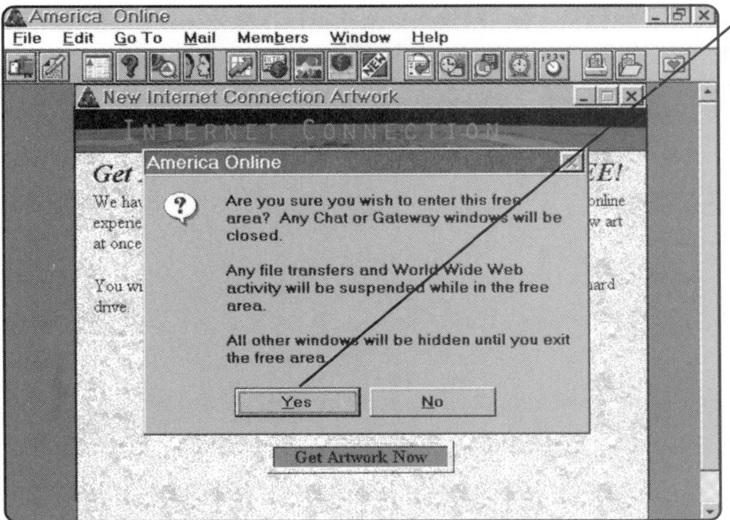

3. **Click** on **Yes**. The America Online Update boxes will appear.

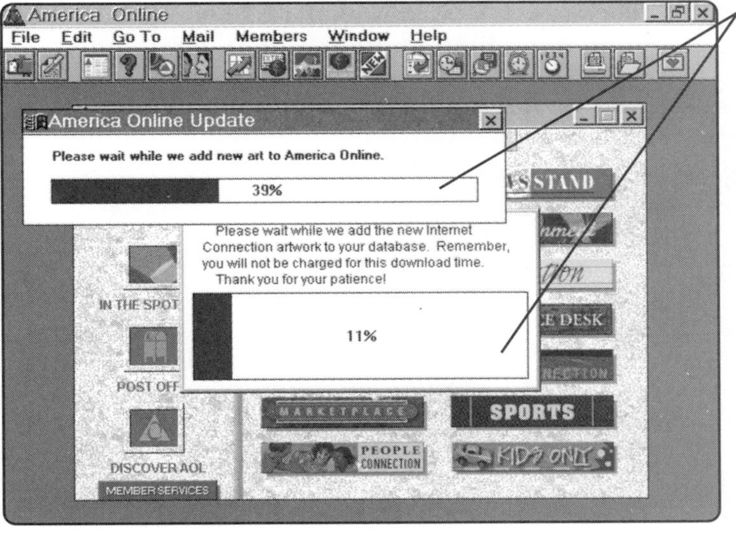

These boxes show the progress of the download. Art files and Web page files (you'll learn more about web pages in Chapter 21) are stored on your computer's hard disk so that they can be redisplayed quickly. This speeds up both AOL and the Web browser. When the download is complete, another America Online dialog box will appear.

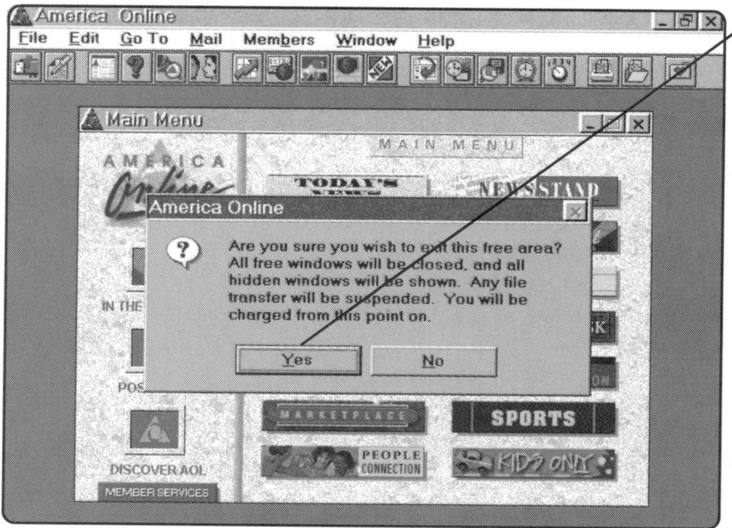

4. **Click** on **Yes**. The Internet Connection dialog box will appear.

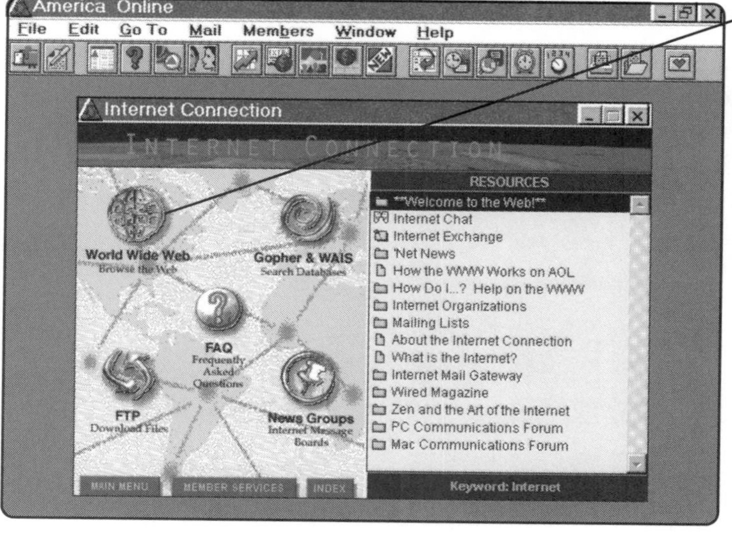

5. **Click** on the **World Wide Web icon**. A Software Update dialog box will appear.

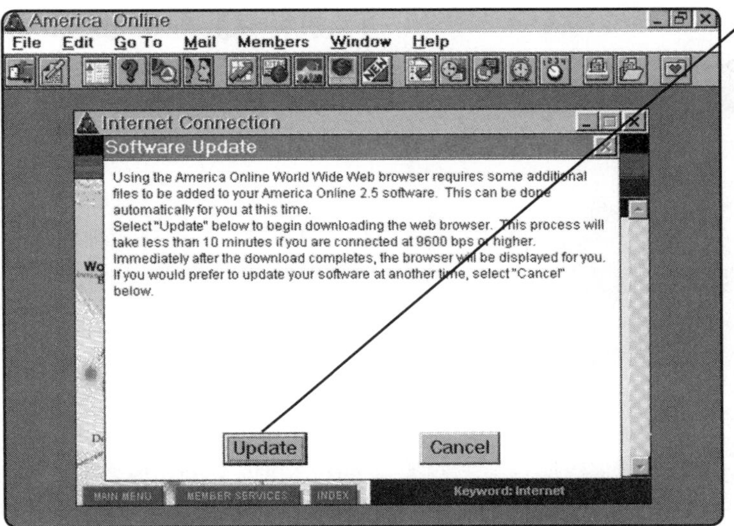

6. **Click** on **Update**. A File Transfer dialog box will appear.

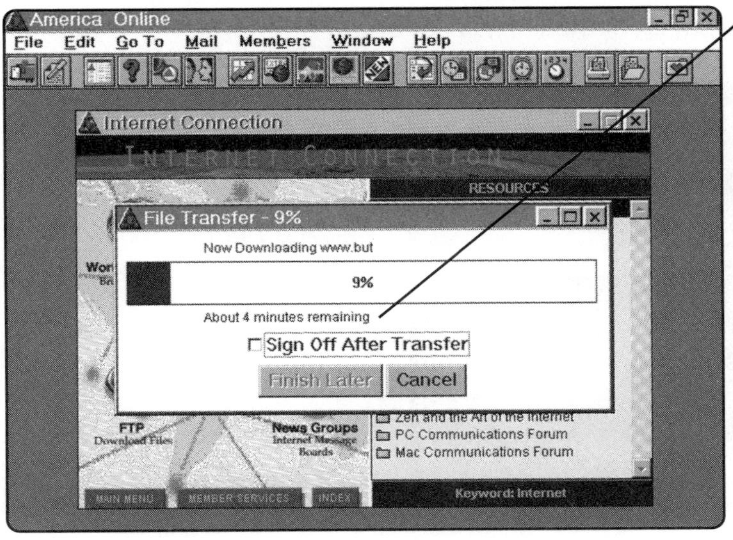

The time remaining for the download is shown here. The download time depends on the speed of your modem. As soon as the file transfer is complete, the Web browser program will open, and the America Online Home Page will begin to be displayed.

TAKING A PEEK AT THE WEB

We're only going to take a quick peek at the Web at this time. In this chapter, we're just getting all the AOL software set up.

The blue AOL logo spins as the AOL Home Page file and its graphics are downloaded and become clear.

The blue bar-graph shows the download's progress.

Once the page has stopped loading, you can continue and explore the Web on your own. Click on the "Help" button if you want information on the World Wide Web and on using the browser. For our example, however, we'll disconnect and check on the added screen name we just set up.

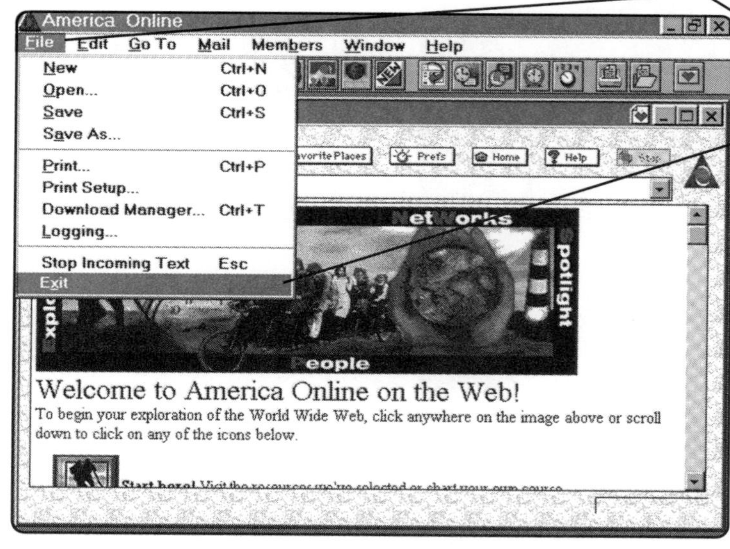

1. **Click** on **File** in the menu bar. A menu will appear.

2. **Click** on **Exit**. An America Online dialog box will appear.

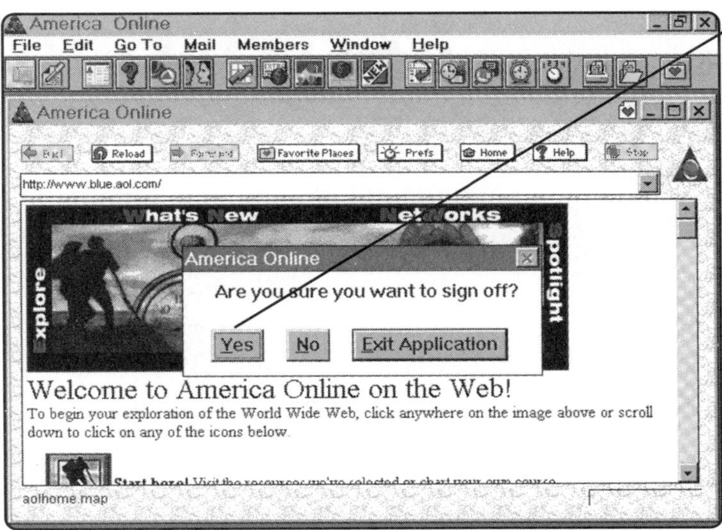

3. **Click** on **Yes**. You will disconnect from America Online's computer, but the AOL program will still be running.

CHECKING A NEW SCREEN NAME

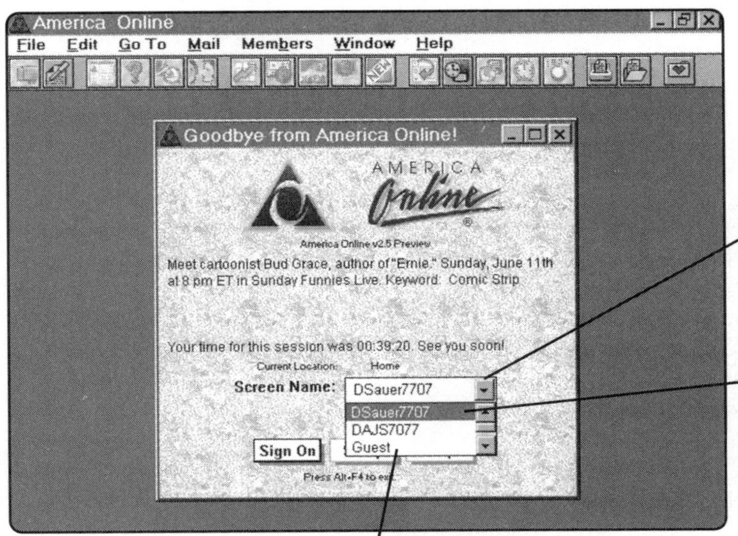

You can change between screen names at the screen you first see when you start the AOL program in Windows.

1. **Click** on the ▼ next to the Screen Name box. A list of screen names will appear.

2. **Click** on the **screen name** you want to use the next time you sign on to AOL. The list will close.

Note: if you have a friend with an AOL account who wants to sign on while visiting at your home, he or she can click on "Guest" here. After connecting to AOL, a screen name and password prompt will appear.

Restricting Children's Access

If you give your children their own screen names and passwords (See Appendix A), you can control how much access your children have to the full range of features in America Online. You can block access to several categories of use: (1) Instant Messages, the private person-to-person conversations shown in Chapter 5; (2) Conference Rooms in various areas such as Reference, Games, and Software; (3) various aspects of Internet Newsgroups; (4) downloading of files; (5) all aspects of the People Connection, the live online chat feature; or (6) only the member-created rooms in the People Connection, which are private online discussions. In this chapter, you will do the following:

✔ Learn how to block access to various features of America Online

EXERCISING PARENTAL CONTROL

Access restrictions can be put into place only through the master account, that is, the screen name you set up for yourself when you initially registered on AOL.

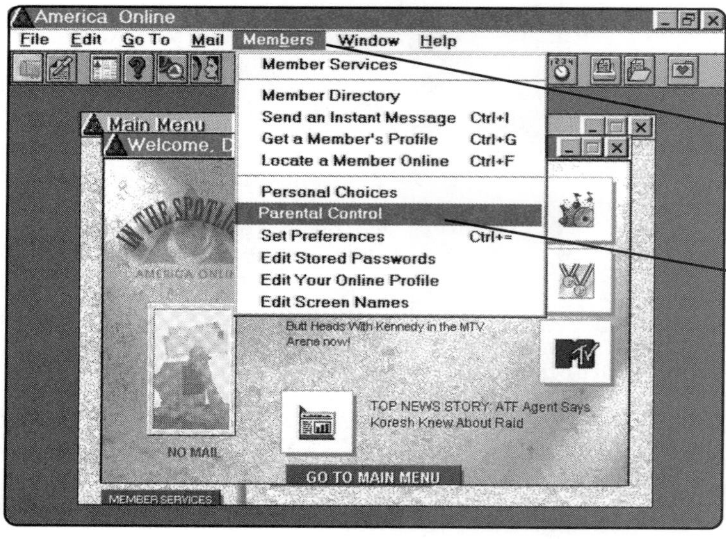

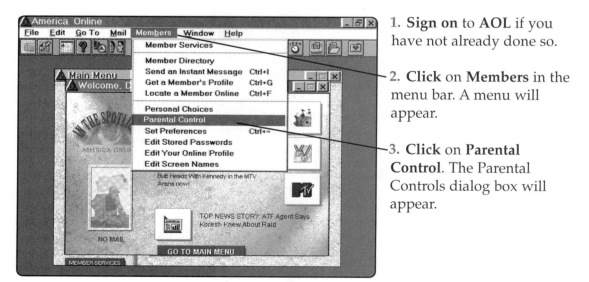

1. **Sign on** to **AOL** if you have not already done so.
2. **Click** on **Members** in the menu bar. A menu will appear.
3. **Click** on **Parental Control**. The Parental Controls dialog box will appear.

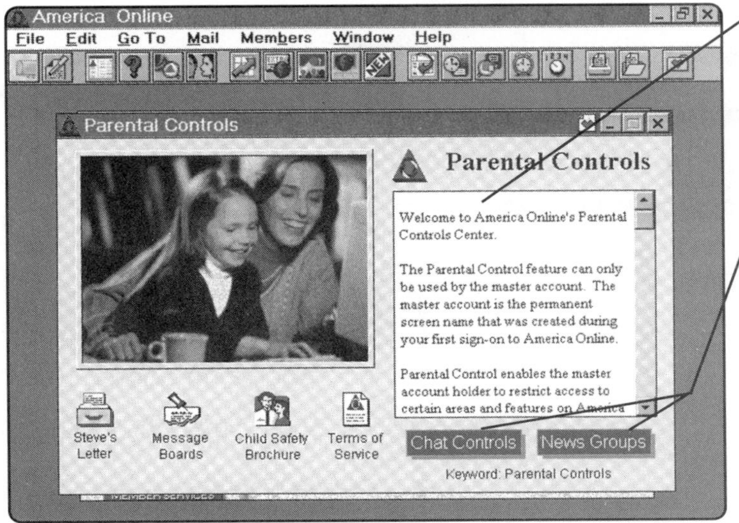

4. **Read** the **welcome message** for Parental Controls. It contains details on the Chat Controls and can be printed or saved.

These buttons take you to the two areas where controls can be used, chats and newsgroups.

Other options available through this screen include a letter from AOL's President, Steve Case; message boards relating to parents' concerns; a child safety brochure that you can print, save, or read online; and a relevant note on parents' responsibilities under the AOL Terms of Service.

5. **Click** on **Message Boards**. The Parental Controls Message Boards dialog box will appear.

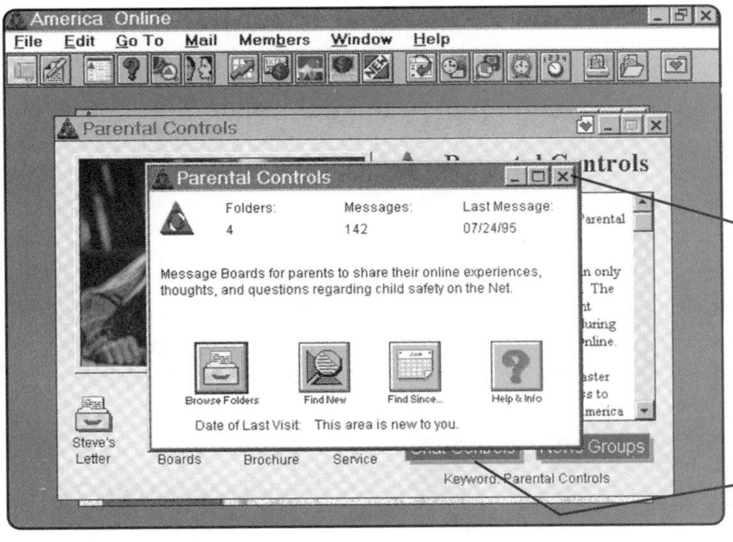

The message boards feature notes posted by parents. They are used the same way that forums are, as shown in Chapter 13.

6. **Click** on the X in the right corner of the title bar, or, if you're using Windows 3.1, **click twice** on the **Control menu box** in the left corner to close the dialog box.

7. **Click** on **Chat Controls**. The dialog box for control over chat areas will appear.

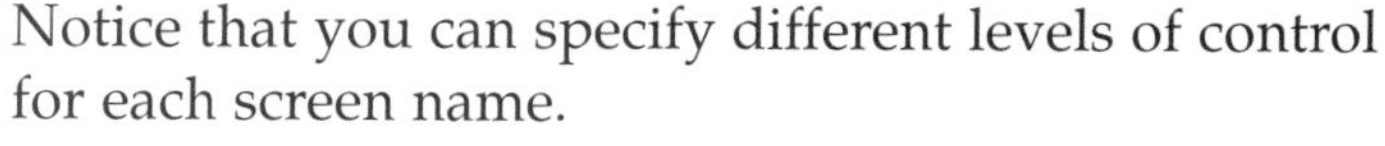

Notice that you can specify different levels of control for each screen name.

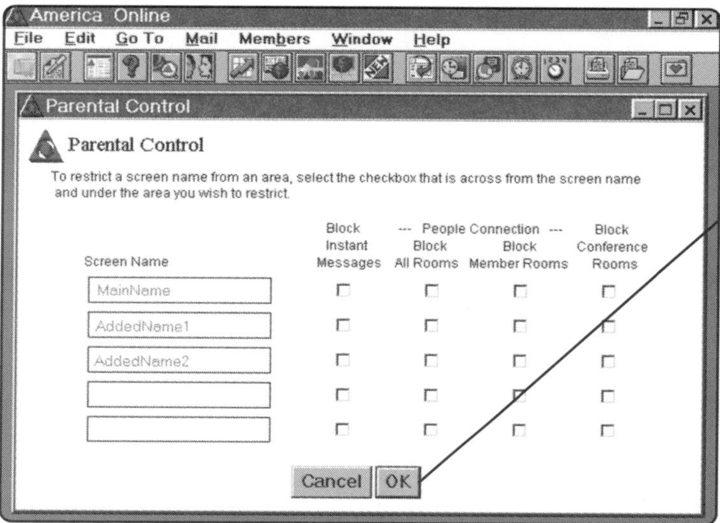

8. **Click** on the **box** that matches the type of control you want to implement. A ✔ will appear in the box.

9. **Click** on **OK** to put the control in place (or Cancel if you don't want to establish any controls). A message box (not shown here) will appear saying that the changes have been saved.

10. **Click** on **OK**. The message box will close.

Controlling Newsgroups

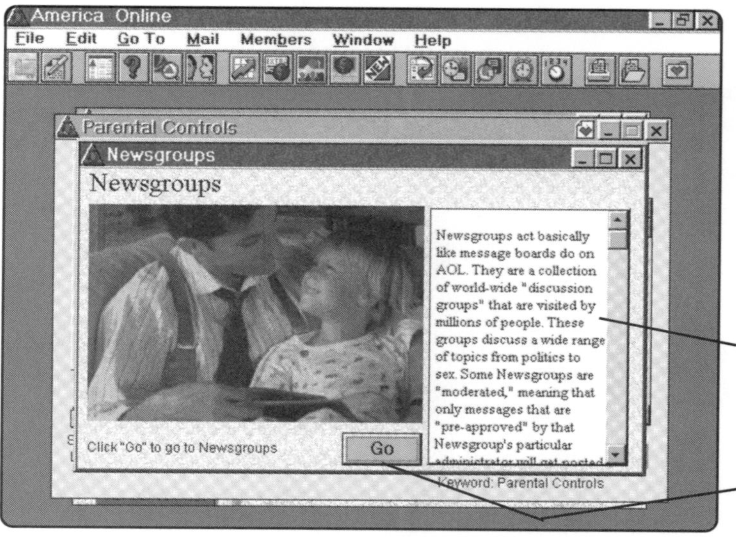

1. **Click** on the **Newsgroups button** in the lower-right corner of the Parental Controls dialog box that is shown at the top of the previous page. The Newsgroups dialog box will appear.

2. **Read** the **Newsgroups message**. It can also be printed or saved.

3. **Click** on **Go**. Another Newsgroups dialog box will appear.

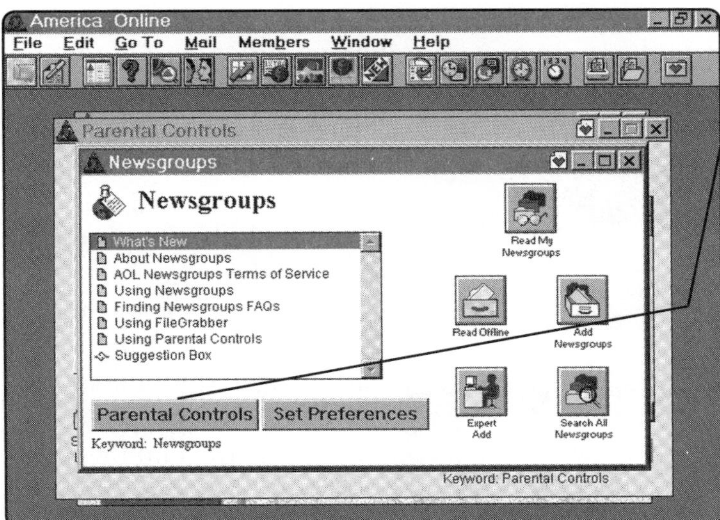

4. **Click** on **Parental Controls**. The Parental Controls dialog box will appear.

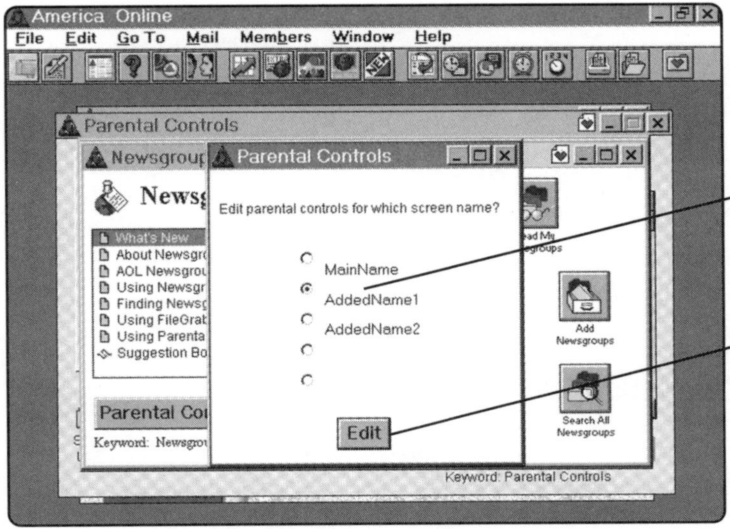

This dialog box lets you specify the screen name for which you are setting up controls.

5. **Click** on a **screen name** to place a dot in the circle next to it.

6. **Click** on **Edit**. The Blocking Criteria dialog box will appear.

Read AOL's Note to Parents for details on these criteria.

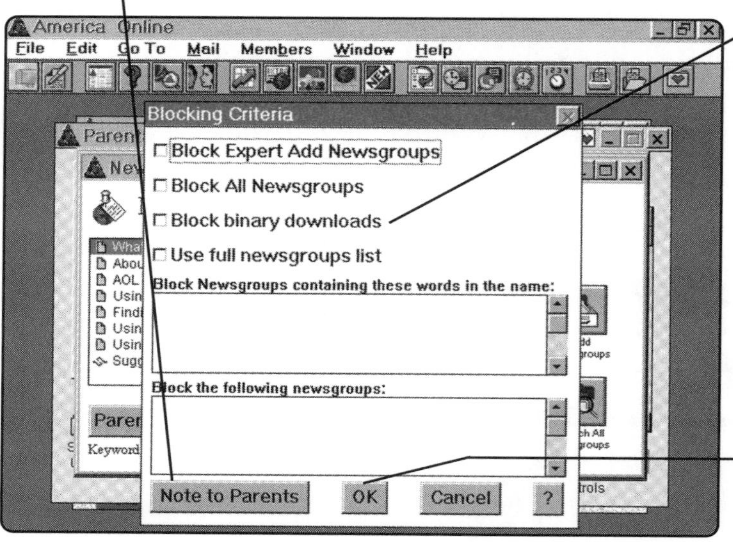

Note: If you block binary downloads, the screen name will not be allowed to download files from AOL's software libraries.

7. **Click** on an **option** to place a ✔ next to it and select it, and/or type specific words into the text boxes.

8. **Click** on **OK** to save your choices and close this dialog box.

9. **Click** on the ☒**s** in the right corners of the titles bars, or (Windows 3.1) click twice on the Control menu boxes in the left corners of the title bars to close the open dialog boxes.

Index

A

B

C

D

J

K

L

M

Q

R

S

T

U

V

W

Y

Z